Perception

BLACKWELL READINGS IN PHILOSOPHY

Series Editor: Steven M. Cahn

Blackwell Readings in Philosophy are concise, chronologically arranged collections of primary readings from classical and contemporary sources. They represent core positions and important developments with respect to key philosophical concepts. Edited and introduced by leading philosophers, these volumes provide valuable resources for teachers and students of philosophy, and for all those interested in gaining a solid understanding of central topics in philosophy.

Perception

Edited by
Robert Schwartz

 **Blackwell**
Publishing

350 Main Street, Malden, MA 02148-5018, USA
108 Cowley Road, Oxford OX4 1JF, UK
550 Swanston Street, Carlton South, Melbourne, Victoria 3053, Australia
Kurfürstendamm 57, 10707 Berlin, Germany

First published 2004 by Blackwell Publishing Ltd

Library of Congress Cataloging-in-Publication Data

Perception / edited by Robert Schwartz.
p. cm. — (Blackwell readings in philosophy ; 12)
Includes bibliographical references and index.
ISBN 0-631-22421-1 (alk. paper) — ISBN 0-631-22422-X (pbk. : alk. paper)
1. Perception (Philosophy) I. Schwartz, Robert, 1940– II. Series.

B828.45 .P46 2003
121'.34—dc21

2002038281

A catalogue record for this title is available from the British Library.

Set in 10/12.5pt Palatino
by Kolam Information Services Pvt. Ltd, Pondicherry, India
Printed and bound in the United Kingdom
by TJ International, Padstow, Cornwall

For further information on
Blackwell Publishing, visit our website:
http://www.blackwellpublishing.com

For Toby,
who teaches me to see so much more

Contents

Acknowledgments

The editor and publisher gratefully acknowledge the permission granted to reproduce the copyright material in this book. The material in chapters 2, 3, and 5 was taken from the public domain:

Chapter 1: Princeton University Press, for the extracts from Aristotle, *On the Soul*, pp. 665–7, 674–5, and 676–80, in J. Barnes (ed.), *Complete Works of Aristotle* (1984); © 1984 by Princeton University Press.

Chapter 2: George Berkeley, for the extracts from *An Essay towards a New Theory of Vision* (Dublin, 1709).

Chapter 3: Thomas Reid, for the extracts from *Essays on the Intellectual Powers of Man* (Edinburgh, 1785).

Chapter 4: Princeton University Press, for the extracts from Ernst Cassirer, *The Philosophy of the Enlightenment* (1962), pp. 108–15; © 1962 by Princeton University Press.

Chapter 5: Johannes Müller, for the Introduction to *Handbuch der Physiologie des Menschen*, Book V (Koblenz, 1838), translated by William Baly as *Elements of Physiology*, vol. 2 (London, 1842).

Chapter 6: Dover Publications, Inc., for the extracts from Hermann von Helmholtz, *Treatise on Physiological Optics*, Book 3, edited by J. Southall (1950), pp. 1–7, 10–13, and 17–22.

Chapter 7: Global Rights Group, a division of Thomson Learning, for the extracts from Kurt Koffka, *Principles of Gestalt Psychology* (New York: Harcourt, Brace and World, 1935), pp. 73, 75–87, and 96–7.

Chapter 8: Houghton Mifflin Company, for the extract from James J. Gibson, *The Senses Considered as Perceptual Systems* (1966), pp. 1–6, © 1966 by Houghton Mifflin Company; and Lawrence Erlbaum Associates, Inc., for the extract from James J. Gibson, *The Ecological Approach to Visual Perception* (Hillsdale, NJ: Lawrence Erlbaum Associates, 1986), pp. 244–6.

Chapter 9: Blackwell Publishing Ltd, for the extract from David W. Hamlyn, *In and Out of the Black Box* (Oxford: Blackwell, 1990), pp. 84–91.

Chapter 10: John Heil, for the extract from *Perception and Cognition* by John Heil (Berkeley: University of California Press, 1983), pp. 4–18.

Chapter 11: Brian O'Shaughnessy, for the extract from *The Will*, vol. 1 (Cambridge: Cambridge University Press, 1980), pp. 167–81. The version reproduced here has been revised by the author.

Chapter 12: Dover Publications, Inc., for the extract from Ernst Mach, *The Analysis of Sensation* (1959), pp. 135–7, note 2.

Chapter 13: Cambridge University Press, for the extracts from Michael J. Morgan, *Molyneux's Question* (1977), pp. 171–80 and 191–3.

Chapter 14: Oxford University Press, for the extracts from "Molyneux's Question" in Gareth Evans, *Collected Papers* (Oxford: Oxford University Press, 1985), pp. 365–6, 372–82, and 388–99; © 1985 by Antonia Phillips.

Chapter 15: Taylor and Francis Books Ltd, for James J. Gibson, "A Theory of Direct Visual Perception," in J. Royce and W. Rozeboom (eds.), *The Psychology of Knowing* (New York and London: Gordon and Breach, 1972), pp. 215–27; and Lawrence Erlbaum Associates, Inc., for the extract from James J. Gibson, *The Ecological Approach to Visual Perception* (Hillsdale, NJ: Lawrence Erlbaum Associates, 1986), pp. 251–3.

Chapter 16: Elsevier Science, for the extracts from Jerry A. Fodor and Zenon W. Pylyshyn, "How Direct is Visual Perception? Some Reflections on Gibson's 'Ecological Approach'" in *Cognition* 9 (1981), pp. 139–60 and 165–6.

Chapter 17: The University of Chicago Press, for Irvin Rock, "Inference in Perception," in *Proceedings of the Philosophy of Science Association* 2 (1982), pp. 525–40; © 1983 by the Philosophy of Science Association.

Chapter 18: The University of Chicago Press, for Patricia Smith Churchland, "Is the Visual System as Smart as it Looks?" in *Proceedings of the*

Philosophy of Science Association 2 (1982), pp. 541–52; © 1983 by the Philosophy of Science Association.

Chapter 19: Cambridge University Press, for Simon Ullman, "Tacit Assumptions in the Computational Study of Vision" in A. Gorea (ed.), *Representations of Vision* (1991), pp. 305–17.

Chapter 20: Leo S. Olschki, for William Epstein, " 'Why Do Things Look as They Do?' What Koffka Might Have Said to Gibson, Marr and Rock," in S. Pogg (ed.), *Gestalt Psychology: Its Origins, Foundations and Influence* (1989), pp. 175–89.

Chapter 21: The MIT Press, for Fred Dretske, "Seeing, Believing, and Knowing," in D. Osherson, S. Kosslyn, and J. Hollerbach (eds.), *Visual Cognition and Action*, vol. II (1990), pp. 129–48.

Chapter 22: Taylor and Francis Books Ltd, for the extract from Robert Fogelin, *Wittgenstein*, 2nd edn. (London: Routledge, 1987), pp. 201–5.

Chapter 23: Cambridge University Press, for the extracts from Norwood Russell Hanson, *Patterns of Discovery* (1965), pp. 4–13 and 15–18.

Chapter 24: Christopher Peacocke, for "Analogue Content," in *The Aristotelian Society*, supplementary vol. LX (1986), pp. 1–17; © 1986 by Christopher Peacocke.

Chapter 25: Elizabeth S. Spelke, for the extracts from "Where Perceiving Ends and Thinking Begins: The Apprehension of Objects in Infancy" by Elizabeth S. Spelke in A. Yonas (ed.), *Perceptual Development in Infancy* (Hillsdale, NJ: Lawrence Erlbaum Associates, 1988), pp. 196–9 and 220–30.

Chapter 26: Oxford University Press, Inc., for "Seeing Is Believing – Or Is It?" in Daniel C. Dennett, *Perception*, edited by Kathleen Akins (1996), pp. 158–72; © 1996 by Oxford University Press, Inc. The illustration *View of Dresden with the Frauenkirche at left*, 1747 by Bernardo Bellotto is reproduced courtesy of North Carolina Museum of Art, purchased with funds from the State of North Carolina.

Every effort has been made to trace copyright-holders and to obtain their permission for the use of copyright material. The publisher apologizes for any errors or omissions in the above list and would be grateful if notified of any corrections that should be incorporated in future reprints or editions of this book.

Introduction

Anthologies are characterized by what they leave out as well as by what they include. The focus of this collection is on conceptual and theoretical problems in the study of vision. Little is to be found specifically on metaphysical and epistemological issues concerning the nature of Reality and our perceptual access to it. Nor is there much on the ontology of subjective experience, qualia, or color. Other books surveying these matters are readily available.

Part I, "Historical Background," introduces the main topics examined in this volume. The frequent and continuing reference in the theory of vision to these older writings serves to indicate their lasting significance. Moreover, knowledge of this history is important for any serious understanding of the issues. Even today, much of the discussion and debate in the theory of vision follows along the contours laid out in these earlier works. Also found in these historical writings are the roots of many of the more metaphysical, epistemological, and ontological questions only skirted in the rest of the volume. The selections in Part I, therefore, should help the reader appreciate the extent to which the conceptual and theoretical issues in the study of vision remain intertwined with, reflect, and are affected positively and negatively by these philosophical concerns.

It is commonplace that vision is a distinct modality and that, like other modalities, it has its own distinct sensory organ or receptor system. Equally commonplace are the assumptions that seeing essentially involves sensations or subjective experiences and that these visual sensations are qualitatively different from the sensations produced by the sense organs of other modalities. Finally, as is apparent in the readings in Part I, it has long been maintained that such sensations play an important role in the generation and constitution of visual percepts.

Part II, "The Senses," questions the suppositions and presuppositions underlying all these claims.

What, for example, does distinguish one sense or sense organ from another? Is it the qualitative features of the associated conscious sensations or is it something more "objective"? Do the various senses each provide distinct and distinctive information about the world? Or are the various senses merely different channels of information for the very same facts. In turn, is it still reasonable to hold that sensations have an explanatory role to play in a scientifically acceptable account of perception? If so, what? If not, might the very idea of there being a "sensory core" to perception be misguided? Of course, any resolution of these issues will have a profound effect on how one understands the nature of the relationship among our various sense modalities. The ending selections of "The Senses" explore the ways in which sight and touch – the senses thought to be most intimately involved in the perception of space – may or may not function together.

Vision typically starts when certain electromagnetic waves strike a light-sensitive retina. The visual end product is something else – a perceptual awareness of the location and properties of objects in the environment. But how do we get from the initial stimulus to the final information-bearing stage? Is the first step a sensation or other sensory representation of the layout? And do the subsequent steps and transitions depend on *cognitive* states or processing? If so, are the mechanisms involved the same or analogous to those that underlie thought and intelligence? Alternatively, is the whole idea of the mind supplementing an impoverished retinal input erroneous? Perhaps the information contained in the stimulus is richer than assumed, and thus there is no need for cognitive elaboration to flesh it out. Perception, then, would not depend on intermediate mental states or processes. Part III, "Direct versus Indirect Theories of Perception," offers accounts and criticisms of three of the major competing approaches to this topic.

There would seem to be an obvious and important difference between basing a judgment on the data vision provides and perceiving the related state of affairs so judged. Sherlock Holmes *deduces* the earlier presence and route of the thief from the footprints he observes. He does not actually see or perceive the thief. And even when the thief is standing before him to be seen, Holmes might not yet realize he is the actual culprit. Holmes only *sees* the thief's size, shape, coloring, and dress, not his past behavior or that his name is "Sam." But where and on what basis is the line to be drawn between what we see and what we otherwise find out by use of our visual sense. And in what terms are we to characterize or describe these supposedly different components of perception? The papers in Part IV, "Perception and Conception," demonstrate both how difficult it is to draw this distinction and how much the topics and problems considered in the previous three sections depend on and assume it.

Although many of the readings in this volume are "classics" in the field, the selections were chosen primarily on pedagogical grounds. The aim was to lay out several core issues in the theory of vision in a way accessible to the non-expert and then to set up a dialogue on the topics among philosophers and psychologists, past and present. In making these selections, I have often opted for the more expository work in place of the most influential or latest statement of the view. It should also be noted that many of the readings are excerpts from much larger works. Undoubtedly, this has its risks and losses. In most cases, excisions could not be avoided: the excerpts are from books. The main constraint overall was one of space. Opting for fuller or complete works would have meant fewer pieces and fewer perspectives. I chose more expansive coverage. I apologize to the authors for any distortions of their ideas and arguments that may be the result of my editorial decisions.

I wish to thank Margaret Atherton and Sidney Morgenbesser for helpful suggestions in putting together this anthology.

Part I

Historical Background

Introduction to Part I

The snippets of history found in this section contain the seeds of much that followed in the theory of vision. At the same time, there has always been a good deal of controversy in the scholarly literature over how best to interpret these works and their authors' ideas. Matters are further complicated by the fact that the views of these historical figures are often distorted in the retelling. Thus it is not unusual to find a writer claim to have refuted Berkeley on a position Berkeley never held or claim to be a follower of Helmholtz, while rejecting many of Helmholtz's core assumptions.

In the selection from *De Anima*, Aristotle maintains that the senses are distinguished by their special objects, the qualities each uniquely presents. Perception of the special objects of sense are always free of error. With the sense of sight, its special object is color. All of the senses, however, perceive figure, size, motion, and number. These "spatial" properties are common sensibles. Aristotle also holds that there are many things we determine on the basis of sense, yet do not strictly perceive. For example, we see an object of a particular shape, color, and size that, in fact, is the son of Diares, but we cannot *directly* perceive that he is Diares's son. To recognize him as the son of Diares requires further information beyond that which the sense of sight can itself immediately provide.

At the beginning of Book III of *De Anima*, Aristotle says there are exactly five senses (sight, hearing, smell, taste, and touch). He then goes on to argue that there could not be any others. Most significantly, there could not be a sense organ that has the common sensibles as its *special* object. The common sensibles, nonetheless, are real objects of sense. They are perceptible in and of themselves, not derivatively or incidentally as when we see that some object is Diares's son. Aristotle argues as well that, strictly speaking, perception must be distinguished from both thinking and understanding. All animals perceive but thinking requires "discourse of reason" (Hamlyn 1968; Sorabji 1971).

The jump through history from Aristotle to Berkeley is no indication of a lack of important work in the years between (Herrnstein and Boring 1968; Lindberg 1976; Hatfield and Epstein 1979). Still, Berkeley's *New Theory of Vision* had a formative and transformative impact on the field. How Berkeley's work on vision fits in with his doctrines of idealism and immaterialism is a subject of continuing discussion (Atherton 1990). Many of his ideas concerning vision were, nevertheless, adopted by realist and materialist thinkers.

At the start of the *New Theory*, Berkeley famously notes that "distance, of itself and immediately, cannot be seen. For distance being a line directed end-wise to the eye it projects only one point on the fund of the eye, which point remains invariably the same, whether the distance be longer or shorter." Although this claim is frequently disparaged when not being simply dismissed, I think J. J. Gibson (1976: 83) is right when he remarks that Berkeley here "states the problem of the third dimension, or depth perception, as it has been studied and puzzled over for 250 years" (Schwartz 1994).

The excerpts from the *New Theory* encapsulate various of Berkeley's most important themes. In these sections are found: an account of distance cues, a critique of the then prevalent geometrical model of distance perception, a motor theory of the development of spatial perception, and a statement of his doctrine of the heterogeneity of the senses. For Berkeley there are no common sensibles that underlie our ideas and perceptions of space.

The view that some ideas are made available by sense while others go beyond what is initially so given is pervasive in the study of vision. Variations of the assumption are found in Aristotle and Berkeley and in the work of most theorists in between. Reid is usually credited with being the first person to formulate the distinction explicitly in terms of a difference between sensation and perception. Sensations are our qualitative experiences *per se*; they have no external reference. Perceptions are the ways we take the actual objects in the world to be. Although few in the end have been totally satisfied with Reid's proposal, finding an acceptable substitute has not been easy. Moreover, until quite recently one version or another of a sensation/perception distinction has figured centrally in most theories of vision.

In this selection, Reid argues that although vision is a two-stage process, the link between sensations and perceptions is irresistible, immediate, and, he suggests, innate. Reid is careful, though, to distinguish these claims. A transition is irresistible and immediate if the mind is forced to make it and deliberation cannot affect the course of such transitions. With qualifications, this characterization of the link between stage one and two was quite common among vision theorists. Reid's innateness claim, however, was and remained much more controversial. It stands, for example, in contrast both to Berkeley's learning-based model and to various theories that attribute the appreciation of space to an innate intuition.

Molyneux asked whether a man born blind and given sight would be able to distinguish a cube from a sphere. Berkeley famously says "no" and believes a negative answer is important to his theory of vision. Philosophers and psychologists to this day have found the problem intriguing and have thought a definitive answer to it should have important implications concerning the nature of sense and the nature of mind in general. Cassirer traces major themes in the history of work on the Molyneux problem and discusses alternative formulations of the question. Cassirer offers, as well, an explanation of how and why the problem took on such widespread theoretical significance.

Much of what Müller says was in the air and can be found, too, in earlier thinkers. Nevertheless, Müller's explicit physiological formulation of these ideas seemed to galvanize scientific thinking on the subject. For the most part, the empirical data Müller cites do not require sophisticated laboratory setups to uncover. The main findings are that: (i) very different stimuli applied to the same sense organ can produce the same sensations, and (ii) the same stimulus can produce totally different sensations when applied to a different sensory system. Although sensations are triggered by physical inputs and vary with the intensity and kind of these stimuli, the nature or quality of the sensation is determined by the characteristic specific energies of the sensory nerves. Thus sensory organs are not mirrors of nature, and sense experience is not a direct reflection of the physical properties of the environment. We do not sense the properties of the world *per se*, but experience responses to them as fixed by the physiological make-up of the affected sense.

Helmholtz is considered by many the founder of modern visual science. The excerpts from his monumental three-volume, *Physiological Optics* begin with Helmholtz's appeal to a sensation/perception distinction to delineate the areas and issues of study. It is in the last volume of the work that Helmholtz actually discusses his "unconscious inference" model of perception in detail. Put roughly, Helmholtz claims perceptions are inferences from sensations. These inferences are grounded in habits, which are themselves based on the experience of past regularities. Helm-holtz makes clear, though, that for him (as for many other theorists) sensations are not readily accessible to the subject, nor are reports of them incorrigible. Considerable skill is needed to detect the qualities of our own sensations.

Helmholtz's model is usually identified as a "cognitive" theory of perception. In broad outline, however, his theory is similar to Berkeley's. True, Berkeley criticized inference accounts of perception, but the sort of visual processes Helmholtz appeals to are little different from the mech-anisms of "suggestion" Berkeley employs. Helmholtz, in fact, specifically says that his perceptual inferences are analogues of the empirical induct-ive associations of ideas Mill discusses. By Helmholtz's time innateness was perhaps *the* central issue of theoretical contention in the theory of vision. Helmholtz came down forcefully on the "empiricist" side. Indeed, Helmholtz maintains that *the* major result of the *Physiological Optics* is to show how very many phenomena claimed to be matters of innate intu-ition were actually the result of learning (Hatfield 1990).

Koffka was one of the founders of the Gestalt school of psychology. Like other members of this school, he placed great emphasis on the idea that experience is not atomistic. Experience always enters awareness as an organized whole. Koffka maintains that introspective reports claiming to reveal elementaristic or punctiform sensory fields are not to be trusted. At the same time, Koffka does not want to throw in with the Behaviorists, who either deny the phenomena of subjective experience or deny that it can be studied scientifically. Koffka argues, instead, that the main ques-tion of visual perception is "Why do things look as they do?" In this chapter, Koffka canvasses a range of answers and finds them all wanting. They each fail to take proper account of the organizing effects our sensory system and brain impose on incoming stimuli.

In reading Koffka it is important not to confuse what he calls the "constancy hypothesis" with the notion of "perceptual constancy." The constancy hypothesis is the assumption that there is some simple point-by-point correspondence between the stimulus array and the experienced visual field. This Koffka rejects, since perception is always organized. Perceptual constancy, by contrast, is the claim that things continue to look the same even though the stimulus changes. For example, I see a book as being the same size whether it is in my hand or lying on the desk several feet away. But the image projected on my retina is much larger when the book is in my grasp. Phenomena of perceptual constancy, therefore, conflict with the constancy hypothesis claim that there is a point-by-point correspondence between the stimulus array and the way things look.

References

Atherton, M. (1990), *Berkeley's Revolution in Vision*, Ithaca, NY: Cornell University Press.

Gibson, J. J. (1976), Three kinds of distance that can be seen, or how Bishop Berkeley went wrong. In *Studies in Perception: Festschrift for Fabio Metelli*, ed. G. Flores D'Arcais, Milan: Martello-Guiunti.

Hamlyn, D. W. (1968), *Aristotle's De Anima Books I and II*, Oxford: Clarendon Press.

Hatfield, G. (1990), *The Natural and the Normative*, Cambridge, MA: MIT Press.

Hatfield, G. and Epstein, W. (1979), The sensory core and the medieval foundations of early modern perceptual theory, *Isis* 70: 363–84.

Herrnstein, R. and Boring, E. (eds.) (1968), *A Source Book in the History of Psychology*, Cambridge, MA: Harvard University Press.

Lindberg, D. (1976), *Theories of Vision from Al-Kindy to Kepler*, Chicago: University of Chicago Press.

Schwartz, R. (1994), *Vision: Variations on Some Berkeleian Themes*, Oxford: Blackwell.

Sorabji, R. (1971), Aristotle on demarcating the five senses, *Philosophical Review* 80: 55–79.

1

From *On the Soul*

Aristotle

Book II

. . .

418ᵃ **6.** In dealing with each of the senses we shall have first to speak of the objects which are perceptible by each. The term 'object of sense' covers three kinds of objects, two kinds of which we call perceptible in themselves, while the remaining one is only incidentally perceptible. Of the 10 first two kinds one consists of what is special to a single sense, the other of what is common to any and all of the senses. I call by the name of special object of this or that sense that which cannot be perceived by any other sense than that one and in respect of which no error is possible; in this sense colour is the special object of sight, sound of hearing, flavour of taste. Touch, indeed, discriminates more than one set of different qual-15 ities. Each sense has one kind of object which it discerns, and never errs in reporting that what is before it is colour or sound (though it may err as to what it is that is coloured or where that is, or what it is that is sounding or where that is). Such objects are what we call the special objects of this or that sense.

Common sensibles are movement, rest, number, figure, magnitude; these are not special to any one sense, but are common to all. There are at any rate certain kinds of movement which are perceptible both by touch and by sight.

20 We speak of an incidental object of sense where e.g. the white object which we see is the son of Diares; here because being the son of Diares is

Aristotle, *On the Soul*, in J. Barnes (ed.), *Complete Works of Aristotle* (Princeton: Princeton University Press, 1984), pp. 665–7, 674–5, 676–80.

incidental to the white which is perceived, we speak of the son of Diares as being incidentally perceived. That is why it in no way as such affects the senses. Of the things perceptible in themselves, the special objects are properly called perceptible and it is to them that in the nature of things the structure of each several sense is adapted.   25

7. The object of sight is the visible, and what is visible is colour and a certain kind of object which can be described in words but which has no single name; what we mean by the second will be abundantly clear as we proceed. Whatever is visible is colour and colour is what lies upon what is in itself visible; 'in itself' here means not that visibility is involved in the 30 definition of what thus underlies colour, but that that substratum contains in itself the cause of visibility. Every colour has in it the power to set in movement what is actually transparent; that power constitutes its very 418ᵇ1 nature. That is why it is not visible except with the help of light; it is only in light that the colour of a thing is seen. . . .

The following makes the necessity of a medium clear. If what has 419ᵃ colour is placed in immediate contact with the eye, it cannot be seen. Colour sets in movement what is transparent, e.g. the air, and that, extending continuously from the object of the organ, sets the latter in movement. Democritus misrepresents the facts when he expresses the 15 opinion that if the interspace were empty one could distinctly see an ant on the vault of the sky; that is an impossibility. Seeing is due to an affection or change of what has the perceptive faculty, and it cannot be affected by the seen colour itself; it remains that it must be affected by what comes between. Hence it is indispensable that there be *something* in 20 between – if there were nothing, so far from seeing with greater distinctness, we should see nothing at all. . . .

12.   Generally, about all perception, we can say that a sense is what has 424ᵃ the power of receiving into itself the sensible forms of things without the matter, in the way in which a piece of wax takes on the impress of 20 a signet-ring without the iron or gold; what produces the impression is a signet of bronze or gold, but not *qua* bronze or gold: in a similar way the sense is affected by what is coloured or flavoured or sounding not insofar as each is what it is, but insofar as it is of such and such a sort and according to its form.

A primary sense-organ is that in which such a power is seated. The sense and its organ are the same in fact, but their essence is not the same. What perceives is, of course, a spatial magnitude, but we must not admit 25 that either the having the power to perceive or the sense itself is a

magnitude; what they are is a certain form or power in a magnitude. This enables us to explain why excesses in objects of sense destroy the organs
30 of sense; if the movement set up by an object is too strong for the organ, the form which is its sensory power is disturbed; it is precisely as concord and tone are destroyed by too violently twanging the strings of a lyre. This explains also why plants cannot perceive, in spite of their having a portion of soul in them and being affected by tangible objects themselves;
424ᵃ1 for their temperature can be lowered or raised. The explanation is that they have no mean, and so no principle in them capable of taking on the forms of sensible objects but are affected together with their matter. The problem might be raised: Can what cannot smell be said to be affected by
5 smells or what cannot see by colours, and so on? Now a smell is just what can be smelt, and if it produces any effect it can only be so as to make something smell it, and it might be argued that what cannot smell cannot be affected by smells and further that what can smell can be affected by it only in so far as it has in it the power to smell (similarly with the proper objects of all the other senses). Indeed that this is so seems clear as
10 follows. Light or darkness, sounds and smells leave bodies quite un-affected; what does affect bodies is not these but the bodies which are their vehicles, e.g. what splits the trunk of a tree is the air which accom-panies thunder. But bodies are affected by what is tangible and by flavours. If not, by what are things that are without soul affected, i.e. altered in quality? Must we not, then, admit that the objects of the other senses also may affect them? Is not the true account this, that all bodies are capable of being affected by smells and sounds, but that some on
15 being acted upon, having no boundaries of their own, disintegrate, as in the instance of air, which does become odorous, showing that some effect is produced on it by what is odorous? What is smelling more than such an affection by what is odorous? Is it that air, when affected quickly, becomes perceptible, but that smelling is actually perceiving?

Book III

1. That there is no sense in addition to the five – sight, hearing, smell, taste, touch – may be established. . . .
425ᵃ   Further, there cannot be a special sense-organ for the common sensi-
15 bles either, i.e. the objects which we perceive incidentally through this or that special sense, e.g. movement, rest, figure, magnitude, number, unity; for all these we perceive by movement, e.g. magnitude by movement, and therefore also figure (for figure is a species of magnitude), what is at

rest by the absence of movement: number is perceived by the negation of continuity, and by the special sensibles; for each sense perceives one class of sensible objects. So that it is clearly impossible that there should be a special sense for any one of the common sensibles, e.g. movement; for, if that were so, our perception of it would be exactly parallel to our present perception of what is sweet by vision. That is so because we have a sense for each of the two qualities, in virtue of which when they happen to meet in one sensible object we are aware of both contemporaneously. If it were not like this our perception of the common qualities would always be incidental, i.e. as is the perception of Cleon's son, where we perceive him not as Cleon's son but as white, and the white thing happens to be Cleon's son.

But in the case of the common sensibles there is already in us a common sensibility which enables us to perceive them non-incidentally; there is therefore no special sense required for their perception: if there were, our perception of them would have been exactly like what has been above described.

The senses perceive each other's special objects incidentally; not because the percipient sense is this or that special sense, but because all form a unity: this incidental perception takes place whenever sense is directed at one and the same moment to two disparate qualities in one and the same object, e.g. to the bitterness and the yellowness of bile; the assertion of the identity of both cannot be the act of either of the senses; hence the illusion of sense, e.g. the belief that if a thing is yellow it is bile.

It might be asked why we have more senses than one. Is it to prevent a failure to apprehend the common sensibles, e.g. movement, magnitude, and number, which go along with the special sensibles? Had we no sense but sight, and that sense no object but white, they would have tended to escape our notice and everything would have merged for us into an indistinguishable identity because of the concomitance of colour and magnitude. As it is, the fact that the common sensibles are given in the objects of more than one sense reveals their distinction from each and all of the special sensibles.

2. Since it is through sense that we are aware that we are seeing or hearing, it must be either by sight that we are aware of seeing, or by some sense other than sight. But the sense that gives us this new sensation must perceive both sight and its object, viz. colour: so that either there will be two senses both percipient of the same sensible object, or the sense must be percipient of itself. Further, even if the sense which perceives sight were different from sight, we must either fall into an infinite regress, or we must somewhere assume a sense which is aware of itself. If so, we ought to do this in the first case. . . .

Each sense then is relative to its particular group of sensible qualities: it
10 is found in a sense-organ as such and discriminates the differences which exist within that group; e.g. sight discriminates white and black, taste sweet and bitter, and so in all cases. Since we also discriminate white from sweet, and indeed each sensible quality from every other, with what do we perceive that they are different? It must be by sense; for what is
15 before us is sensible objects. (Hence it is also obvious that the flesh cannot be the ultimate sense-organ: if it were, the discriminating power could not do its work without immediate contact with the object.)

Therefore discrimination between white and sweet cannot be effected by two agencies which remain separate; both the qualities discriminated must be present to something that is one and single. On any other supposition even if I perceived sweet and you perceived white, the
20 difference between them would be apparent. What says that two things are different must be one; for sweet is different from white. Therefore what asserts this difference must be self-identical, and as what asserts, so also what thinks or perceives. . . .

427ᵃ **3.**   There are two distinctive peculiarities by reference to which we characterize the soul – (1) local movement and (2) thinking, understand-
20 ing, and perceiving. Thinking and understanding are regarded as akin to a form of perceiving; for in the one as well as the other the soul discriminates and is cognizant of something which is. Indeed the ancients go so far as to identify thinking and perceiving; e.g. Empedocles says 'For tis in respect of what is present that man's wit is increased', and again 'Whence it befalls them from time to time to think diverse thoughts', and Homer's
25 phrase 'For suchlike is man's mind' means the same. They all look upon thinking as a bodily process like perceiving, and hold that like is understood as well as perceived by like, as I explained at the beginning of our discussion. Yet they ought at the same time to have accounted for error
427ᵇ1 also; for it is more intimately connected with animal existence and the soul continues longer in the state of error. They cannot escape the dilemma: either whatever seems is true (and there are some who accept this) or error is contact with the unlike: for that is the opposite of the
5 knowing of like by like.

But it seems that error as well as knowledge in respect to contraries is one and the same.

That perceiving and understanding are not identical is therefore obvious; for the former is universal in the animal world, the latter is found in

only a small division of it. Further, thinking is also distinct from perceiving – I mean that in which we find rightness and wrongness – rightness in 10
understanding, knowledge, true opinion, wrongness in their opposites;
for perception of the special objects of sense is always free from error, and
is found in all animals, while it is possible to think falsely as well as truly,
and thought is found only where there is discourse of reason....

2

From *An Essay towards a New Theory of Vision*

George Berkeley

1. My design is to shew the manner wherein we perceive by sight the distance, magnitude, and situation of objects. Also to consider the difference there is betwixt the ideas of sight and touch, and whether there be any idea common to both senses.

2. It is, I think, agreed by all that distance, of itself and immediately, cannot be seen. For distance being a line directed end-wise to the eye, it projects only one point in the fund of the eye, which point remains invariably the same, whether the distance be longer or shorter.

3. I find it also acknowledged that the estimate we make of the distance of objects considerably remote is rather an act of judgment grounded on experience than of sense. For example, when I perceive a great number of intermediate objects, such as houses, fields, rivers, and the like, which I have experienced to take up a considerable space, I thence form a judgment or conclusion that the object I see beyond them is at a great distance. Again, when an object appears faint and small, which at a near distance I have experienced to make a vigorous and large appearance, I instantly conclude it to be far off: And this, 'tis evident, is the result of experience; without which, from the faintness and littleness I should not have inferred anything concerning the distance of objects.

4. But when an object is placed at so near a distance as that the interval between the eyes bears any sensible proportion to it, the opinion of speculative men is that the two optic axes (the fancy that we see only with one eye at once being exploded) concurring at the object do there make an angle, by means of which, according as it is greater or lesser, the object is perceived to be nearer or farther off.[1]

George Berkeley, *An Essay towards a New Theory of Vision* (Dublin, 1709).

5. Betwixt which and the foregoing manner of estimating distance there is this remarkable difference: that whereas there was no apparent, necessary connexion between small distance and a large and strong appearance, or between great distance and a little and faint appearance, there appears a very necessary connexion between an obtuse angle and near distance, and an acute angle and farther distance. It does not in the least depend upon experience, but may be evidently known by anyone before he had experienced it, that the nearer the concurrence of the optic axes, the greater the angle, and the remoter their concurrence is, the lesser will be the angle comprehended by them.

6. There is another way mentioned by optic writers, whereby they will have us judge of those distances, in respect of which the breadth of the pupil hath any sensible bigness: And that is the greater or lesser divergency of the rays, which issuing from the visible point do fall on the pupil, that point being judged nearest which is seen by most diverging rays, and that remoter which is seen by less diverging rays: and so on, the apparent distance still increasing, as the divergency of the rays decreases, till at length it becomes infinite, when the rays that fall on the pupil are to sense parallel. And after this manner it is said we perceive distance when we look only with one eye.

7. In this case also it is plain we are not beholding to experience: it being a certain, necessary truth that the nearer the direct rays falling on the eye approach to a parallelism, the farther off is the point of their intersection, or the visible point from whence they flow.

8. Now though the accounts here given of perceiving near distance by sight are received for true, and accordingly made use of in determining the apparent places of objects, they do nevertheless seem very unsatisfactory: and that for these following reasons.

9. It is evident that when the mind perceives any idea, not immediately and of itself, it must be by the means of some other idea. Thus, for instance, the passions which are in the mind of another are of themselves to me invisible. I may nevertheless perceive them by sight, though not immediately, yet by means of the colours they produce in the countenance. We often see shame or fear in the looks of a man, by perceiving the changes of his countenance to red or pale.

10. Moreover it is evident that no idea which is not itself perceived can be the means of perceiving any other idea. If I do not perceive the redness or paleness of a man's face themselves, it is impossible I should perceive by them the passions which are in his mind.

11. Now from sect. 2 it is plain that distance is in its own nature imperceptible, and yet it is perceived by sight. It remains, therefore, that

it be brought into view by means of some other idea that is itself immediately perceived in the act of vision. . . .

16. Now, it being already shewn that distance is suggested to the
mind by the mediation of some other idea which is itself perceived in
the act of seeing, it remains that we inquire what ideas or sensations there
be that attend vision, unto which we may suppose the ideas of distance
are connected, and by which they are introduced into the mind. And *first*,
it is certain by experience that when we look at a near object with both
eyes, according as it approaches or recedes from us, we alter the disposition of our eyes, by lessening or widening the interval between the
pupils. This disposition or turn of the eyes is attended with a sensation,
which seems to me to be that which in this case brings the idea of greater
or lesser distance into the mind.

17. Not that there is any natural or necessary connexion between the
sensation we perceive by the turn of the eyes and greater or lesser
distance, but because the mind has by constant experience found the
different sensations corresponding to the different dispositions of the
eyes to be attended each with a different degree of distance in the object,
there has grown an habitual or customary connexion between those two
sorts of ideas, so that the mind no sooner perceives the sensation arising
from the different turn it gives the eyes, in order to bring the pupils
nearer or farther asunder, but it withal perceives the different idea of
distance which was wont to be connected with that sensation; just as
upon hearing a certain sound, the idea is immediately suggested to the
understanding which custom had united with it. . . .

21. *Secondly*, an object placed at a certain distance from the eye, to
which the breadth of the pupil bears a considerable proportion, being
made to approach, is seen more confusedly: and the nearer it is brought
the more confused appearance it makes. And this being found constantly
to be so, there ariseth in the mind an habitual connexion between the
several degrees of confusion and distance; the greater confusion still
implying the lesser distance, and the lesser confusion the greater distance
of the object. . . .

27. *Thirdly*, an object being placed at the distance above specified, and
brought nearer to the eye, we may nevertheless prevent, at least for some
time, the appearances growing more confused, by straining the eye. In
which case that sensation supplies the place of confused vision in aiding
the mind to judge of the distance of the object; it being esteemed so much
the nearer by how much the effort or straining of the eye in order to
distinct vision is greater.

28.   I have here set down those sensations or ideas that seem to be the constant and general occasions of introducing into the mind the different ideas of near distance. It is true in most cases that divers other circumstances contribute to frame our idea of distance, to wit, the particular number, size, kind, etc., of the things seen. Concerning which, as well as all other the forementioned occasions which suggest distance, I shall only observe they have none of them, in their own nature, any relation or connexion with it: nor is it possible they should ever signify the various degrees thereof, otherwise than as by experience they have been found to be connected with them. . . .

41.   From what hath been premised it is a manifest consequence that a man born blind, being made to see, would, at first, have no idea of distance by sight; the sun and stars, the remotest objects as well as the nearer, would all seem to be in his eye, or rather in his mind. The objects intromitted by sight would seem to him (as in truth they are) no other than a new set of thoughts or sensations, each whereof is as near to him as the perceptions of pain or pleasure, or the most inward passions of his soul. For our judging objects perceived by sight to be at any distance, or without the mind, is (*vid.* sect. 28) entirely the effect of experience, which one in those circumstances could not yet have attained to. . . .

45.   In [the case of normal vision] the truth of the matter stands thus: having of a long time experienced certain ideas, perceivable by touch, as distance, tangible figure, and solidity, to have been connected with certain ideas of sight, I do upon perceiving these ideas of sight forthwith conclude what tangible ideas are, by the wonted ordinary course of Nature like to follow. Looking at an object I perceive a certain visible figure and colour, with some degree of faintness and other circumstances, which from what I have formerly observed, determine me to think that if I advance forward so many paces or miles, I shall be affected with such and such ideas of touch: so that in truth and strictness of speech I neither see distance itself, nor anything that I take to be at a distance. I say, neither distance nor things placed at a distance are themselves, or their ideas, truly perceived by sight. This I am persuaded of, as to what concerns myself: and I believe whoever will look narrowly into his own thoughts and examine what he means by saying he sees this or that thing at a distance, will agree with me that what he sees only suggests to his understanding that after having passed a certain distance, to be measured by the motion of his body, which is perceivable by touch, he shall come to perceive such and such tangible ideas which have been usually connected with such and such visible ideas. But that one might be deceived by these suggestions of sense, and that there is no necessary connexion between visible and tangible ideas suggested by them, we need go no farther than the next looking-glass or pictures to be convinced. Note that when I speak of tangible ideas, I take the word idea for any the immediate object of sense or understanding, in which large signification it is commonly used by the moderns.

46.   From what we have shewn it is a manifest consequence that the ideas of space, outness, and things placed at a distance are not, strictly speaking, the object of sight; they are not otherwise perceived by the eye than by the ear. Sitting in my study I hear a coach drive along the street; I look through the casement and see it; I walk out and enter into it; thus, common speech would incline one to think I heard, saw, and touched the same thing, to wit, the coach. It is nevertheless certain, the ideas intromitted by each sense are widely different and distinct from each other; but having been observed constantly to go together, they are spoken of as one and the same thing. By the variation of the noise I perceive the different distances of the coach, and know that it approaches before I look out. Thus by the ear I perceive distance, just after the same manner as I do by the eye. ...

129.   ...[L]ight and colours are allowed by all to constitute a sort or species entirely different from the ideas of touch: nor will any man, I presume, say they can make themselves perceived by that sense: but there is no other immediate object of sight besides light and colours. It is therefore a direct consequence that there is no idea common to both senses. ...

132.   A farther confirmation of our tenet may be drawn from the solution of Mr Molyneux's problem, published by Mr Locke in his *Essay*: which I shall set down as it there lies, together with Mr Locke's opinion of it, "'Suppose a man born blind, and now adult, and taught by his touch to distinguish between a cube and a sphere of the same metal, and nighly of the same bigness, so as to tell, when he felt one and t'other, which is the cube and which the sphere. Suppose then the cube and sphere placed on a table, and the blind man to be made to see: *quaere*, whether by his sight, before he touched them, he could now distinguish and tell which is the globe, which the cube?" To which the acute and judicious proposer answers: "Not. For though he has obtained the experience of how a globe, how a cube, affects his touch, yet he has not yet attained the experience that what affects his touch so or so must affect his sight so or so: or that a protuberant angle in the cube that pressed his hand unequally shall appear to his eye as it doth in the cube." I agree with this thinking gentleman, whom I am proud to call my friend, in his answer to this his problem; and am of opinion that the blind man at first sight would not be able with certainty to say which was the globe, which the cube, whilst he only saw them' (*Essay on Human Understanding*, B. ii. C. 9. S. 8). ...

147. Upon the whole, I think we may fairly conclude that the proper objects of vision constitute an universal language of the Author of Nature, whereby we are instructed how to regulate our actions in order to attain those things that are necessary to the preservation and well-being of our bodies, as also to avoid whatever may be hurtful and destructive of them. It is by their information that we are principally guided in all the transactions and concerns of life. And the manner wherein they signify and mark unto us the objects which are at a distance is the same with that of languages and signs of human appointment, which do not suggest the things signified by any likeness or identity of nature, but only by an habitual connexion that experience has made us to observe between them. ...

Note

1 See what Descartes and others have written on this subject.

3

From *Essays on the Intellectual Powers of Man*

Thomas Reid

Chapter V: Of Perception

...

If, therefore, we attend to that act of our mind which we call the perception of an external object of sense, we shall find in it these three things: *First,* Some conception or notion of the object perceived; *Secondly,* A strong and irresistible conviction and belief of its present existence; and, *Thirdly,* That this conviction and belief are immediate, and not the effect of reasoning.

First, It is impossible to perceive an object without having some notion or conception of that which we perceive. We may, indeed, conceive an object which we do not perceive; but, when we perceive the object, we must have some conception of it at the same time; and we have commonly a more clear and steady notion of the object while we perceive it, than we have from memory or imagination when it is not perceived. Yet, even in perception, the notion which our senses give of the object may be more or less clear, more or less distinct, in all possible degrees.

Thus we see more distinctly an object at a small than at a great distance. An object at a great distance is seen more distinctly in a clear than in a foggy day. An object seen indistinctly with the naked eye, on account of its smallness, may be seen distinctly with a microscope. The objects in this room will be seen by a person in the room less and less distinctly as the light of the day fails; they pass through all the various degrees of distinctness according to the degrees of the light, and, at last, in total darkness they are not seen at all. What has been said of the objects of sight

---

Thomas Reid, *Essays on the Intellectual Powers of Man* (Edinburgh, 1785), chs V, XVI.

is so easily applied to the objects of the other senses, that the application may be left to the reader.

In a matter so obvious to every person capable of reflection, it is necessary only farther to observe, that the notion which we get of an object, merely by our external sense, ought not to be confounded with that more scientific notion which a man, come to the years of understanding, may have of the same object, by attending to its various attributes, or to its various parts, and their relation to each other, and to the whole. Thus, the notion which a child has of a jack for roasting meat, will be acknowledged to be very different from that of a man who understands its construction, and perceives the relation of the parts to one another, and to the whole. The child sees the jack and every part of it as well as the man. The child, therefore, has all the notion of it which sight gives; whatever there is more in the notion which the man forms of it, must be derived from other powers of the mind, which may afterwards be explained. This observation is made here only that we may not confound the operations of different powers of the mind, which by being always conjoined after we grow up to understanding, are apt to pass for one and the same.

Secondly, In perception we not only have a notion more or less distinct of the object perceived, but also an irresistible conviction and belief of its existence. This is always the case when we are certain that we perceive it. There may be a perception so faint and indistinct as to leave us in doubt whether we perceive the object or not. Thus, when a star begins to twinkle as the light of the sun withdraws, one may, for a short time, think he sees it without being certain, until the perception acquire some strength and steadiness. When a ship just begins to appear in the utmost verge of the horizon, we may at first be dubious whether we perceive it or not; but when the perception is in any degree clear and steady, there remains no doubt of its reality; and when the reality of the perception is ascertained, the existence of the object perceived can no longer be doubted....

I observed, *Thirdly,* That this conviction is not only irresistible, but it is immediate, that is, it is not by a train of reasoning and argumentation that we come to be convinced of the existence of what we perceive; we ask no argument for the existence of the object, but that we perceive it; perception commands our belief upon its own authority, and disdains to rest its authority upon any reasoning whatsoever.

The conviction of a truth may be irresistible, and yet not immediate. Thus, my conviction that the three angles of every plain triangle are equal to two right angles, is irresistible, but it is not immediate; I am convinced of it by demonstrative reasoning. There are other truths in mathematics of which we have not only an irresistible but an immediate conviction. Such are the axioms. Our belief of the axioms in mathematics is not grounded upon argument – arguments are grounded upon them; but their evidence is discerned immediately by the human understanding.

It is, no doubt, one thing to have an immediate conviction of a self-evident axiom; it is another thing to have an immediate conviction of the existence of what we see; but the conviction is equally immediate and equally irresistible in both cases. No man thinks of seeking a reason to believe what he sees; and, before we are capable of reasoning, we put no less confidence in our senses than after....

The account I have given of our perception of external objects, is intended as a faithful delineation of what every man, come to years of understanding, and capable of giving attention to what passes in his own mind, may feel in himself. In what manner the notion of external objects, and the immediate belief of their existence, is produced by means of our senses, I am not able to shew, and I do not pretend to shew. If the power of perceiving external objects in certain circumstances, be a part of the original constitution of the human mind, all attempts to account for it will be vain. No other account can be given of the constitution of things, but the will of Him that made them. As we can give no reason why matter is extended and inert, why the mind thinks and is conscious of its thoughts, but the will of Him who made both; so I suspect we can give no other reason why, in certain circumstances, we perceive external objects, and in other do not.

The Supreme Being intended that we should have such knowledge of the material objects that surround us, as is necessary in order to our supplying the wants of nature, and avoiding the dangers to which we are constantly exposed; and he has admirably fitted our powers of perception to this purpose. If the intelligence we have of external objects were to be got by reasoning only, the greatest part of men would be destitute of it; for the greatest part of men hardly ever learn to reason; and in infancy and childhood no man can reason: Therefore, as this intelligence of the objects that surround us, and from which we may receive so much benefit or harm, is equally necessary to children and to men, to the ignorant and to the learned, God in his wisdom conveys it to us in a way that puts all upon a level. The information of the senses is as perfect, and gives as full conviction to the most ignorant as to the most learned....

Chapter XVI: Of Sensation

HAVING finished what I intend, with regard to that act of mind which we call the perception of an external object, I proceed to consider another, which, by our constitution, is conjoined with perception, and not with perception only, but with many other acts of our minds; and that is sensation. . . .

Almost all our perceptions have corresponding sensations which constantly accompany them, and, on that account, are very apt to be confounded with them. Neither ought we to expect that the sensation, and its corresponding perception, should be distinguished in common language, because the purposes of common life do not require it. Language is made to serve the purposes of ordinary conversation; and we have no reason to expect that it should make distinctions that are not of common use. Hence it happens, that a quality perceived, and the sensation corresponding to that perception, often go under the same name.

This makes the names of most of our sensations ambiguous, and this ambiguity hath very much perplexed philosophers. It will be necessary to give some instances, to illustrate the distinction between our sensations and the objects of perception.

When I smell a rose, there is in this operation both sensation and perception. The agreeable odour I feel, considered by itself, without relation to any external object, is merely a sensation. It affects the mind in a certain way; and this affection of the mind may be conceived, without a thought of the rose, or any other object. This sensation can be nothing else than it is felt to be. Its very essence consists in being felt; and, when it is not felt, it is not. There is no difference between the sensation and the feeling of it – they are one and the same thing. It is for this reason that we before observed that, in sensation, there is no object distinct from that act of the mind by which it is felt – and this holds true with regard to all sensations.

Let us next attend to the perception which we have in smelling a rose. Perception has always an external object; and the object of my perception, in this case, is that quality in the rose which I discern by the sense of smell. Observing that the agreeable sensation is raised when the rose is near, and ceases when it is removed, I am led, by my nature, to conclude some quality to be in the rose, which is the cause of this sensation. This quality in the rose is the object perceived; and that act of my mind by which I have the conviction and belief of this quality, is what in this case I call perception.

But it is here to be observed, that the sensation I feel, and the quality in the rose which I perceive, are both called by the same name. The smell of a rose is the name given to both: so that this name hath two meanings; and the distinguishing its different meanings removes all perplexity, and enables us to give clear and distinct answers to questions about which philosophers have held much dispute.

Thus, if it is asked, whether the smell be in the rose, or in the mind that feels it, the answer is obvious: That there are two different things signified by the smell of a rose; one of which is in the mind, and can be in nothing but in a sentient being; the other is truly and properly in the rose. The sensation which I feel is in my mind. The mind is the sentient being; and, as the rose is insentient, there can be no sensation, nor anything resembling sensation in it. But this sensation in my mind is occasioned by a certain quality in the rose, which is called by the same name with the sensation, not on account of any similitude, but because of their constant concomitancy.

All the names we have for smells, tastes, sounds, and for the various degrees of heat and cold, have a like ambiguity; and what has been said of the smell of a rose may be applied to them. They signify both a sensation, and a quality perceived by means of that sensation. The first is the sign, the last the thing signified. As both are conjoined by nature, and as the purposes of common life do not require them to be disjoined in our thoughts, they are both expressed by the same name: and this ambiguity is to be found in all languages, because the reason of it extends to all.

The same ambiguity is found in the names of such diseases as are indicated by a particular painful sensation: such as the toothache, the headache. The toothache signifies a painful sensation, which can only be in a sentient being; but it signifies also a disorder in the body, which has no similitude to a sensation, but is naturally connected with it.

Pressing my hand with force against the table, I feel pain, and I feel the table to be hard. The pain is a sensation of the mind, and there is nothing that resembles it in the table. The hardness is in the table, nor is there anything resembling it in the mind. Feeling is applied to both; but in a different sense; being a word common to the act of sensation, and to that of perceiving by the sense of touch.

I touch the table gently with my hand, and I feel it to be smooth, hard, and cold. These are qualities of the table perceived by touch; but I perceive them by means of a sensation which indicates them. This sensation not being painful, I commonly give no attention to it. It carries my thought immediately to the thing signified by it, and is itself forgot, as if it had never been. But, by repeating it, and turning my attention to it, and abstracting my thought from the thing signified by it, I find it to be merely a sensation, and that it has no similitude to the hardness, smoothness, or coldness of the table, which are signified by it.

It is indeed difficult, at first, to disjoin things in our attention which have always been conjoined, and to make that an object of reflection which never was so before; but some pains and practice will overcome this difficulty in those who have got the habit of reflecting on the operations of their own minds. . . .

Sensation, taken by itself, implies neither the conception nor belief of any external object. It supposes a sentient being, and a certain manner in which that being is affected; but it supposes no more. Perception implies an immediate conviction and belief of something external – something different both from the mind that perceives, and from the act of perception. Things so different in their nature ought to be distinguished; but, by our constitution, they are always united. Every different perception is conjoined with a sensation that is proper to it. The one is the sign, the other the thing signified. They coalesce in our imagination. They are signified by one name, and are considered as one simple operation. The purposes of life do not require them to be distinguished. . . .

4

From *The Philosophy of the Enlightenment*

Ernst Cassirer

. . .

2

A survey of the special problems of eighteenth century epistemology and psychology shows that in all their variety and inner diversity they are grouped around a common center. The investigation of individual problems in all their abundance and apparent dispersion comes back again and again to a general theoretical problem in which all the threads of the study unite.[1] This is the problem which Molyneux first formulated in his *Optics*, and which soon awakened the greatest philosophical interest. Is the experience derived from one field of sense perception a sufficient basis on which to construct another field of perception that is of qualitatively different content and of specifically different structure? Is there an inner connection which permits us to make a direct transition from one such field to another, from the world of touch, for instance, to that of vision? Will a person born blind – who has acquired an exact knowledge of certain corporeal forms by means of experience and so can distinguish accurately among them – have the same power to distinguish objects if, as a result of a successful operation, he gains possession of his visual faculty, and is required to judge concerning these forms on the basis of purely optical data without the aid of his sense of touch? Will he be able immediately to distinguish a cube from a sphere by sight, or will a long and difficult period of adjustment be necessary before he succeeds in

Ernst Cassirer, *The Philosophy of the Enlightenment* (Princeton, NJ: Princeton University Press, 1962), pp. 108–15.

establishing a connection between the tactile impression and the visual form of these two objects? No uniform solution of all these problems was found at once, but now that the problems had been formulated, their influence reached far beyond the sphere of the special sciences. Berkeley's philosophical diary shows how much these problems occupied his mind, and how they form, as it were, germinating cells from which his whole theory of perception developed. The *Essay towards a New Theory of Vision*, which forms the prelude to Berkeley's philosophy and contains all of his ideas implicitly, is nothing but an attempt at a complete systematic development and elucidation of Molyneux's problem. For decades thereafter the strength and fruitfulness of this problem are still evident in French philosophy. Voltaire, in his *Elements of the Philosophy of Newton*, gives an extensive exposition of the problem;[2] Diderot makes it the central point of his first psychological and epistemological essay, *Letter on the Blind* (1749). As for Condillac, he is so much under the spell of this question that he even declares that it contains the source and key to all modern psychology; for it was this question which drew attention to the decisive role of the faculty of judgment in the simplest act of perception as well as in the developing structure of the perceptual world.[3] The decisive systematic significance of Molyneux's problem is thus clearly indicated; the individual example which this problem presents called attention to the general question as to whether sense as such can produce the physical world which we find in consciousness, or whether to this end it requires the cooperation of other powers of the mind, and as to how these powers are to be determined.

Berkeley in his *New Theory of Vision* and his *Principles of Human Knowledge* had proceeded from the paradox that the only material available for the erection of the structure of our perceptual world consists in simple sense perceptions, but that, on the other hand, these perceptions do not contain the slightest indication of those 'forms' in which perceptual reality is given. We believe that we see this reality before us as a solid structure in which every individual element has its assigned place, and in which its relation to all other parts is exactly determined. The fundamental character of all reality lies in this definite relationship. Without the presence of order in the co-existence and sequence of our individual perceptions, without a definite spatial and temporal relationship among the various perceptions, there can be no objective world, no 'nature of things.' And not even the most determined idealist can deny this nature of things; for he too must postulate an inviolable order among phenomena, or else his phenomenal world will dissolve into mere illusion.[4] Thus the cardinal question of all theory of knowledge is that of the meaning of this order, while the cardinal question of all genetic psychology is that of its derivation. But here experience, from which alone we can expect reliable guidance, seems to leave us in the lurch. For it always shows us the world of products, not the world of process; it confronts us with objects bearing definite shapes, especially in respect to a certain spatial arrangement, without telling us how they acquired these shapes. The first glance we cast on things enables us to discover not only certain sense qualities, but certain spatial relations as well; we ascribe to every individual object a certain magnitude, a certain position, and a certain distance from other objects. But if we try to establish the foundation of all these assertions, we find that it is not to be discovered among the data given us by the visual sense. For these data are merely differentiated according to quality and intensity and contain nothing that would lead us to the concept of magnitude or of pure quantity. The ray of light which passes from the object to my eye can tell me nothing directly about the object's shape or its distance from me. For all the eye knows is the impression on the retina. But from the quality of this impression no knowledge can be had of the cause which produced it, nor of the distance of the object from the eye. The conclusion to be drawn from all this is that what we call distance, position, and magnitude of objects is itself something invisible. Berkeley's fundamental thesis now seems to be reduced to an absurdity; the equation of being (*esse*) and being perceived (*percipi*) seems to have vanished. In the midst of phenomena which are immediately perceived by our senses, and which we cannot avoid, something has been discovered which lies beyond all the limits of perception. The distance between objects appears by its very nature to be imperceptible, and yet it is an element which is absolutely essential to the structure of our conception of the world. The spatial form of perceptions is fused with its sense material; and yet it is not given in the material alone, nor can it be analytically reduced to this material. Thus the form of perceptions constitutes a foreign body in the only accessible world of immediate sense data which cannot be eliminated without causing this world to collapse. In the assertion: '...distance is in its own nature imperceptible and yet it is perceived by sight,'[5] Berkeley in his *New Theory of Vision* gives the most poignant expression of the dilemma with which sensationalist psychology and epistemology are confronted at the very start.

Berkeley overcomes this dilemma by giving a broader meaning to his basic concept of perception, by including in its definition not only simple sensation but also the activity of representation. Every sense impression possesses such a power of representation, of indirect reference. It not only presents itself with its specific content to consciousness but it causes all other content with which it is joined by a strong empirical bond to be visible and present in consciousness. And this reciprocal play of sense impressions, this regularity, with which they recall each other and represent each other in consciousness, is also the ultimate basis of the idea of space. This idea is not given as such in a particular perception; it belongs neither to the sense of vision nor to that of touch alone. Space is no specific qualitative element as originally given as color or tone; it is that which results from the relationship among various sense data. Since in the course of experience visual and tactile impressions are firmly joined, consciousness acquires the ability to pass from one type of sensation to another according to certain rules. It is in this transition that we must look for the origin of the idea of space. The transition itself must of course be understood as a purely empirical, not as a rational, transition. It is not a bond of a logical and mathematical kind; it is not reasoning which leads us from certain perceptions of visual sensation to those of touch, or from the latter to the former. Habit and practice alone weave this bond, and they make it progressively firmer. The idea of space is not, therefore, strictly speaking an element of sense consciousness but an expression of a process which goes on in consciousness. Only the speed and regularity of this process cause us to overlook the intermediate stages in ordinary introspection and to anticipate the end of the process at the very start. But closer psychological and epistemological analysis reveals these intermediary steps and teaches us how indispensable they are. It shows us that the same connection exists between different fields of sensory experience as between the symbols of our language and their meaning. Just as the speech symbol is in no sense similar to the content to which it refers nor is connected with it by any objective necessity, yet fulfills its function nevertheless, so the same relation holds for the connection among generically different and qualitatively disparate impressions. It is only the universality and regularity of their arrangement which distinguish the symbols of sense impressions from those of speech. Elucidating Berkeley's idea Voltaire writes: 'We learn to see just as we learn to speak and read.... The quick and almost uniform judgments which all our minds form at a certain age with regard to distances, magnitudes, and positions make us think that we need only open our eyes in order to see things as we actually do perceive them. This is an illusion.... If all men spoke the same language, we should always be inclined to believe that there is a necessary connection between words and ideas. But all men speak the same language with respect to the imagination. Nature says to all: When you have seen colors for a certain length of time, your imagination will represent to you in the same manner the bodies to which these colors seem to belong. The prompt and involuntary judgment which you will form, will be useful to you in the course of your life.'[6]

Berkeley's theory of vision was recognized and adopted in its main aspects by almost all leading psychologists of the eighteenth century. Condillac and Diderot[7] modify it in certain details; both point out, for instance, that visual impressions in themselves include a certain 'spatiality.' To the sense of touch they attribute merely the function of clarification and fixation of our visual experience; they consider tactile sensations as indispensable not for the origin, but for the growth of our conception of space. But this modification does not affect Berkeley's strictly empirical thesis as such. All apriority of space is vigorously rejected; hence the question of its generality and necessity appears in a new light. If we owe our insight into the structural relations of space merely to experience, it is not inconceivable that a change of experience, as for instance in the event of an alteration of our psychophysical organization, would affect the whole nature of space. Henceforth the concept of space is indefatigably pursued through all its ramifications. What is the significance of that constancy and objectivity which we are accustomed to attribute to the forms of perception and of the understanding? Does this constancy predicate anything concerning the nature of things, or is not all that we understand by this term related and limited to our own nature? Are the judgments which we base on this conception valid, as Bacon would say, by analogy with the universe (*ex analogia universi*) or rather exclusively by analogy with man (*ex analogia hominis*)? With this question the problem of the origin of the idea of space develops far beyond its initial limits. We see now the circumstance which caused psychological and epistemological thought in the eighteenth century to recur again and again to this problem. For on it the fate of the concept of truth in general seemed to depend. If space, which is a fundamental element of all human perception, consists merely of the fusion and correlation of various sensory impressions, then it cannot lay claim to any other necessity and any higher logical dignity than the original elements of which it is composed. The subjectivity of sensory qualities, which is known to and generally acknowledged by modern science, accordingly draws space too into its sphere. But the development cannot stop here, for what is true of space is true in the same sense and with the same justification of all the other factors on which the 'form' of knowledge is based. Even the psychology of antiquity distinguished sharply among the various classes of sensory content, between colors and sounds, tastes and smells, on the one hand, and between the pure 'form concepts' on the other. The latter – among which were included besides space, especially duration, number, motion, and rest – were given a special place in that they were not attributed to a particular sense but to a 'common sense,' αἰσθητήριον κοινὸν. The rationalistic theory of knowledge in modern times went back to this psychological distinction among the sources of sense impressions in order to establish a specific difference in validity between the ideas derived from the two classes of sensory content. Leibniz points out that the ideas which one usually attributes to 'common sense' (*sensus communis*), really belong to and are derived from the mind: '... they are ideas of pure reason, but such as have an external reference and are perceivable by the senses; hence they are capable of definitions and proofs.'[8] This view appeared to have been conclusively overthrown by the exact analysis of Molyneux's problem. In the year 1728, when Cheselden successfully operated on a fourteen year old boy who had been blind from birth, Molyneux's theoretical problem seemed to have found an empirical solution. Observations on this boy who had suddenly acquired visual organs seemed to confirm the empirical argument on all points. Berkeley's theoretical predictions were completely verified. It was found that the patient by no means obtained full visual power as soon as his eyesight began to function, and that he had to learn gradually and laboriously to distinguish between the corporeal forms which were presented to his vision. The theory that there is no inner affinity between the data of touch and those of vision but that the relation between them is merely the result of their habitual connection is thus verified by experience. But if this conclusion is valid, then we can no longer speak of a uniform space underlying all the senses and serving, as it were, as a homogeneous substratum. This homogeneous space, which Leibniz had looked upon as a creation of the mind, now proves to be a mere abstraction. We do not find any such unity and uniformity of space in experience but rather just as many qualitatively different kinds of space as we have different fields of sensory experience. Optical space, tactile space, kinesthetic space, all have their own unique structure; they are not connected or related by virtue of a common essence or an abstract form but merely by the regular empirical connection existing between them, by means of which they can reciprocally represent one another. A further conclusion now seems inescapable. The question as to which of all these sensory spaces is to be considered the 'true' space, now loses all meaning. They all possess equal validity; none can claim a higher degree of certainty, objectivity, and generality than any other. Accordingly, what we call objectivity or truth or necessity, has no absolute, but merely a relative meaning. Each sense has its own world, and there is no other alternative than to understand and analyze all these worlds in a purely empirical manner without attempting to reduce them to a common denominator. The philosophy of the Enlightenment never tires of inculcating this relativity....

Notes

1 There is no place here for discussion of these problems. For a fuller treatment, see the author's *Erkenntnisproblem*, vol. II.
2 *Éléments de la Philosophie de Newton*, ch. VII, *Oeuvres*, vol. XXX, pp. 138ff.
3 Condillac, *Traité des sensations*, ed. Lyon, p. 33.
4 Cf. Berkeley, *A Treatise concerning the Principles of Human Knowledge*, sect. 34; *Three Dialogues between Hylas and Philonous*, Third Dialogue.
5 Berkeley, *New Theory of Vision*, sect. II.
6 Voltaire, *Éléments de la Philosophie de Newton*, part II, ch. VII; *Oeuvres*, vol. XXX, p. 147.
7 See Diderot, *Lettre sur les Aveugles*, and Condillac, *Traité des Sensations*, part I, chaps VII, XIff.
8 Leibniz, *Nouveaux Essais sur l'entendement humain*, Book II, ch. v.

5

From *Elements of Physiology*

Johannes Müller

On the Specific Energies of Nerves

The senses, by virtue of the peculiar properties of their several nerves, make us acquainted with the states of our own body, and they also inform us of the qualities and changes of external nature as far as these give rise to changes in the condition of the nerves. Sensation is a property common to all the senses; but the kind of sensation is different in each: thus we have the sensations of light, of sound, of taste, of smell, and of feeling, or touch. By feeling, or touch, we understand the peculiar kind of sensation of which the ordinary sensitive nerves generally – as, the nervus trigeminus, vagus, glossopharyngeus, and the spinal nerves – are susceptible; the sensations of itching, of pleasure and pain, of heat and cold, and those excited by the act of touch in its more limited sense, are varieties of this mode of sensation. That which through the medium of our senses is actually perceived by the sensorium, is indeed merely a property or change of condition of our nerves; but the imagination and reason are ready to interpret the modifications in the state of the nerves produced by external influences as properties of the external bodies themselves. This mode of regarding sensations has become so habitual in the case of the senses which are more rarely affected by internal causes, that it is only on reflection that we perceive it to be erroneous. In the case of the sense of feeling or touch, on the contrary, where the peculiar sensations of the nerves perceived by the sensorium are excited as frequently by internal as by external causes, it is easily conceived that the feeling of pain or pleasure, for example, is a condition of the nerves, and

Johannes Müller, Introduction to *Handbuch der Physiologie des Menschen*, Book V (Koblenz, 1838), tr. William Baly as *Elements of Physiology*, vol. 2 (London, 1842).

not a property of the things which excite it. This leads us to the consideration of some general laws, a knowledge of which is necessary before entering on the physiology of the separate senses.

I.   In the first place, it must be kept in mind that *external agencies can give rise to no kind of sensation which cannot also be produced by internal causes, exciting changes in the condition of our nerves. ...*

...The sensations of the sense of vision, namely, colour, light, and darkness, are also perceived independently of all external exciting cause. In the state of the most perfect freedom from excitement, the optic nerve has no other sensation than that of darkness. The excited condition of the nerve is manifested, even while the eyes are closed, by the appearance of light, or luminous flashes, which are mere sensations of the nerve, and not owing to the presence of any matter of light, and consequently are not capable of illuminating any surrounding objects. Everyone is aware how common it is to see bright colours while the eyes are closed, particularly in the morning when the irritability of the nerves is still considerable. These phenomena are very frequent in children after waking from sleep. Through the sense of vision, therefore, we receive from external nature no impressions which we may not also experience from internal excitement of our nerves; and it is evident that a person blind from infancy in consequence of opacity of the transparent media of the eye, must have a perfect internal conception of light and colours, provided the retina and optic nerve be free from lesion....

II.   *The same internal cause excites in the different senses different sensations, in each sense the sensations peculiar to it.*

One uniform internal cause acting on all the nerves of the senses in the same manner, is the accumulation of blood in the capillary vessels of the nerve, as in congestion and inflammation. This uniform cause excites in the retina, while the eyes are closed, the sensation of light and luminous flashes; in the auditory nerve, humming and ringing sounds; and in the nerves of feeling, the sensation of pain. In the same way, also, a narcotic substance introduced into the blood excites in the nerves of each sense peculiar symptoms; in the optic nerves the appearance of luminous sparks before the eyes; in the auditory nerves, 'tinnitus aurium'; and in the common sensitive nerves the sensation of ants creeping over the surface.

III.   *The same external cause also gives rise to different sensations in each sense, according to the special endowments of its nerve.*

The mechanical influence of a blow, concussion, or pressure excites, for example, in the eye the sensation of light and colours. It is well known that by exerting pressure upon the eye, when the eyelids are closed, we can arouse the appearance of a luminous circle; by more gentle pressure the appearance of colours may be produced, and one colour may be made to change to another. . . .

IV. *The peculiar sensations of each nerve of sense can be excited by several distinct causes internal and external.*

The facts on which this statement is founded have been already mentioned. . . .

V. *Sensation consists in the sensorium's receiving through the medium of the nerves, and as the result of the action of an external cause, a knowledge of certain qualities or conditions, not of external bodies, but of the nerves of sense themselves; and these qualities of the nerves of sense are in all different, the nerve of each sense having its own peculiar quality or energy.*

The special susceptibility of the different nerves of sense for certain influences – as of the optic nerve for light, of the auditory nerve for vibrations, and so on – was formerly attributed to these nerves having each a specific irritability. But this hypothesis is evidently insufficient to explain all the facts. The nerves of the senses have assuredly a specific irritability for certain influences; for many stimuli, which exert a violent action upon one organ of sense, have little or no effect upon another: for example, light, or vibrations so infinitely rapid as those of light, act only on the nerves of vision and common sensation; slower vibrations, on the nerves of hearing and common sensation, but not upon those of vision; odorous substances only upon the olfactory nerves. The external stimuli must therefore be adapted to the organ of sense – must be 'homogeneous': thus light is the stimulus adapted to the nerve of vision; while vibrations of less rapidity, which act upon the auditory nerve, are not adapted to the optic nerve, or are indifferent to it; for if the eye be touched with a tuning-fork while vibrating, a sensation of tremors is excited in the conjunctiva, but no sensation of light. We have seen, however, that one and the same stimulus, as electricity, will produce different sensations in the different nerves of the senses; all the nerves are susceptible of its action, but the sensations in all are different. The same is the case with other stimuli, as chemical and mechanical influences. The hypothesis of a specific irritability of the nerves of the senses for certain stimuli, is therefore insufficient; and we are compelled to ascribe, with Aristotle, peculiar energies to each nerve – energies which are vital qualities of the nerve, just as contractility is the vital property of muscle....

The sensation of sound, therefore, is the peculiar 'energy' or 'quality' of the auditory nerve; the sensation of light and colours that of the optic nerve; and so of the other nerves of sense. An exact nature it is always our own sensations that we become acquainted with, and from them we form conceptions of the properties of external objects, which may be relatively correct; but we can never submit the nature of the objects themselves to that immediate perception to which the states of the different parts of our own body are subjected in the sensorium.

VI.   *The nerve of each sense seems to be capable of one determinate kind of sensation only, and not of those proper to the other organs of sense; hence one nerve of sense cannot take the place and perform the function of the nerve of another sense....*

VII.   *It is not known whether the essential cause of the peculiar 'energy' of each nerve of sense is seated in the nerve itself, or in the parts of the brain and spinal cord with which it is connected; but it is certain that the central portions of the nerves included in the encephalon are susceptible of their peculiar sensations, independently of the more peripheral portion of the nervous cords which form the means of communication with the external organs of sense.*

The specific sensibility of the individual senses to particular stimuli – owing to which vibrations of such rapidity or length as to produce sound are perceived, only by the senses of hearing and touch, and mere mechanical influences, scarcely at all by the sense of taste – must be a property of the nerves themselves; but the peculiar mode of reaction of each sense, after the excitement of its nerve, may be due to either of two conditions. Either the nerves themselves may communicate impressions different in quality to the sensorium, which in every instance remains the same; or the vibrations of the nervous principle may in every nerve be the same and yet give rise to the perception of different sensations in the sensorium, owing to the parts of the latter with which the nerves are connected having different properties. The proof of either of these propositions I regard as at present impossible.

VIII.   *The immediate objects of the perception of our senses are merely particular states induced in the nerves, and felt as sensations either by the nerves themselves or by the sensorium; but inasmuch as the nerves of the senses are material bodies, and therefore participate in the properties of matter generally occupying space, being susceptible of vibratory motion, and capable of being* *changed chemically as well as by the action of heat and electricity, they make known to the sensorium, by virtue of the changes thus produced in them by external causes, not merely their own condition, but also properties and changes of condition of external bodies. The information thus obtained by the senses concerning external nature, varies in each sense, having a relation to the qualities or energies of the nerve.*

Qualities which are to be regarded rather as sensations or modes of reaction of the nerves of sense, are light, colour, the bitter and sweet tastes, pleasant and unpleasant odours, painful and pleasant impressions on the nerves of touch, cold and warmth: properties which may belong wholly to external nature are 'extension', progressive and tremulous motion, and chemical change.

All the senses are not equally adapted to impart the idea of 'extension' to the sensorium. The nerve of vision and the nerve of touch, being capable of an exact perception of this property in themselves, make us acquainted with it in external bodies. In the nerves of taste, the sensation of extension is less distinct, but is not altogether deficient; thus we are capable of distinguishing whether the seat of a bitter or sweet taste be the tongue, the palate, or the fauces. In the sense of touch and sight, however, the perception of space is most acute. The retina of the optic nerve has a structure especially adapted for this perception.

6

From *Treatise on Physiological Optics*

Hermann von Helmholtz

Subdivisions of the Subject

Physiological Optics is the science of the visual perceptions by the sense of sight. The objects around us are made visible through the agency of light proceeding thence and falling on our eyes. This light, reaching the retina, which is a sensitive portion of the nervous system, stimulates certain sensations therein. These are conveyed to the brain by the optic nerve, the result being that the mind becomes conscious of the perception of certain objects disposed in space.

Accordingly, the theory of the visual perceptions may be divided into three parts:

1   *The theory of the path of the light in the eye.* Since we are here chiefly concerned with the refraction of the rays, and only incidentally with regular or diffuse reflection, this subdivision of the subject may be entitled *the dioptrics of the eye.*
2   *The theory of the sensations of the nervous mechanism of vision;* in which the sensations are considered by themselves without taking account of the possibility which they afford of recognizing external objects.
3   *The theory of the interpretation of the visual sensations;* dealing with the impressions which these sensations enable us to form of the objects around us. . . .

Hermann von Helmholtz, *Treatise on Physiological Optics*, ed. J. Southall (New York: Dover, 1950), Book 3, pp. 1–7, 10–13, 17–22.

Concerning the Perceptions in General

The sensations aroused by light in the nervous mechanism of vision enable us to form conceptions as to the existence, form and position of external objects. These ideas are called *visual perceptions*. In this third subdivision of Physiological Optics we must try to analyze the scientific results which we have obtained concerning the conditions which give rise to visual perceptions.

Perceptions of external objects being therefore of the nature of ideas, and ideas themselves being invariably activities of our psychic energy, perceptions also can only be the result of psychic energy. Accordingly, strictly speaking, the theory of perceptions belongs properly in the domain of psychology. This is particularly true with respect to the mode of the mental activities in the case of the perceptions and with respect to the determination of their laws. Yet even here there is a wide field of investigation in both physics and physiology, inasmuch as we have to determine, scientifically as far as possible, what special properties of the physical stimulus and of the physiological stimulation are responsible for the formation of this or that particular idea as to the nature of the external objects perceived. In this part of the subject, therefore, we shall have to investigate the special properties of the retinal images, muscular sensations, etc., that are concerned in the perception of a definite position of the observed object, not only as to its direction but as to its distance; how the perception of the form of a body of three dimensions depends on certain peculiarities of the images; and under what circumstances it will appear single or double as seen by both eyes, etc. Thus, our main purpose will be simply to investigate the material of sensation whereby we are enabled to form ideas, in those relations that are important for the perceptions obtained from them. . . .

Here I shall merely indicate at the outset certain general characteristics of the mental processes that are active in the sense-perceptions, because they will be constantly encountered in connection with the various subjects to be considered. Without some previous explanation of their general significance and wide range of activity, the reader might be apt in some special case to regard them as paradoxical and incredible.

The general rule determining the ideas of vision that are formed whenever an impression is made on the eye, with or without the aid of optical instruments, is that *such objects are always imagined as being present in the field of vision as would have to be there in order to produce the same impression on the nervous mechanism, the eyes being used under ordinary normal conditions.* To employ an illustration... suppose that the eyeball is mechanically stimulated at the outer corner of the eye. Then we imagine that we see an appearance of light in front of us somewhere in the direction of the bridge of the nose. Under ordinary conditions of vision, when our eyes are stimulated by light coming from outside, if the region of the retina in the outer corner of the eye is to be stimulated, the light actually has to enter the eye from the direction of the bridge of the nose. Thus, in accordance with the above rule, in a case of this kind we substitute a luminous object at the place mentioned in the field of view, although as a matter of fact the mechanical stimulus does not act on the eye from in front of the field of view nor from the nasal side of the eye, but, on the contrary, is exerted on the outer surface of the eyeball and more from behind. ...

The psychic activities that lead us to infer that there in front of us at a certain place there is a certain object of a certain character, are generally not conscious activities, but unconscious ones. In their result they are equivalent to a *conclusion*, to the extent that the observed action on our senses enables us to form an idea as to the possible cause of this action; although, as a matter of fact, it is invariably simply the nervous stimulations that are perceived directly, that is, the actions, but never the external objects themselves. But what seems to differentiate them from a conclusion, in the ordinary sense of that word, is that a conclusion is an act of conscious thought. An astronomer, for example, comes to real conscious conclusions of this sort, when he computes the positions of the stars in space, their distances, etc., from the perspective images he has had of them at various times and as they are seen from different parts of the orbit of the earth. His conclusions are based on a conscious knowledge of the laws of optics. In the ordinary acts of vision this knowledge of optics is lacking. Still it may be permissible to speak of the psychic acts of ordinary perception as *unconscious conclusions*, thereby making a distinction of some sort between them and the common so-called conscious conclusions. And while it is true that there has been, and probably always will be, a measure of doubt as to the similarity of the psychic activity in the two cases, there can be no doubt as to the similarity between the results of such unconscious conclusions and those of conscious conclusions.

These unconscious conclusions derived from sensation are equivalent in their consequences to the so-called *conclusions from analogy.* Inasmuch as in an overwhelming majority of cases, whenever the parts of the retina in the outer corner of the eye are stimulated, it has been found to be due to external light coming into the eye from the direction of the bridge of the nose, the inference we make is that it is so in every new case whenever this part of the retina is stimulated; just as we assert that every single individual now living will die, because all previous experience has shown that all men who were formerly alive have died.

But, moreover, just because they are not free acts of conscious thought, these unconscious conclusions from analogy are irresistible, and the effect of them cannot be overcome by a better understanding of the real relations. . . .

Another general characteristic property of our sense-perceptions is, that *we are not in the habit of observing our sensations accurately, except as they are useful in enabling us to recognize external objects. On the contrary, we are wont to disregard all those parts of the sensations that are of no importance so far as external objects are concerned.* Thus in most cases some special assistance and training are needed in order to observe these latter subjective sensations. It might seem that nothing could be easier than to be conscious of one's own sensations; and yet experience shows that for the discovery of subjective sensations some special talent is needed, such as Purkinje manifested in the highest degree; or else it is the result of accident or of theoretical speculation. For instance, the phenomena of the blind spot were discovered by Mariotte from theoretical considerations. . . .

When a person's attention is directed for the first time to the double images in binocular vision, he is usually greatly astonished to think that he had never noticed them before, especially when he reflects that the only objects he has ever seen single were those few that happened at the moment to be about as far from his eyes as the point of fixation. The great majority of objects, comprising all those that were farther or nearer than this point, were all seen double.

Accordingly, the first thing we have to learn is to pay heed to our individual sensations. Ordinarily we do so merely in case of those sensations that enable us to find out about the world around us. In the ordinary affairs of life the sensations have no other importance for us. Subjective sensations are of interest chiefly for scientific investigations only. If they happen to be noticed in the ordinary activity of the senses, they merely distract the attention. Thus while we may attain an extraordinary degree of delicacy and precision in objective observation, we not only fail to do so in subjective observations, but indeed we acquire the faculty in large measure of overlooking them and of forming our opinions of objects independently of them, even when they are so pronounced that they might easily be noticed. . . .

Consequently, it may often be rather hard to say how much of our apperceptions (*Anschauungen*) as derived by the sense of sight is due directly to sensation, and how much of them, on the other hand, is due to experience and training. The main point of controversy between various investigators in this territory is connected also with this difficulty. Some are disposed to concede to the influence of experience as much scope as possible, and to derive from it especially all notion of space. This view may be called the *empirical theory* (*empiristische Theorie*). Others, of course, are obliged to admit the influence of experience in the case of certain classes of perceptions; still with respect to certain elementary apperceptions that occur uniformly in the case of all observers, they believe it is necessary to assume a system of innate apperceptions that are not based on experience, especially with respect to space-relations. In contradistinction to the former view, this may perhaps be called the *intuition theory* (*nativistische Theorie*) of the sense-perceptions.

In my opinion the following fundamental principles should be kept in mind in this discussion.

Let us restrict the word *idea* (*Vorstellung*) to mean the image of visual objects as retained in the memory, without being accompanied by any present sense-impressions; and use the term *apperception* (*Anschauung*) to mean a perception (*Wahrnehmung*) when it is accompanied by the sense-impressions in question. The term *immediate perception* (*Perzeption*) may then be employed to denote an apperception of this nature in which there is no element whatever that is not the result of direct sensations, that is, an apperception such as might be derived without any recollection of previous experience. Obviously, therefore, one and the same apperception may be accompanied by the corresponding sensations in very different measure. Thus idea and immediate perception may be combined in the apperception in the most different proportions. . . .

Now in my opinion we are justified by our previous experiences in stating that no indubitable present sensation can be abolished and overcome by an act of the intellect; and no matter how clearly we recognize that it has been produced in some anomalous way, still the illusion does not disappear by comprehending the process. The attention may be diverted from sensations, particularly if they are feeble and habitual; but in noting those relations in the external world, that are associated with these sensations, we are obliged to observe the sensations themselves. Thus we may be unmindful of the temperature-sensation of our skin when it is not very keen, or of the contact-sensations produced by our clothing, as long as we are occupied with entirely different matters. But just as soon as we stop to think whether it is warm or cold, we are not in the position to convert the feeling of warmth into that of coldness; maybe because we know that it is due to strenuous exertion and not to the temperature of the surrounding air. In the same way the apparition of light when pressure is exerted on the eyeball cannot be made to vanish simply by comprehending better the nature of the process, supposing the attention is directed to the field of vision and not, say, to the ear or the skin.

On the other hand, it may also be that we are not in the position to isolate an impression of sensation, because it involves the composite sense-symbol of an external object. However, in this case the correct comprehension of the object shows that the sensation in question has been percieved and used by the consciousness.

My conclusion is, that *nothing in our sense-perceptions can be recognized as sensation which can be overcome in the perceptual image and converted into its opposite by factors that are demonstrably due to experience.*

Whatever, therefore, can be overcome by factors of experience, we must consider as being itself the product of experience and training. By observing this rule, we shall find that it is merely the qualities of the sensation that are to be considered as real, pure sensation; the great majority of space-apperceptions, however, being the product of experience and training. ...

I am aware that in the present state of knowledge it is impossible to refute the intuition theory. The reasons why I prefer the opposite view are because in my opinion:

1 The intuition theory is an unnecessary hypothesis.
2 Its consequences thus far invariably apply to perceptual images of space which only in the fewest cases are in accordance with reality and with the correct visual images that are undoubtedly present. ... The adherents of this theory are, therefore, obliged to make the very questionable assumption, that the *space sensations*, which according to them are present originally, are continually being improved and overruled by knowledge which we have accumulated by experience. By analogy with all other experiences, however, we should have to expect that the sensations which have been overruled continued to be present in the apperception as a conscious illusion, if nothing else. But this is not the case.
3 It is not clear how the assumption of these original *"space sensations"* can help the explanation of our visual perceptions, when the adherents of this theory ultimately have to assume in by far the great majority of cases that these sensations must be overruled by the better understanding which we get by experience. In that case it would seem to me much easier and simpler to grasp, that all apperceptions of

space were obtained simply by experience, instead of supposing that
the latter have to contend against intuitive perceptual images that are
generally false. ...

Our apperceptions and ideas are *effects* wrought on our nervous system
and our consciousness by the objects that are thus apprehended and
conceived. Each effect, as to its nature, quite necessarily depends both
on the nature of what causes the effect and on that of the person on whom
the effect is produced. To expect to obtain an idea which would reproduce the nature of the thing conceived, that is, which would be true in an
absolute sense, would mean to expect an effect which would be perfectly
independent of the nature of the thing on which the effect was produced;
which would be an obvious absurdity. Our human ideas, therefore, and
all ideas of any conceivable intelligent creature, must be images of objects
whose mode is essentially co-dependent on the nature of the consciousness which has the idea, and is conditioned also by its idiosyncrasies.

In my opinion, therefore, there can be no possible sense in speaking of
any other truth of our ideas except of a *practical* truth. Our ideas of things
cannot be anything but symbols, natural signs for things which we learn
how to use in order to regulate our movements and actions. Having
learned correctly how to read those symbols, we are enabled by their
help to adjust our actions so as to bring about the desired result; that is, so
that the expected new sensations will arise. Not only is there *in reality* no
other comparison at all between ideas and things – all the schools are
agreed about this – but any other mode of comparison is entirely *unthink-
able* and has no sense whatever. This latter consideration is the conclusive
thing, and must be grasped in order to escape from the labyrinth of
conflicting opinions. To ask whether the idea I have of a table, its form,
strength, colour, weight, etc., is true *per se*, apart from any practical use I
can make of this idea, and whether it corresponds with the real thing, or
is false and due to an illusion, has just as much sense as to ask whether a
certain musical note is red, yellow, or blue. Idea and the thing conceived
evidently belong to two entirely different worlds, which no more admit
of being compared with each other than colours and musical tones or
than the letters of a book and the sound of the word they denote. ...

Hence there is no sense in asking whether vermilion as we see it, is
really red, or whether this is simply an illusion of the senses. The sensation of red is the normal reaction of normally formed eyes to light
reflected from vermilion. A person who is red-blind will see vermilion
as black or as a dark grey-yellow. This too is the correct reaction for an
eye formed in the special way his is. All he has to know is that his eye is

simply formed differently from that of other persons. In itself the one sensation is not more correct and not more false than the other, although those who call this substance red are in the large majority. In general, the red colour of vermilion exists merely in so far as there are eyes which are constructed like those of most people. Persons who are red-blind have just as much right to consider that a characteristic property of vermilion is that of being black. As a matter of fact, we should not speak of the light reflected from vermilion as being red, because it is not red except for certain types of eyes. When we speak of the properties of bodies with reference to other bodies in the external world, we do not neglect to name also the body with respect to which the property exists. Thus we say that lead is soluble in nitric acid, but not in sulphuric acid. Were we to say simply that lead is soluble, we should notice at once that the statement is incomplete, and the question would have to be asked immediately, Soluble in what? But when we say that vermilion is red, it is implicitly understood that it is red for our eyes and for other people's eyes supposed to be made like ours. We think this does not need to be mentioned, and so we neglect to do so, and can be misled into thinking that red is a property belonging to vermilion or to the light reflected from it, entirely independently of our organs of sense. The statement that the waves of light reflected from vermilion have a certain length is something different. That is true entirely without reference to the special nature of our eye. Then we are thinking simply of relations that exist between the substance and the various systems of waves in the aether.

7

From *Principles of Gestalt Psychology*

Kurt Koffka

. . .

On the phenomenological method

Before we continue, a methodological remark may be in place. One can read many American books and articles on psychology without finding any . . . description [of the behavioral environment], whereas in German works one will meet with them quite frequently. This difference is not superficial, but reveals a thoroughgoing difference in the character of American and German work. Americans will call the German psychology speculative and hairsplitting; Germans will call the American branch superficial. The Americans are justified, when they find an author introducing such descriptions, refining them, playing with them, without really doing anything to them. The Germans are right, because American psychology all too often makes no attempt to look naïvely, without bias, at the facts of direct experience, with the result that American experiments quite often are futile. In reality experimenting *and* observing must go hand in hand. A good description of a phenomenon may by itself rule out a number of theories and indicate definite features which a true theory must possess. We call this kind of observation "phenomenology," a word which has several other meanings which must not be confused with ours. For us phenomenology means as naïve and full a description of direct experience as possible. In America the word "introspection" is the only one used for what we mean, but this word has also a very

Kurt Koffka, *Principles of Gestalt Psychology* (New York: Harcourt, Brace and World, 1935), pp. 73, 75–87, 96–7.

different meaning in that it refers to a special kind of such description, namely, the one which analyzes direct experience into sensations or attributes, or some other systematic, but not experiential, ultimates.

I can save myself and my readers the trouble of discussing this kind of introspection, since Köhler has done that admirably well in the third chapter of his *Gestalt Psychology*. This kind of introspection became un-popular in America because American psychologists saw its barrenness. But in their justified criticism they threw out the baby with the bath, substituting pure achievement experiments and tending to leave out phenomenology altogether. That phenomenology is important, however, should appear from the preceding discussion. Without describing the environmental field we should not know what we had to explain.

There remains the question how this description is possible, what phenomenology as a part of behaviour is. The difficulties inherent in this problem have been frequently discussed; I may refer the reader to two articles of mine in which they are fully treated and in which a solution of these difficulties is attempted ([Koffka] 1923, 1924). ...

Why Do Things Look as They Do?

And now we can take up the functional problem as to the relationship between the geographical and the behavioural environment. Concentrat-ing on the world of sight we can formulate our problem thus: *Why do things look as they do?*

Two aspects of this question

This question has two aspects. Taken literally it refers to the things in our behavioural environment quite regardless of their being "veridical," i.e., leading us to reasonable actions, to adapted behaviour. In this first sense, then, the problem would apply to a world of pure illusion as well as to a realistic world. Illusory perceptions fall under it in the same way as non-illusory ones. If our world were such that all appearances were deceptive, the solution of this problem would have to be the same as it is now. If a pencil which we picked up for taking notes behaved like a snake, a bar of iron which we grasped turned out to be a ball of wax, a stone on which we stepped jumped at us like a wolf, and so on, still we would have to ask the question: Why does the pencil look like a pencil, the iron bar like a bar, the stone like a stone? But in reality our world is, fortunately, not such a burlesque nightmare; as a rule, things are what they look like, or otherwise expressed, their looks tell us what to do with them, although as...optical illusions...show, perception may be deceptive. And thus arises the second aspect of our question: Why is it that our behaviour, directed as it is by the objects in the behavioural environment, is, as a rule, also adapted to the objects in the geographical environment? This is a new question.... It is important not to confuse these two aspects of our general question, not to introduce facts which belong to the second aspect into our solution of the first. An example will make clear what I mean by this last warning. We shall later on raise the question: Why to the spectator does this actor on the stage *look* furious or embarrassed or grief-stricken? and in answering this question we must not introduce our knowledge of what he feels, whether he actually experiences the emotions of his part or whether he remains detached or full of glee. Only when we have answered our question can we turn to this second fact and try to explain why in this case our perception was possibly illusory. That means the second, the cognitive, aspect of perception can only be treated after we have exhausted the first, the qualitative aspect.

The First Answer

Why, then, do things look as they do? We shall systematically take up various answers that may be given to this question, although they have been implicitly refuted in our previous discussion. A first answer would be: things look as they look because they are what they are.

Although this answer seems banal, it is not only utterly inadequate, but in many cases literally wrong. Let us single out a few aspects of behavioural things and compare them with the real ones. The pen with which I am writing is a unit in my behavioural environment and so is the real pen in the geographical. So far, so good. But if our proposition were true, to be a real unit would be a necessary and sufficient condition for a thing to be also a behavioural unit. But it is easy to show that it is neither necessary nor sufficient. If it were a necessary condition, it would mean: to every unit in my behavioural field there corresponds a unit in the geographical environment; for if behavioural units could exist without corresponding geographical ones, then the existence of the latter would no longer be necessary for the existence of the former. Nothing, however, is easier to point out than behavioural units to which no geographical units correspond. Look at figure 7.1. In your behavioural field it is a unit, a cross; in reality, in the geographical environment, there is no cross,

Figure 7.1

there are just eleven dots in a certain geometrical arrangement, but there is no connection between them that could make them a unit. This is, of course, true of all pictures, equally true of the stellar constellations like Charles's Wain, a case which Köhler has chosen as an illustration of this point.

If the visible existence of real units were the *sufficient* condition for the appearance of a behavioural unit it would mean that whenever our eyes were directed on a physical unit we should perceive a behavioural one. But this is not true either. Certainly, in most cases, this correspondence exists, but there are exceptions. As a matter of fact, it is possible to interfere with the real units in such a way that they will no longer look like units, an effect which we try to produce when we want to conceal certain well-known objects. If a gun is covered with paint in such a way that one part of it will "fuse" with the bole of a tree, another with the leaves, a third with the ground, then the beholder will no longer see a unit, the gun, but a multiplicity of much less important objects. Camouflage was an art well developed during the war, when even big ships were destroyed as real units in the behavioural world of the scouting enemy. Thus existence of a real unity is neither the necessary nor the sufficient cause of behavioural unity.

If we choose size as the aspect in which we should find correspondence we see at once that no direct relation between real and apparent size can exist, for the moon looks large on the horizon and small on the zenith.

And even for the aspect of motion it is easy to prove that the existence, within the field of vision, of real motion is neither a necessary nor a sufficient condition for the perception of motion. It is not a necessary condition, for we can see motion when no real motion occurs, as on the cinematographic screen, but neither is it sufficient, for apart from the fact that too slow and too fast real motions produce no perception of motion, there are many cases where the apparently moving object is really at rest, as the moon that seems to float through the clouds.

We forbear discussing other aspects because our material is sufficient to prove the first answer to our question wrong. That things are what they are does not explain why they look as they look.

Consequences implied in the first answer

Before we discuss another answer to our question we may for a moment consider what it would mean if the first answer were right. If things looked as they do because they are what they are, then the relation between the behavioural and the geographical environment would be simple indeed. Then for all practical purposes we could substitute the latter for the former. Conversely, since we know that the answer is wrong, we must guard against this confusion, which is not as easily avoided as one might think. To show how a disregard of our warning has influenced psychological theory, we will formulate our conclusion in still another manner. If things looked as they do because they are what they are, then perception would not contain in its very make-up a cognitive problem. Perception would, barring certain unusual conditions, be cognitive of the geographical environment. A cognitive problem might arise in the field of generalized thought, but as long as we remained in the field of direct perception we ought to be face to face with objective reality. The proposition, included in many philosophical systems, that the senses cannot lie, is a special form of this more general idea. To be sure, the existence of special cases where perception was deceptive was generally admitted. But these cases were treated as exceptions to the general rule, and for this reason the so-called geometric optical illusions received so much attention in the development of psychology. And when one reads the older literature on the subject, and some of the recent too, one will find explanations of this kind: if of two equal lines, one looks longer than the other, then we must look for special conditions which mislead our *judgment* about the relative length of these lines. Remove these distracting circumstances and the judgment will be correct, the normal state of affairs, in which the behavioural world corresponds to the geographical one, will be re-established. That is to say, illusory perceptions were not accorded the same rank as non-illusory ones; they presented a special problem, whereas the normal appearance presented no problem at all. This distinction between two kinds of perception, normal and illusory, disappears as a psychological distinction as soon as one becomes thoroughly aware of the fallacy which it implies, much as it may remain as an epistemological distinction. For each thing we have to ask the same question, "Why does it look as it does?" whether it looks "right" or "wrong."

Two meanings of the term stimulus

These last considerations ought to have shown that our refutation of the first answer is not so banal as might have been thought. At the start it might well have been argued, How can the first answer be right, when the geographical things are not in direct contact with the organism? When I see a table, this table *qua* table does not affect my senses at all; they are affected by processes which have their origin in the sun or an artificial source of light, and which are only modified by the table before they excite the rods and cones in our retinae. Therefore, these processes, the light waves, and not the geographical objects, are the direct causes of our perceptions, and consequently we cannot expect a very close relationship between behavioural and geographical things. For the light waves do not depend only upon the things *qua* things, but also upon the nature of the source of light (which only in the case of self-luminous bodies belongs to them as their own property) and on the position of the things with regard to our own bodies. This last relation is regulated by the laws of perspective, the first by laws of light absorption and reflection. But perspective, light absorption, and reflection remain outside our organisms. The retinae receive a pattern of excitations, and it can make no difference to the retinae how these excitations have been produced. If, without a table and even without light (for instance, by electrical stimulation of the rods and cones), we could produce the same pattern of excitation with the same curvature of the lenses which is ordinarily produced on our retinae when we fixate a table, then the person on whose retinae these excitations were produced should and would see a table. This leads us to introduce a new terminological distinction. The causes of the excitations of our sense organs are called stimuli. We see now that this word has two different meanings which must be clearly distinguished from each other: on the one hand the table in the geographical environment can be called a stimulus for our perception of a table; on the other hand the excitations to which the light rays coming from the table give rise are called the stimuli for our perception. Let us call the first the *distant* stimulus, the second the *proximal* stimuli. Then we can say that our question why things look as they do must find its answer not in terms of the distant, but of the proximal, stimuli. By a neglect of this difference real problems have been overlooked, and explanations proffered which are no explanations at all. We shall see this presently in detail, but we can point out here how the confusion of distant and proximal stimuli can have such a fatal effect on psychological theory. The danger of this confusion lies in the fact that for each distant stimulus there exists a practically infinite number of proximal stimuli; thus, the "same stimulus" in the distant sense may not be the same stimulus in the proximal sense; as a matter of fact it very seldom is. Thus the sameness of the former conceals a difference of the latter, and all arguments based on identical stimulation are spurious if they refer to identity of the distant stimulus only.

The Second Answer

The introduction of our term proximal stimulus has, however, given us a clue to the second answer to our question: things look as they do because the proximal stimuli are what they are. Now in its broadest interpretation this proposition is certainly true, but the interpretation usually given to it is distinctly limited and therefore false. In the widest interpretation our proposition means no more than this: any change in the proximal stimulation will, provided it be not too small, produce *some* change in the look of things, but *what kind* of change in the behavioural world will follow upon a change in the proximal stimulation cannot be derived from our proposition; whereas in the narrower interpretation the proposition also contains implicitly a statement about the kind of this change. Two objects project retinal images of different size on our retinae and appear to be at the same distance. Then the one which corresponds to the larger retinal image will look larger. We see two adjacent surfaces at an equal distance in front of us, the one looks a lighter, the other a darker, grey; then the retinal image corresponding to the former will contain more light than that of the latter. From these examples two conclusions might be drawn: the larger the retinal image, the larger the perceived object, and the greater the intensity of the image the more white will the object look; consequently when I change the stimulus corresponding to one object by making it smaller, the object should look smaller too, and if I reduce the intensity of stimulation the object should look blacker. These conclusions which have been actually accepted as axioms of sense psychology will seem very plausible. But neither do they follow from our examples, nor are they true. They do not follow from our examples because they only take in a part of the conditions of these examples and they are continually contradicted by the facts. Look at a white surface and then reduce the illumination of this surface; for a long time the surface will remain white, and only when you have reduced your illumination to a very low point will it become greyish. As a matter of fact a surface which still looks white under a low illumination may send much less light into our eyes than a black surface in good illumination. Disregard for the moment such plausible explanations as that when the light is decreased the pupil dilates so as to allow more of the incoming light to fall on our retinae, and that simultaneously the sensitivity of our retinae increases so as to make the effect of light greater. As we shall see later, both these factors, which are admittedly real, have been ruled out as sufficient explanations of our effect, so for simplicity's sake we neglect them altogether in our present discussion. Have we then shown that a change in the stimulus, in our case a diminution of light, has no effect at all on the look of things? If we had, we should have contradicted our general interpretation of the proposition: things look as they do because the proximal stimuli are what they are, an interpretation which we have accepted. But we have shown no such thing; we have only shown that the particular effect which would follow from the narrower interpretation of our proposition has failed to materialize. But there is an effect notwithstanding. For when the illumination is reduced, we become aware of a *darkening* of the *room*. Comparing this case with our former example we see that a change in the intensity of the retinal image may have at least two different effects: it may make the particular object look whiter or blacker, or it may make the whole room appear brighter or darker.

And the same is true of our other example. Look at the moon, particularly when it is at the horizon, and compare its size with that of a shilling held at arm's length. You will find the moon looking very much larger, whereas the retinal image of the shilling is larger than that of the moon. At the same time you see the moon at a much greater distance. Therefore decrease in size of a retinal image may either produce a shrinking or a receding of the corresponding object in the behavioural environment.

Two old experiments confirm this conclusion. In both, the observer looks monocularly at a screen with a circular hole in it. At some distance behind the screen there is a well illuminated homogeneous white wall part of which is visible through the hole. In the first experiment... a taut vertical black thread between the screen and the wall passes through the centre of the circle exposed by the hole. This thread is attached to stands which can be moved backwards and forwards in a sagittal line from the observer in such a way that the thread, whatever its distance from the hole, divides the circle into equal halves, the stands being invisible behind the screen. A movement of the thread has then no other effect than an increase or decrease of the width of its retinal image, apart from a possible blurring due to insufficient accommodation. Under these conditions the observer sees, as a rule, a sagittal motion of a thread with *constant* thickness, and not an increase or decrease of the thickness of an immovable thread. In the second experiment there is no thread at all, and the room is totally dark so that the light circular hole is the only visible object in it. The variable is this time the opening of the hole itself which is made by an iris diaphragm which can be opened or closed. The retinal conditions are still simpler than in the first case, the retinal area on which the light falls increasing or decreasing. Accompanying these retinal changes the observers see either a forward or backward movement of the light circle, or its expansion or contraction, or finally a joint effect in which expansion and approach, contraction and recession, are combined.

We can now present our argument in a more generalized form. If the answer: things look as they do because the proximal stimuli are what they are, were true in the narrower sense, two propositions should hold. (1) Changes in the proximal stimulation unaccompanied by changes of the distant stimulus-object should produce corresponding changes in the *looks* of the behavioural object, and (2) any change in the distant object which produces no effect in the proximal stimulation should leave the looks of the behavioural object unchanged.

That (1) is not true follows from the example we have discussed. A white surface continues to look white, a black one black even when the proximal stimulation to which they give rise varies over a very wide range; my pencil looks no bigger when I hold it in my hand than when it is at the other end of my desk, when its retinal image may be less than half the size of the image of the pencil in my hand; the seat of a chair looks rectangular, although its retinal image will be rectangular in a negligibly small number of occasions only. In other words the behavioural things are conservative; they do not change with every change of the proximal stimulation by which they are produced. The constancy of real things is to a great extent preserved in the constancy of the *phenomenal* things despite variations in their proximal stimuli.

Relation of the two answers

When we compare this argument with the one given in our discussion of the first answer which explained the look of behavioural things by the nature of the real things, we are struck with a somewhat curious relation between the two answers: According to the first the correspondence between real and behavioural things should have been much better than it really is, and according to the second it should be much worse.

Refutation of second answer continued

Let us now turn to the second point. It is quite true that changes of the distant stimuli unaccompanied by any change in the proximal stimulation can have no effect on the look of things. Thus a third variant of the experiment just described has been introduced.... The hole in the screen is constant, and behind it is a movable black surface with a very sharp and smooth straight edge which cuts through the centre of the visible circle just as the thread did in the first modification. Howsoever this surface is moved backwards and forwards, the observer will see a semicircle bounded by a sharp contour, and in this case, much more frequently, motion of the surface will remain entirely unnoticed, in accordance with the fact that, again apart from possible blurring of the edge due to inaccurate accommodation, the proximal stimulation remains unaltered by the process of moving the surface.

And yet the proposition of our point (2) does not tell us the whole truth, because its conversion is no longer true. The conversion of our proposition (2) would be: no change can occur in the looks of things without corresponding changes in the proximal stimuli. But this is not true. Figure 7.2 will not preserve its appearance when you continue to look at it; if you see at first a black cross on white, you will later see a white cross on black, and these two phases will alternate. Puzzle pictures, reversible perspectives, demonstrate the same fact, and so does the experiment with the iris diaphragm described above in which the observer may at one time see a displacement, at another time a change of the size of the hole. From this we must draw the conclusion that the looks of things cannot alone depend upon the proximal stimulation, even if this dependence is considered in the broadest sense, but also upon sets of other conditions which must lie within the real organism.

Finally, many of the arguments used to disprove the first answer apply equally well to the second. Since the mosaic of proximal stimulation possesses no unity, the unity within our behavioural world cannot be explained by a corresponding unity in the proximal stimulation. And the

Figure 7.2

argument derived from the cinema applies to proximal stimulation as well as to distant, so that, in this respect, the second answer is in the same boat with the first.

Reasons for the survival of the second answer

It may seem strange that the view according to which there is a point-to-point correspondence between proximal stimulation and the look of things should have survived the evidence which we have presented and which is not at all new. But it is not difficult to explain the tenacity of this view which has by no means disappeared from present-day psychology. Two general features of traditional psychological thought mutually supported each other to keep it alive. The first is connected with the old physiological hypotheses about conscious phenomena.... It may be presented like this: the simplest experiments reveal that under standard conditions whiteness depends upon intensity of light, and apparent size on the size of the retinal image. If under other less simple conditions other correlations seem to obtain, these cannot be true correlations in the same sense in which our first are. For how should it be possible that one and the same nerve fibre should react once in one way, the next time in another way, when it receives the same stimulation in the two cases? The physiological hypotheses had no place for such a change (Stumpf 1890: 10).

Current theory a combination of the two first answers; sensation and perception

Strongly entrenched as the physiological hypotheses were, this theory could hardly have survived the damning evidence of the facts without the second general feature mentioned above. The damning evidence consists in the fact that the things do not look as they ought to on the ground of pure proximal stimulation, and they differ from such an expectation by looking more like the distant stimuli, like the things with which we have real dealings. Therefore it was assumed that the *real* properties of things, that the distant stimuli, have something to do with the looks of things after all. The answer, that things look as they do because the proximal stimulation is what it is, had to be supplemented by the first answer, viz., that the fact that things are what they are must be included also in a final explanation. Current theory was, in this way, a sort of combination of our two answers, in which the second answer accounted for the immediate effect, the first for a secondary one. For according to this way of thinking, in dealing with things we acquire experience about them, and this experience enters our whole perception. Thus, according to this view, we must really distinguish between two kinds of behavioural fields, a primary and a secondary one, the field of sensations and the field of perceptions. The original primary field, the field of sensations, corresponded completely to the proximal stimuli – there was only one notable exception... – for this primary field the answer that it looked as it did because the proximal stimuli were what they were, was true in a very narrow sense. But experience has changed this primary field and has substituted for it the secondary by virtue of the numberless experiences which we have had.

The network of traditional hypotheses   Let us see how this theory worked. Not so very long ago, in 1920, Jaensch explained Wundt's experiment of the approaching and receding thread whose motion we perceive, in the following manner: "In the case of the thread, judgment can rest only upon a change in the magnitude of the retinal dimensions which accompanies the alteration of the thread's distance, and although this change is too small to be directly noticed as a change of magnitude, still it must determine the judgment of distance." Several features of this explanation are worth noting. First it distinguishes between *effects* which can be *directly noticed* – even if they are not noticed at the time – viz., the change of the apparent thickness of the thread corresponding to a change of breadth in the retinal image – and *judgments* determined by such directly noticeable effects – viz., the greater or smaller distance of the thread. If we express this distinction by saying: the increasing thickness of the behavioural thread means, is interpreted as, approach, its decreasing thickness as recession, then we see that this is a clear-cut example of the "meaning theory" which Köhler has discussed with great brilliance in his book. What, so any unbiased person ought to ask, is the reason for distinguishing in Wundt's experiment between a sensory, though unnoticed, breadth and a judgmental distance? Admittedly, experience presents us only with one fact, the change of distance; admittedly, because the change of breadth is called unnoticed, i.e., unexperienced; neither do we experience this movement as a judgment, but as a change of the same palpability as a change of width which we may experience at another time. That this particular change of distance is interpreted by Jaensch as a judgment is due to the fact that the proximal stimulation changed in breadth, and therefore implies the relation between proximal stimulation and the behavioural field assumed in the second answer. Thus we see the circular nature of this interpretation: in order to call the experienced change of distance a judgment, Jaensch must assume that a change of breadth in the retinal image produces primarily a change of breadth in the perceived object; but in order to reconcile this assumption with the observed facts he must interpret the actual experience of changed distance as a judgment.

Constancy and interpretation hypothesis   The general name for this assumption is "constancy hypothesis" – to be explained presently; we shall call the other the interpretation hypothesis – preferring this term to Köhler's "meaning theory" for no intrinsic reasons but merely for the practical one that we use the word "meaning," just as Köhler, in a very different sense and do not want to confuse the reader by an avoidable ambiguity. Then we can say: the interpretation hypothesis presupposes the constancy hypothesis, but also the latter the former. At the risk of appearing frivolous I will tell a joke which seems to me to give a perfect picture of the relation between the two hypotheses. A man and his small son are viewing with great interest an acrobat walking on the tight rope and balancing himself with a long pole. The boy suddenly turns to his father and asks: "Father, why doesn't that man fall?" The father replies: "Don't you see that he is holding on to the pole?" The boy accepts the authority of his parent, but after a while he bursts out with a new question: "Father, why doesn't the pole fall?" Whereupon the father replies: "But don't you see that the man holds it!"

Non-noticed sensations   Köhler, who has shown up this same vicious circle (1913), has emphasized what pernicious consequences it had for research, a conclusion which is also illustrated by our anecdote. But there is another point in Jaensch's explanation that deserves a special comment; the direct sensory experience is, according to him, too small to be noticed! And yet it is supposed to determine a judgment. This removes the last vestige of plausibility from this theory. We could at least understand what is meant by a judgment based on a perceived sensory experience. In the particular case under discussion the process would then be like this: the observer experiences a change in the thickness of the thread; he has learned, we do not know how, that often such a change is not a real change of the thread but merely due to a change of its position with regard to himself. Therefore he judges that in the present case too the thread has moved without changing its volume. I say that such a description would at least have a meaning, even though it must appear as a pure construction unsupported by facts which contain nothing of such an inferential judgment. But now the change of thickness is assumed to be unnoticed. Since I cannot judge about something I am not aware of, the term judgment must have a meaning different from the ordinary one; in fact it can have no definite meaning any more over and above the very general one: non-sensory process. But then it will not explain anything. For though we can understand how a judgment based upon a sensory experience may lead to a certain interpretation of this experience – we see smoke and we judge there must be a fire – we do not understand how a non-sensory process produces out of an unnoticed sensory process a noticed datum which has all the direct characteristics of a sensory process and is different from the non-noticed one.

Furthermore, the assumption of the non-noticed sensory experience is necessary only because of the constancy hypothesis which derives the looks of things from a universal point-to-point relation with the proximal stimulation. We have again the man on the tight rope and the pole. Without the constancy hypothesis we would not assume unnoticed experiences, and without unnoticed experiences we could not preserve the constancy hypothesis. ...

Constancy hypothesis and traditional physiological theory. Local stimulation   In the beginning of this discussion we have claimed that the interpretation hypothesis is closely bound up with the traditional physiological hypotheses about brain processes. We can now make this claim more explicit. The interpretation hypothesis was demanded by the constancy hypothesis which we shall now formulate in a somewhat different manner. Recalling the arguments on which it was based we see that it correlated behavioural characteristics not with the total proximal stimulation but only with such parts of it as corresponded to the distant stimulus objects under discussion. In other words, it derived the characteristics of behavioural objects from the properties of *local* stimulations. In its consistent form the constancy hypothesis treats of sensations, each aroused by the local stimulation of one retinal point. Thus the constancy hypothesis maintains that the result of a local stimulation is constant, provided that the physiological condition of the stimulated receptor is constant (e.g., adaptation). This implies that all locally stimulated excitations run their course without regard to other excitations, in full accord with the traditional physiological hypotheses. When now we see that the constancy hypothesis has to be abandoned we know already what has to take its place, for we have demonstrated ... that physiological processes must be considered as processes in extension. But that means that no local stimulation can determine the corresponding excitation by itself, as the constancy hypothesis implied, but only in connection with the totality of stimulation. The form of the process in extension must depend upon the whole extended mosaic of stimulation, and all its parts become what they are as a result of the organization of the extended process. Only when we know the kind of organization in which a local process occurs can we predict what it will be like, and therefore the same change in local stimulation can produce different changes in the behavioural world according to the total organization which is produced by the total stimulation. Thus we can say: only when the total conditions are such that two visible objects will appear in *one* frontal vertical plane will the one whose retinal image is larger also look larger. The abandonment of the constancy hypothesis does not mean that we put in its place an arbitrary connection between proximal stimulation and the looks of things. All we intend to do is to replace laws of local correspondence, laws of machine effects, by laws of a much more comprehensive correspondence between the total perceptual field and the total stimulation, and we shall, in the search for these laws, find at least indications of some more specific constancies, though never one of the type expressed by the constancy hypothesis. . . .

References

Jaensch, E. R. (1920), Einige allgemeinere Fragen der Psychologie und Biologie des Denkens, erläutert an der Lehre vom Vergleich, *Arb. z. Psych. und Philos.* her. von E. R. Jaensch, 1: 1–31.

Koffka, K. (1924), Introspection and the method of psychology, *Brit. J. Psych.* 15: 149–61.

———(1923), Zur Theorie der Erlebniswahrnehmung, *Ann. d. Philos.* 3: 375–99.

Köhler, W. (1913), Über unbemerkte Empfindungen und Urteilstäuschungen, *Zts. f. Psych.* 66: 51–80.

Stumpf, C. (1883), *Tonpsychologie.* I, Leipzig.

———(1890), *Tonpsychologie.* II, Leipzig.

Part II

The Senses

Introduction to Part II

The view that the senses are distinguished by the qualitative nature of the experiences they each uniquely present strikes many as self-evident. For reasons related to those articulated by Müller, it has also seemed reasonable to assume that the way a sense responds to a particular stimulus is pretty much fixed by the physiological makeup of the sense organ. But then the sensations so triggered would appear to have rather limited content. In and of themselves, they could not tell us very much about the location and properties of objects in the world around us. Sensations serve only as signs or the initial building blocks upon which full-blown perceptions are constructed. The primary goal of vision theory, then, is to figure out how the brain/mind converts these impoverished sensory data into the far richer informational states that constitute our perception of the environment. Part I of this volume contains some of the historical underpinnings for this picture of sensing and perceiving.

James J. Gibson finds the main outlines of the story largely in place in the middle of the twentieth century. He believes, however, that progress in the theory of vision requires its complete dismantling. Some of the critical work had already been done by others, especially the Gestalt theorists. They argued against the prevalent atomistic conception of sensations and sensory processes. Gestaltists claimed that what we typically see are organized wholes. We do not build perceptions upon a mosaic of elementary sensations that correspond point for point with local retinal stimuli.

Gibson's criticism of the tradition goes much further than that found in Gestalt writings. He argues that it is necessary to: (1) replace talk of "sense organs" with that of "perceptual systems," (2) abandon all explanatory appeal to, if not the very idea of, "sensations," and (3) reconceive the whole notion of a "stimulus." Stimuli should be thought of in terms of the information contained in higher-order invariant properties of arrays of ambient light, particularly those that result from movement. Adopting this framework, Gibson believes, dissolves the traditional problem of explaining how the mind turns impoverished sensations into rich perceptions. The information in the stimulus is *not* impoverished. In a selection printed in Part III of this volume, Gibson spells out in more detail what a theory of vision looks like from this new perspective.

Hamlyn recognizes there are problems with traditional accounts of the sensation/perception distinction, but he is afraid Gibson and other theorists go too far in renouncing the study of sensory qualities (Clark 1993). Hamlyn joins many in arguing that some appeal to sensations is needed to capture what is special or distinctive of perception in general and vision in particular. And, of course, only if sensuous qualities do have a defining role or status would it be plausible to individuate the senses on their basis. Hamlyn, however, sees the need to defend his position against problems posed by the phenomena of blind-sight and tactile visual substitution. Such cases, it has been argued, demonstrate that there can be "vision" without visual sensations. Detailed consideration of these clinical phenomena has become increasingly prevalent in debates over the nature of sensory qualities and conscious awareness (Vision 1998). Hamlyn argues that in abnormal cases like blind-sight and tactile visual substitution, something essential to seeing is missing. Furthermore, he contends that a proper appreciation of these matters can help clarify and deepen our understanding of important aspects of normal spatial vision and the experiences of stereoscopic depth perception.

The selection from Heil's book explores in more detail the question of how to distinguish among or individuate the senses. Grice's (1962) paper, "Some Remarks about the Senses" is the *locus classicus* of contemporary philosophical worries on the topic. Heil examines Grice's analysis and finds it unsatisfactory. Unlike Hamlyn, however, Heil is more sympathetic to Gibson's program. Relying on Gibsonian notions of stimulus information, Heil maintains that the senses are distinguished by the type of information they access, not by their attendant sensory qualities. The implications of this approach for a taxonomy of the senses are radical. And whereas phenomena like tactile visual substitution seem to pose a problem for Hamlyn to overcome, Heil takes cases of this sort to support his own position.

The selection of O'Shaughnessy is an update of the much discussed and challenged chapter 6 of his two-volume book, *The Will*. O'Shaughnessy, here, reaffirms his earlier position that there are some very good reasons to postulate the existence of sensations. He also believes that the sensations so countenanced do have a real role to play in an account of perception. Moreover, he defends a version of Berkeley's claim that the array of visual sensations is two-dimensional, not three-dimensional. In this new version of his chapter, O'Shaughnessy cautions that his arguments may only hold for *monocular* vision, but he does not elaborate much on the implications of this restriction.

In any case, O'Shaughnessy maintains that the character and order of visual sensations is distinct from the character and order of touch sensations. This, in turn, raises issues about the nature of our spatial concepts, the spatiality of sight and touch, and how the sensory realms of vision and touch are coordinated. O'Shaughnessy explores various of these issues further in developing his account of the will.

Once it was put forth, the Molyneux problem, as Cassirer documents, grew in importance, and it has never left the stage. Still, questions about the relationship among the senses would seem ill-posed until there is agreement on what constitutes a sense and what distinguishes one sense from another (Hamlyn 1996). But there are also other roadblocks to resolving the dispute. In the insightful footnote reprinted here, Mach provides a concise review of several alternative approaches to the Molyneux problem. He then indicates some worries he has about the relevance of the evidence often thought pertinent to settling matters. For example, Mach calls our attention to the fact that people may and do have difficulty on shape transfer tasks within even a single modality. Thus the failure to transfer shape appreciation between modalities, as might happen in a Molyneux test, cannot by itself be taken to imply the heterogeneity of the senses.

Morgan's book, from which the selection here comes, provides extensive historical and contemporary evidence concerning the Molyneux problem. Real-life Molyneux subjects (blind from birth and now recovered), however, are hard to find. Accordingly, other means have usually been employed to test the competing positions. In the excerpt presented here, Morgan explores questions about the relationship between sight and touch more broadly taken. He reviews experimental evidence concerning: adaptation to inverting and distorting lens, space perception in infants, cases of conflict between visual and tactile information, and cross-modal matching and transfer tasks (Welsch 1986).

Empirical studies of this sort have often owed their inspiration to Berkeley's writings. The more recent findings that Morgan discusses, for instance those of Rock, have been taken to refute Berkeley's account of visual space and his claims about the heterogeneity of the senses. Morgan argues that this is a mistake. As he sees it, these experiments may require some changes or restatement of Berkeley's thesis, but they do not undermine its core tenets. Although one may agree here with Morgan's criticism of Rock on Berkeley, Rock's book, *The Nature of Perceptual Adaptation*, should be required reading for anyone interested in conceptual issues concerning the relationships among sight, touch, and space perception.

Evans point out that there are numerous non-equivalent versions of the Molyneux problem in circulation. Some like Morgan's, he believes, do not get to the heart of the issue. After an initial ground-clearing, Evans attempts to spell out what he, himself, takes to be the crucial issue at stake. Evans formulates the Molyneux debate in terms that he claims to find in Berkeley's *New Theory*. The critical controversy for Evans is over the nature of the ability that underlies mastery of spatial concepts, especially those of shape. For example, does the use of the word "square" tap a single unified conceptual ability that is applied both by sight and by touch? Or are there separate conceptual abilities at work, a distinct one for each modality? Evans thinks he can establish that the conceptual ability presupposed in attributions of shape concepts insures that sight and touch localize objects in a single inter-modal, behavioral space. Obviously, much depends on one's analysis and understanding of the notion of "conceptual ability." Evans's solution, perhaps, speaks less to an empirical resolution of the Molyneux problem than it does to the ideas about the nature of space and spatial competence that underlie and fuel many of the debates over the integration of the senses (Eilan et al. 1993).

References

Clark, A. (1993), *Sensory Qualities*, Oxford: Clarendon Press.

Eilan, N., McCarthy, R. and Brewer, B. (eds.) (1993), *Spatial Representation: Problems in Philosophy and Psychology*, Oxford: Blackwell.

Grice, H. P. (1962), Some remarks about the senses. In *Analytical Philosophy* (first series), ed. R. J. Butler, Oxford: Blackwell, pp. 133–53.

Hamlyn, D. W. (1996), *Understanding Perception*, Aldershot: Avebury.

Rock, I. (1966), *The Nature of Perceptual Adaptation*, New York: Basic Books.

Vision, G. (1998), Blindsight and philosophy, *Philosophical Psychology* 11: 137–59.

Welsch, R. (1986), Adaptation of space perception. In *Handbook of Perception and Human Performance*, vol. 1, ch. 24, ed. K. Boff, L. Kaufman and J. Thomas, New York: Wiley.

8

From *The Senses Considered as Perceptual Systems,* and *The Ecological Approach to Visual Perception*

James J. Gibson

THE SENSES CONSIDERED AS PERCEPTUAL SYSTEMS

What are the Senses?

It has always been assumed that the senses were channels of sensation. To consider them as systems for perception, as this book proposes to do, may sound strange. But the fact is that there are two different meanings of the verb *to sense*, first, *to detect something*, and second, *to have a sensation*. When the senses are considered as perceptual systems the first meaning of the term is being used.

In the second meaning of the term there is a vast difference between sensations and perceptions. In 1785, Thomas Reid wrote:

> The external senses have a double province; to make us feel, and to make us perceive. They furnish us with a variety of sensations, some pleasant, others painful, and others indifferent; at the same time they give us a conception, and an invincible belief of the existence of external objects. This conception of external objects is the work of nature. The belief of their existence, which our senses give, is the work of nature; so likewise is

James J. Gibson, *The Senses Considered as Perceptual Systems* (Boston: Houghton Mifflin, 1966), pp. 1–6.

the sensation that accompanies it. This conception and belief which nature produces by means of the senses, we call perception. The feeling which goes along with the perception, we call sensation. The perception and its corresponding sensation are produced at the same time. In our experience we never find them disjoined. Hence we are led to consider them as one thing, to give them one name, and to confound their different attributes. It becomes very difficult to separate them in thought, to attend to each by itself, and to attribute nothing to it which belongs to the other. (*Essays on the Intellectual Powers of Man*, II, p. 17)

That province of the senses which is to "furnish us with a variety of sensations" is by no means the same as that which is to "make us perceive." Reid was right. The part of this passage that might be objected to is the suggestion that perception of objects must depend on "conception and belief." It will here be suggested that the senses can obtain information about objects in the world without the intervention of an intellectual process – or at least that they can do so when they operate as perceptual systems.

In this book I will distinguish the input to the nervous system that evokes conscious sensation from the input that evokes perception. I will not even speak of the ingoing impulses in nerves as "sensory," so as not to imply that all inputs arouse sense impressions. For it is surely a fact that *detecting* something can sometimes occur without the accompaniment of sense impressions. An example is the visual detection of one thing behind another. . . . There will be many examples of the principle that stimulus information can determine perception without having to enter consciousness in the form of sensation.

The reader should make allowance for the double meaning of the verb *to sense*. The detecting of stimulus information without any awareness of what sense organ has been excited, or of the quality of the receptor, can be described as "sensationless perception." But this does not mean that perception can occur without stimulation of receptors; it only means that organs of perception are sometimes stimulated in such a way that they are not specified in consciousness. Perception cannot be "extrasensory," if that means without any input; it can only be so if that means without awareness of the visual, auditory, or other quality of the input. An example of this is the "obstacle sense" of the blind, which is felt as "facial vision" but is actually auditory echo detection. The blind man "senses" the wall in front of him without realizing what sense has been stimulated. In short, there can be sensationless perception, but not informationless perception.

The seemingly paradoxical assertion will be made that perception is not based on sensation. That is, it is not based on having sensations, as in the second meaning, but it is surely based on detecting information, as in the first meaning.

There are two different levels of sensitivity.... the so-called sense organs are of at least two different sorts: the passive receptors that respond each to its appropriate form of energy, and the active perceptual organs, better called systems, that can search out the information in stimulus energy. The receptors have measurable thresholds below which they are not excited; the organs and systems do not have fixed thresholds except as they depend on receptors.

Similarly, there are different levels of stimulation. The stimulus energy of optics, mechanics, and chemistry is coordinate with receptors, but the stimulus information to be described is coordinate with perceptual systems. Stimulus energy varies along simple dimensions like intensity and frequency, but stimulus information varies along innumerable complex dimensions, not all amenable to physical measurement.

When the senses are considered as channels of sensation (and this is how the physiologist, the psychologist, and the philosopher have considered them), one is thinking of the passive receptors and the energies that stimulate them, the sensitive elements in the eyes, ears, nose, mouth, and skin. The experimenters in physiology and psychology have been establishing the conditions and limits at this level of stimulation for more than a century. A vast literature of sensory physiology has developed and a great deal is known about the receptors. It is a highly respected branch of science. But all this exact knowledge of sensation is vaguely unsatisfactory since it does not explain how animals and men accomplish sense perception.

It can be shown that the easily measured variables of stimulus energy, the intensity of light, sound, odor, and touch, for example, vary from place to place and from time to time as the individual goes about his business in the environment. The stimulation of receptors and the presumed sensations, therefore, are variable and changing in the extreme, unless they are experimentally controlled in a laboratory. The unanswered question of sense perception is how an observer, animal or human, can obtain constant perceptions in everyday life on the basis of these continually changing sensations. For the fact is that animals and men do perceive and respond to the permanent properties of the environment as well as to the changes in it.

Besides the changes in stimuli from place to place and from time to time, it can also be shown that certain higher-order variables – stimulus energy, ratios, and proportions, for example – do *not* change. They remain invariant with movements of the observer and with changes in the intensity of stimulation.... And it will be shown that these invariants of the energy flux at the receptors of an organism correspond to the permanent properties of the environment. They constitute, therefore, information about the permanent environment.

The active observer gets invariant perceptions despite varying sensations. He perceives a constant object by vision despite changing sensations of light; he perceives a constant object by feel despite changing sensations of pressure; he perceives the same source of sound despite changing sensations of loudness in his ears. The hypothesis is that constant perception depends on the ability of the individual to detect the invariants, and that he ordinarily pays no attention whatever to the flux of changing sensations.

The ways in which animals and men pick up information by looking, listening, sniffing, tasting, and touching are the subject of this book. These five perceptual systems overlap one another; they are not mutually exclusive. They often focus on the same information – that is, the same information can be picked up by a combination of perceptual systems working together as well as by one perceptual system working alone. The eyes, ears, nose, mouth, and skin can orient, explore, and investigate. When thus active they are neither passive senses nor channels of sensory quality, but ways of paying attention to whatever is constant in the changing stimulation. In exploratory looking, tasting, and touching the sense impressions are incidental symptoms of the exploration, and what gets isolated is information about the object looked at, tasted, or touched. The movements of the eyes, the mouth, and the hands, in fact, seem to keep changing the input at the receptive level, the input of sensation, just so as to isolate over time the invariants of the input at the level of the perceptual system.

The Senses and the Sensory Nerves

What about the input of the sensory nerves? We have been taught that the impulses in these fiber bundles comprised the messages of sense and that they were the only possible basis for perception. This doctrine is so generally accepted that to challenge it seems to fly in the face of physiology. There is said to be a receptor mosaic for each sense connecting with the central nervous system and projecting the pattern of excited receptors to the brain. But let us note that if the perceptual organs are normally exploratory, as they are, this anatomical projection of receptors is quite simply irrelevant for the process of normal perception. It is not false, for it explains after-images, as well as many of the curiosities of subjective sensory experience that occur when stimuli are imposed on a passive observer by an experimenter. Experiments on sensation are usually of this sort. But the neural input of the mobile eyes in the mobile head of a mobile animal, for example, cannot be thought of as the anatomical pattern of the nerve cells that are excited in the fiber bundle. This anatomical pattern changes from moment to moment. Neurophysiologists in the past have been reluctant to face up to this difficulty in explaining perception, for they know more about the anatomy of the eyes, ears, and skin than they do about the physiology of looking, listening, and touching.

What might be a physiological or functional equivalent of the external information, if it cannot be anatomical? How could invariants get into the nervous system? The same incoming nerve fiber makes a different contribution to the pickup of information from one moment to the next. The pattern of the excited receptors is of no account; what counts is the external pattern that is temporarily occupied by excited receptors as the eyes roam over the world, or as the skin moves over an object. The individual sensory units have to function *vicariously*, to borrow a term from Lashley, a neuropsychologist.

The answers to these questions are not yet clear, but I am suggesting new directions in which we may look for them. Instead of looking to the brain alone for an explanation of constant perception, it should be sought in the neural loops of an active perceptual system that includes the adjustments of the perceptual organ. Instead of supposing that the brain constructs or computes the objective information from a kaleidoscopic inflow of sensations, we may suppose that the orienting of the organs of perception is governed by the brain so that the whole system of input and output resonates to the external information.

If this formula is correct, the input of the sensory nerves is not the basis of perception as we have been taught for centuries, but only half of it. It is only the basis for passive sense impressions. These are not the data of perception, not the raw material out of which perception is fashioned by the brain. The active senses cannot be simply the initiators of *signals* in nerve fibers or *messages* to the brain; instead they are analogous to tentacles and feelers. And the function of the brain when looped with its perceptual organs is not to decode signals, nor to interpret messages, nor to accept images. These old analogies no longer apply. The function of the brain is not even to *organize* the sensory input or to *process* the data, in modern terminology. The perceptual systems, including the nerve centers at various levels up to the brain, are ways of seeking and extracting information about the environment from the flowing array of ambient energy.

The Improvement of Perception with Learning

The elementary colors, sounds, smells, tastes, and pressures that were supposed to be the only data of sense (and that are indeed obtained when a passive observer is stimulated by carefully measured applications of energy in a laboratory) have been thought of as an inborn repertory of experience on which a baby's later perception is founded. Learning to perceive, then, had to be some such process as the associating of memories with these bare impressions, or the interpreting of them, or the classifying of them, or the organizing of them. Theories of perception have been concerned with operations of this sort.

If the senses are perceptual systems, however, the infant does not have sensations at birth but starts at once to pick up information from the world. His detection equipment cannot be exactly oriented at first, and his attention is imprecise; nevertheless, he looks at things, and touches and mouths them, and listens to events. As he grows, he learns to use his perceptual systems more skillfully, and his attention becomes educated to the subtleties of stimulus information. He does learn to perceive but he does *not* have to learn to convert sense data into perception.

On the assumption that the senses are channels of sensation, the process of learning has been thought of by stimulus-response psychologists as an attaching of new responses to a fixed set of possible inputs. On the assumption that the senses are perceptual systems, however, the emphasis is shifted to the discovery of new stimulus invariants, new properties of the world, to which the child's repertory of responses can be applied. This is perceptual learning as distinguished from performatory learning. Both kinds of learning occur in the child, but perceptual learning is the more in need of study because it is the more neglected. . . .

THE ECOLOGICAL APPROACH
TO VISUAL PERCEPTION

The Concept of a Perceptual System

The theory of information pickup requires perceptual systems, not senses. Some years ago I tried to prove that a perceptual system was radically different from a sense,[1] the one being active and the other passive. People said, "Well, what I mean by a sense is an *active* sense." But it turned out that they still meant the passive inputs of a sensory nerve, the activity being what occurs in the brain when the inputs get there. That was not what I meant by a perceptual system. I meant the activities of looking, listening, touching, tasting, or sniffing. People then said, "Well, but those are responses to sights, sounds, touches, tastes, or smells, that is, motor acts resulting from sensory inputs. What you call a perceptual system is nothing but a case of feedback." I was discouraged. People did not understand.

I shall here make another attempt to show that the senses considered as special senses cannot be reconciled with the senses considered as perceptual systems. The five perceptual systems correspond to five modes of overt attention. They have overlapping functions, and they are all more or less subordinated to an overall orienting system. A system has organs, whereas a sense has receptors. A system can orient, explore, investigate, adjust, optimize, resonate, extract, and come to an equilibrium, whereas a sense cannot. ... Five fundamental differences between a sense and a perceptual system are given below.

1. A special sense is defined by a bank of receptors or receptive units that are connected with a so-called projection center in the brain. Local stimuli at the sensory surface will cause local firing of neurons in the center. The adjustments of the organ in which the receptors are incorporated are not included within the definition of a sense.

A perceptual system is defined by an organ and its adjustments at a given level of functioning, subordinate or superordinate. At any level, the

---

James J. Gibson, *The Ecological Approach to Visual Perception* (Hillsdale, NJ: Lawrence Erlbaum Associates, 1986), pp. 244–6.

incoming and outgoing nerve fibers are considered together so as to make a continuous loop.

The organs of the visual system, for example, from lower to higher are roughly as follows. First, the lens, pupil, chamber, and retina comprise an organ. Second, the eye with its muscles in the orbit comprise an organ that is both stabilized and mobile. Third, the two eyes in the head comprise a binocular organ. Fourth, the eyes in a mobile head that can turn comprise an organ for the pickup of ambient information. Fifth, the eyes in a head on a body constitute a superordinate organ for information pickup over paths of locomotion. The adjustments of accommodation, intensity modulation, and dark adaptation go with the first level. The movements of compensation, fixation, and scanning go with the second level. The movements of vergence and the pickup of disparity go with the third level. The movements of the head, and of the body as a whole, go with the fourth and fifth levels. All of them serve the pickup of information.

2. In the case of a special sense, the receptors can only receive stimuli, passively, whereas in the case of a perceptual system the input-output loop can be supposed to obtain information, actively. Even when the theory of the special senses is liberalized by the modern hypothesis of receptive units, the latter are supposed to be triggered by complex stimuli or modulated in some passive fashion.

3. The inputs of a special sense constitute a repertory of innate sensations, whereas the achievements of a perceptual system are susceptible to maturation and learning. Sensations of one modality can be combined with those of another in accordance with the laws of association; they can be organized or fused or supplemented or selected, but *no new sensations can be learned*. The information that is picked up, on the other hand, becomes more and more subtle, elaborate, and precise with practice. One can keep on learning to perceive as long as life goes on.

4. The inputs of the special senses have the qualities of the receptors being stimulated, whereas the achievements of the perceptual systems are specific to the qualities of things in the world, especially their affordances. The recognition of this limitation of the senses was forced upon us by Johannes Müller with his doctrine of specific "nerve energies." He understood clearly, if reluctantly, the implication that, because we can never know the external causes of our sensations, we cannot know the outer world. Strenuous efforts have to be made if one is to avoid this shocking conclusion. Helmholtz argued that we must deduce the causes of our sensations because we cannot detect them. The hypothesis that sensations provide clues or cues for perception of the world is similar. The popular formula that we can interpret sensory signals is a variant of it. But it seems to me that all such arguments come down to this: we can perceive the world only if we already know what there is to be perceived. And that, of course, is circular. . . .

The alternative is to assume that sensations triggered by light, sound, pressure, and chemicals are merely incidental, that information is available to a perceptual system, and that the qualities of the world in relation to the needs of the observer are experienced directly.

5. In the case of a special sense the process of attention occurs at centers within the nervous system, whereas in the case of a perceptual system attention pervades the whole input-output loop. In the first case attention is a consciousness that can be focused; in the second case it is a skill that can be educated. In the first case physiological metaphors are used, such as the filtering of nervous impulses or the switching of impulses from one path to another. In the second case the metaphors used can be terms such as *resonating, extracting, optimizing,* or *symmetricalizing* and such acts as orienting, exploring, investigating, or adjusting. . . .

Note

1 *The Senses Considered as Perceptual Systems.* Boston, MA: Houghton Mifflin.

9

From *In and Out of the Black Box*

David W. Hamlyn

Sensation

It was Thomas Reid in the eighteenth century who has been most insist-
ent both on the distinction between sensation and perception and on the
necessary dependence of perception on sensation.[1] It is desirable to
emphasize both the distinction and the necessary dependence, because
there has been a tendency in the history of thought to conflate sensation
and perception in a way that distorts both concepts. It is that conflation
that leads to the notion of sense-data or analogous notions, such as that of
Hume's 'impressions'. Sense-data are supposed to be 'of' something; they
have content and provide information about the world thereby. They are
taken to constitute what is supposedly 'given' immediately to and by the
senses. It is a question for epistemology whether there is any such thing,
but that need not be our concern at present; for there is a place for the
concept of sensation which is quite distinct from that, and this is something which Reid clearly saw.

Reid defined 'sensation' by saying (*Essays*, I. 1) that it 'is a name given
by philosophers to an act of mind which may be distinguished from all
others by this, that it hath no object distinct from the act itself'. There may
be various things which one could object to in this, including the use of
the word 'act'. Reid went on to say, however, that 'there is no difference
between the sensation and the feeling of it'; that, with minor qualifications, seems evidently true of the most obvious candidate for the title of
'sensation' in ordinary parlance – pain. (The minor qualifications result
from the fact that we might sometimes want to speak of a pain continuing

David W. Hamlyn, *In and Out of the Black Box* (Oxford: Blackwell, 1990), pp. 84–91.

when our attention is diverted from it and thus when, strictly speaking, we do not feel it. This connection with attention is important in itself and I shall return to it.)

Apart from pain, the occurrence of sensations of this kind is most evident in the case of other forms of bodily sensitivity, for example, in connection with touch. When we pass our hand over a textured surface we may receive certain sensations in our finger-tips, which will depend on the nature of the texture. To the extent that we are aware thereby of the texture of the surface, the less are we likely to be aware of the sensations as such. That is clearly a function of the 'direction' of our attention – whether our attention is concentrated on the surface of the object or on what is happening in our finger-tips. There may indeed be a certain vacillation of attention in this respect. I suggest that it is implausible to think that the sensations occur only when our attention is concentrated on them, as distinct from the surface of the object which produces them.

I have therefore argued elsewhere[2] that it is a reasonable thesis that the sensations occur even when our attention is not on them and we are not explicitly aware of them as such. Indeed the sensations in question affect the quality of the total experience which we are having when we feel the texture of the surface. They 'colour' it, so to speak, so giving the experience a totally different quality from that involved when we perceive the surface by some other means. A further point in this connection is the possible explanation, referred to in the second of the papers mentioned above, of the fact, which I am assured obtains, that panel-beaters usually put a cloth or tissue between their fingers and the panel, the smoothness of which they are trying to check. I suggest that they do this in order to obviate the possibility of their receiving distracting sensations in their finger-tips when they are anxious to concentrate all their attention on the surface of the panel. This also provokes questions about the role of a medium for a given form of perception.

It might be argued, and has been argued, that even if it is the case that one might justifiably speak of sensations of touch and suppose them to occur in some way when we use the sense of touch, this is no reason for thinking that sensations occur in the case of other senses, particularly vision. Gilbert Ryle, indeed, argued that there were no such things as visual sensations, except perhaps when our senses go wrong, as when we 'see stars'.[3] What makes touch different in this respect is that it is a contact sense, and in that way it is directly dependent on the effects that objects have on the body and on bodily sensitivity. By contrast, vision is a distance sense and has no necessary or even customary dependence on bodily sensations in the eyes. (Extremes of brilliance or intensity of light may produce such, as do analogous extremes in connection with hearing, but that does not affect the rule.)

All that is true, but it does not really affect the question whether there is a sensuous aspect to vision, involving something akin to what are evidently sensations in the case of touch. If there was nothing of that sort, there would be no special characteristic belonging to visual experience, other than what results from the fact that it is mediated by sense-organs of a particular kind, with a particular location and situation. But it is clear that visual experience does have a special quality of the kind in question, so that the analogy with touch, even if only partial, justifies our thinking in terms of visual sensation or sensations. (If one uses the plural here, it is evident that there are problems about how individual visual sensations are to be distinguished and identified, but no matter. In the history of thought on these matters the conflation of sensations with sense-data made the distinction between sensations derived from sight only too easy; but one should not be misled by this.)

That there is a sensuous aspect to perception, including visual perception, has also been argued recently by Christopher Peacocke, on a variety of grounds of varying persuasiveness.[4] Peacocke thinks, however, that such sensations are to be characterized in terms of an analogy between their qualities and those possessed by the objects of the corresponding perception. Thus the perception of a red object has a sensuous aspect which can be characterized only via an analogy with the quality of redness which the object possesses. For this reason he introduces the notion of 'primed predicates', such as 'red'' ('red prime'), which can be applied to the sensuous element or sensation which the corresponding perception involves. The perception of a red object involves a red' (red prime) sensation.

This seems to me a mistake. A burning sensation is not so called because of any feature of its cause, as a red' sensation is presumably so called because its cause is red. Burning does not necessarily produce burning sensations, and those which are so called are so because there is an analogy between their characteristics and the physical process of burning (which, of course, need have nothing to do with their origin). Hence, whatever sensations are brought about by the visual perception of something red may have no properties which can be characterized as amounting to redness or to anything which has an analogy with that. The way in which analogy enters into our characterization of sensations is quite different from that supposed by Peacocke.

For present purposes this is, perhaps, a minor point, although there are philosophical issues connected with it concerning the way in which terms like 'red' get a meaning for us, and what relation that meaning has to the sensations which occur when we see things as red. What is clear is that without those sensations someone could have at best only a partial understanding of what it is for things to be red; and if perception involves, as I believe it does, some such understanding, he could not perceive things as red in the way in which normal-sighted people do. Similar considerations apply, with modifications, to the perception of other properties of things, including their spatial properties.

It is worth noting that point because of the attention that has been given recently to the phenomenon of so-called 'blind sight'.[5] Weiskrantz discovered (and others have followed up the discovery) that some people suffering from certain forms of brain damage leading to apparent blindness over a part of the visual field can identify points of light in the part of the field of vision to which they are ostensibly blind at a level which is much better than chance. On the other hand, they have no consciousness of the points of light and do not believe that they are seeing them; they are simply, as they suppose, guessing. If the issue is put in that way, it might be suggested that these are cases of unconscious seeing, however that is to be explained. But the implication is that the lack of consciousness is due to the fact that there is no sensory or sensational aspect to the 'seeing'. Hence the term 'blind sight'.

There is a conceptual issue as to whether 'sight' is the right word to use in these circumstances, though psychologists might prefer to pay more attention, in effect, to the word 'blind'. The use of the word 'sight' presents an issue simply because some philosophers, as we shall see in more detail later, have tried to analyse 'sight', and 'perception' generally, entirely in terms of a specific form of causation of beliefs. It might be argued that the patients in question do not have beliefs about the points of light – they think they are guessing. But they might conceivably come to have such beliefs if they were convinced of the reliability of their supposed 'guesses'. If that were so, they would be caused to have such beliefs by, *inter alia*, the points of light. But the only reason for speaking of sight would be that the eyes were involved; they would be the means, causally, whereby the patients acquired the relevant information. It is not clear that this would be enough to justify speaking of 'sight', given that there were no visual experiences.

Moreover, it remains true that if someone were born without any visual experience whatever, he would never come to have any more than a partial understanding of what it is for things to have colour or brightness, or a whole host of other 'visual' properties of objects. Gibson ... rejected any appeal, in a theory of perception, to cognitive processes. He also rejected an appeal to sensations.[6] But, certain kinds of information about objects is crucially dependent on the fact that it is mediated by processes involving sensation. For the possession of the requisite concepts in an adequate way depends on having visual experiences (and in some cases experiences connected with other senses). Moreover, although this is not a point which need be our immediate concern, someone who has no sensations cannot have any perception or appreciation of the aesthetic characteristics of things.

It must be noted that I have not said above that someone who lacks the relevant sensations can have no understanding whatever of the corresponding properties of things. The blind can have *some* conception of colour, particularly an understanding of the formal relationships between colours and, for example, any analogies which exist between colours and sensory properties the perception of which depends on the use of other senses, for example, the idea of warm and cold colours. Moreover, it might be possible for them to discriminate between colours in other ways than by sight, if, for example, any correlation exists between colour and some other detectable property. None of this belies the fact that they cannot have the understanding of colour that sighted people have, unless they have at some stage enjoyed the experience of sight. The same does not apply to spatial perception, since the perception of spatial properties and relationships is possible through other senses than sight, for example, touch. But, as is indicated by the reported experiences of those who have had their sight restored after congenital cataract, the spatial perception of the congenitally blind may well not be quite like that of sighted people.[7]

The relation between the sensations that a person may be having in perceiving things and how they look or otherwise appear to him is a complex one. There is, for example, the phenomenon of perceptual adaptation – the fact that sometimes when experience is distorted in some way things can come in course of time to 'look right'. It is reported, for example, that when subjects wear distorting spectacles or prisms, which invert or otherwise spatially distort the look of things by altering the pattern of excitation on the retina, things do after a time come to 'look right'.[8] It is never entirely clear what this means, but there is undoubtedly some sense in which this is so.

The same kind of thing occurs in the use of certain prosthetic devices, the immediate purpose of which is not to distort sense perception, but to supplement it when, for example, a specific sense is missing. There is a device entitled a 'tactile visual substitution system' (TVSS), whereby blind people are enabled to perceive what is in front of them by means of a television camera connected to a system of vibrating rods which stimulate the skin on their backs. After a time such people not only come to be able to detect by its means the spatial distribution of objects in front of them; they also report that they become less and less aware of the distribution of sensations on their back and more and more aware of how objects in front of them are distributed – to the extent that they feel inclined to speak of 'seeing' the objects or of their looking such to them.[9]

The sensations on their backs no doubt have what F. H. Bradley called 'volume' or 'voluminousness', in the sense that they are, as it were, spatially distributed over the skin; but they are not thereby distributed in the space in which the objects are eventually perceived as existing.[10] No doubt the subjects who underwent these experiences would never have had any spatial perception at all if they had no conception of space derived from the use of other senses. It remains true that the TVSS enabled them to have a form of spatial perception which they would not otherwise have had, that things came to appear to them in ways which would not otherwise have been available, and that this way of appearing was mediated by sensations which had voluminousness through their bodily location but which did not in themselves constitute a form of spatial perception.

It is arguable that one of the things which led Marr to the idea of the $2\frac{1}{2}$-D sketch – the fact that random-dot stereograms devised by Bela Julesz, when viewed so that a pattern of randomly distributed dots is presented to one eye and a slightly shifted pattern is presented to the other, produce through retinal disparity an impression of one pattern or part of it floating in front of the other – is another example of the phenomenon of voluminousness and not, strictly speaking, an instance of spatial perception proper. Marr thinks otherwise and uses it as an example of how stereopsis can come about by computation from the details of the primal sketch. If I am right, however, the mechanisms involved in the reaction of the optical system to the retinal disparities produced by the random-dot stereograms might well afford sensory experiences which have voluminousness. Where a person already has the idea of depth, the sensory experience could manifest itself as an impression of depth; but that would depend on the existence of forms of spatial perception proper.

By itself, therefore, the so-called impression of depth which occurs in the case in question or in analogous cases is merely the having of sensations which have voluminousness. More is required for spatial perception proper than that, even when the spatial perception is restricted to surfaces. Voluminousness applies to sensations only, and it might be objected that the experience in the random-dot stereogram case does not consist merely of voluminous sensations but is an experience *of* volume. I have already noted, however, the effect on the situation that may be brought about by possession of a concept of space. It is worth noting in this connection the situation which holds good over after-images. In their case too, an experience consisting of sensations is naturally taken by the person concerned as an experience *of* certain things, for example, a pattern on the wall at which he is looking. Voluminousness in sensations can, when part of a perceptual experience, produce an experience of *as it were* spatial characteristics. But all that depends upon the possession of a concept of space.[11] ...

Notes

1   See T. Reid, *Essays on the Intellectual Powers of Man*, ed. A. D. Woozley (Macmillan, London and Basingstoke, 1941). There is a section on Reid, as well as a general discussion of the concepts of sensation and perception, in D. W. Hamlyn, *Sensation and Perception* (Routledge and Kegan Paul, London, 1961). See also D. W. Hamlyn, *Experience and the Growth of Understanding* (Routledge and Kegan Paul, London, 1978), ch. 5.

2   See my 'Unconscious inference and judgment in perception' and 'Perception, information and attention', in D. W. Hamlyn, *Perception, Learning and the Self* (Routledge and Kegan Paul, London, 1983), pp. 11–29 and 57–68.

3   G. Ryle, *The Concept of Mind* (Hutchinson, London, 1949), pp. 240ff. and his 'Sensation', in *Contemporary British Philosophy*, 3rd Series, ed. H. D. Lewis (Allen and Unwin, London, 1956), pp. 427–43.

4   C. Peacocke, *Sense and Content* (Clarendon Press, Oxford, 1983), ch. 1.

5   See, e.g., L. Weiskrantz, 'Trying to bridge the neuropsychological gap between monkey and man', *British Journal of Psychology*, 68 (1977), pp. 431–45, and L. Weiskrantz and others, 'Visual capacity in the hemianopic field following a restricted ablation', *Brain*, 97 (1974), pp. 709–28. I have had a few words to say about the phenomenon in my 'Perception, information and attention', in Hamlyn, *Perception, Learning and the Self*, pp. 57–68, esp. p. 59.

6   See J. J. Gibson, *The Senses Considered as Perceptual Systems* (Houghton Mifflin, Boston, MA, 1966 and Allen and Unwin, London, 1968), p. 2, and my discussion of these issues in my 'The concept of information in Gibson's theory of perception', in Hamlyn, *Perception, Learning and the Self*, pp. 30–42.

7   See e.g. M. Von Senden, *Space and Sight*, trans. P. Heath (Methuen, London, 1960). This affects the question of the possible solutions to 'Molyneux's problem' (the question that Molyneux put to Locke in the eighteenth century, as to whether a congenitally blind person would, on having his sight restored, be able to perceive the properties of things which he had previously perceived by

touch). See M. J. Morgan, *Molyneux's Question* (Cambridge University Press, Cambridge, 1977), and D. W. Hamlyn, *The Psychology of Perception* (Routledge and Kegan Paul, London, 1957), pp. 96–7.

8 See I. Rock, *The Nature of Perceptual Adaptation* (Basic Books Inc., New York and London, 1966). For an interesting discussion of the notion of 'looks' see A. Millar, 'What's in a look?', *Proc. Arist. Soc.*, 86 (1985/6), pp. 83–97.

9 See e.g. the report of this and the further references given, including an account of the experience by a blind philosophy student, by John Heil, *Perception and Cognition* (University of California Press, Berkeley, Los Angeles and London, 1983), pp. 15ff. and 74ff. He also has things to say about 'blind sight'.

10 See F. H. Bradley, 'In what sense are psychical states extended?', in his *Collected Papers* (2 vols, Clarendon Press, Oxford, 1935), vol. 2, pp. 349ff. Bradley was reacting to James Ward, who spoke of the 'extensity' of sensations. See also Hamlyn, *Sensation and Perception*, pp. 160–2, and, for more detail, D. W. Hamlyn, 'Bradley, Ward and Stout', in *Historical Roots of Contemporary Psychology*, ed. B. B. Wolman (Harper and Row, New York, 1968), pp. 298–320.

11 See D. W. Hamlyn, 'The visual field and perception', *Proc. Arist. Soc.*, supp. vol., 31 (1957), pp. 107–24.

10

From *Perception and Cognition*

John Heil

Sensory Modalities

What is it, then, that distinguishes the several senses? How many senses are there? Might there be creatures with senses other than those with which we are familiar? What constitutes a "sensory modality?"

Grice (1962: 135 ff.) has provided an inventory of ways in which these and similar questions might be answered. There are, he contends, at least four distinct criteria to which one might appeal.

(1) The senses might perhaps be distinguished by reference to the "features that we become aware of by means of them." Thus one becomes aware of colors, for instance, by means of sight, of sounds by means of hearing, of odors by way of one's sense of smell. (Such a view may be traced back at least to Aristotle; see *De Anima*, bk ii.)

(2) It might be the case that each sense has a characteristic *experience* associated with it: certainly the experience of seeing something differs enormously from the experience of feeling or hearing it. And it seems possible that such differences afford a means of identifying and distinguishing sensory modes.

(3) One could, instead, focus on the "differing general features of the external physical conditions on which the various modes of perceiving depend, to differences in 'stimuli' connected with different senses: the sense of touch is activated by contact, sight by light rays, hearing by sound waves, and so on" (Grice 1962: 135).

John Heil, *Perception and Cognition* (Berkeley: University of California Press, 1983), pp. 4–18.

(4) Finally, one might wish to identify senses by reference to the organs involved. Seeing is what is done with eyes, hearing is accomplished by means of ears, smelling requires a nose.

I shall not here attempt to elucidate the view that emerges in Grice's discussion. I wish instead to offer an alternative account, one that avoids both the pitfalls and the inevitable complexities of views that attempt (as Grice's ultimately does) to distinguish among the senses by reference to some set of *internal* features of perceptual experiences or qualia.

The notion that the senses are to be defined and distinguished by reference to the phenomenal characteristics of sensory experiences – sensations – has a long and honorable history (one rehearsed admirably in Boring 1942). Implicit in such views has been the belief that the senses comprise *pathways* (or "channels") that culminate in the production of sensations. The latter are, according to some theorists, specific to pathways: sensations arising from stimulation of the visual pathway differ phenomenally from those produced when the auditory pathway is activated (see Müller 1838).[1] Awareness of sensations has been thought in this way to mediate perception of things and events outside the body. Perception, as distinguished from sensation, turns out on such a view to be always indirect, inferential.

Theories of this sort, however, theories that peg differences in sensory modes to characteristics of sensations or experiences (one may call them *internal feature* theories), are burdened with two major, and a host of minor, liabilities. In the first place, they are obliged to produce some *non-circular* account of those components of perceptual experiences or qualia that mark them off as experiences or qualia of one particular sense rather than another. This task (as Grice's paper attests) is by no means a simple one.

Second, an internal feature theory must provide a characterization of perceptual experiences that is suitably *universal*. Pre-analytically it seems not unreasonable to suppose, for example, that both honeybees and human beings may correctly be said to *see* various features of the world. It is far from obvious, however, that we should want to say that a honeybee's visual experiences are very much like our own, or that the qualia encountered by a honeybee resemble the visual qualia with which we are familiar. More dramatically, there is nothing obviously wrong with the supposition that another person (or, if that seems implausible, a Martian) might, in seeing something, have the sorts of experience we have when we hear something. In any case, it would be disturbing to *begin* theorizing about the senses on the assumption that such things are impossible. The question seems largely (though perhaps not exclusively) an empirical one.

Further, the Aristotelian notion – embodied in Grice's first suggestion – that the senses are to be distinguished by differences in (as he says) "features that we become aware of by means of them," runs afoul of the evident fact that one may become aware of some one property in utterly different ways. Thus one may tell by feeling an object or by looking at it that it is warm or smooth. Difficulties here lead one back to the notion of distinctive internal features of sensory experiences.[2]

It might, at first glance, appear more promising to pursue the notion that the senses are to be distinguished by reference to their respective "organs." Seeing, on this view, is what one does with one's eyes, hearing requires the use of ears. This is, of course, indisputably correct, though for the purposes at hand it is largely unhelpful. It is a matter of contingent empirical fact that most of the creatures with which we are familiar have eyes and ears with certain definite anatomical features. Even here, however, there are difficulties. The compound eye of a honeybee, to take but one example, is in most ways unlike the eye of a human being.

It is surely imaginable, in any case, that there are creatures elsewhere in the universe who (we should wish to say) see and hear perfectly well, yet who lack anything physiologically similar to the eyes and ears of terrestrial species. Confronted with a race of such creatures, the most natural course for a scientific investigator to take would be to decide which anatomical bits are to be counted as eyes, which might be called ears, by determining, first, which portions of the creatures' anatomy enabled them to see and which enabled them to hear. And this requires that an investigator begin with some independent idea of what seeing and hearing are and how they are different.

Characteristics of "Stimuli"

There is reason, then, to regard with suspicion Grice's options (1), (2), and (4), that is, to resist theories that attempt to identify senses by reference to properties of objects perceived, to internal features of sensory experiences, or to anatomical characteristics of perceptual organs. What of option (3)? Might the senses be identified and distinguished by reference to "the differing general features of the external physical conditions on which the various modes of perceiving depend," might they, that is, be distinguished by tracing out their connections to certain sorts of "proximal" stimulus?

Curiously, Grice spends little time exploring this possibility. It seems to me, however, at least if I understand rightly what Grice means by "stimuli" here, that this option affords a key to the solution of the problem. Very roughly, what I should like to suggest is that sensory modalities are to be identified and distinguished (insofar as this is possible) by reference to the kinds of "physical stimulation" from which a sentient creature extracts information about its surroundings.

On this account, seeing involves the activity of extracting information from light radiation; hearing occurs when a creature gains information from pressure waves of certain sorts; smell and taste involve the extraction of information from chemical features of the environment (the former from features borne through the creature's medium – the air or water through which it moves – the latter from chemical features of things ingested); touch incorporates the capacity to obtain information about things via mechanical contact of some sort.

I do not, I hasten to add, wish to defend the view that the senses can, in all cases, be distinguished *sharply* from one another. I want rather to suggest that to the extent that the senses can be distinguished at all, they are best distinguished by reference to characteristics of the physical stimuli that affect them, their respective sources of information.

Before taking things further, there are a number of features of the suggested taxonomy that are worth mentioning. First, it is a relatively simple matter to move from this way of talking about the senses to a classification of sensory "organs" or "receptors." An eye, for example, is a collection of receptors sensitive to light, an ear, one sensitive to vibration in the medium.

Second, it is clear that there may be a variety of ways to "build" receptors sensitive to the sorts of stimulation mentioned. What creatures that see have in common is the capacity to respond to and make intelligent use of a particular source of stimulation – light. What they need not have in common is a particular anatomical doodad nor, it seems, a particular sort of experience.

Third, I do not mean to imply that it is a necessary truth that seeing involves a creature's sorting through electromagnetic radiation. It may be that present-day theories of light propagation are false. I do, however, want to advance the notion that seeing, whatever else it is, is a matter of information-extraction from available light. It is the task of the physicist to determine what light is. I do not know whether the claim that seeing involves the picking up of information in the light, if true, is a necessary truth. It is, at least, a promising conceptual hypothesis.

These same points are meant to apply, of course, to the other senses. That hearing, for example, is the extracting of information from pressure waves transmitted through the medium, that smell is the picking up of information borne by chemicals dispersing through the same medium; these are partly empirical claims, partly something more. The empirical part concerns one's characterization of the physical stimuli and one's account of the receptors (and deeper-lying mechanisms) that make information contained in the stimuli available to the perceiver. The remaining part concerns the less straightforwardly empirical notion that the senses are a creature's means of finding out about its world. Information about that world transmitted in the light is picked up by way of devices we call eyes; information transmitted by pressure waves rippling through the medium is extracted by means of ears; and so on.

This approach provides an answer to a question sometimes posed by philosophical skeptics (and others) with certain theoretical axes to grind: "Couldn't one imagine a being able to see with its ears, hear with its eyes?" If one characterizes an eye as a bank of receptors used to extract information from light radiation, then any organ that allows for this *is* an eye. And, of course, there are (presumably) very good physiological reasons why one cannot do this with one's ears (or perform the opposite feat with one's eyes). If, in contrast, the questioner is in doubt about the sorts of experience perceivers might conceivably have when they look about themselves or listen, then, if I am right, his question is badly put. Seeing need not be distinguished from hearing by reference to features of the respective experiences. I suspect that there are solid empirical reasons for adopting the view of common sense here. Thus it seems somehow *likely* that the particular character of a creature's perceptual experience is a function of the character of its sensory receptors and their associated mechanisms. It seems correspondingly unlikely that two creatures, physiologically very similar, might experience the world in thoroughly different ways.

I cannot prove this, of course, but I do not need to. On the view endorsed here, the peculiar flavor of the experiences had by perceivers is just irrelevant to the question at hand. We are entitled to say that *S* and *T* see the same thing without committing ourselves to any theory at all about the internal character of their respective experiences. We may say that a visual experience is one arising from the process of extracting information from available light; an auditory experience is one brought about when information is obtained from the oscillating medium. . . .

Gibson's Account

The view I have begun sketching here owes much to the work of J. J. Gibson (see e.g., Gibson 1966, 1979; Schiffman 1976). Gibson's fundamental notion is that perceiving is the picking up of information about the world made available to the perceiver by various sorts of physical stimulation. Such an approach is, I am convinced, essentially correct. I wish for the moment, however, to align myself with Gibson in just two respects. First, although Gibson does not directly appeal to characteristics of perceptual stimuli in constructing a taxonomy of the senses, such an account seems implicit in much of what he says (see for example, Gibson 1966, ch. 3). Second, Gibson's characterization of perceiving as the picking up of information seems sound. I have tried already to make a case for the first point; now I should like to say a word about the second.

I have spoken repeatedly of the senses as devices (or, to use Gibson's term, "systems") enabling creatures to "extract information" about the world from various sorts of stimulation. This way of talking may offend some, but I think it need not. The information that a creature picks up may, in general, be characterized propositionally: that a certain object is green or rectangular, that it is loud or coarse, that it is sweet or warm. To say that a creature has picked up information describable in this way comes very close to saying that it has acquired a belief similarly describable.

I am not, I should say, suggesting that Gibson means by "information" what one ordinarily means by "belief." Information in the present context is a feature of a mode of stimulation; it may be picked up, or overlooked or ignored altogether. Information, in this sense, is "in the world," not (as a belief surely is) "in the perceiver." Nevertheless it seems right to say that the *picking up* of information is so close as to be indistinguishable from what I should prefer to call the acquiring of belief. Very crudely: we are able to acquire the beliefs we do about the world because the world is the way it is and because we are the way we are.

This way of putting the point is apt to seem spectacularly uninformative, but for all that it may be right. If light, for example, behaved differently from the way it does, it would *not* provide us with reliable information about such things as colors and shapes. Our visual apparatus, not surprisingly, evolved to take advantage of the information-providing characteristics of light: that light reflected from a smooth surface has different properties from light reflected from a rough surface;

that light reflected by a tomato differs in systematic ways from that reflected by a cucumber. ...

It is not, of course, that one perceives light radiation or pressure waves rather than tomatoes and thunderclaps. When one looks about the world, for instance, *what* one sees are objects and events illuminated by (or, in some cases, emitting) light. The notion that one might see *light* (a notion once fostered by impressionist painters) is, I am inclined to think, something very close to a category mistake.

Gibson's suggestion is that "ambient light" is structured by the objects and events it illuminates in such a way that it affords a creature, suitably equipped, with information about its surroundings. Light so structured at a "point of observation" (a point that may or may not be occupied) is labeled by Gibson the "optic array" (see Gibson 1979, ch. 5). The latter may be thought of as embodying information about the objects and events that determine its structure. My suggestion is that the extraction of such information may usefully be regarded as a matter of belief-acquisition. The idea is that a creature's senses enable it to discover properties of its surroundings by way of such information-bearing stimuli as light radiation and pressure waves.

It is perhaps worth emphasizing that, for Gibson, it is not simply a range of stimulation (light radiation, pressure waves, and the like) that conveys information, but *structured* stimulation. Unstructured light results in a luminous fog or *Ganzfeld* (Metzger 1930) that is visually impenetrable, unstructured sound in so-called white noise.

Concentrating for the moment on vision, it may be noted that the structure of the "optic array"

> can be described in terms of visual solid angles with a common apex at the point of observation. They are angles of intercept, that is, they are determined by the persisting environment. And they are nested, like the components of the environment itself. (Gibson 1979: 92)

As a perceiver explores his environment, the point of observation changes and the visual solid angles comprising the optic array are transformed. The systematic character of the resulting transformations "specifies" an underlying pattern of permanence.

The details of all this may be found in Gibson's writings (in e.g., Gibson 1966, 1979), and I shall not take the time to rehearse them here. For our purposes the point to be emphasized is that it is structured stimulation, over time, that produces in us reliable perceptual beliefs about our surroundings. Earlier, I volunteered somewhat unhelpfully that we discover properties of our environment "by way of" structured stimuli. I am now suggesting that one take "by way of" in a causal sense: structured stimuli *produce* certain beliefs in (suitably equipped) perceivers.

Experimental Support: "Tactile Vision"

Perhaps all this can be brought into focus by considering a recent development in the applied psychology of perception. It is a virtue, I think, of the sort of view I have been advancing that it allows one to take account of the phenomenon I shall describe, and to do so in a way that seems perfectly natural.

In a paper entitled (in my view, perspicuously) "Seeing with the skin" (White et al. 1970; see also Guarniero 1974; Morgan 1977; Reed and Jones 1978), a group of researchers discusses a device characterized as a "tactile visual substitution system" (TVSS). The device consists of a television camera (its "eye") coupled to a mechanism that converts the visual image produced by the camera into an "isomorphic cutaneous display" in the form of a pattern of vibration produced by a collection of tiny vibrating pins arranged in a grid and brought into contact with the skin (usually on the back or the stomach) of experimental subjects. Practice in the use of this device enables persons who are blind to detect reasonably fine differences among objects and events that appear in front of the camera.

The details of this experimental work are fascinating, but this is not the place to go into them (see above for references). I wish only to raise the question of how we are to describe such cases. My suggestion is that a person making intelligent use of a TVSS may be said to be *seeing* (though perhaps only dimly) features of his environment. This, surely, is what we should say were we to discover a creature whose "visual system" turned out to be a biological analogue of the mechanism described.

Let us call a person armed with a TVSS (or a creature biologically equipped with such a system) a *T-perceiver*. On my view it would be proper to say that a T-perceiver *sees* his surroundings because the T-perceiver makes use of information contained in reflected light.

There are two matters worth noting here. First, T-perceivers will enjoy a range of capacities and limitations thoroughly analogous to the capacities and limitations attributable to ordinary sighted creatures. Thus, for example, both ordinary sighted observers and T-perceivers will be able to describe the shapes and orientation of things without having to touch them, both will find it difficult to make out objects and events that are dimly illuminated.

Second, although T-perceivers and persons with ordinary eyesight may well describe what they see (or "T-perceive") in the same way, it is unlikely that we should want to attribute to them the same sorts of experience. If a T-perceiver were sufficiently practiced and well equipped, the fact (if indeed it is a fact) that his perceptual experiences were different from those of an ordinary perceiver would not necessarily be detectable from the ways in which he described his perceptions. Indeed a T-perceiver might well be at a loss to describe the character of his "visual experiences" without simply describing what he T-perceived.

In this regard at least, a T-perceiver would be no different from an ordinary (sighted) perceiver. As Grice puts it,

> such experiences (if experiences they be) as seeing and feeling seem to be, as it were, diaphanous: if we were asked to pay close attention, on a given occasion, to our seeing or feeling as distinct from what was being seen or felt, we should not know how to proceed; and the attempt to describe the differences between seeing and feeling seems to dissolve into a description of what we see and what we feel.   (Grice 1962: 144)

The view I have set out here appears to provide one with a way of accounting for this difficulty; more, it leads one precisely to *expect* it. The point of perceptual talk is to describe things perceived, not to describe experiences of things perceived. It makes clear, in addition, just why the character of perceptual experiences – sensations – seems so often beside the point.

It is interesting to compare these musings with the testimony of one who has himself employed a TVSS, a living, breathing T-perceiver. G. Guarniero, a graduate student (in philosophy!) who had been blind from birth, was given a three-week training session in the use of the device. He recounts his impressions in a paper entitled "Experience of tactile vision" (Guarniero 1974).

It is perhaps significant that Guarniero himself elects to describe what he has learned to do as *seeing*, rather than as feeling things. "Only when I first used the system did the sensations seem as if they were on my back" (1974: 101). Later he came to be aware, as it were, not of vibrations, but of objects existing apart from himself.

> Very soon after I had learned how to scan, the sensations no longer felt as if they were located on my back, and I became less and less aware that vibrating pins were making contact with my skin. By this time objects had come to have a top and a bottom; a right side and a left.   (1974: 104)

These observations again make clear a difficulty inherent in attempts to describe perceptual experiences without simply describing characteristics of objects perceived. They provide, as well, a certain amount of support for the "information pickup" view of perception advocated by Gibson. The function of sensory systems is to extract information from some particular stimulatory source (in the case of vision, from ambient light radiation), not to create distinct experiences, sensations or internal models of what is perceived. Given suitable equipment and proper training, evidently one can learn to extract visual information by way of the skin.[3]

I concede that it is, to an extent, misleading to describe a TVSS-user as *seeing* in an unqualified sense. Such a person, one might say, is employing a device that *enhances* or *extends* his senses. But *which* sense is thereby enhanced or extended? That will be determined, on the view defended here, by the character of the "intervening stimulation" sampled.

In putting it this way, it may appear that I have missed a crucial point. After all, one deploying a TVSS seems to be making use of *two* sorts of physical stimulation – the light radiation that reaches the lens of the apparatus and the vibration of pins against his skin. One might thus suppose that, given the tenets of my view, I ought to describe the case as one comprised of both touch and vision.[4]

This, I think, is partly correct, but, insofar as it *is* correct, it is perfectly unobjectionable. To the extent that one wishes to describe a TVSS-user as availing himself of his sense of touch, the *objects* felt are not those in front of the television camera, but the vibrating pins put in contact with his skin. If, in contrast, one takes the objects of his sensing to be those scanned by the camera, it is more plausible, surely, to describe them as (in some sense) seen, the beliefs thus acquired as (in some sense) visual.

It should be noted that a device such as a TVSS is workable chiefly because it establishes a partial isomorphism between an "optic array" and a gridwork of vibrating pins, *not* one between the scanned items and the gridwork.[5] It is the optic array as sampled by the television camera that determines the character of the vibrations. This is why the former may be taken as, in a certain sense, primary, and *this* is why it seems not altogether unnatural to describe a person employing a TVSS as *seeing*.

If I am right about this, then another interesting conclusion appears to follow. As was earlier noted, the notion that particular senses depend on particular neural pathways or mechanisms is a longstanding one (see Müller 1838). Thus vision has been associated not only with retinal occurrences, but in addition with goings-on in the optic nerve and the visual cortex. This seems, however, unnecessarily restrictive. Not only does it appear to rule out – unreasonably – the possibility that creatures built in ways different from us might properly be said to see (or hear, or taste, or smell) their environment, it confuses as well questions about the ways in which sensory mechanisms are in fact realized with questions about how they might be realized – what is essential to a certain mode of sensing.

This confusion is associated by Gibson with the doctrine of "specific nerve energies" formulated in the nineteenth century by Johannes Müller (see Müller 1838; Gibson 1979: 33 ff.). If the function of perception is, as I have suggested, to produce in the perceiver certain cognitive or doxastic states, and if the senses are distinguished chiefly by features of the world that produce these states, then particular characteristics of the internal mechanisms that mediate this process are strictly inessential. Perception may depend upon a causal process, but it is important to be clear about what is and what is not intrinsic to that process. This requires, among other things, a specification of its beginning and end states. My suggestion is that the process begins with physical stimulation structured by objects and events in the environment, and ends with the production of a belief (or belief-like cognitive state). Different senses are distinguished by differences in one of these boundary states, not by differences in neural pathways or by differences in the sorts of sensation generated by the activation of these.

Notes

1 If such a view were correct, it would be possible, perhaps, to conflate Grice's methods (2) and (4): commonalities and differences among sensory qualia would be accounted for by reference to biological features of perceivers.
2 In fact the route back to perceptual experiences is more tortuous than this way of putting it suggests. Roxbee Cox (1970) has attempted to construct a theory in which the senses are distinguished by reference to certain "directly" apprehended "key features" of perceived states of affairs. I shall not discuss this possibility here (though see below). The view I shall offer appears to account for the facts cited in support of the notion of key features and to do so in a much simpler, less *ad hoc* way.
3 Further, cases such as these suggest difficulties for theories that tie modes of sensing to particular psychological or physiological "channels".
4 I owe this observation to Gary Monnard.
5 Properties of the optic array are determined by, but are not identical to, properties of illuminated objects and events. An object in motion relative to an observer, for example, may systematically transform the array without

itself changing. Thus, an approaching object will "loom large," an object moving away will eventually "vanish." According to Gibson, visual information is conveyed largely by means of these and similar *transformations* of the optic array that occur as the perceiver observes, moves about in, and manipulates his environment.

References

Boring, E. G. (1942), *Sensation and Perception in the History of Experimental Psychology*, New York: Appleton-Century.

Gibson, J. J. (1966), *The Senses Considered as Perceptual Systems*, Boston: Houghton Mifflin.

Gibson, J. J. (1979), *The Ecological Approach to Visual Perception*, Boston: Houghton Mifflin.

Grice, H. P. (1962), Some remarks about the senses. In *Analytical Philosophy* (First Series), ed. R. J. Butler, Oxford: Basil Blackwell.

Guarniero, G. (1974), Experience of tactile vision, *Perception* 3: 101–4.

Metzger, W. (1930), Optische in Ganzfeld II, *Psychologische Forschung* 13: 6–29.

Morgan, M. J. (1977), *Molyneux's Question*, London: Cambridge University Press.

Müller, J. (1838), On the specific energies of nerves. In *A Sourcebook in the History of Psychology*, ed. R. J. Herrnstein and E. G. Boring, Cambridge, MA: Harvard University Press, 1965.

Reed, E. S. and Jones, R. K. (1978), Gibson's theory of perception: a case of hasty epistemologizing? *Philosophy of Science* 45: 519–30.

Roxbee Cox, J. W. (1970), Distinguishing the senses. *Mind* 79: 530–50.

Schiffman, H. R. (1976), *Sensation and Perception*, New York: John Wiley.

White, B. W., Saunders, F. A., Scadden, L., Bach-y-Rita, P., and Collins, C. C. (1970), Seeing with the skin, *Perception and Psychophysics* 7: 23–7.

11

From *The Will*

Brian O'Shaughnessy

The Location of Sensations

We stand to our limbs in a relation of *awareness*. A concrete or *intuitional* awareness. And since that awareness ceases when feeling ceases, and despite the fact that feeling is not the evidential ground of the object of awareness, it must be a *sensuous* intuition. Then what information do we acquire in being thus aware? We learn of the presence of the limb, and of such properties as that it is straight or moving away from the body, i.e. of certain *spatial properties* of the limb. Now it was for reasons of this kind that I came... to conjecture that the proprioceptive 'given' might be sensations and their position in three-dimensional physical space. And this led naturally to the supposition that a 'skin' of spaced sensations is both the 'given' *and* the fundamental framework wherein sensations are located *and* the explanation of proprioceptive illusions *and* the X that is laid nakedly open to view in the phenomenon of 'phantom' limb.

This is a piece of philosophical mythology. It rests, I think, in the final analysis on an unexamined thesis concerning the *location of sensations*. Namely, that sensations are given immediately to their owners as autonomously positioned in physical three-dimensional space. Then while this claim is mistaken, I have yet to demonstrate precisely why. To do so, I need to come by the criteria by which we manage to locate a sensation at some point in the body. Now such an enterprise has an especial relevance to the overall project... – which is an investigation into the actual nature of, and the preconditions of the givenness of, the bodily

Brian O'Shaughnessy, *The Will* (Cambridge: Cambridge University Press, 1980), vol. 1, pp. 167–81 (revised version, by the author, of chapter 6).

will's immediate object – and is in effect a continuation of the project . . . of uncovering the criterial conditions of willing phenomena in an object. The special relevance is this. [It seems clear] that the above theoretical account must be radically false. The proprioceptive 'given' is a rich and unitary whole which encompasses *both* the presence and spatial proper-ties of the limb *and* the bodily location of the very sensations that ensure such a 'given'. That is, the givenness of the will's immediate object is inextricably linked with the givenness of the location of just those sensa-tions that help to make it thus 'given'. This strongly suggests that un-covering what it is that enables a sensation to have a bodily position, should help reveal what enables the bodily will to have its bodily object given to it, and in the immediate primitive manner that it requires. We shall in any case see that it does.

1   A Theory of Sense Perception

(a)   *A short proof of the existence of perceptual sensations*

It will greatly assist my account of the location of bodily sensations, such as itches and pains, if we can be certain of the existence, and the role in sense perception generally, of another category of sensation: namely, the type of sensation that is involved in such perceptual experiences as seeings and hearings. That is, what might be termed 'perceptual sensa-tions'. A short proof of their existence now follows.

A man with sinusitis may of a sudden notice a faint 'ringing', and that 'ringing' may persist without respite for days. This phenomenon, not of *noticing* 'ringing', but of *'ringing'* itself, which is the material object of the noticing event, is an instance of the type in question. And it has every right to be characterized as a *sensation*. I say so, because it is endowed with the requisite battery of typifying properties. Thus, (1) it is capable of greater or lesser intensity, and it has location and extension of a kind; (2) it is not the product of the belief or concept systems, it absolutely must have an extra-psychological bodily cause, and one can state causally sufficient bodily conditions for it; (3) one can notice or fail to notice it, and one can actively attend to it, so that it can be a possible immediate material object for the attention; and (4) because it can elude awareness and yet continue in existence it cannot be the hypostatized internal object of an intentional perceptual consciousness. So much for the reality of this type of phenomenon and its general character as a sensation. The next thing is to demonstrate that a phenomenon of this kind is an ingredient of the veridical perceptual situation.

Now when a man hears some real and particular sound, let us say *as* the word 'I', air waves must have caused some physical phenomenon, call it p, in his auditory nerves, which then caused a mental event of noticing a sound of type 'I' *as* an occurrence of the word 'I'. Then had just such a bodily p been caused instead merely by sinusitis, and had that man's attention been riveted elsewhere, p would, I suggest, still then be causing some auditory psychological *something*. My reason for saying this is that, were that man's attention to be diverted away from its present 'riveting' object and into the auditory channel, he must surely then notice, not of course a real sound, since none was there to be heard, but something real and internal that sounds exactly as 'I' sounds: after all, this merely replicates the situation described in the previous paragraph in which a property of this kind obtained. It follows that such a sinusitis-originated and continuing p must be continually causing an auditory psychological something that exists independently of his noticing it. Now evidently that psychological something is the same in general type as the 'ringing' mentioned above, i.e. a sensation. It seems, therefore, that absolutely any example of the p-phenomenon will cause an auditory sensation provided the right conditions obtain: those conditions being, first the inherence of the state of consciousness, second the presence of satisfactorily functioning auditory cerebral equipment. Then since p and the above conditions obtained when the subject in question veridically heard the real sound 'I', p must have caused that sensation in that veridical situation. Moreover, since there cannot simultaneously occur two absolutely identical experiences of seeming to hear 'I', the noticing of the sensation as 'I' and the noticing of the sound 'I' must be one and the same event. In short, there are such items as auditory sensations, and they are an essential element of the veridical perceptual situation. The sound is one thing, the auditory sensation a second, the noticing-of-the-auditory-sensation event – which *is* the event of hearing that sound – a third. All three phenomena occur when we veridically hear sounds.

This argument can be generalized through the phenomenon of after-images and/or phosphenes to visual perception, wherein a visual field of visual sensations which are (at the least) two-dimensionally arrayed mediates one's perception of the environment, and thence of sense perception generally. One should not be deflected in this argument by the heavy interpretational, spatial (etc.) load that is placed upon the visual field of visual sensations in visual perceptual experience: these are merely additions to a situation that is basically the same as the auditory situation.

(b)   *A defence of this theory of sense perception*

Objection might be taken to this account of sense perception, and particularly visual sense perception, (1) because of my use of the concept sensation, (2) concerning the assumption that visual sensations are arrayed in two-dimensional space, (3) over difficulties presented by hallucinations. Before I move on in section 2 to the main business of considering the location of sensations, I shall offer a brief comment on these three topics: (1) sensations, (2) the two-dimensionality of visual sensations, and (3) hallucinations.

(1)   I have in section (a) above listed a number of properties that are essential to sensations. These can be assembled into groups which help to display the distinctive character of sensations. The first group is of some real significance: intensity, together with location and extension (of a kind). More important still is the relation of the sensation to the attention; for the sensation is a *possible* but not certain immediate object for the attention, and is such that in specifiable optimum circumstances (say, wakeful sanity, attention free, a hunt on for the sensation) it is under some description or other a *certain* immediate object for the attention. Finally, and perhaps most important of all is the absolute *senselessness* of the sensation, which is a product of the special type of its origin. For since the sensation fails to exhibit intentionality (unlike, it may be, one's awareness of sensations), and since its very last cause is of necessity physical non-psychological, concepts play no part in its genesis, whether causally or constitutively. It is neither 'made out of' concepts, nor 'made by' concepts. It is, one might therefore say, a mere meaningless 'it', simply 'there' in consciousness as nothing else psychological is, lying about the mind like junk, almost indeed a sort of stuff. This seems to be unique to sensation.

Then this trio of properties: intensity and location (of a kind), being a possible immediate material object for the attention and a certain such object in optimum circumstances, and being both intrinsically and extrinsically senseless, apply alike to after-images and 'ringings' in the ears. This ensures that it is no mere conventionalist stipulation when we characterize these latter as sensations, and reminds us that sense-perception derives its title precisely because of the presence of the sensation in this epistemological transaction. It seems to me evident that such a senseless, or intrinsically and extrinsically intentionally undirected psychological 'it', occurs therein – and in particular in the sense of sight.

A word on this last, far and away the most useful and impressive of the senses. Thus, precisely what are the main phenomena in the visual perceptual situation? and what are they called? and how do they relate? They are, I believe, two in number: one consisting in *visual sensations* distributed in (at least) two-dimensional body-relative physical space, the other being a phenomenon in the *attention*, namely, its taking the above two-dimensional array as object (for all sense perceivings are events in which sensations come to the attention). The first phenomenon has no name, but is in normal circumstances characterizable under multiple headings as (essentially) 'sensation entering visual field'/ (inessentially) 'light entering visual field'/ (inessentially) 'physical object entering visual field'. Then this groundwork phenomenon in the visual perceptual situation is the cause of, the necessary but insufficient condition of, and at the same time the necessary and immediate material object of, the second phenomenon. That second phenomenon does have a name, since it is for this that we usually reserve the term 'see'. Inactive occurrences of the phenomenon, which is to say noticings, are 'seeings' 'glimpsings' 'catching sight of' (etc.); while active occurrences, which is to say processive attendings, are 'lookings', 'watchings', 'starings' (etc.). Then this second phenomenon, what one might very naturally dub 'the impression' or 'the visual experience', and which unlike the sensory array is indeed constitutively dependent upon the concepts resident in the mind of its owner, takes the form 'see *as* ... '. Now philosophers concerned with what they call 'sense-datum theory' can take their pick from these two phenomena: they can describe either the first, or the second, though not both! (in a mental 'blur'), as the 'sense-datum'; but let them make the distinction in the first place, and then let them avoid the snare of hypostatizing the intentional object of the impression, or worse of denying the existence of the sensation on the grounds of the non-existence of such a hypostatic object!

(2) Granted the existence of these sensuous entities in sense perception generally, why should we assume that in visual perception they form a 2D array in body-relative physical space? Well, I say in body-relative physical space, because the psychological datum is not merely a set of simultaneous visual sensations, and not just the fact that those sensations are given as standing to one another in relations like next-to and farther-off-than, but in addition that they are given to one as lying in real physical directions out from the body. Then why 2D? Why not 1D or 3D? Now it is evident that *any* visual experience will present to awareness, not merely colour instances and various measures of proximity between simultaneous colour instances, but 2D shapes like roundness and triangularity, and suchlike. Clearly, the psychological given must be either 2D or 3D. Then why not 3D? Does not that accord better with experience? Well, it may be that in binocularity it is so. But if we confine the discussion to monocular vision – as I propose to do throughout this entire discussion – then two simple facts decisively put paid to the suggestion that the visual given might be 3D: the first is, that the last cause of the visual sensation is necessarily physical non-psychological; the second, that psychological factors like concepts and knowledge of the look of things (and conceivably also evolution-determined interpretational propensities) all play a causal part in the genesis of monocular visual depth experience. For if the entry of depth into a visual field *is* the entry of an array of visual sensations all of which have non-psychological causes, and if it is also true that concepts and knowledge of the look of things (etc.) play a part in the genesis of the experience of depth in the monocular visual impression, then it is certain that those sensations cannot *in themselves* make visible the depth that they bring forward for visual consciousness. If only mental factors like concepts / knowledge of types / knowledge of the look of types / etc. can unlock to view the depth that is potentially visible through the medium of sensations, those sensations cannot in themselves lie in a depth that matches the depth they bring to view; and that is to say that *a representative theory of visual depth is unacceptable* in the case of monocular vision (binocular vision being a different story altogether). Indeed, since *any* visual depth experience depends upon seeing one's visual sensations *as* contributing the colour of physical items situated at some distance from one, and therefore upon the swinging into play of one's conceptual apparatus, it seems certain that visual sensations cannot in themselves lie in psychological depth. In short, monocular visual sensations must be distributed in two rather than three dimensions. (I emphasize once more that these considerations apply, not to binocular visual experience, but to monocular experience only. The Julesz experiment reveals a very different situation in the case of binocular vision, for here the uniformity of depth-experience transcends the knowledge and concepts (etc.) present in the mind of the perceiver.)

The claim that monocular visual sensations are merely two-dimensionally distributed finds corroboration in the fact that, just as two completely indistinguishable and wholly veridical coloured photographs can be of different scenes presenting different depth situations, so two visual fields of sensations could be internally indistinguishable and yet, thanks to the diverse concepts and beliefs of their owners, cause different *veridical* visual depth-impressions, i.e. different depth-*perceivings*. Does not this show that those sensations must lie in an order that, in being independent of the concepts / knowledge / beliefs / etc. resident in the minds of their owners, and therefore also of the depth content of any resulting visual impression, must itself lack depth?

And the optical facts further corroborate this account of monocular depth experience. Thus, consider (figure 11.1) the light from a scene approaching an eye: a transit that is so rapid that it seems stationary and homogeneous down the line of sight. Then a full specification of the optical data coming through space is given entirely in 2D terms. For if we were to set up a screen S to intercept the beams of light, we would manage to collect all the data simply by specifying the colour-and-brightness value of each point on the two-dimensional surface S. A dimension more and we collect the same, a dimension less and we collect no more than a line. Then note that nothing represents the gulf between P and Q. Indeed, it is clear that, just as those two indistinguishable photographs can represent different depth situations, so the light coming from P and Q is theoretically consistent with diverse depth causes. It follows that the optical data coming from P and Q must be, depending on the prevailing circumstances, evidence for different depth situations. So how can the sensations that these light beams cause lie in a depth that matches the reality? And how can they lie in any depth of their own if only concepts/knowledge/expectations can unlock the experience of depth? Then it is precisely those concepts and beliefs etc. in the mind that do justice to the prevailing circumstances (which may even include the spatial layout of the physical setting in which the species evolved), while the purely sensuous contents of the visual field do justice to the

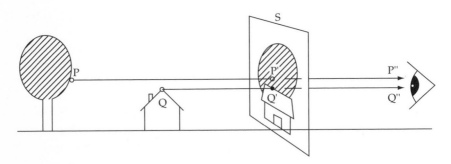

Figure 11.1

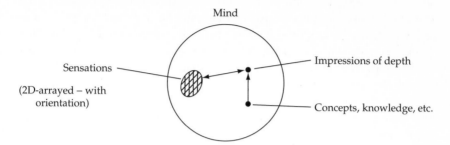

Figure 11.2

factor of sight. The product of their interaction is the visual impression (see figure 11.2).

3 This account of sense perception has a difficulty to face in the hallucination. For if the sensation is both immediate cause and immediate necessary material object of the perceptual experience, must not this also be true of the hallucination? For is not the hallucination indistinguishable from the visual experience? Yet surely the cause of the hallucination is a state of the mind rather than a sensation?

The mistake here lies in the assumption that because the hallucination *seems* the same as perceiving, it must *be* the same experience as perceiving; this probably derives from assuming that all 'seeming seeings' are so in the sense that they are the same experience as the experience of seeing. Yet it is clear that this is false. For a mental image is a seeming seeing, but not in the sense of being the same experience as seeing. Likewise the hallucination. While the image is a seeming seeing in the sense of being some kind of duplicate of seeing, hallucinatory seeing is a seeming seeing in the sense of seeming to its owner to be the same experience, i.e. such that he would say it was the same were he to believe he could trust his judgement. Yet it *is not* the same experience. For it is not a *visual* experience. Like the mental image, it is an event in the *visual imagination*; it differs from the mental image, not in that one need believe either in its content or even that it is the same experience as seeing, but in its being *experienced as* the same experience. A necessary condition of visual experience is that the attention is causally and attentively engaged by visual sensations, and the hallucination is not so engaged. And so hallucinatory situations must be differently structured from perceptual situations. Whereas visual perception is a five-term relation, between subject-awareness-sensation-light-object, the visual hallucination is at most three-term, between subject-hallucination-object. Hallucinations do not take sensations as their external or material object, even though one can hallucinate the having of sensations. Indeed, they have neither sensation objects nor causes. Accordingly, they constitute no difficulty for the theory of perception which I am proposing.

A few general comments. Whereas some episodes in the visual imagination are merely victories for the imagination over a firm sense of reality, e.g. seeming to see faces in the fog during trench warfare, all hallucinations necessarily are caused by a diminution in one's sense of reality, e.g. even the slight hallucinations of mescalin takers that involve no delusions. Then some hallucinations manifest damage to but not loss of the sense of reality, e.g. Macbeth asked 'Is this a dagger...?' and that he voiced a *question* beautifully demonstrates in the instant, first that he has not yet left us (the world), second that he is not properly with us (in the world). But some hallucinations carry all before them, as when Macbeth addresses Banquo's ghost with the words 'Never shake thy gory locks at me!', which is indicative of total delusion and complete loss of the sense of reality. The schema (figure 11.3) summarily represents these facts.

2   The Actual Physical Location of Sensations

(a)   *The actual physical location of after-images*

Let us return to the main problem of this chapter. Thus, we wish to know what is, and how properly to determine, the location of bodily sensations. Then we would do well to ask a comparable question concerning another type of sensation, namely, the visual sensation: for example, the after-image (or phosphene, etc.). For it seems to me that, just as the mind automatically 'projects' the after-image on to walls and skies, so it 'projects' the bodily sensation on to the *unique framework* available for items of this kind. That is, the human body. Indeed, as we shall see, it first and foremost 'projects' it on to the *body-image*, and thence, and only secondly, albeit immediately, on to the *body itself.*

Where is the after-image? Not on the retina or on the eye. Not on the wall on which we see it; for demolition of the wall only releases further spaces for it. Not merely in a certain direction; for how can a phenomenon lie in no more than a direction? Not merely in the middle of the visual field; for that gives no information about the spatial locality of the item itself. Then is it a *reality*? Or is the reality instead merely *one's having* an after-image? It is a true individual: an entity that can be

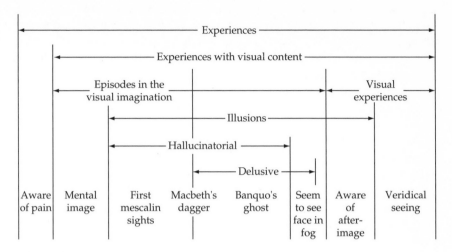

Figure 11.3

differentially singled out by the attention, though one that, like motion, necessarily is attached to some something that owns it, namely, its owner. Yet I reject the supposition that the after-image has no more refinable a location than its owner. After all, the one after-image could persist even if its owner were to lose his feet – while his brain remained intact – an instant after the after-image came into being, which surely implies that it occurred somewhere between hair and ankles; so that it must have happened in a differentiable sector of the body. Doubtless, in the brain. For where else?

This conclusion may seem a trifle paradoxical in the light of the fact that we locate it on walls (etc.). But this is because we fail to take note of the *heterogeneity* of 'where'-questions. For consider: 'Where is the pebble?' 'in his shoe'; 'Where do thoughts occur?' 'in the mind'; 'Where does the letter "z" occur?' 'at the end of the alphabet'; 'Where is the phosphene?' 'in the middle of the visual field'; 'Where do after-images occur?' 'on the surface of whatever physical object happens to share some part of the visual field with them'. Thus, 'Where?' might ask for (i) the region of *space* they occupy, (ii) their *domain of being*, (iii) the *part of the domain of being* in which they occur, (iv) the sector of a *sense field*, (v) the point in real physical space at which they are *experienced to be*. So we ought not to assume in the case of after-images that because they are experienced at some real place p, and because that gives a true answer to a genuine 'where?'-question, their location in physical space must be p. Indeed, it seems to me that to the question 'Where are after-images?', we might simultaneously offer *five different true answers*. Either: in the brain, in the domain of the psychological, in the less mental subsector of the domain of the psychological, in a sector of the visual field, on whatever physical object happens to share with it a sector of the visual field.

It should be noted that when we locate the after-image in the visual field, we commit ourselves to no particular thesis concerning its actual physical location, for the position of a sensation in a sense field need stand in no systematic or projective relation to the actual position in space of that sensation. Now the visual field is a sense field, i.e. a two-dimensional psychological map wherein sensations stand to one another in merely two-dimensional relations like 'adjacent-to-left' 'less-adjacent-to-right' 'above' 'below', which are such that a continuous path through contemporaneous sensations of that type leads from any one point in that field to any other point: a schema which allows for boundaries, blind spots, etc. Thus, after-images occur in a two-dimensional sensuous spatial system. Yet why should there be a systematic relation between the two-dimensional relations within that system and their actual positions in physical space?

There is probably one and only one, answer to the question: 'Which region of physical space is occupied by after-images?' Namely: a region in the brain.

(b)   *The actual physical location of bodily sensations*

This discussion assists us when we turn to the bodily sensation. It counsels us to recognize that the sentence 'Where is the bodily sensation?' has several interpretations. So let us begin the inquiry by addressing ourselves to the question of the first and most basic type, namely, a (i)-type 'where'-question. Thus: 'Which region of physical space is occupied by the bodily sensation?'

We know that the bodily sensation is a phenomenal reality, with physical event causes and effects and a determinate location in time. Accordingly, it seems likely that it has a determinate location in physical space. But where? Well, a pain in the foot that is caused by a pin-prick has not even begun until the neurological message reaches the brain, and were the foot to be removed when that message had travelled but to the knee the pain would still occur, and we cannot suppose that the brain effects of that message cause a psychological phenomenon in the foot, let alone a psychological phenomenon in the foot that necessarily cannot occur if the brain does not exist or is dead! And how in any case can a psychological phenomenon be set in a foot? Thus, the pain can hardly be in the foot! Moreover, pain necessarily requires pheno-mena in the brain of its owner if it is to occur, and necessarily has all-but-contemporaneous physical causes therein. So surely it is somewhere. But surely the pain in the foot is located either in the *brain* or the *foot* or *nowhere*. Then since it is not in the foot, and not nowhere, it must be in the brain. I take this to be its actual position in three-dimensional physical space.

Yet we are inclined to insist that really a pain in the foot *must* be in the same space as the foot. After all, 'the place of the pain' and 'the part of the body that hurts', are logically equivalent, and the latter expression singles out a real body part. So must not the former? Of course it must – but so what? Why must that real place in physical space be *occupied* by the sensation? In any case the above two descriptions evoke *different theoretical expectations*. The former suggests autonomy for the sensation, of the kind one might impute to a sooty smudge situated on a limb; the latter suggests that a sensation gets its position in space only through the position of the item that supports it. Now each of these suggestions is seriously awry, though the former more so. For the former leads us to suppose that what we call 'the place of the pain' is the position in space of an autonomous phenomenon that happens con-tingently to coincide with the position in space of the limb wherein we site it, and that the position of the pain has no essential link with the seeming position of seeming parts of the body, thereby generating an entire mythology of a body-image composed of such luminous will-o'-the-wisp entities. While the latter leads us to suppose that what we call 'the place of a pain' is the actual position in physical space of a phenom-enal something that necessarily is *of* something with which necessarily it shares position (as happens with movement). This account, in tightly linking 'the place of a sensation' with the real place on the limb, is to that extent insightful, but misguided in supposing that that is where it actually is.

Now the fact that we use 'the place of the pain' and 'the part of the body that hurts' interchangeably, leads us naturally to suppose that, as the latter place is the real physical place of that body part, so therefore must the first-mentioned 'place, of the pain' be the real physical place of the pain. But after all, 'on the wall' cites a real physical place, and is truly assigned to a real after-image. And yet the after-image is not a psycho-logical something that wanders on walls! 'The place of the after-image', which mentions a real place and a real after-image, so uses 'of' that it does not state the sector of space in which the after-image occurs. Like-wise, 'the place of the pain'.

3   Projection and Psychological Space

From this point on I shall be concerned expressly and differentially with the location of sensations, taken not in the sense in which we locate physical phenomena in physical space, but in the usual and vastly familiar sense in which we position feelings in various parts of the body. Thus, bodily sensations, which literally occupy a space in the brain, get located nonetheless in such disparate places as teeth and hands. Two very interesting questions then suggest themselves. *In what sense* or by what means do these items which are actually in one place come to be set in these different places? And to what extent is their being sited in bodily extremities due to their standing to one another in psychological spatial relations which match the spatial relations holding between these body parts? The first of these questions leads me into a brief consideration of a phenomenon that I call '*projection*', the second to the topic of sensory or *psychological space*. Through these concepts we manage significantly to relate and simultaneously significantly to distinguish the location of bodily sensations and the location of visual sensations. At the same time this puts us in a position to provide a very general and merely preliminary answer to the question: What do we mean in speaking of 'the location of a sensation'?

(a)   *Projection*

When ordinarily we locate sensations, we mention a real place, a real sensation, and assign one to the other. 'My pain is here', one says, pointing to a tooth. Yet we are not saying where in space it is, since it is in the brain. Then if this real place in a tooth is not the place of the *sensation*, of *what* is it the real place?

The most illuminating comparison is with 'the after-image is on the wall', for it seems that the bodily sensation must be projected on to the limb as the image is on to the wall, where to be 'projected' is for a psychological item to be experienced *as* inhabiting some physical something that lies outside the mind of the experiencer. It seems that the place of the sensation must be the place it is experienced to be, that place being of necessity a part of the body. As the after-image is projected on to whatever physical item occupies its sector of the visual field – and items in physical space projectively sustain visual sensations when eyes are open – so the bodily sensation is projected on to the one physical landscape capable of sustaining it, namely, the animal body that is veridically given to the awareness of its owner.

Thus, as the array of purple-ish visual sensations had with closed eyes gives way on opening those eyes to an array presenting to awareness the real contents of physical space, so the bodily sensations produced (say) by brain stimulation in one whose brain has temporarily been all but disconnected neurologically from the rest of the body, gives way to an array of sensations projected successfully on to the now reconnected torso and limbs. Then in either successful case, sensations that are seemingly of some something – round red object (in sight) – paining big toe at end of leg (in feeling) – manage veridically both to bring something to awareness (sun, toe) *and* to land successfully projectively on to that projective sustainer (sun, toe). In short, we become aware of the contents of space and of individual points on our body, through projecting these brain-located phenomena on to the unique items that can support them, namely, the physical world, and one's body. Thus, the phenomenon of projection proves paradoxically to be the device whereby concrete intuitional awareness of the *projective sustainer* is realized! It is that through which we become aware of the spatially removed. Like a fisherman we throw out the two-dimensional net of the visual field, and like him again we haul back to consciousness the whatever the net managed appropriately to fit, while it is as a sort of spear fisherman that we throw out the bodily sensation, and haul back to consciousness the whatever bodily place it was destined to skewer.

Roughly, as visual sensation is to physical objects at large, the bodily sensation is to particular points in the body.

(b)   *The unlikeness of sight and touch in respect of psychological space*

We can imagine a permanently blind man learning to single out and to identify the colour of various visual sensations in his visual field which have been induced in him by ocular stimulation. And we can in addition imagine him learning to order those sensations in terms which are spatial and yet sensuous, as when he singles out a blue triangle or a red circle under those concepts. Finally, we must recognize that those various sensations will be given to him as lying in specific directions in relation to his body: for example, he may experience (say) the blue triangle as lying a little to his left and a little above the red circle. Now one important fact that this 'thought-experiment' demonstrates is that visual sensations can be individuated and spatially structured independently of any material object 'receivers'. This is because monocular visual sensations form a merely two-dimensionally ordered sense-field, which paradoxically is given simultaneously in intra-sensuous psychological terms wherein the concepts of extent and shape find instantiation *and* directionality in body-relative physical space. Thus, a permanently blind man might be able to see (say) that one yellow point is separated by a greater extent of black visual sensation from a blue point than it is from a red point – *and also* be perceiving in so doing the diverse measures of two physical angular directions out from his body – for he will simultaneously be perceiving the directions in body-relative physical space in which lie the several coloured points. It is a tempting but serious error to suppose that he would be perceiving *no more than* a sensuous extent, a sensuous extent which happens wholly contingently to relate in regular fashion to bodily extent: in effect, to postulate the existence of an autonomous 'visual space', a sensuous domain wherein spatial relations like circularity and linearity exist, which is distinct from physical space. Rather, in perceiving sensuous extent he is *at the same time* perceiving an angular sector of physical space. This perplexing double property of sensations, whereby there exists sensuous extent which is simultaneously physical extent, is a direct consequence of the fact that we individuate sensations of absolutely all kinds – whether they be bodily, visual or auditory – by assigning them appropriate sites in body-relative physical space. It is this latter fundamental principle of individuation which permits us to have two simultaneous, indistinguishable bodily sensations – say, a dull ache in one's left thumb and a dull ache in one's right thumb – as we cannot simultaneously harbour two thoughts with identical content.

Then despite this important congruence of sensory extent and physical directional extent, the fact remains that visual sensations can be individuated and spatially arranged altogether independently of any material object 'receivers'. And there can be no analogue of this property in the case of the sense of touch, even though, because the skin envelope convolutes as a two-dimensional surface in three-dimensional space, and because touch sensations get located thereon and can be adjacent and so form a continuum, one is inclined to postulate the existence of an autonomous two-dimensional touch sense-field convoluting in three-dimensional physical space. Even more mysteriously, one is inclined to postulate an autonomous touch sense-field that is set convoluting in a purely psychological three-dimensional space, exactly as visual sensations seemed at first blush to be set in a purely psychological two-dimensional sensory space. Now the major unlikenesses of sight and touch in these particular spatial respects are as follows (always remembering that we are speaking of experienced and not of actual place).

(1a)   While monocular visual sensations are two-dimensionally arrayed in body-relative physical space, the given distances therein have no linear measure in millimetres or miles, but

(1b)   the only places in which touch sensations are set are real places in physical space that are separated by real distances, or putative examples of such.

(2a)   Visual sensations are set in their two-dimensional system independently of landing upon material object 'receivers', but

(2b)   a touch sensation has a place in three-dimensional physical space only if it is at and of a body part.

(3a)   Each part of the visual field has a sensation value, but

(3b)   each point on the skin surface is in fact not the continuing bearer of a sensation.

(4a)   The visual sensation is simply 'red and bright' (say), and is not as such putatively of some physical object (e.g. a balloon), but

(4b)   each bodily sensation is either merely putatively or else actually of a body part (e.g. headache, toothache, earache).

So there is no autonomous 2D 3D touch sense-field, set either in physical space and independent of the body-thing, or else set in a purely psychological space which likewise is independent of the body-thing, on to which the bodily sensation is projected. Then while sight shares some of these properties, there exist significant differences between the two senses. Thus, in the case of visual sensations one could start 'inside', let us say if one were blind from birth, and be aware of those sensations and even order them spatially in a two-dimensional field which is at once psychological-sensuous *and* physical-directional, and *only then*, with the late advent of the normal powers of sight, proceed 'outside' and 'project' them on to items in the physical world. But there could be no analogous working from 'inside' to 'outside' in the case of tactile and bodily sensations, even in one whose brain happened temporarily to be neurologically disengaged from the rest of the body. Those sensations are from the start necessarily putatively of body-parts. And the *one and only* physical or else psychological spatial systems into which they fit is the one that has application when they successfully 'project'. That is, the *public physical space* of the body. Thus, the bodily sensation, set in fact in the brain, gets its one and only possible experienced space either through successfully 'projecting' on to a limb or else putatively doing so; whereas the visual sensation, set likewise in fact in the brain, first of all has a two-dimensional experienced space which is at once psychological/sensuous *and* physical-directional, and thence and only secondly 'projects' on to the objects whose seen colour and contour it displays. A major difference.

This discussion enables me to offer a provisional and very general characterization of 'the location of a bodily sensation' in the sense under investigation. The location of a bodily sensation is and can never be anything but the real point on the presently existing body-part of its owner at which it really and not merely seemingly is experienced to be. Accordingly, if the body-part is not there, or if the sensation fails to successfully 'project' on to an existing part and is hence not really experienced at any body-part, then in the sense under consideration the sensation has *no* location. It merely seemingly has. Why not? This is the resolution of the problem of the location of 'phantom' limb sensations.

Now despite the lack of a location in the usual familiar sense for a sensation which fails to 'project' on to the body, such a sensation has a sensuous location in relation to other contemporaneous sensations: for example, it may be nearer to a tickle than a twinge. However, this sensuous proximity is not autonomously just that and nothing else: it is not a sensuous proximity in a purely sensuous domain. Rather, it is a sensuous proximity which is simultaneously putatively a nearness in the body (that happens not to be actualized). While bodily sensations are not directionally given to their owner as are auditory sensations, since they are not experienced 'from' anything other than the body in which they are set, so that no physical angular measure is perceived in perceiving the sensuous extent separating them, that sensuous extent is nonetheless putatively also a body-distance.

12

From *The Analysis of Sensation*

Ernst Mach

[2] The view that the sense of sight and the sense of touch involve, so to speak, the same space-sense as a common element, was advanced by Locke and contested by Berkeley. Diderot also (*Lettres sur les aveugles*) is of opinion that the space-sense of the blind is altogether different from that of a person who sees. Compare on this point the acute remarks of Dr Th. Loewy (*Common Sensibles. Die Gemeinideen des Gesichts- und Tastsinnes nach Locke und Berkeley*, Leipzig, 1884), with whose results, however, I cannot agree. The circumstance that a man blind from birth does not, after being operated upon, in accordance with the experiment proposed by Molyneux, *visually* distinguish the cubes and spheres with which he is familiar from touch, proves to my mind nothing at all against Locke and nothing in favor of Berkeley and Diderot. Even persons who see recognize figures that are turned upside down only after much practice. The fact is that at the first moment of sight all the associations connected with the optical process, which may subserve its application intellectually, are wanting. A further point is that, when optical stimuli have been absent for a long period in early youth, the development of the central visual spheres may be arrested, or perhaps degeneration may even take place, as has been shewn by Schnabel's beautiful observations ("Beiträge zur Lehre von der Schlechtsichtigkeit durch Nichtgebrauch der Augen," *Berichte des naturwissenschaftlich-medikalischen Vereins in Innsbruck*, vol. XI, p. 32), and by Munk's experiments on new-born puppies (*Berliner klinische Wochenschrift*, 1877, no. 35). Even in the case of people who are not actually blind, the visual sphere may be so little developed that a special education is required to enable them to turn

Ernst Mach, *The Analysis of Sensation* (New York: Dover, 1959), pp. 135–7, note 2.

their sight-sensations to account. The case of the boy described by S. Heller, the Director of the Vienna Institute for the Blind (*Wiener klinische Wochenschrift*, 25 April 1901), is probably such a case of partial optical idiotism. It is only with great caution, therefore, that conclusions should be drawn from the behaviour, after operations, of those born blind. Chesselden, for instance, gave an account of an operation performed on a man blind from birth, who at first believed that everything he saw was in contact with his eyes; from this the false conclusion was drawn that the perception of the dimension of depth depends on extra-optical experiences. An accident put me in the way of understanding this phenomenon. Once when I was walking on a dark night in a district with which I was unfamiliar, I was all the time afraid of running up against a large black object. This turned out to be a hill several kilometres distant, which brought about this phenomenon through my being unable to fix and accommodate my sight, in much the same way as people who have been newly operated must be unable to do. If any one is not convinced by his own stereoscopy that the dimension of depth also is optically given, he is not likely to be convinced by the experiences of truncated people without arms and legs, such as Eva Lark and Kobelkoff (G. Hirth, *Energische Epigenesis*, 1898, p. 165).

All systems of space-sensation, however different they may be, are connected by a common associative link – the movements which they serve to guide. If Locke was wrong, how could the blind Saunderson have written a geometry intelligible to those who are not blind? Without doubt there are analogies between the sense of space given through sight and that given through touch.... Many of these phenomena were known to the Aristotelian school. Thus in the *Parva Naturalia* we find mentioned the experiment by which a little ball is felt as double when touched by the index-finger and the middle finger placed across it. With me this experiment produces an even more striking effect when I cross my fingers and move them up and down a little stick; and when I take two parallel sticks, and arranging my fingers in this way, run them between them, I feel the two sticks as single. The analogy with seeing the single as double and seeing the double as single is here complete. But the differences also are so great that the man of normal sight finds it difficult to picture to himself a blind man's space-presentation, since he is always introducing his own visual presentations by way of interpretation. Even so acute a mind as Diderot's can fall on occasion into the strange error of denying that the blind can imagine space. Cf. Loeb's work on tactual space (Über den Fühlraum der Hand, *Pfluger's Archiv*, vols XLI and XLVI), and Heller's *Studien zur Blindenpsychologie* (Leipzig, 1895).

13

From *Molyneux's Question*

Michael J. Morgan

Movement and Perceptual Adaptation

Commentators are unanimous in ascribing to the empiricists the belief that space is primarily a tactile phenomenon. They are equally unanimous that the belief is mistaken. This conclusion is important, if true. Therefore it must be asked what the empiricists actually said about this question, and why they went so wrong in answering it, according to modern views.

Since for Berkeley there is no such thing as visual space, the possibility scarcely arises of different spaces coming into conflict, or of one being formed from the other. It is puzzling, then, to find a recent writer speaking of 'Berkeley's theory of the derivation of visual space from tactual space'.[1] If Berkeley anywhere says something that encourages this interpretation, he was guilty of some rather muddled thinking, since for him there could hardly be any question of *deriving* something which he had shown not to exist. Rock's interpretation is all the more puzzling because he handsomely credits Berkeley with the discovery of the irrelevance of the inverted retinal image. Even more difficult to understand is why Rock claims to refute Berkeley by experiments in which touch and vision are put into conflict without the subject being aware of it. These experiments grew out of others on adaptation to distorted vision, which it will now be necessary to describe in some detail.

At the end of the nineteenth century, G. M. Stratton attempted to test Berkeley's theory of the inverted retinal image, by 'reinverting' the image

---

Michael J. Morgan, *Molyneux's Question* (Cambridge: Cambridge University Press, 1977), pp. 171–80, 191–3.

with an arrangement of lenses. He reasoned that, if Berkeley were right, his subjects should eventually come to see the world the right way up, since the inverted optic array would come to suggest, or be the 'mark' for (as Berkeley would have said) normally oriented actions and tactile experiences. The following description of what happened is taken from Merleau-Ponty:[2]

> If a subject is made to wear glasses which correct the retinal image, the whole landscape appears at first unreal and upside down; on the second day of the experiment normal perception begins to reassert itself, except that the subject has the feeling that his own body is upside down. In the course of a second set of experiments lasting a week, objects at first appear inverted, but less unreal than the first time. On the second day the landscape is no longer inverted, but the body is felt to be in an abnormal position. From the third to the seventh day, the body progressively rights itself, and finally seems to occupy a normal position, particularly when the subject is active. When he is lying motionless on a couch, the body still presents itself against the background of the former space, and, as far as the unseen parts of the body are concerned, right and left preserve their former localisation to the end of the experiment. External objects increasingly have the look of 'reality'. From the fifth day, actions which were at first liable to be misled by the new mode of vision, and had to be corrected in the light of the general visual upheaval, now go infallibly to their objective. The new visual appearances which, at the beginning, stood out against a background of previous space, develop round themselves, at first (third day) only through a great effort of will, later (seventh day) with no effort at all, a horizon with a general orientation corresponding to their own. On the seventh day, the placing of sounds is correct so long as the sounding object is seen as well as heard. It remains unreliable, and with a double, or even inaccurate, representation, if the source of the sound does not appear in the visual field. At the end of the experiment, when the glasses are removed, objects appear not inverted, it is true, but 'queer' and motor actions are reversed: the subject reaches out his right hand when it should be his left.

There has been endless argument since then about whether subjects with a reinverted retinal image *really* ever see the world the right way up. It has indeed been the most interesting result of these experiments that argument has been possible. For the plain fact is that, if the subjects are asked which way up they *really* 'see' the world, they find it difficult to reply. When one of the investigators was asked whether things looked upside down, he replied that, *although he had not thought of them as such until the question was asked,* he could see that they were upside down with respect to what they had been before the reinversion. Further experiments by Kohler clarified this extraordinary state of affairs. He found that adaptation proceeded in a haphazard and piecemeal fashion; some objects in the visual field might appear the right way up and others still look wrong. An object could suddenly change its orientation, as when an upside-down candle snapped into the upright when it was lit (an amusing film of Kohler's experiments attempts to show these effects). Vehicles were seen correctly as driving on the right-hand side of the road but with their licence numbers reversed, and so on. Similarly, in an experiment on left–right inversion described by Taylor a subject who had learned to move his left or right hand and foot appropriately when the side of the body was indicated by a stick, failed to do so with his knees, shoulders and elbows.[3]

The conclusion from these phenomena is that Berkeley was right: there is indeed no such thing as a specifically visual space. If there were, it is hard to see how a person could be in doubt as to its orientation, or how some objects in it should be 'correctly' and others 'incorrectly' oriented. More generally, if it is a question of *visual* space, the phenomenon of adaptation is inexplicable. Rock's theory, for example, is that we remember how the world used to look on our retina, and compare it with the reinverted image to find the latter 'upside down'. Merleau-Ponty describes this theory as 'unintelligible' because it says nothing about the experiences of upside down and right way up. Even if (as seems unlikely) the stored representations of visual images could literally be rotated with respect to present input, why should *that* cause them to be seen upside down – unless they suggest to us a whole new set of actions which are the reverse of those we habitually associate with the objects? And unless the new objects we see, instead of being the same objects, actually appear 'queer' and 'different', as subjects report.

The results in fact show that perceptual space is not at all like the space of the physicist, an indifferent, isomorphic three-dimensional manifold, in which objects are situated sensible to feeling as to sight, and in which things are the same no matter how oriented. Instead, we see objects in relation to us; they differ according to their orientation. A face seen upside down is not the same face incomprehensibly maintaining all its properties but its position in a featureless container; it is a different face, even 'queer' and 'frightening', as subjects with reinverting spectacles say. Thus, when the visual image is reinverted, it at first looks odd partly because there is difficulty in recognizing the objects in it (try looking at a television picture upside down to convince yourself of this); partly because such objects as are identifiable seem to call for an unaccustomed set of actions. As time goes on, objects are identified again, and appropriate new responses are learned to them; the world seems more and more familiar, and the subject is less preoccupied with its 'strangeness'; he may even forget that it is upside down unless specifically asked. Since behavioural adaptation to the new images takes time, and can happen at different rates to objects depending on amount of exposure, it is natural that the process should be piecemeal. The behavioural theory of adaptation therefore accounts for the facts perfectly; they only pose a problem if we think of some internal space that has to be inverted – and this error can be avoided once we realize with Berkeley that spatial perception is *not* some consequence of a spatial world, miraculously laid out there in front of our vision, with all the properties ascribed to it by the believers in transcendental matter.

Recent research on perceptual adaptation has grown away from the drastic changes imposed by reinversion of the image, and has concentrated instead on the more easily measured changes that occur when the apparent location of objects with respect to our bodies is changed by putting prisms in front of the eyes. As Helmholtz was the first to report, laterally displacing prisms cause one initially to grab to one side of an object when one tries to pick it up, but in a matter of minutes this misreaching tendency is overcome. When the prisms are then removed, the learned compensation persists for a while, with the result that one misreaches in the reverse of the original misreaching error. Practice with one hand transfers to the other hand, but not completely. Prisms may also cause an error in pointing at the location of an auditorily experienced signal, but the amount of this adaptation, and the extent to which it depends upon prior experience with the pointing hand, is in some dispute.

Research has concentrated on assessing the contribution to adaptation of various factors, such as: (a) active versus passive movement; (b) task-oriented versus 'informal' movement; (c) importance of seeing the moving limb; (d) knowledge of results, of various kinds; (e) transformation of the optic array during movement. Reviews of the relevant research will be found in Rock,[4] Freedman,[5] Howard and Templeton,[6] and Hochberg.[7] The safest conclusion from the mass of research is that the adaptation will be the faster to the extent that the subject is given reason to think that adaptation is necessary; in other words, if you go to bed with prisms on, you will not do much adapting. Few investigators dissent from this truism, which Wallach calls the 'information hypothesis'. The role of the subject's own movements has been stressed by Richard Held and his collaborators; in a long series of experiments they have shown that walking about, moving the head and eyes, actively touching objects and so on speed up the process of adaptation but are not absolutely mandatory; some adaptation can occur even if the subject is moved around in a wheelchair. Movement of the observer or of objects in the visual field is a useful cue, for when prisms are worn by the observer, objects do not move in the usual way on the retina. In one ingenious experiment, subjects showed a misreaching compensation when the only adaptation stimulus had been a homogeneous field of spheres; in this case, transformations of the optic array during head movements must have been the cause.

Obviously the result of adaptation must be that at least some objects change their apparent positions with respect to our selves. But the phrase 'our selves' is not very precise here, and trying to make it so has provoked much research. One possibility is that our self is our whole self, as it were, and objects which before adaptation seem in one position with respect to our whole self, now seem somewhere else. This predicts that adaptation of one limb of the body should completely transfer to another, and, as Helmholtz knew, this is not strictly true. Therefore there has been much said in favour of the alternative *proprioceptive shift* hypothesis, according to which the change occurs in the perceived location of one body part with respect to the others. Suppose, for example, we initially see an object straight in front of our nose and two feet away, and we feel our right hand to be thirty degrees and two feet away from this position. We send an appropriate command to the hand to reach for the object, and, because we are wearing prisms, we get a handful of empty air. To get it right on a future occasion we could *either* see the object in a different position with respect to the nose (or whatever else is supposed to be the centre of a coordinate system to which both object and hand are referred) *or* we could modify the position in which the hand is felt to be. The former is the possibility we rejected previously because it implies complete transfer to the other hand; the latter is the proprioceptive shift hypothesis. It predicts that adaptation will be unique to the hand which has done the reaching. Since this is not exactly true either, we may conclude that each hypothesis is probably a bit right, and that there is doubtless more than one kind of adaptation. There is no real question of principle involved, anyway; both hypotheses concede that it is felt position of an object with respect to *at least* a part of the body which alters. The dispute concerns definition of 'our self'.

As Hochberg notes concerning this conflict; 'What is important to us here is that in one explanation the motor-proprioceptive system of one arm has changed, and in the other, it is the correlation between the motor-proprioceptive system of the arm and that of the head, in judging visual direction, that has altered. Neither explanation predicates a change in vision itself.' It is indeed difficult to see how a change in the apparent position of objects could occur as a result of a change in 'vision itself', if by that is meant a change having no reference to bodily position at all.

The results of modern research therefore confirm Berkeley's assertion that there is no such thing as visual space. Why then has his theory fallen into disrepute?

There are two reasons, one serious, and the other based upon a misunderstanding. The latter arises from studies of 'visual capture', in which (so it is said) vision and touch are made to give conflicting information. For example, in an experiment described by Rock, subjects were shown a square object through a lens that made it appear like a rectangle, and were simultaneously allowed to feel it with a hand. Rock believed that this was a situation in which visual and tactile space were in conflict, and thought that, according to Berkeley, the tactile spatial impression ought to dominate. In fact, the visual impression dominated, and the subjects reported seeing and feeling, not a square, but a rectangle.[8]

The premise behind this refutation is quite mistaken. We have seen that according to Berkeley there is no such thing as visual space, so there is no question of a conflict between visual and tactile space. What we have in Rock's experiment, according to Berkeley, is a conflict between two kinds of tactile information: the one coming directly from the hands, and the other coming from memory images aroused by information from the retinal image. The retinal image is one that has always been associated in the past with tactile rectangles. The fact that the subject perceives a rectangle and not a square thus indicates that previous experience dominates over current impressions; there is nothing unreasonable about this hypothesis, and nothing inconsistent with Berkeley's position. It is exactly what Rock himself assumes when he argues that the reinverted retinal image looks upside down because memory traces dominate over present sensory information. Rock may have refuted the 'derivation of visual space from tactile space', but, since this has nothing to do with Berkeley's hypothesis, the refutation is not damaging.

It is otherwise with recent claims that very young children have well-developed depth perception and object constancy. T. G. R. Bower[9] has claimed to show this by conditioning babies to make responses to visual cues, which are subsequently altered in systematic ways to see which cues the baby treats as most like the original. For example, the baby is trained to respond to a large circle and not to a smaller one, and then a large circle is shown at a greater distance so that its retinal image is the size of the previous 'small' circle. Does the baby respond to the retinal size or to the real size? According to Berkeley's view it is difficult to see that the baby has any basis for responding at all, since size is not a visual impression as such, and the baby has had no previous experience allowing it to relate retinal size to object size. (The young baby is like Condillac's statue before it has started to move.) Nevertheless, Bower's data show that the baby correctly recognizes the circle as the larger of the two. Other data show that the baby is 'surprised' when its hands close on the purely visual image provided by a 3-D shadowcaster, and fail to find an object there; as Bower says, it appears that the baby expected to find a tactile object on the basis of purely visual information. Bower has explicitly stated that his results dispose of Berkeley's speculations.

Inevitably, however, questions must arise about the nature of the babies' previous experience. Although they were only a few months old, they had presumably experienced the visual consequences of moving their arms and feet. Held and Bauer have shown that if monkeys are prevented from seeing their moving limbs during the first few months of life, they subsequently react to the appearance of those limbs with fascination, and are unable to use them for the executing of visually guided movement.[10] Given that Bower's infants reacted with fascination, not to their limbs, but to the failure of these limbs to do what was expected, it seems likely that they had watched their limbs moving before. If this was the case, the argument against the empiricists collapses. It is only fair to point out that this appeal to hypothetical early experience can be carried to any lengths desired, and can only be rejected in the end on the grounds of common sense. But given the conflict between Bower's conclusions and those of Held and his colleagues, not to mention those of Piaget and the Genevan school, we are justified in adopting an attitude of caution towards the data at this stage.

What if Bower proves to be right? There would be one refuge for Berkeley, and that would be to reverse his position and say that space is visual and not tactile. According to common interpretations of his hypothesis, this would be to abandon it entirely; but I hope to have shown that this is far from being the case. Berkeley's essential position was that there are no ideas common between the senses; given any one idea, he had to decide to which sense it should be assigned. With space he chose touch, not vision; and although he gave many reasons for his choice, it was not made on ideological but on factual grounds; therefore it would be modified if further evidence made it untenable. A final refutation of Berkeley would consist, not in demonstrating the origin of space in vision, which indeed would support his general position, but in showing that it was an idea common to the senses. And it is fitting that

Rock expresses the view which really is the reverse of Berkeley's, when he concludes that 'perhaps we should think of space as a basic category of mind, as Kant suggested'. In other words, Rock is really a transcendental idealist, and this explains his disagreement with Berkeley. That modern psychology, after its brief flirtation with behaviourism, should return to talking about 'basic categories of mind' (and Rock is no isolated example in this respect) indicates how very well founded was the empiricists' distrust of general ideas. To any psychologist still trying to be a behaviourist – that is, trying to avoid a radical distinction between the mental and physical – Rock's 'basic category of mind' will be infinitely less congenial than the theory which Berkeley finally summarizes as follows:

> Upon the whole, I think we may fairly conclude, that the proper objects of vision constitute a universal language of the Author of nature, whereby we are instructed how to *regulate our actions*, in order to attain those things that are necessary to the preservation and well-being of our bodies, as also to avoid whatever may be hurtful and destructive of them. It is by their information that we are principally guided in all the transactions and concerns of life.   (*New Theory of Vision*, italics added)

. . .

Cross-modal Transfer Experiments

The experimental evidence has been reviewed by Ettlinger,[11] and a recent report by Cowey and Weiskrantz[12] has added useful information. Ettlinger divides the relevant studies into two classes: (1) cross-modal matching or recognition and (2) cross-modal transfer. In the *matching* task the subject is specifically given the task of comparing seen and felt objects. For example, a monkey might have a sphere in its hand, and would see before it a sphere and a cube. Choices of the sphere would be rewarded by a piece of food. Ettlinger concludes that there is no certain evidence for transfer in these circumstances, either in monkeys or in apes. Therefore it appears that these primates, like Locke, reply 'Not' to Molyneux's question.

Babies in their first year, however, show evidence of transfer in such a task, according to Bryant.[13] The technique in Bryant's experiments was to permit the baby to handle a distinctively shaped object that emitted a noise. This object, not now emitting sound, was then placed along with a new object on a table, where both were visible but could not be touched. The babies tended to reach for the object that had previously been held in the hand. This confirmed a previous finding that babies prefer one of a pair of visible objects which had previously emitted sound, and further suggested that an object could be visually recognized despite having been experienced previously only by touch. This, of course, is not an affirmative answer to Molyneux's question, because the babies had not been born blind, but it does show that we have 'general ideas' very early in our lives, certainly before we have words in which to express them. Locke would probably have been a bit put out by the experiment, and might have asked for it to be repeated in babies with controlled prior experiences of objects.

In cross-modal *transfer* tasks, the subject is taught to discriminate between two objects presented in one sense-modality only, and is then presented with the same objects in another modality. For example, a blindfolded monkey might be trained to find a peanut hidden under a cube, but not under a sphere, and then be shown the sphere and cube with blindfold removed. The expectation, if the monkey has 'general ideas', is that he will look first under the cube. The crucial difficulty in this argument was raised by Diderot, who pointed out that, even if a person seeing objects for the first time recognized the similarity between them and the objects he had previously felt, still he would have no grounds for assuming that he was supposed to behave similarly towards them in all respects:

> 'My good Sirs,' he would conclude, 'this object seems to be a circle and this one a square; but I have no guarantee that they will be the same to touch as to sight.'[14]

Ettlinger puts the same point as follows:

> However, it can be seen that transfer testing, although particularly conveni-
> ent and time-saving in animal experiments, suffers from being too special a
> case of the cross-modal exchange of information. Its basic defect lies in
> the ambiguity of the requirements when the stimuli are introduced in the
> second modality: no indication is given to the subject that the previous
> experience with these (or analogous) stimuli is to be taken into account.

Diderot, it may be recalled, suggested that a rather stupid person would show transfer, while a reflective philosopher, for the reason mentioned, would not. His guess seems to have been inspired, for the facts reviewed by Ettlinger reveal that transfer is within the capacity of bush-babies, but not within that of monkeys, or of children before they have learned to

128 Michael J. Morgan

talk. This area is still controversial (Cowey and Weiskrantz, for example, found positive results in monkeys),[15] but it certainly does not appear that a negative result can be taken to indicate stupidity. In this respect, all the difficulties of a practical nature that Diderot and Condillac spoke about in relation to Molyneux's question have been amply justified. ...

Notes

1 I. Rock, *The Nature of Perceptual Adaptation* (New York: Basic Books, 1966) 18 note 5.
2 *Phenomenology of Perception*, 244–5.
3 *Behavioral Basis of Perception*, ch. 9.
4 *Nature of Perceptual Adaptation*.
5 S. J. Freedman (ed.), *The Neuropsychology of Spatially Oriented Behavior* (Homewood, Ill.: Dorsey Press, 1968).
6 I. P. Howard and W. B. Templeton, *Human Spatial Orientation* (London: John Wiley, 1966) ch. 15.
7 J. Hochberg, 'Perception II: space and movement', in J. W. Kling and L. A. Riggs (eds), *Woodworth and Schlosberg's Experimental Psychology* (London: Methuen, 1972).
8 The same phenomenon has recently been demonstrated in a group of people presumably well accustomed to judging shapes by touch: potters. See R. P. Power and A. Graham, 'Dominance of touch by vision: generalisation of the hypothesis to a tactually experienced population', *Perception* 5 (1976) 161–6.
9 An excellent general account of these experiments will be found in T. G. R. Bower's own book *Development in Infancy* (San Francisco: W. H. Freeman, 1974). Concerning the infants' reactions when their hands failed to make contact with the illusory 3-D object, Bower states, 'All the infants were surprised and upset when their hand reached the location of the intangible object and failed, of course, to make contact with it' (p. 94). Again, the babies are said to 'howl' at the experience (p. 114). Bower has said in several places that experiments of this kind pose difficulties for Berkeley: for example, 'Contrary to the Berkeleian tradition, the world of the infant would seem to be inherently tridimensional' ('Object perception in infants', *Perception* 1 (1972) 15–30).
10 R. Held and J. A. Bauer, 'Visually guided reaching in infant monkeys after restricted rearing', *Science, New York* 155 (1967) 718. In a similar experiment with cats it was shown that reaching established under the control of one eye did not transfer to the eye that had not seen the limb previously: A. Hein, R. Held and E. C. Gower, 'Development and segmentation of visually controlled movement by selective exposure during rearing', *Journal of Comparative and Physiological Psychology* 73 (1970) 181–7.

11   G. Ettlinger, 'The transfer of information between sense-modalities: a neuro-psychological review', in *Memory and Transfer of Information*, ed. H. P. Zippel (New York: Plenum Press, 1973) 43–64. I am grateful to Dr Ettlinger for sending me a copy of his paper, on which the first part of this section is largely based.

12   A. Cowey and L. Weiskrantz, 'A demonstration of cross-modal transfer in Rhesus Monkeys, *Macaca Mulatta*', *Neuropsychologia* 13 (1975) 117–20.

13   Cf. Ettlinger, *op. cit*; also P. E. Bryant, P. Jones, V. Claxton, and G. M. Perkins, 'Recognition of shapes across modalities by infants', *Nature, Lond.* 240 (1972) 303–4.

14   *Letter on the Blind*; see above, p. 55.

15   *Op. cit*. Their technique was to use edible objects, which presumably mean more to the monkey than bits of wood and plastic. The monkeys first learned to select edible from inedible objects on the basis of their felt shape, and subsequently proved able to select the same edible objects when they were presented visually.

14

Molyneux's Question

Gareth Evans

...I want to make two points about the terms in which the question is posed. First, I shall make a simplification of the situation originally suggested by Diderot.[1] Molyneux asked whether or not the blind man would be able to apply three-dimensional spatial concepts, such as *sphere* and *cube*, upon the basis of his newly acquired vision; he also seems to have been interested in whether the blind man would see things as at various distances from him.[2] There is nothing wrong with these questions, but they are in a sense less interesting than whether he would be able to extend two-dimensional concepts, like *square* and *circle*, since there is less antecedent expectation that the newly sighted man would be able to appreciate the depth cues available in visual perception. Although most disputants in the controversy retained the terms in which Molyneux originally posed it, it transpires that their fundamental disagreement is about whether the blind man would be able to extend his two-dimensional concepts.[3]

Secondly, I must stress that Molyneux's Question is about whether a born-blind man *who can see* a circle and a square would extend his concepts to them. It is not a question about how soon after the operation, and via what process, a newly sighted man would be able to see. Molyneux's Question requires only that the newly sighted man would be able to have visual experiences of circles and squares without his, or his brain's, having had a chance to establish correlations between the old and the new information.

Several thinkers have returned a negative answer to Molyneux's Question not because they held a view about the difference between the spatial

Gareth Evans, "Molyneux's Question." In *Collected Papers* (Oxford: Oxford University Press, 1985), pp. 365–6, 372–82, 388–99.

concepts of the blind and those connected with visual experience, but because they held that the blind do not have any genuinely spatial concepts at all. ... The line of thought behind this position can be seen in the following passage from von Senden, the most recent, and most dogmatic, of its proponents:

> Nothing is given to the blind man simultaneously, either by touch or the other senses; everything is resolved into successions...Only the variety furnished by a temporally ordered series of experiences can furnish him with knowledge. ...
>
> Since nothing is given simultaneously to his senses as spatial, it must be mentally strung together in time...A spatial line must be replaced by a temporal sequence.[4]

But I do not think that Berkeley held that the *two*-dimensional concepts which we are able to form on the basis of touch – like the concept he called *tangible square* – were concepts of succession, and so I do not think that his reason for giving a negative answer to Molyneux's Question is the same as von Senden's. Berkeley is quite explicit:

> Sounds, for example, perceived at the same instant, are apt to coalesce, if I may so say, into one sound: but we can perceive at the same time great variety of visible objects, very separate and distinct from each other. Now *tangible extension being made up of several distinct co-existent parts*, we may hence gather another reason that may dispose us to imagine a likeness or an analogy between the immediate objects of sight and touch.[5]

In view of this, it is certain that in answering Molyneux's Question negatively, Berkeley was taking up a position upon the most fundamental issue posed by that question – an issue which only arises on the assumption that the blind do have simultaneous spatial concepts. It is to that issue that I now turn.

To bring it out, let us consider first the position of a philosopher, whom I shall call 'V', who insists that, on the conditions given, the newly sighted man must be able to apply his concepts to the visually presented array – must, to use a convenient term, 'generalize'. (Curiously enough, there is no historical figure who has taken exactly this position; as I will explain, even Leibniz's 'Yes' to Molyneux's Question indicates a position weaker than V's.) For V, the case presented by Molyneux's Question is no different from that involved in the following speculation: whether a man born deaf, and taught to apply the terms 'continuous' and 'pulsating' to stimulations made on his skin, would, on gaining his hearing and being presented with two tones, one continuous and the other pulsating, be able to apply the terms correctly. Few of us have a doubt about the outcome of this experiment, but, more important, if the born-deaf man failed to apply the terms in this new case, we should feel obliged to interpret this as casting doubt upon his understanding of the terms which we thought we had introduced to him, just as if he had, incomprehensibly, been unable to apply the terms to stimulations made on a hitherto unused part of his skin. We should say that he had not fully mastered the concept of *pulsation* simply because he had been presented with a case to which the concept manifestly applied, and had failed to apply it. No obligation attaches to one who holds this position to provide an alternative interpretation of the subject's previous utterances; it is not, indeed, part of his position that they are intelligible. What he does claim is that there is a unitary conceptual capacity which most people have with the word 'pulsating' which this born-deaf man must be acknowledged to lack.[6]

In the same way, V holds, there is a unitary conceptual ability associated in the case of most adults with the word 'square' – mastery of a single concept. Now, the fact of the matter is that this concept *applies* in the case of a visually presented square, or in the case of four points of light arranged in a square. If a man does not perceive the shape, or the points of light, then his inability to apply the term 'square' in no way casts doubt upon his understanding of it. But if we build into the description of the case that the newly-sighted man does see the square, or the four dots – does, if you like, have a visual experience of the same character as leads the normally sighted to apply the term – then he is presented with something which falls under the concept, and an incapacity to apply the term in this new case must show that he does not possess the (unitary) concept of a square.

V finds it impossible to conceive of a coherent concept which applies to items simultaneously existing, which is therefore exercised most directly in connection with perceptual representations of several distinct objects existing simultaneously, and yet which stops short of applying in the case where the items are visually perceived. V simply cannot find room for *two* genuine, i.e. simultaneous, concepts of a square, or for *two* genuine concepts of *between, straight line*, etc., each set of concepts generating its own geometry.

If V is sophisticated, he will make no appeal to the notion of *similarity*. His position is not that the tactual perceptual representation of a square *resembles* the visual perceptual representation of a square. His point is that if both are simultaneous representations, the only concept which he can understand applies (or seems to apply) in both cases.[7]

The opposing position is essentially that advanced by Berkeley in the *New Theory of Vision*, though I shall call its proponent 'B' so as to allow him to deviate a little from the historical Berkeley. B denies that there is a single concept *square*, which may or may not be possessed by the blind man, and whose possession is tested by whether he generalizes when he regains his sight. The sighted adult's use of the word 'square' rests upon two separable and conceptually unconnected abilities.[8] Both of the concepts apply to arrangements of simultaneously existing objects, but nevertheless they are distinct.

No one can say that B's position is, on the face of it, a wildly attractive one: to see why it has attracted so many adherents, we must look at the reason B can advance for opposing V's simple idea of the single conceptual capacity. Many reasons have been advanced, but the one I want to focus upon as being particularly important arises from the way B regards visual experience. B supposes that a subject could enjoy visual experience without regarding it as *of* a world distinct from himself at all. In this condition, the subject would not conceive of the items of which he was aware as *outside* himself, or as located at any distance from himself, but even so, B thinks, his visual experience would acquaint the subject with a two-dimensional mosaic of colours. Now, B supposes that it would be possible for the subject to abstract from this experience colour concepts, such as 'red', 'blue', etc., and B supposes that the subject might respond in a similar way to shape-resemblances in the colour mosaics, and thereby form (two-dimensional) shape concepts. Such are the concepts which B terms *visible square*, *visible circle* – abstracted from an experience which has no reference to an external reality at all. These concepts, B thinks, are the concepts which V is prepared to ascribe to the blind man. But this is what B cannot understand. How is it possible for a man who cannot form the least idea of visual experience to acquire a concept capable of being abstracted so directly from it – related to it in the same way in which colour concepts are related to it?

These reflections certainly do not constitute a decisive argument against V's position, but they do focus attention upon an unease which will not be removed until visual experience and its spatiality are fundamentally rethought. ...

If I have identified in the dispute between B and V the central issue raised by Molyneux's Question, then we can see that this issue was missed by two contemporary discussions of the question.

In a recent book on Molyneux's Question, the psychologist M. J. Morgan writes as though the main issue was one of *innateness*. He writes, for example:

> Locke replied 'Not' to Molyneux's Question to avoid postulating a common representational scheme for the different senses, because such a schema implies an innate supra-sensible structure to the mind.[9]

The reasoning comes out in the following passage:

> The real question was whether he could name what he saw. And the answer to this was 'Not' because to name the visual impression he would have to compare it to some other idea, an idea common between touch and vision. Plainly, such an idea could not be a simple 'sensory impression'; it would have to be something transcending individual impressions, and to which these individual impressions could be referred. The *Essay* was written against such innate ideas...[10]

It seems to me that the issue of innateness cuts right across the dispute between B and V. In the first place, I see no particular reason why the concept which V attributes to the blind man has to be innate. Whether it can be accounted for by empiricist learning mechanisms depends upon what we conceive those mechanisms to be. I suppose that, according to the most radical empiricist position, an organism has an innate similarity-space defined over *sensations*, and concepts simply result from a partitioning of that space.[11] It is perfectly true, on that position, that no account can be given of the spatial concepts which V attributes to the blind man. This is not because the required concept is supra-sensible (i.e. a-modal). There is nothing on the radical empiricist view that precludes sensations produced by the stimulation of different sense modalities being sufficiently close together in the innate similarity space for responses conditioned to the one to generalize to the other. There is nothing particularly upsetting to an empiricist theory of concept formation in the suggestion that human subjects who are trained with the use of 'harmonious' in the case of sounds might generalize its use (without further training) to the case of certain combinations of colours. Rather, the difficulty arises in the case of shape concepts because on the simple model there is no way for the gap between succession and simultaneity to be bridged. However, such a radical empiricism is not an attractive position, nor is it clear that B could appeal to it, since he too acknowledges that the concept *tangible square* is a simultaneous concept.

A much more reasonable position would be to suppose that spatial concepts can be learned through the subject's capacity to *perceive* spatially. A perceptual spatial representation, although it embodies spatial information, is not a *conceptual* representation, and there is room for the explanation of our acquisition of *concepts* like *square*, with their characteristic generality, in terms of our exposure, in perception, to a range of squares.[12] It is not clear why the concept which V attributes to the blind man, and which is open to generalization, could not have been acquired in this way. Of course, it is B's thesis that no concept acquired in this way can be directly applied on the basis of vision, but that, V holds, is because B fails to take into account what is involved in tactual-kinaesthetic spatial perception, and has a false view about the nature of visual experience. Their dispute is about these things, not about innate ideas.[13]

In the second place, far from innateness being an essential ingredient of V's position, it is an element of a perfectly possible variant of B's position. B holds that there is no *conceptual* connection between *tangible square* and *visible square*, but this leaves it open how the move from the visible to the tangible is made. Berkeley held that we *learn* the connection by experience, but an alternative hypothesis is that the connection is pre-programmed into the brain. (I assume that it is a coherent hypothesis with respect to anything which is learned that it should have been innate.) It follows from this observation that Molyneux's Question is not in fact a crucial experiment in the dispute between B and V, for although a negative answer would refute V, a positive answer would be consistent both with V's position, and with this nativist version of B's position.

In a second recent work on Molyneux's Question, Judith Jarvis Thompson takes the central issue to be whether a world is conceivable in which tactual circles give rise to the visual impression of a square, and tactual squares give rise to the visual impression of a circle. She writes:

> I am inclined to think that what was in Molyneux's mind, because of which he drew that conclusion [that the blind man would not generalize] from those premises [the blind man has not yet attained the experience that what affects his touch so or so, must affect his sight so and so], was this: that what affects one's touch so or so *could* have affected one's sight such and such instead of so and so.[14]

Borrowing an idea from Grice,[15] she attempts to show that no such world is conceivable. For example, when three tactual circles are brought together, empty space can be felt between them, but there is nothing corresponding to this in the case of three visual squares. I shall not go into detail here, because this line of thought seems to me to be beside the point. For what position would this reflection support on the debate between B and V? If Mrs Thompson's reasoning is cogent, and if the blind man can be expected to rehearse it, it follows that he can *work out* which visual shape corresponds to which tactual shape, *on the assumption that he knows that some such correspondence exists*. But, according to V, no such assumption is necessary. V holds that, on seeing the square or the four points arranged in a square, the blind man is confronted with an instance of his antecedently existing concept, and hence should be disposed to apply it without any additional information or instruction at all. There is no question of his having to *work out* how to apply it. We don't suppose that the man who regained his hearing would need to be told that one of the sounds he was to hear was going to be continuous and the other pulsating in order to be able to apply his concept in the new case, and this is the position V takes on Molyneux's Question.

Although she does not mention any of this work, Mrs Thompson's paper is the last in a long line, beginning with Leibniz, of answers to Molyneux's Question. Leibniz held that the blind man would be able to work out which was which, on the ground:

> that in the globe there are no points distinguishable on the side of the globe itself, all being level there without angles, whereas in the cube there are eight points distinguished from all the others.[16]

Hence, Leibniz thought that if one was to set up a correspondence between the visual and the tactual, one could not map the visual circle on to the tactual square in such a way as to generate analogues in the visual world to each structural property and relation perceivable in the tactual world. Mrs Thompson and Leibniz focus on different examples of properties that would not be representable in the visual domain in the unnatural correspondence, but their arguments have the same structure. However, Leibniz realized the limitations of this argument, in a way which Mrs Thompson apparently does not. Leibniz wrote:

> Perhaps Molyneux and the author of the *Essay* are not so far from my opinion as at first appears...If you will weigh my answer, ['Yes' to Molyneux's Question] you will find that I have put a condition upon it which can be considered as included in the question: it is, that the only thing in question is that of distinguishing, and the blind man knows that the two figured bodies which he must distinguish are there, and thus that each of the appearances which he sees is that of the cube or that of the globe.[17]

In other words, Leibniz was refusing to support V's position, since by implication, he suggests that in the absence of instruction, the newly sighted man might enjoy visual experiences of squares and circles without being put in mind of the shapes discernible by touch at all. Hence, Leibniz's qualified affirmative answer shows him to be an adherent of a version of B's position. After all, Berkeley himself was prepared to allow that 'the visible square is fitter than the visible circle to represent the tangible square'[18] on the ground that the visible square had, as the visible circle did not, several distinguishable parts, and it would not matter to the fundamental disagreement that he has with V that the visible square is *uniquely* fitted to represent the tangible square. It remains the case that the one *represents* the other, rather than being both instances of a common concept. It remains the case, that is, that there is an intelligible and separable conceptual capacity whose range is restricted to the set of tactually perceived squares.

As we have seen, the result of Molyneux's experiment bears somewhat indirectly upon what I have identified as the main issue raised by his question. (See figure 14.1.) It is true that a negative result to the experiment does undermine V's position, and it might be thought that enough negative answers had been collected to make further speculation unnecessary. However, almost all of the experiments which are cited as providing a negative result to Molyneux's Question do no such thing, for while it is true that subjects cannot name the circle and the square, this is because they do not have any visual figure perception at all but are restricted to a confusing succession of experiences of light and colour. Even Berkeley missed this point, and cites Chiselden's case in defence of his position; quite unsuitably for even as Berkeley reported it, the subject in that case 'knew not the shape of anything, nor any one thing from another, however different in shape or magnitude'.[19] Von Senden cites only one or two cases in which it is claimed that the subject could distinguish the circle from the square, yet could not name them correctly, but even these results are not guaranteed to be relevant to the central issue, since a capacity to make gross 'same/different' judgements is far from establishing visual perception of the figure. A more recent case studied by Gregory seems to confirm a positive answer to Molyneux's Question, but unfortunately the experiments were only carried out a considerable time after the operation.[20] I have been able to track down only two reports of relevant experiments since then, and neither bears unequivocally upon the issue.[21] In view of the delicacy of the experimental conditions, it might be thought to be worth while to make a more theoretical examination of the issue by considering what background

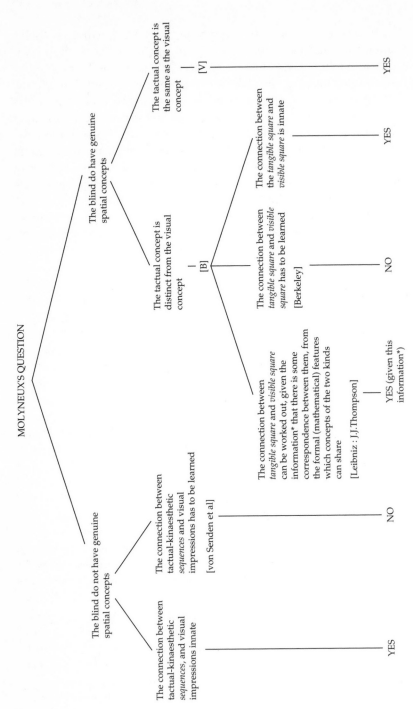

MOLYNEUX'S QUESTION

The blind do not have genuine spatial concepts

The connection between tactual-kinaesthetic sequences, and visual impressions innate

YES

The connection between tactual-kinaesthetic sequences and visual impressions has to be learned

[von Senden et al]

NO

The blind do have genuine spatial concepts

The tactual concept is distinct from the visual concept

[B]

The connection between tangible square and visible square can be worked out, given the information* that there is some correspondence between them, from the formal (mathematical) features which concepts of the two kinds can share

[Leibniz : J.J.Thompson]

YES (given this information*)

The connection between tangible square and visible square has to be learned

[Berkeley]

NO

The connection between the tangible square and visible square is innate

YES

The tactual concept is the same as the visual concept

[V]

YES

Figure 14.1

theories of perception might sustain the respective positions of B and V, and whether any arguments might be offered for or against them. . . .

Let us bring [our reflections on hearing] to bear upon the 'simultaneous' perceptual representations of space, which earlier we argued the blind man could possess. The spatial information available to him upon the basis of tactual-kinaesthetic perception is much *richer* than that available by hearing, and quite different perceptible phenomena, of course, are specified as located at different positions. However, there is a fundamental point of similarity; when we think of the spatial content of tactual-kinaesthetic perception, we also think of it as specifiable in egocentric terms. Indeed, when he uses his hand, the blind man gains information whose content is partly determined by the disposition he has thereby exercised – for example, that *if* he moves his hand forward such-and-such a distance and to the right he will encounter the top part of a chair. And when we think of a blind man synthesizing the information he receives by a sequence of haptic perceptions of a chair into a unitary representation, we can think of him ending the process by being in a complex informational state which embodies information concerning the egocentric location of each of the parts of the chair; the top *over there, to the right* (here, he is inclined to point or reach out), the back running from *there* to *here*, and so on. Each bit of the information is directly manifestable in his behaviour, and is equally and immediately influential upon his thoughts. One, but not the only, manifestation of this latter state of affairs is the subject's judging that there is a chair-shaped object in front of him.

We started off by thinking about what is involved in perceptions which specify the egocentric position of a stimulus, and we find that we have captured perceptions which convey, at least in a rudimentary way, *shape* or *figure* – i.e. perceptions upon the basis of which shape concepts could be applied. To make the transition, it is necessary to move from auditory spatial perception, which specifies the direction but not the distance of a sound, to a mode of perception which also conveys information about the distance of perceptible phenomena from the subject, so that he can think of a series of points as lying on a plane, and as all being equidistant from him. But no new theoretical departure is made; the content of this information is still specifiable egocentrically – we are still dealing with behavioural space.

It is a consequence of the fact that the spatial content of auditory and tactual-kinaesthetic perceptions must be specified in the same, egocentric, terms, that perceptions from both systems will be used to build up a unitary picture of the world, and hence that spatial concepts applicable upon the basis of one mode of perception must generalize to the other. There is only one behavioural space.[22]

There is nothing in the description that I have offered of the spatiality of tactual-kinaesthetic perception with which either party need disagree. Berkeley himself emphasized the egocentricity of the spatial information provided by the tactual-kinaesthetic mode of perception. For example, in the *New Theory of Vision* he writes:

> by touch he [the blind man] could not perceive any motion but what was up or down, to the right or left, nearer or farther from him; besides these and their several varieties or complications, it is impossible he should have any idea of motion.[23]

And it becomes clear that one of Berkeley's main arguments for his negative answer to Molyneux's Question is precisely that the spatiality of vision has nothing to do with the egocentrically specifiable spatial information. In the same section, he continues:

> He [the blind man] would not therefore think anything to be motion, or give the name motion to any idea which he could not range under some or other of those particular kinds thereof. But...it is plain that by the mere act of vision he could not know motion upwards or downwards, to the right or left, or in any other possible direction.

An angel, or unembodied spirit, who had no sense of touch, and who could not act, would have no notions of *up, down, left, right, forwards,* and *backwards,* but, says Berkeley, it could see perfectly well: 'i.e. having a clear perception of the proper and immediate objects of sight'.[24]

We come here to a theoretical disagreement about the nature of visual perception which might be seen to underlie the dispute between B and V. For, suppose one took a view of the nature of visual perception radically different from the one expressed by Berkeley, by holding that the spatiality of vision is not a primitive datum, but something to be explained in the way we have explained the spatiality of auditory and tactual-kinaesthetic perception. To hold this is to hold that any visual experience of distinct but spatially related phenomena must consist in the subject's possession of spatial information specifiable in egocentric terms. This would then provide a common basis for the application of at least certain fundamental spatial concepts. To explore this possibility further, I want to concentrate upon a streamlined version of Molyneux's Question.

It has been known for many years that direct electrical stimulation of the visual cortex in human subjects produces the experience of a flash of light, or a 'phosphene'.[25] It is also known that phosphenes can be produced in this way in subjects who have been blind for many years,[26] though, to the best of my knowledge, no attempt has ever been made to produce phosphenes by direct cortical stimulation of the congenitally blind.[27] The repeated stimulation of a given site of the visual cortex with a given intensity reliably produces a phosphene located at the same position in the visual field, and the simultaneous stimulation of two or more distinct sites produces the experience of simple patterns. However, as with the after-images, the phosphenes are experienced as moving when the eye moves. There has been a certain amount of research devoted to the possibility of exploiting this fact to provide a visual prosthesis for the blind.[28] G. S. Brindley, the pioneer of this work, has made long-term cortical implants in two patients, and used them to produce recognizable patterns corresponding to letters of the alphabet, including a fairly good question mark.[29]

The simplified version of Molyneux's Question that I want to consider is this. Suppose it is possible to produce in a congenitally blind man, by the use of a Brindley implant, a pattern of phosphenes exemplifying a shape which previously he had been able to name when he tactually perceived it (for example, a square, or the letter 'A'), would he then be able to name the shape correctly? This version of Molyneux's Question avoids certain difficulties in the original question which arise from the complexity of the information which a newly sighted man would receive upon opening his eyes, from the confusion introduced by the movement of his eyes and head, and from the need to separate figure and ground. But the essence of the question is preserved. And I am suggesting that one way in which V could defend his expectation that the blind man will be able to generalize is by arguing as follows. To have the visual experience of four points of light arranged in a square amounts to no more than being in a complex informational state which embodies information about the egocentric location of those lights; for example, one is perceived up and off to the left, another below it, a third up and off to the right, and so on. Now, we are assuming that the subject has been able to form simultaneous perceptual representations of the locations of tactually perceived objects, and this means that he has been in a complex informational state of just this kind before, perhaps when he felt the four corners of a wire square to be occupying these, or similarly related, positions in behavioural space. Of course, the perceptible phenomena apparently located at the various positions in behavioural space in the two cases are different, but the spatial ingredient of the information would be specifiable in the same vocabulary, so that if receipt of such information was sufficient to prompt application of the concept *square* in the tactual case, it is not clear why it should not do so in the visual case.

There is a complication. Although phosphenes are assigned positions 'in the visual field', the position does not involve the specification of distance from the observer; in this very pared-down case, visual localization is like auditory localization:

Sperling: Could the woman equate those phosphenes with any prior visual experience?
Brindley: Yes, certainly. She said that they were like stars in the sky. This raises the question of whether they appear to be distant or close to her, but when I tried to probe her on that, and when other people questioned her on that, she was not very consistent. I do not think that she has a definite impression that they are a long way away, or that they are close.[30]

If the blind man was to apply the two-dimensional concept *square*, he would have to think of the points of light as equally far away. Although this is a natural assumption for sighted people when looking at the night sky, since none of the normal distance cues, like occlusion, is present, we cannot say that this would be a natural assumption for the blind man, who has never responded to those cues. So, strictly speaking, a defence of V's position based upon the view of the spatiality of vision being outlined, carries with it the need to enter a slight qualification to his affirmative answer to Molyneux's Question. However, I do not think that it significantly diminishes the interest of his conclusion.

V's position is therefore essentially that advanced by the great Scottish philosopher, Thomas Reid:

To set this matter in another light, let us distinguish betwixt the *position* of objects with regard to the eye, and their *distance* from it. Objects that lie in the same right line drawn from the centre of the eye, have the same position, however different their distances from the eye may be: but objects which lie in different right lines drawn from the eye's centre, have a different position; and this difference of position is greater or less, in proportion to the angle made at the eye by the right lines mentioned. Having thus defined what we mean by the position of objects with regard to the eye, it is evident, that as the real figure of a body consists in the situation of its several parts with regard to one another, so its visible figure consists in the position of its several parts with regard to the eye; and as he that hath a distinct conception of the situation of the parts of the body with regard to one another, must have a distinct conception of its real figure; so he that conceives distinctly the position of its several parts with regard to the eye, must have a distinct conception of its visible figure.[31]

Visual localization is complicated in the normal case by the fact that the eyes can move, so that, even given a single orientation of the head, there is no simple correspondence between points on the two retinas and points in behavioural space. It is not necessary, however, for V to argue that the mechanism whereby account is taken of eye position in computing position in behavioural space must be present at the inception of visual experience. His position is that apparent location in behavioural space is an essential feature of any visual experience which permits the application of two-dimensional spatial concepts, not that the apparent location is accurate, or likely to be accurate, were the visual cortex to be connected to the retina in the standard way.

Nor is it necessary for V to argue that the capacity to apply visual shape concepts rests upon no more than the capacity for visual localization. It obviously does not. I have already mentioned the separation of figure and ground, which is closely tied to the capacity to perceive an object as the same as it moves about in the visual field. Furthermore, sighted people clearly have a capacity to respond to the purely visual similarities of things, as when they recognize a friend by his face, or detect a family resemblance in the faces of father and son, and the application of many visual shape concepts depends upon this capacity. V's position is that if a visual system is capable of providing the experience of distinct but spatially related phenomena then it is *at least* a system which provides the subject with information about the position such phenomena occupy in behavioural space, and that this fact provides a basis for the application of certain very fundamental spatial concepts which is common to vision and touch. What matters to V is that the application of concepts like *straight, square, between* etc., should be independent of the capacity to respond to the characteristic look that things have, and not that the application of all shape concepts should be independent of that capacity.

There is certainly nothing in the literature on direct cortical stimulation that contradicts V's contention. What experimenters mean by 'point in the visual field' is 'apparent point in behavioural space'; when they map cells on to points in the visual field, the subject is asked to point to the apparent source of the light. This, however, may not impress B, since all those studied are late-blind; but it is extremely difficult to see how the spatiality of the experience could be established experimentally in the absence of any links with behavioural space. There *is* a certain amount of evidence that visual localization, and visual shape perception are subserved by different parts of the brain in certain mammals, and that with suitable lesions, they can be separated. Schneider claims that 'undercutting the superior colliculus [in a hamster] abolishes the ability to orient toward an object, but not the ability to identify it according to tests of pattern discrimination learning'.[32] However, I do not think that this undermines V's position, which concerns the nature of conscious visual experience. It is not difficult to envisage feature detectors of the Hubel and Wiesel type, capable of responding selectively to certain pattern and shape features of the retinal stimulus, operating in the absence of any of the links between stimulus and behaviour which we earlier saw were necessary if the stimulus is to embody localization information. These feature detectors could then be exploited in discriminatory behaviour. But such a system could not provide the basis for the visual experience of shape. When we have the experience of seeing a square, we do not unaccountably find ourselves inclined to judge that there is a square somewhere in the vicinity; we possess information about each of the parts of the square and their relations to one another. The experience of seeing a square, we might say, is a *complex* psychological state. And this, V argues, is because it involves the possession of information about the location of each of the parts of the square in behavioural space. To this claim, Schneider's findings are plainly irrelevant.[33]

So far, I have considered the position on the spatiality of vision which might sustain V's answer to Molyneux's Questions to be an empirical theory about the visual system in humans. I want to end by canvassing the possibility that the position can be defended on *conceptual* grounds – the possibility that there are grounds for holding that it does not *make sense* to talk of a subject's perceiving spatially distinct points of light in an extended visual field, unless this can be explained in terms of the subject's receiving information about the location of phenomena in behavioural space. Now, I think sighted people *do* have an incapacity to conceive (i.e. imagine) a visual experience of an array of lights which are not at the same time referred to points in behavioural space, but I do not think that we can rest any weight on this incapacity, which B will argue shows nothing more than our extreme familiarity with the association of points in visual and behavioural space. However, there are weightier considerations.

The first argument is very familiar, and I shall only mention it briefly. B's notion of a visual field generates what we may call *necessarily private facts*. B presumably thinks of the subject's visual field as having an orientation – four distinguishable sides – so that the experience of A is distinguishable from the experience of ∀. (Were this not so, it would not make sense to speak of the motion of something across, or the rotation of something in, the visual field.) The visual field, then, has four sides, *a*, *b*, *c*, *d*, which can be identified from occasion to occasion, and what makes the experience of A different from that of ∀ is that in the first case the apex of the A is closest to the *a*-side, and in the second it is closest to the *c*-side. Now, on B's theory, the sides of the visual field cannot be distinguished by reference to anything outside the field, and consequently, in identifying them from occasion to occasion, the subject is engaged in the application of a necessarily private concept, something which I believe Wittgenstein has shown to be highly problematic. For there does not appear to be a distinction between the correct and the incorrect application of the names 'a', 'b', 'c', and 'd'. As I said, this argument is very familiar, and since the present application of the argument introduces nothing new, I shall not say anything further about it.

One who uses this argument of Wittgenstein's plays along with B's notion of the visual field, only to discredit it, so to speak, from the inside. The second argument I want to mention questions the legitimacy of B's describing the visual experience in spatial terms at all. We may start by taking note of the fact that many of the spatial descriptions of visual experience which we are inclined to give are obviously metaphorical. For example, I myself have been speaking of cortical stimulation 'producing a pattern of phosphenes arranged in a square', and the literature is replete with such metaphorical talk. It is clear that such descriptions cannot be taken literally; there are not literally four points of light, or indeed four things of any kind, arranged in a square. To think that when a subject seems to see four points of light arranged in a square, there really are four (mental) items *actually* arranged in a square is to commit the sense-datum fallacy. It might be better to call it 'the homunculus fallacy', to which it inescapably gives rise. One commits the homunculus fallacy when one attempts to explain what is involved in a subject's being related to objects in the external world by appealing to the existence of an inner situation which recapitulates the essential features of the original situation to be explained – by introducing a relation between the subject and inner objects of essentially the same kind as the relation existing between the subject and outer objects. Thus, we start by wondering what is involved in a subject's gaining knowledge of the spatial relations of outer objects, and we appeal, quite correctly, to an inner, psychological, state – a perceptual experience 'of items disposed in the visual field'. We cannot then go on to take the 'visual field' description literally, by supposing that there are certain items which *in fact* stand in spatial relations. For the question arises again: how are we to understand the subject's capacity to gain knowledge of these relations?[34]

We must therefore always be prepared to replace our metaphorical descriptions of experience in terms of mental items – colour patches, phosphenes, and the like – with conceptually more innocent descriptions. V's way of thinking about the spatiality of visual experience enables him to do this; 'the subject experiences four phosphenes arranged in a square' describes a subject as being in a complex informational state embodying the (non-conceptual) information (or misinformation) that there are four lights located at various positions in his immediate vicinity. Notice: the subject *has* this information, he does not confront it on an inner screen.

How can B cash the metaphor of the four lights in the visual field? He can certainly do nothing along V's lines. It is essential to V's way of avoiding the inner screen that he thinks of a visual experience as an informational, or representational, state – a state which can be assessed as true or false, and hence which refers to something outside itself. The spatiality of the experience is explained in terms of its embodying information about the spatial relations of things. But on B's view, points in the blind man's visual field bear no relation to points in physical space, and this precludes him from conceiving of visual experience as representational. If the existence and spatial relations of objects in the subject's immediate vicinity are not represented, it is difficult to believe that the existence and spatial relations of any other group of objects can be.

B wishes to hold that cortical stimulation of a congenitally blind man may cause him to have an experience which can be described in spatial terms, even though he does not perceive points of light as having positions in behavioural space. When we were content with metaphorical descriptions, there did not seem to be any difficulty – the stimulation produced four phosphenes arranged in a square. But once we attempt to dispense with the metaphor, it is not clear that the description of the experience in spatial terms can be defended. If 'arranged in a square' cannot come in literally, as a description of the position of phosphenes, and if it cannot come in indirectly, as a description of the apparent position of lights in space, it is not clear that it can come in at all. It certainly cannot come in by virtue of the fact that it is the description that the subject himself is inclined to offer – at least not if B is to continue to give a negative answer to Molyneux's Question.

Much more needs to be said about both of the arguments against B's position which I have mentioned. For example, a full treatment of the subject would involve an extended discussion of the results of the inverting prism experiments.[35] I shall be content if I have shown how Molyneux's Question is linked to these other fundamental issues in the philosophy of mind and perception, and if I have shown that V is not entirely without resources to defend himself.

Notes

1 Diderot, *Lettre sur les Aveugles*, trans. in M. J. Morgan's *Molyneux's Question* (Cambridge: Cambridge University Press, 1977), p. 108.
2 See the original letter Molyneux sent to Locke in 1688, four years before the one Locke cites in the *Essay* (in the Bodleian Library (MS Locke c. 16, fol. 92)). I owe this reference to W. von Leyden, *Seventeenth Century Metaphysics* (London: Duckworth, 1968), p. 277. See also the letter no. 1064 in *The Correspondence of Locke*, vol. 3, ed. E. de Beer (Oxford: Clarendon Press, 1978).
3 John Mackie claims, in his *Problems from Locke* (Oxford: Clarendon Press, 1976), p. 30, that Locke's negative answer was only to Molyneux's original question, and that he would have answered 'Yes' to Diderot's later version. I do not think that this interpretation of Locke can be sustained. See especially the passage immediately following the discussion of Molyneux's Question: '...sight...conveying to our minds the ideas of light and colours which are peculiar only to that sense; and also the far different ideas of space, figure and motion, the several varieties whereof change the appearance of *its proper object*, viz., light and colours; we bring ourselves *by use* to judge of the one by the other' (*Essay* II, ix, 9 – my italics). This seems to express the straight Berkeleyan position on visual perception of space, and would obviously require a negative answer to Diderot's version of Molyneux's Question also.
4 M. von Senden, *Space and Sight*, trs. P. Heath (London: Methuen, 1960), pp. 285–6.
5 *New Theory of Vision*, ed. Ayers, sect. 145, p. 51 (my italics).
6 [Evans subsequently noted that there is a disanalogy between this case and Molyneux's, for in the former the concepts *continuous* and *pulsating* apply literally to the experience itself, rather than figuring in the specification of its representational content – Ed.] [This note, and the other editorial notes through this chapter, were added by an earlier editor. – RS.]
7 The qualification 'seems to apply' is designed to take account of the possibility that either representation might be illusory. [Evans was dissatisfied with this paragraph and probably would have rewritten it – Ed.]
8 The qualification 'conceptually unconnected' is required so as to preclude a trivialization of B's position; *tangible square* and *visible square* must not be analysable as *square and tangible*, and as *square and visible* respectively.
9 Op. cit., p. 14.

10   Ibid., p. 7. In fairness to Morgan, it should be pointed out that he ends the book with the view that the nativist/empiricist distinction is not a very useful one in terms of which to think of approaches to Molyneux's Question.

11   For the notion of 'innate similarity-space' see, e.g., W. V. O. Quine, *Roots of Reference* (La Salle, Ill.: Open Court, 1973), sect. 5. 'Some implicit standard... for ordering our episodes as more or less similar must therefore antedate all learning, and be innate.' See also Quine's 'Linguistics and Philosophy', in S. Hook, *Language and Philosophy* (New York: New York University Press, 1969), pp. 95–8.

12   For further explanation of the distinction between conceptual and perceptual representations, see the Appendix to this paper. [This Appendix must be one that Evans planned to write, for as far as I know it does not exist. See instead *The Varieties of Reference* (Oxford: Clarendon Press, 1982), chap. 5, pp. 122–9. Ed.]

13   Nor is the innateness of the blind man's capacity to perceive spatially the ground of the dispute between them. On my construal of the debate, both B and V attribute to the blind man this capacity, hence arguments, or evidence, for the innateness of this capacity affects both of them equally.

14   'Molyneux's Question', *Journal of Philosophy* 71 (1974), p. 637.

15   H. P. Grice, 'Some Remarks about the Senses', in R. J. Butler (ed.), *Analytical Philosophy* (Oxford: Blackwell, 1962).

16   *New Essays on the Human Understanding*, IX, 8.

17   Ibid.

18   Berkeley, *New Theory of Vision*, sect. 142.

19   *The Theory of Vision Vindicated and Explained*, sect. 71.

20   R. L. Gregory and J. Wallace, 'Recovery from Early Blindness – a case study', in R. L. Gregory, *Concepts and Mechanisms of Perception* (London: Duckworth, 1974), pp. 65–129.

21   A. Valvo, *Sight Restoration after Long Term Blindness* (New York: American Foundation for the Blind, 1971); H. Umezu, S. Torii, and Y. Uemura, 'Postoperative Formation of Visual Perception in the Early Blind', *Psychologia* 18 (1975), pp. 171–86.

22   See S. J. Freedman and J. H. Rekosh, 'The Functional Integrity of Spatial Behaviour', in S. J. Freedman (ed.), *The Neuropsychology of Spatially Oriented Behaviour* (Homewood, Ill.: Dorsey, 1968).

23   *New Theory of Vision*, sect. 137.

24   Ibid., sect. 95.

25   For a review, see G. S. Brindley 'Sensory Effects of Electrical Stimulation of the Visual and Paravisual Cortex', in R. Jung (ed.), *Visual Centres of the Brain*, Handbook of Sensory Physiology 7, 3, *b* (Berlin: Springer-Verlag, 1973), ch. 26.

26   W. H. Dobelle, M. G. Mladejovesky, and J. P. Girvan, 'Artificial Vision for the Blind', *Science* 183 (1974), pp. 440–4.

27 The closest we come to a study of phosphenes in the congenitally blind is in the report of W. Schodtman ('Ein Beitrag zur lehre von der Optischen Lokalisati bei Blindgebronen', *Archiv für Ophthalmologie* 54 (1902), pp. 256–67) who claimed that 'pressure phosphenes' could be produced in such subjects by pressure on their eyes, and that these phosphenes were located in behavioural space; located 'up' if the pressure was on the lower part of the eyeball, and 'down' if on the upper. However, there is a certain amount of doubt about whether this claim can be believed. I owe the reference to I. Rock.

28 For a recent review, see W. H. Dobelle, 'Current State of Research on Providing Sight to the Blind by Electrical Stimulation of the Brain', *Journal of Impairment and Blindness* 71 (1977), pp. 290–7. See also T. D. Sperling (ed.), *Visual Prosthesis* (New York: Academic Press, 1971).

29 G. S. Brindley and W. S. Lewin, 'The Sensations Produced by Electrical Stimulation of the Visual Cortex', *Journal of Physiology* 196 (1968), pp. 479–93.

30 Telephone conversation with G. S. Brindley, in *Visual Prosthesis*, op. cit., p. 48.

31 Thomas Reid, *An Inquiry into the Human Mind*, ed. T. Duggan (Chicago, Ill.: University of Chicago Press, 1970), p. 113. I presume Reid must mean to be referring to 'the Cyclopean eye'.

32 G. S. Schneider, 'Two Visual Systems', in *Science* 163 (1969), p. 901. A similar but by no means identical distinction between 'ambient' and 'focal' perception has been suggested by C. Trevarthen, Two mechanisms of perception in primates, *Psychologische Forschung*, 31 (1968).

33 The considerations of this paragraph strongly suggest that a great deal of the work on computer vision – computer simulation of visual perception – is based upon a mistake. The problem is conceived to be that of simulating the human subject's capacity to describe his environment, and so, fundamentally a problem of devising a sufficiently complicated pattern-recognizing program. Whatever it is that one may reach by this route, it does not remotely resemble the psychology of a conscious human subject, since there is nothing which corresponds to the human's non-conceptual representation of his environment – i.e. nothing which corresponds to visual experience. If the argument of this paper is along anything like the right lines, that defect will not be rectified until attention shifts to the study of programs for computers which control behaviour in a spatial world.

34 The link between the sense-datum fallacy and the homunculus fallacy is brought out well in Ryle's *Concept of Mind* (Harmondsworth: Penguin, 1963), pp. 200–11.

35 For such a discussion, see I. Rock, *The Nature of Perceptual Adaptation* (New York: Basic Books, 1966).

Part III

Direct versus Indirect
Theories of Perception

Introduction to Part III

Although there were always serious dissenters, the consensus in vision theory well into the twentieth century was that perception of the spatial layout was, in one way or another, a multi-stage process. First comes the registration by the visual sense of the *cues* found in the light stimuli striking a two-dimensional retina. Next, these data are processed by higher-level mechanisms that combine and supplement what is given by sense to turn it into veridical three-dimensional perceptions of the environment. The sensory registration of cues is immediate and physiologically determined. Perception of the environment is non-immediate. It is indirect, since it is derived from the initial data made available by sense.

Part II of this volume contained a selection by Gibson outlining his reasons for rejecting the standard view of the senses as providing the experiential base for perception. In the reading that now follows, Gibson further elaborates his theory of direct perception. According to Gibson, once the concept of a "stimulus" is properly expanded, it can be shown that the invariant properties of arrays of light contain all the information needed to perceive the physical layout veridically. The stimulus, in and of itself, accurately reflects the way the world is. Thus there is no need to derive or infer environmental properties from sense-registered cues. We immediately and directly see how things are without the aid of intervening mental states and processes.

Gibson allows that in many instances we may have to learn to see. The expert can see things and properties the untutored cannot discern. Learning, though, is not a matter of bringing in past experience to alter or enrich the interpretation of the sensory data. Perceptual learning is the honing of an ability to pick up *directly* the information present in the light array (Gibson and Gibson 1955) Gibson frequently describes his opponents as subscribing to the view that perceptions are based on sensations. In the brief addendum piece taken from his book, *The Ecological Approach to Perception*, Gibson makes clear that it is not just this more traditional position he rejects. He finds equally misguided *any* theory, including newer computational theories, that understands vision as a process of data registration plus mental representation and supplementation. Indeed, it is these wider implications that many of Gibson's opponents find the least palatable.

Fodor and Pylyshyn recognize the importance of Gibson's contributions to vision theory, and they agree with his criticisms of various alternative approaches. Nonetheless, they believe Gibson's claim that perception is direct is untenable. Significantly, it conflicts with core tenets of their own favored representational (or as they call it "Establishment") theory of mind. Fodor and Pylyshyn believe Gibson is in a bind he cannot escape. They argue that even Gibson must admit that not everything we determine by sight can be contained in the stimulus. There are no invariants in the light array corresponding to the property "painted by Da Vinci" or, one might say, to the property "son of Diares." So Gibson has to constrain his notion of "direct pickup" to rule out these cases. At the same time, he cannot be too restrictive. For then he will not be able to sustain his claim that layout information is fully contained in the stimulus and can be accessed without intermediaries.

Fodor and Pylyshyn canvas a range of possible responses Gibson might give and argue that they all are faulty. The moral they relentlessly draw is that the Establishment is right; perception must be a matter of *inference*. Fodor and Pylyshyn recognize that they themselves are left with a problem related to the one they thrust on Gibson. If vision is a matter of inference, what is to count as the premises or evidence upon which perception is inferred? In the remainder of their paper (only parts of which are included here), Fodor and Pylyshyn attempt to cope with this dilemma. Their solution depends on distinguishing processes of transduction, that provide the initial data, from cognitive computational processes, that make inferences thereon. Commentators have questioned both Fodor and Pylyshyn's account of Gibson's views and whether their own transduction/inference distinction can actually do the job they assign it (Turvey et al. 1981; Bennett et al. 1991).

Rock, too, recognizes the significance of Gibson's expanded conception of the stimulus and the significance of Gibson's stress on the added information movement provides. Rock thinks, however, there are a wide range of important visual phenomena a Gibsonian approach cannot handle. He believes there is much empirical evidence that vision, including basic aspects of spatial and color perception, depends on mechanisms and processes that evaluate and combine different kinds of information (Rock 1997). Size perception, for example, is determined by the visual system "taking account of" retinal image angle and registered distance. On the basis of this information and in accord with geometrical/optical principles, magnitude is then calculated. Rock thinks that this sort of account can also explain non-veridical perception, as for example the Moon Illusion. Gibsonians, by contrast, generally have more difficulty applying their theory of direct vision to cases of misperception.

Rock likens his own cognitive theory of vision to Helmholtz's unconscious inference model (Rock 1977). A major difference, however, is that Rock is not committed to Helmholtz's empiricism. Rock is willing to allow that the principles underlying his posited mental transitions are hard-wired. Still, Rock believes it is useful and proper to conceive of the working of the visual system as displays of intelligence. Perception can be understood as a form of logical reasoning and inference to the best explanation. The visual system seeks solutions to the problems of interpretation the retinal image poses (Rock 1983).

Churchland questions the aptness of Rock's picture of the working of the visual system. She claims that what seems to be intelligent problem-solving may simply be the result of low-level interactions that do not reflect thought-like processes. Churchland's criticism of Rock is not a result of her adopting the Gibsonian model. In this paper, Churchland rests her case primarily on the computational theory of vision championed by Marr and his followers. She thinks that Marr-type explanations of Rock's phenomena drain them of their intellectual aura.

To provide background for her argument, Churchland offers an outline of Marr's computational model. The Churchland piece thus provides a useful introduction to some of the main features of his approach. Churchland, nonetheless, expresses qualms about various aspects of Marr's program. She develops her own views and her critique of the Marr model more fully in later works (Churchland et al. 1994). It is worth noting, too, that Churchland's criticism of Rock stands in marked contrast to Anscombe's (1974) earlier and more epistemological rejection of Gregory's (1974) proposal to talk of vision in terms of "hypothesis formation" and "intelligence."

Like Gibson and Rock, Marr's work has had a profound effect on the field. Yet here, too, on many if not most of his central claims and proposals there is considerable dissent. Marr's approach is clearly not the only game in town. Ullman has long been a major proponent and contributor to the computational vision program (Ullman 1979). And his (1980) paper "Against direct perception" has been one of the most cited and influential criticisms of Gibsonian doctrines. Ullman recognizes, however, that all is not smooth sailing for his own and Marr's computational approach to vision. In this piece, he lays out six core assumptions of the computational program along with assorted challenges to each of them. Ullman judiciously evaluates the pros and cons of the competing positions and the prospects for resolving the issues at stake.

The Gestalt theorist Koffka posed as the central topic for the study of visual perception the question "Why do things look as they do?" In numerous works Koffka and fellow Gestalt theorists attempted to answer it. Epstein makes use of Koffka's question and the Gestaltist perspective to explore the positions of Gibson, Rock, and Marr. He compares and contrasts their views and evaluates them against the background of Koffka's theory. Although Epstein has reservations about all of these approaches, he recommends a Gibsonian search for stimulus invariants as the default position. Moreover, Epstein believes there are empirical grounds for questioning the existence or "psychological reality" of the symbolic representations that lie at the heart of the computational model (Epstein 1993). These, though, are the very posits that have been a central attraction to many who wish to promote "Establishment" representational theories of mind (Kitcher 1988; Egan 1995; Hatfield 1988).

In addition to the three main approaches to vision theory discussed above, several others may be briefly noted. Ramachandran and his co-workers have opted for something they call a "bag of tricks" model (Ramachandran 1990). They believe their approach is biologically more realistic than that of Marr. Ullman, in the piece reprinted, suggests that the differences may not be as great as Ramachandran thinks. In a book and series of articles Cutting has argued that the information available in the stimulus is even richer than Gibson supposed. It is not only sufficient for determining the layout, it is redundant. Cutting calls his model "directed perception." The visual system does not have to supplement the data, it must select or combine the more than sufficient information available (Cutting 1986; Schwartz 1996). Most recently there has been an effort to describe perception within the framework of Bayesian decision theory (Knill and Richards 1996). Perception is a form of probabilistic inference. Although much of this work is undertaken within a computational framework, proponents of the Bayesian approach recognize the debt they owe to the inference, hypothesis-testing models of Rock and Gregory. The full implications of the Bayesian model for the issues discussed in this volume remain to be explored.

References

Anscombe, E. (1974), Comments on Professor R. L. Gregory's paper. In *Philosophy of Psychology*, ed. S. C. Brown, London: Macmillan, pp. 211–20.

Bennett, B., Hoffman, D. and Prakash, C. (1991), Unity of perception, *Cognition* 38: 295–334.

Churchland, P., Ramachandran, V. S. and Sejnowski, T. (1994), A critique of pure vision. In *Large Scale Neuronal Theories of the Brain*, ed. C. Koch and J. Davis, Cambridge, MA: MIT Press, pp. 23–60.

Cutting, J. (1986), *Perception with an Eye for Motion*, Cambridge, MA: MIT Press.

Egan, F. (1995), Computation and content, *Philosophical Review* 104, 2: 181–203.

Epstein, W. (1993), The representational framework in perceptual theory, *Perception and Psychophysics* 53: 704–9.

Gibson, J. J. and Gibson, E. J. (1955), Perceptual learning: differentiation or enrichment? *Psychological Review* 62: 32–41.

Gregory, R. L. (1974), Perception as hypothesis. In *Philosophy of Psychology*, ed. S. C. Brown, London: Macmillan, pp. 195–210.

Hatfield, G. (1988), Representation and content in some (actual) theories of perception, *Studies in the History and Philosophy of Science* 19: 175–214.

Kitcher, P. (1988), Marr's computational theory of vision, *Philosophy of Science* 55: 1–24.

Knill, D. and Richards, W. (eds) (1996), *Perception as Bayesian Inference*, Cambridge: Cambridge University Press.

Ramachandran, V. S. (1990), Visual perception in people and machines. In *AI and the Eye*, ed. A. Blake and T. Troscianko, New York: John Wiley, pp. 21–77.

Rock, I. (1977), In defense of unconscious inference. In *Stability and Constancy in Visual Perception*, ed. W. Epstein, New York: Wiley, pp. 321–73.

Rock, I. (1983), *The Logic of Perception*, Cambridge, MA: MIT Press.

Rock, I. (ed.) (1997), *Indirect Perception*, Cambridge, MA: MIT Press.

Schwartz, R. (1996), Directed perception, *Philosophical Psychology* 9: 81–91.

Turvey, M., Shaw, R., Reed, E. and Mace, W. (1981), Ecological laws of perceiving and acting: in reply to Fodor and Pylyshyn (1981), *Cognition* 9: 237–304.

Ullman, S. (1979), *The Interpretation of Visual Motion*, Cambridge, MA: MIT Press.

Ullman, S. (1980), Against direct perception, *Behavioral and Brain Sciences* 3: 373–415.

15

A Theory of Direct Visual Perception, and from *The Ecological Approach to Visual Perception*

James J. Gibson

A THEORY OF DIRECT VISUAL PERCEPTION

The theory to be outlined is partly developed in *The Senses Considered as Perceptual Systems* (Gibson 1966), especially in chapters 9–12 on vision. It is related to, although a considerable departure from, the theory presented in *The Perception of the Visual World* (Gibson 1950). Some of its postulates go back 20 years to that book, but many are new.

What is "direct" visual perception? I argue that the seeing of an environment by an observer existing in that environment is direct in that it is not mediated by visual sensations or sense data. The phenomenal visual world of surfaces, objects, and the ground under one's feet is quite different from the phenomenal visual field of color-patches (Gibson 1950, ch. 3). I assert that the latter experience, the array of visual sensations, is not entailed in the former. Direct perception is not based on the having of sensations. The suggestion will be that it is based on the pickup of information.

So far, all theories have assumed that the visual perception of a stable, unbounded, and permanent *world* can only be explained by a process of correcting or compensating for the unstable, bounded, and fleeting sensations coming to the brain from the retinal images. That is to say, all extant theories are sensation-based. But the theory here advanced as-

James J. Gibson, "A Theory of Direct Visual Perception," in J. Royce and W. Rozeboom (eds.), *The Psychology of Knowing* (New York and London: Gordon and Breach, 1972), pp. 215–27.

sumes the existence of stable, unbounded, and permanent stimulus-information in the ambient optic array. And it supposes that the visual system can explore and detect this information. The theory is information-based, not sensation-based.

Perception and Proprioception

Simplifying a distinction made by Sherrington, the term *perception* will be used to refer to any experience of the environment surrounding the body of an animal, and the term *proprioception* for any experience of the body itself (including what Sherrington called *interoception*). Far from being one of the senses, then, proprioception is a kind of experience cognate with perception. Proprioception *accompanies* perception but it is not the same thing as perception.

An awareness of the body, however dim, does in fact seem to go along with an awareness of the world. Conversely, an awareness of the body, however intense, even an experience of pain, is never wholly without some awareness of the environment. And this reciprocity is only to be expected since the very term "environment" implies something that is surrounded, and the term "observer" implies a surrounding world.

The difference between perception and proprioception, then, is one of function, not a difference between the receptors stimulated as Sherrington assumed, that is, the exteroceptors and the proprioceptors. Perception and proprioception both depend on stimulation, but the visual system, for example, can isolate from the flux of stimulation that which is exterospecific (specifies the world) from that which is propriospecific (specifies the body). Vision, in other words, serves not only awareness of the environment but also awareness of self.

For example, the motion of an object relative to the stationary environment can be detected by vision, and this is a case of *perception*. Likewise the motion of one's body relative to the stationary environment, whether active or passive, can be detected by vision, and this is a case of *proprioception*. Locomotion, as distinguished from object motion, is specified by transformation of the ambient optic array as a whole. An observer can ordinarily distinguish the two cases with no difficulty, and so can animals, even species with very simple eyes.

Note that proprioception, as here defined, it not to be confused with *feedback* in the modern usage of the word, that is, a return input to the nervous system from a motor action. The movements and postures of the body are detected (in several independent ways) whether they are imposed by outside forces or are obtained by an action of the observer himself. Proprioception can be passive or active, just as perception can be passive or active. The above hypothesis is elaborated in chapter 2 of *The Senses Considered as Perceptual Systems*. The classical doctrine that proprioception is one of the sense modalities is familiar, and is still taught, but it simply will not work. The evidence is against it.

It should already be evident that this theory of perception does not accept the usual analogy between the brain and a computer, and rejects the idea that perception is a matter of processing the information fed into a computer. No one has suggested that a computer has the experience of being "here."

Optical Stimulation and Optical Information

The theory distinguishes between stimulation by light and the information in light. The difference is between light that is seen and the light by which *things* are seen. Light as energy is treated by physical optics. Light as information is treated by an unfamiliar discipline called ecological optics (Gibson 1961; 1966, ch. 10). The facts of physical optics are sufficient for a psychophysics of the light sense, and of the elementary visual sensations. But the facts of ecological optics are required for an understanding of direct visual perception.

The relation between optical stimulation and optical information seems to be as follows. The stimulation of photoreceptors by light is a necessary condition for visual perception. The activity of the visual system depends on ambient light; there is no vision in darkness. But *another* necessary condition for visual perception is an *array* of ambient light. It must be structured or differentiated, not homogeneous. With homogeneous ambient light, perception fails although the sensation of light remains. Such is the case in dense fog, empty sky, or in the experiment of wearing plastic diffusing eye-caps, an experiment that we repeat every year at Cornell. In homogeneous darkness, perception fails because stimulation is absent. In homogeneous light, perception fails because stimulus *information* is absent although stimulation is present. We conclude that stimulus energy is a necessary but by no means sufficient condition of stimulus information.

The meaning of the term "information." There are currently two radically different usages of the word "information" in psychology. One I will call *afferent-input information* and the other *optic-array information*. The former is familiar; it is information conceived as impulses in the fibers of the optic nerve. Information is assumed to consist of *signals*, and to be *transmitted* from receptors to the brain. Perception is a process that is supposed to occur *in* the brain, and the only information for perception must therefore consist of neural inputs *to* the brain.

Optic-array information is something entirely different. It is information in light, not in nervous impulses. It involves geometrical projection to a point of observation, not transmission between a sender and a receiver. It is outside the observer and available to him, not inside his head. In my theory, perception is *not* supposed to occur in the brain but to arise in the retino-neuro-muscular system as an activity of the whole system. The information does not consist of signals to be interpreted but of structural invariants which need only be attended to.

It has long been assumed by empiricists that the only information for perception was "sensory" information. But this assumption can mean different things. If it means that the information for perception must come through the senses and not through extrasensory intuition, this is the doctrine of John Locke, and I agree with it, as most of us would agree with it. But the assumption might mean (and has been taken to mean) that the information for perception must come over the sensory nerves. This is a different doctrine, that of Johannes Müller, and with this we need *not* agree. To assume that visual information comes through the visual sense is not to assume that it comes over the optic nerve, for a sense may be considered as an active system with a capacity to extract information from obtained stimulation. The visual system in fact does this. Retinal inputs lead to ocular adjustments, and then to altered retinal inputs, and so on. It is an exploratory, circular process, not a one-way delivery of messages to the brain. This hypothesis is elaborated in chapters 2 and 3 of *The Senses Considered as Perceptual Systems*.

The Main Principles of Ecological Optics

The term *ecological optics* was introduced in a paper (Gibson 1961) and the subject was further developed in a chapter on environmental information (Gibson 1966, ch. 10). But the concepts and postulates are not yet wholly established, and what follows must be regarded as tentative.

Ecological optics attempts to escape the reductionism of physical and geometrical optics. It introduces a new concept, *ambient light*, which goes beyond the physicist's conception of radiant light, and it postulates a notion of space-filling illumination that extends the classical meaning of illuminance.

1   *The unlimited reflecting of light waves*

In a medium of water or air, in which animals live and move and have evolved, light not only propagates as it does in empty space but also reverberates. It is rapidly reflected back and forth between earth and sky, and also between the facing surfaces of semi-enclosed spaces. Given the speed of light and the fact of sunlight, it almost instantly reaches an equilibrium in the medium, that is, a steady state. The light moves in all directions at once. This steady state of multiply reflected light has very interesting properties. First, at every point in the medium there is ambient light and, second, the ambient light at every such point will be structured by the reflecting surfaces facing that point.

2   *Projection to a point*

At any point in a medium there will exist a bundle of *visual solid angles* corresponding to the components or parts of the illuminated environment. The *faces* and *facets* of reflecting surfaces are such components; what we call *objects* are others; and the *patches of pigment* on a flat surface are still others. Note that the bundle of *solid angles* postulated above is not the same as a pencil of rays, which is a concept of *geometrical* optics. The cross-section of a solid angle always has a "form," no matter how small, whereas the cross-section of a ray is a formless point. And the cross-section of a *bundle* of solid angles always has a pattern whereas the cross-section of a pencil of rays does not.

3   *The ambient optic array*

A bundle of visual solid angles at a point (a point of observation) is called an *ambient optic array*. Such an array is invariant under changes in the illumination from noon to sunset. It is an arrangement of components, not an assemblage of points, and the components are nested within others of larger size. It is analyzed by topology or perspective geometry, not by analytic geometry. The array can be said to exist at a point of observation whether or not an eye is stationed at that point. In this respect the array is quite unlike a retinal image, which occurs only if a chambered (vertebrate) eye is put there and aimed in a certain direction. The array is also unlike an image inasmuch as the image is usually said to be an assemblage of focus points each corresponding to a luminous radiating point (presumably an atom) in the environment.

4 Projected surfaces and occluded surfaces at a point of observation

Given that surfaces are in general *opaque*, not transparent, some of the surfaces of the world will be hidden at a given point of observation (occluded) and the remainder will be unhidden (projected at the point). This holds for any layout of surfaces other than a flat plane unobscured to its horizon. But any hidden surface may become unhidden by a change of the point of observation. The occlusion of one surface by another entails an *occluding edge*.

5 Connected sets of observation points

A path of locomotion in ecological space consists of a connected set of observation points. To each connected set of observation points there corresponds a unique family of perspective transformations in the ambient optic array. In short the changing optic array at a moving point of observation specifies the movement of the point (i.e., the path of locomotion of the observer).

The optical transition between what I call two "vistas" of the world (as when an observer goes from one room to another) entails the progressive occlusion of some parts of the world and the disocclusion of others. The transition, however, arises from a path of locomotion which is reversible, and the transition is itself reversible. What went out of sight in going comes back into sight on returning. This reversible optical transition is to be distinguished from an *irreversible* transition such as occurs when an object is melted or dissolved or destroyed. The study of the two different ways in which an object can go out of sight, by being hidden or by being destroyed, suggests that they are clearly distinguishable on the basis of optical information.

6 The family of perspectives for an object

Given an illuminated object with several faces (a polyhedron for example) it will be surrounded by an unlimited set of points of observation. Each *perspective* of the object (its projection in each optic array) is unique at each point of observation. The family of perspectives is unique to the object. An observer who walked around the object (looked at it "from all sides") would obtain the whole family.

The features of the object that make it different from other objects have corresponding features in the family of perspectives that are *invariant* under perspective transformations. These invariants constitute information about the object. Although the observer gets a different form-sensation at each moment of his tour, his information-based perception can be of the same object. This hypothesis provides new reasons for realism in epistemology (Gibson 1967).

7   *Correspondence of structure between an ambient optic array and the environment*

There is evidently some correspondence between the structure of the environment and the structure of the ambient light at a stationary point of observation. It is by no means a simple correspondence. It is not point-to-point but component-to-component. There are subordinate and superordinate components of the world and corresponding subordinate and superordinate forms in the array, each level of units being nested within larger units. But some components of the environment are missing from a frozen array, because of occlusion. All components of the environment, however, could be included in the changing array over time at a moving point of observation.

8   *Invariant information in an ambient optic array*

A list of the *invariants* in an array as the amount of illumination changes, as the type of illumination changes, as the direction of the prevailing illumination changes, and (above all) as the point of observation changes cannot yet be drawn up with any assurance. But a few facts seem to be clear. The *contours* in an array are invariant with most of the changes in illumination. The *textures* of an array are reliably invariant with change of observation-point. The property of a contour being *closed* or *unclosed* is always invariant. The *form* of a closed contour in the array is independent of lighting but highly variant with change of observation point. A great many properties of the array are *lawfully* or *regularly* variant with change of observation point, and this means that in each case a property defined by the law is *invariant*.

9   *Summary*

Eight main principles of ecological optics have been outlined. They are perhaps enough to show that the new optics is not just an application of the accepted laws of physical and geometrical optics, inasmuch as different laws emerge at the new level. And it should now be clear why ecological optics is required for a theory of direct visual perception instead of what is taught in the physics textbooks.

The Sampling Process in Visual Perception

The theories of sensation-based perception presuppose the formation of a retinal image and the transmission of it to the brain. The theory of direct perception presupposes the sampling of the ambient array by the ocular system. What is this sampling process?

No animal has wholly panoramic vision (although some approximate to having it) and therefore no animal can perceive the whole environment at once. The successive sampling of the ambient array is carried out by head-movements, the eyes being stabilized to the structure of the array by compensatory eye-movements (see Gibson 1966, ch. 12, for an explanation of head-movements and compensatory eye-movements). The point to be noted is that vertebrate animals with chambered eyes must perform *sample-taking* in order to perceive the environment. Invertebrates with compound eyes probably do the same, although very little is known about visual perception in arthropods. The sampling of the optical environment is a more general process than the fixating of details. The latter arises in evolution only when the eyes develop concentrated foveas.

Along with the taking of stabilized samples of the spherical array there goes a process of optimizing the pickup of information in the sample. Accommodation of the lens, the centering of the retinal fovea on an item of the sample, and the adjustment of the pupil for an optimal level of intensity, together with the adaptation of the retina, are all cases of the adjustment of the ocular system to the requirements of clear vision.

From the earliest stage of evolution, therefore, vision has been a process of exploration in time, not a photographic process of image registration and image transmission. We have been misled about vision by the analogy between eye and camera. Physical optics, and the physiological optics that depends on it, do not now conceive the eye in any way except as a camera. But a camera is not a device with which one can perceive the whole environment by means of sampling, whereas an eye does perceive the environment by sampling it.

If the visual system is exploratory we can assume that it extracts the information in successive samples; we do not have to speculate about how the brain could "store" the sequence of images transmitted to it and combine them into a total image of the world. The experience of the visual world is not compounded of a series of visual fields; no one is aware of the *sequence* but only of the total *scene*. Presumably this is because the ocular system detects the invariants over time that specify the scene.

I once assumed (Gibson 1950) that the only way one can be aware of the environment behind one's back is to remember it, in the sense of having a *memory image* of it. Similarly, I supposed that, when I look out of the window, my lawn, only part of which is projected through the window to my eyes, must be filled out by images of the remainder. But I no longer believe this theory. Awareness of the room behind my back and the lawn outside my window cannot depend on imagery. I doubt if it depends on *memory*. I apprehend part of the room as *occluded by my head*, and part of the lawn as *occluded by the edges of the window*. And the perception of occlusion, it seems to me, entails the perception of *something* which is *occluded*.

A memory image of a room or of a lawn is something quite different from the perception of surfaces that are temporarily hidden from sight. I can summon up a memory image of the house and the lawn where I lived as a child. This is not at all like the awareness I have of the room behind my back and the lawn outside my window. The theory of information-based perception differs from the theory of sensation-based perception in many ways but in none more radical than this: it does not require the assumption that memories of the past must somehow be mixed with sensations of the present.

The False Problem of Depth Perception and the True Problem of Environment Perception

For centuries, the problem of space perception has been stated as the puzzle of how "depth" or the "third dimension" could be seen when the sensations for the perception were depthless or two-dimensional. Three kinds of solution have been offered, one by nativism (intuition), one by empiricism (past experience), and a third by Gestalt-theory (spontaneous organization in the brain). But none of them has been convincing. In the light of the present theory the puzzle of depth perception is insoluble because the problem is false; we perceive the layout of the environment, not the third dimension of space. There is nothing special about "depth" in the environment. As Merleau-Ponty somewhere pointed out, "depth is nothing but breadth seen from the side." We have been misled by taking the third dimension of the Cartesian coordinate system to be a phenomenal fact of perception. And if the flat patchwork of visual sensation is not the basis of visual perception in any case, a third dimension does not *have* to be added to the two dimensions they already possess.

Perception of the *environment* differs from a perception of *space*. An environment implies points of observation in the medium, whereas a space does not. The points of geometrical space are abstract fictions, whereas the points of observation in an environment are the positions where an observer might be stationed. Perception of the environment is thus accompanied by an awareness of the perceiver's existence in the environment (and this is what I call proprioception) whereas a perception of space in its purest form need not be accompanied by any awareness of the thinker's existence in that space.

Geometrical optics is based, of course, on geometrical space. This is everywhere transparent, and it is composed of ghostly points, lines, and planes. It is impersonal and lifeless. Ecological optics is based on a space of solid opaque surfaces with a transparent medium in which living animals get about, and which permits the reverberation of reflected light. The surfaces are textured and pigmented. They are flat or curved. They have corners and occluding edges. There are objects and the inter-spaces between objects. In short, the environment has a layout.

The so-called *cues* for the perception of depth are not the same as the *information* for the perception of layout. The former are called *signs* or *indicators* of depth, or *clues* for an inference that depth exists in the world. Their meaning has to be learned by association. They are sensations in the visual field of the observer, noticeable when he introspects. The latter, the available kinds of information, are *specifiers* of layout, not signs or indicators or clues. They have to be distinguished or discriminated, but their meaning does not have to be learned by association. They are not sense impressions or sense data. When the information for occlusion of one surface by another is picked up there is no sensation for the occluded surface but it is nevertheless perceived. And the information for the occlusion of one surface by another *is* picked up by vision.

The surface layout of the world is thus perceived *directly* when the information is available and when the cycle of action from retina to brain to eye to retina again is attuned to this information. The information must be *attended to*, of course, and this may depend on the maturation of the system, and on practice in looking, and even on the education or training of attention. But the meanings of an edge, of a falling-off-place, of an obstacle in one's path, or of the solid ground under one's feet are given in the ambient optic array and do not have to be memories of past experience attached to present sense-data, or memories of touching aroused by sensations of seeing.

False questions in the perception of the environment

We have seen that the old question of why the phenomenal environment has depth whereas the retinal images are depthless is a false question. There are other false questions of this same sort. One is the question made famous by Stratton's experiment in 1897, *why is the phenomenal world upright whereas the retinal image is inverted on the retina?* Another, going back at least to Helmholtz, is *why is the phenomenal world stationary when the retinal image continually moves with respect to the retina?* Still another (connected with the fact of sampling) is, *why is the phenomenal environment unbounded when each retinal image is bounded by the margins of the retina?* In another form, this is the question, *why does the phenomenal world seem to persist when the retinal images are impermanent?* The answer to all the above questions is this: we do not *see* our retinal images. We see the environment. The doctrine of Müller that all we can see is our retinal images (or at least all we can ever see *directly*) is quite false. If we saw our retinal images we would perceive two worlds, not one, since there is a separate image of it in each eye.

The False Puzzle of the Constancy of Phenomenal Objects

The so-called "constancy" of objects in perception despite changing stimulation and changing sensation has long been considered a puzzle. For the past century, experimenters have studied the perceived size of an object with retinal size variant, the perceived form of an object with retinal form variant, and the perceived surface-color of an object with variation of the intensity and wavelength of the light in the retinal image. There is always some tendency to perceive the "real" size, form, and color of the surface of the object, the amount of constancy depending on experimental conditions. Explanations of this result differ with different theorists but they all begin with one assumption, namely, that the perceived size, form, and color are based on retinal size, form, and color respectively – that the process of perception must *start with* these stimulus variables of the image.

According to the present theory this assumption is mistaken. There is information in the optic array for the size, shape, and color of a surface in a layout of other surfaces. The information is a matter of complex invariant ratios and relations; it is not easy to isolate experimentally. But the size, the form, and the color of the image impressed on the retina, when they are experienced at all, are not relevant to and not commensurable with the dimensions and slant and pigmentation of the surface. If I am right, a whole century of experimental research on the *amount* of constancy obtained by an observer is pointless. Insofar as these laboratory experiments have impoverished the stimulus information for perception they are not relevant to perception.

The Effect on Perception of Impoverishing the Stimulus Information

If perception is a process of operating on the deliverances of sense, it has seemed obvious that one way of investigating the process is to *impoverish* the stimulation, to *minimize* the cues, and observe what happens. Visual perception is supposed to come into its own when the input is reduced. Perception then has more work to do. Experiments with a tachistoscope, or with blurred pictures, or with very faint images on a screen are therefore common in the psychology laboratory.

According to the present theory, however, this is not the best way of investigating the process, for perception is frustrated when the stimulus information is impoverished. If the visual system is not allowed to "hunt" for the external specifying information, all sorts of internal processes begin to occur. They are very interesting processes, worthy of investigation, but they should not be confused with the normal process of perceiving.

The situation is similar when contradictory information in the same display is presented to an observer, "conflicting cues." The ambiguous figures and reversible perspectives that have been so frequently studied are of this sort. Ink blots are a combination of impoverished and inconsistent information. I argue that the *guessing* that goes on in these experiments, the attempt to fill out or complete a perception by supplementing the almost meaningless data, is not indicative of what goes on in ordinary perception. The process does not reach an equilibrium state of *clarity* as it does in ordinary perception. And the achieving of precise awareness is the aim of perception.

Orthodox theories assume that there is always an "objective contribution" to perception (the sensations) and a "subjective contribution" to perception (innate ideas, or memories, or field-forces in the brain), the two contributions being combined in various proportions. I reject this assumption. If unequivocal stimulus information is made available to an observer in an experiment, his perception will be determined by it and by nothing else. When *ambient* stimulus information is available to an observer outside the laboratory he can *select* the information that interests him; he can give attention to one part instead of another, but his perception will be determined by the information he attends to.

When *no* stimulus information is allowed to reach the eyes of an observer, as when the eyes are covered by diffusing plastic caps (which can be made of halved ping-pong balls) he is *deprived* of visual perception, although not of sensation. The subject does not like the situation; it is worse than being blindfolded. The only visual experience is that of "nothing." His perceptual system acts a little like a motor running without a load. If he is not allowed to go to sleep, experiences resembling hallucinations may arise.

Summary and Conclusions

This theory of vision asserts that perception is direct and is not mediated by retinal images transmitted to the brain. Most theories assume that perception of the world is *indirect*, and that all we ever *directly* perceive is our retinal images.

Now it is perfectly true that when an observer looks at a painting, photograph, sculpture, or model, he gets an *indirect* visual perception, a *mediated* experience, an awareness *at second hand*, of whatever is represented. A human artifact of this sort is an *image* in the original meaning of the term. It is a light-reflecting object in its own right but it displays *information* to specify a quite different object (Gibson 1966, ch. 11). An image in this straightforward meaning of the term is something to be looked at, and it has to be looked at, of course, with eyes. Thus there can be a direct perception of a man's portrait accompanied by an indirect perception of the man himself.

The fallacy of the standard theories of perception consists of taking as a model for vision the kind of indirect visual perception that uses pictures as substitutes for things. The false analogy should now be evident. Direct perception of a retinal image implies an eye inside the head, in the brain, with which to look at the image. But there is no little man anywhere in the brain who can do this. We do not look at our retinal images and perceive the world in the way that we look at a portrait and perceive the sitter. Putting the objection another way, the so-called image on the retina is not an image at all, properly speaking, since it cannot be looked at, as a picture can be looked at, and cannot therefore mediate perception. The famous experiment of looking at the back of the excised eye of a slaughtered ox and observing an image is profoundly misleading. The eye is a biological device for sampling the information available in an ambient optic array. The vertebrate eye does it in one way and the insect eye does it in another way but both register differences of light in different directions at a point of observation.

The availability of information in ambient light and the possibility that it can be picked up directly have implications for epistemology. They lend sophisticated support to the naive belief that we have direct knowledge of the world around us. They support direct realism (Gibson 1967). If these hypotheses prove correct, they justify our deep feeling that *the senses can be trusted*. At the same time they explain the seemingly contrary conviction *that the senses cannot be trusted*. For a distinction has been drawn between what might be called the *useful* senses, the perceptual systems, and the *useless* senses, the channels of sensation.

References

Gibson, J. J. (1950), *The Perception of the Visual World*. Boston: Houghton Mifflin.
Gibson, J. J. (1961), Ecological optics, *Vision Research* 1: 253–62.
Gibson, J. J. (1966), *The Senses Considered as Perceptual Systems*. Boston: Houghton Mifflin.
Gibson, J. J. (1967), New reasons for realism, *Synthese*, 17: 162–72.

FROM *THE ECOLOGICAL APPROACH TO VISUAL PERCEPTION*

The Traditional Theories of Perception: Input Processing

The theory of information pickup purports to be an alternative to the traditional theories of perception. It differs from all of them, I venture to suggest, in rejecting the assumption that perception is the processing of inputs. *Inputs* mean sensory or afferent nerve impulses to the brain.

Adherents to the traditional theories of perception have recently been making the claim that what they assume is the processing of information in a modern sense of the term, not sensations, and that therefor they are not bound by the traditional theories of perception. But it seems to me that all they are doing is climbing on the latest bandwagon, the computer

James J. Gibson, *The Ecological Approach to Visual Perception* (Hillsdale, NJ: Lawrence Erlbaum Associates, 1986), pp. 251–3.

bandwagon, the computer bandwagon, without reappraising the traditional assumption that perceiving is the processing of inputs. I refuse to
let them pre-empt the term *information*. As I use the term, it is not
something that has to be processed. The inputs of the receptors have to
be processed, of course, because they in themselves do not specify anything more than the anatomical units that are triggered.

All kinds of metaphors have been suggested to describe the ways in
which sensory inputs are processed to yield perceptions. It is supposed
that sensation occurs first, perception occurs next, and knowledge occurs
last, a progression from the lower to the higher mental processes. One
process is the filtering of sensory inputs. Another is the organizing of
sensory inputs, the grouping of elements into a spatial pattern. The
integrating of elements into a temporal pattern may or may not be
included in the organizing process. After that, the processes become
highly speculative. Some theorists propose mental operations. Others
argue for semilogical processes or problem-solving. Many theorists are
in favor of a process analogous to the decoding of signals. All theorists
seem to agree that past experience is brought to bear on the sensory
inputs, which means that memories are somehow applied to them.
Apart from filtering and organizing, the processes suggested are cognitive. Consider some of them.

Mental operations on the sensory inputs

the a priori categories of understanding possessed by the perceived,
    according to Kant
the perceiver's presuppositions about what is being perceived
    innate ideas about the world

Semilogical operations on the sensory inputs

unconscious inferences about the outer causes of the sensory inputs,
    according to Helmholtz (the outer world is deduced)
estimates of the probable character of the "distant" objects based on the
    "proximal" stimuli, according to Egon Brunswik (1956), said to be a
    quasirational, not a fully rational, process

Decoding operations on the sensory inputs

the interpreting of the inputs considered as signals (a very popular
    analogy with many variants)

the decoding of sensory messages
the utilizing of sensory cues
the understanding of signs, or indicators, or even *clues*, in the manner
of a police detective

The application of memories to the sensory inputs

the "accrual" of a context of memory images and feelings to the core of
sensations, according to E. B. Titchener's theory of perception (1924)

This last hypothetical process is perhaps the most widely accepted of all,
and the most elaborated. Perceptual learning is supposed to be a matter
of enriching the input, not of differentiating the information (Gibson and
Gibson 1955). But the process of combining memories with inputs turns
out to be not at all simple when analyzed. The appropriate memories
have to be retrieved from storage, that is, aroused or summoned; an
image does not simply accrue. The sensory input must fuse in some
fashion with the stored images; or the sensory input is assimilated to a
composite memory image, or, if this will not do, it is said to be assimilated to a class, a type, a schema, or a concept. Each new sensory input
must be categorized – assigned to its class, matched to its type, fitted to its
schema, and so on. Note that categories cannot become established until
enough items have been classified but that items cannot be classified until
categories have been established. It is this difficulty, for one, that compels
some theorists to suppose that classification is a priori and that people
and animals have innate or instinctive knowledge of the world.

The error lies, it seems to me, in assuming that either innate ideas or
acquired ideas must be applied to bare sensory inputs for perceiving to
occur. The fallacy is to assume that because inputs convey no knowledge
they can somehow be made to yield knowledge by "processing" them.
Knowledge of the world must come from somewhere; the debate is over
whether it comes from stored knowledge, from innate knowledge,

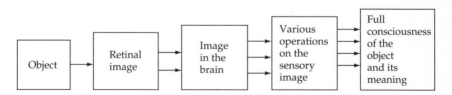

Figure 15.1   The commonly supposed sequence of stages in the visual perceiving
of an object.

or from reason. But all three doctrines beg the question. Knowledge of the world cannot be explained by supposing that knowledge of the world already exists. All forms of cognitive processing imply cognition so as to account for cognition.

All this should be treated as ancient history. Knowledge of the environment, surely, develops as perception develops, extends as the observers travel, gets finer as they learn to scrutinize, gets longer as they apprehend more events, gets fuller as they see more objects, and gets richer as they notice more affordances. Knowledge of this sort does not "come from" anywhere; it is got by looking, along with listening, feeling, smelling, and tasting. The child also, of course, begins to acquire knowledge that comes from parents, teachers, pictures, and books. But this is a different kind of knowledge.

References

Brunswik, E. (1956), *Perception and the Representative Design of Psychological Experiments*, Berkeley: University of California Press.

Gibson, J. J., and Gibson, E. J. (1955), Perceptual learning: differentiation or enrichment? *Psychological Review* 62: 32–41.

Helmholtz, J. (Translated 1925), *Physiological Optics*, vol. 3, ed. J. P. C. Southall, Optical Society of America.

Titchener, E. B. (1924), *A Textbook of Psychology*, New York: Macmillan.

How Direct is Visual Perception?
Some Reflections on Gibson's
"Ecological Approach"

Jerry A. Fodor and Zenon W. Pylyshyn

1   Introduction

. . .

The current Establishment theory (sometimes referred to as the "information processing" view) is that perception depends, in several respects presently to be discussed, upon *inferences*. Since inference is a process in which premises are displayed and consequences derived, and since that takes time, it is part and parcel of the information processing view that there is an intrinsic connection between perception and memory. And since, finally, the Establishment holds that the psychological mechanism of inference is the transformation of mental representations, it follows that perception is in relevant respects a computational process.

What makes Gibson's position seem outrageous from the Establishment perspective is that it is presented as an outright denial of every aspect of the computational account, not merely as a reformulation of parts of it. According to Gibson, the right way of describing perception is as the "direct pickup" of "invariant properties." (More precisely, we are taking Gibson to be claiming this: for any object or event x, there is some property P such that the direct pickup of P is necessary and sufficient for the perception of x.) Now, what is "direct" is *ipso facto* not mediated; in particular, according to Gibson, perception is not mediated by memory,

Jerry A. Fodor and Zenon W. Pylyshyn, "How Direct is Visual Perception? Some Reflections on Gibson's 'Ecological Approach,'" in *Cognition* 9 (1981), pp. 139–60, 165–6.

nor by inference, nor by any other psychological processes in which mental representations are deployed. Moreover, Gibson insists upon the radical consequences of his unorthodoxy: "The ecological theory of direct perception ... implies a new theory of cognition in general" (p. 263).[1]

In his last book, which will serve as the basis for our discussion, Gibson elaborates on the views he has arrived at after thirty years of research on perception, and on the bases of his disagreement with the Establishment position. The tone of the book, when it comes to Gibson's relation to received psychological theorizing is pretty intransigent:

> The simple assumption that the perception of the world is caused by stimuli from the world will not do. The more sophisticated assumption that perceptions of the world are caused when sensations triggered by stimuli are supplemented by memories will not do. ... Not even the current theory that the inputs of the sensory channels are subject to "cognitive processing" will do. The inputs are described in terms of information theory, but the processes are described in terms of old-fashioned mental acts: recognition, interpretation, inference, concepts, ideas and storage and retrieval of ideas. These are still the operations of the mind upon the deliverances of the senses, and there are too many perplexities entailed by this theory. It will not do, and the approach should be abandoned. ... What sort of theory, then, will explain perception? Nothing less than one based on the pickup of information. (p. 238)

> The theory of information pickup differs radically from the traditional theories of perception. First, it involves a new notion of perception, not just a new theory of the process. Second, it involves a new assumption about what there is to be perceived. Third, it involves a new concept of the information for perception. ... Fourth, it requires the new assumption of perceptual systems with overlapping functions. ... Finally, fifth, optical information pickup entails an activity of the system not heretofore imagined by any visual scientist... (p. 239)

> Such is the ecological approach to perception. It promises to simplify psychology by making old puzzles disappear. (p. 304)

We will suggest that there is a way of reading Gibson which permits the assimilation of many of his insights into the general framework of Establishment psychological theorizing. Moreover, given this conciliatory reading, much that Gibson says is seen to be both true and important; and it does indeed differ in significant respects from what has generally been assumed by psychologists who accept the information processing framework. But, as should be clear from the preceding quotes, Gibson *does not want* to be read in a conciliatory way. And for good reason: if the program as he presents it were to succeed, it would constitute a conceptual revolution on the grand scale. Many of the deepest problems in cognitive psychology and the philosophy of mind would be bypassed, and the future of research in both disciplines would be dramatically altered. Such a possibility may seem particularly attractive to those who believe that our current understanding of psychological processes has been too much influenced by the achievements of computer technology. And it will appeal, too, to those who feel that the antibehaviorist revolution in cognitive psychology has gone too far; a sentiment with which Gibson is by no means unsympathetic.

We will argue, however, that Gibson's claim to have achieved, or even to have initiated, such a fundamental reformulation of the theory of mind simply cannot be sustained. The main line of our argument will go like this: Gibson's account of perception is empty *unless* the notions of "direct pickup" and of "invariant" are suitably constrained. For, patently, if *any* property can count as an invariant, and if any psychological process can count as the pickup of an invariant, then the identification of perception with the pickup of invariants excludes nothing. We will show, however, that Gibson has no workable way of imposing the required constraints consonant with his assumption that perception is direct. To put the same point the other way around, our argument will be that the notion of "invariant" and "pickup" can be appropriately constrained only on the assumption that perception is inferentially mediated. This is hardly surprising: Gibson and the Establishment agree that pickup and inference exhaust the psychological processes that could produce perceptual knowledge; hence, the more pickup is constrained, the more there is left for inference to do.

It will turn out, in the case of visual perception, that at least two constraints upon pickup are required. First, nothing can be picked up except a certain restricted class of properties of the ambient light. Second, spatio-temporal bounds on the properties that are picked up are determined by what stimuli turn out to be "effective"; i.e., sufficient to cause perceptual judgments. The consequence of the first restriction is that all visual perception must involve inferences based upon those properties of the light that are directly detected; in particular, all visual perception of features of objects in the environment requires such inferences. The consequence of the second restriction is that visual perception typically involves inference from the properties of the environment that are (to use Gibson's term) "specified" by the sample of the light that one has actually encountered to those properties that would be specified by a more extensive sample. This sort of inference is required because the causally effective stimulus for perception very often underdetermines what is seen. These two kinds of inference are, however, precisely the ones that information processing theories have traditionally assumed must mediate visual perception. We will therefore conclude that Gibson has not offered a coherent alternative to the Establishment view; indeed, that the Establishment view falls out as a consequence of the attempt to appropriately constrain Gibson's basic theoretical apparatus.

2   The Trivialization Problem

The easiest way to see that constraints on the notion of invariant and pickup are required is to notice that, in the absence of such constraints, the claim that perception is direct is *bound* to be true simply because it is empty. Suppose that under certain circumstances people can correctly perceive that some of the things in their environment are of the type P. Since you cannot correctly perceive that something is P unless the thing is P, it will always be trivially true that the things that can be perceived to be P share an invariant property: namely, *being* P. And since, according to Gibson, what people do in perceiving is directly pick up an appropriate invariant, the following pseudoexplanation of any perceptual achievement is always available: to perceive that something is P is to pick up the (invariant) property P which things of that kind have. So, for example, we can give the following disarmingly simple answer to the question: how do people perceive that something is a shoe? There is a certain (invariant) property that all and only shoes have – namely, the property of being a shoe. Perceiving that something *is* a shoe consists in the pickup of this property.

It is quite true that if you do psychology this way, the old puzzles tend to disappear. For example many psychologists have wondered how somebody like Bernard Berenson managed to be so good at perceiving (i.e., telling just by looking) that some painting was an authentic Da Vinci. This problem is one of those that disappears under the new dispensation, since there is obviously some property that all and only genuine Da Vincis share; namely, the property, *having been painted by Da Vinci*. What Berenson did was simply to pick up this invariant.[2]

Clearly this will not do, and we do not suppose that Gibson thinks it will. Although he never discusses the issues in quite these terms, it is reasonably evident from Gibson's practice that he wishes to distinguish between what is *picked up* and what is *directly perceived*. In fact, Gibson ultimately accepts something like our first constraint – that what is picked up in visual perception is only certain properties of the ambient light array. Gibson is thus faced with the problem of how, if not by inferential mediation, the pickup of such properties of light could lead to perceptual knowledge of properties of the environment. That is: how, if not by inference, do you get from what you pick up about the light to what you perceive about the environmental object that the light is coming from? If Gibson fails to face this difficulty, it is because of a curious and characteristic turn in his theorizing: when he is being most careful, Gibson says that what is picked up is the *information* about the environment which is contained in the ambient array. We shall see that it is close to the heart of Gibson's problems that he has no way of construing the notion *the information in the ambient array* that will allow it to do the job that is required.

Pursuing the main course of Gibson's attempt to constrain the notion of pickup will thus bring us, eventually, to the notion of the "information in the light." There are, however, other passages in Gibson's writings that can also plausibly be viewed as attempts to impose constraints on the notions of pickup and invariance. We will discuss several of these proposals, but we want to emphasize that it is not clear which, if any, of them Gibson would endorse. This deserves emphasis because the constraints are not only non-coextensive, they are not even mutually consistent; and none of them is consistent with *all* of the things that Gibson describes as being directly perceived. So this is very much a matter of our reconstruction of Gibson's text. The reason it is worth doing is that we will argue that there is, in fact, *no* satisfactory way of constraining the notions of invariant and of pickup so as both to exclude the sort of trivialization discussed above and at the same time to sustain the thesis of unmediated perception; and to make such an argument one has to consider all the possible ways of interpreting Gibson's views.

2.1 First gambit: only the ecological properties of the environment are directly perceived

Gibson's last book starts with the observation that "Physics, optics, anatomy and physiology describe facts, but not facts at the level appropriate for the study of perception" (p. xiii). The first section of the book is then devoted to sketching an alternative taxonomy in terms of *ecological* properties of environmental objects and events. Gibson provides many examples of properties that are to count as ecological and some examples of properties that are not. The former include some properties of objects (for example, texture, shape, illumination, reflectance, and resistance to deformation are mentioned). There are also ecological properties of arrangements of objects and of surfaces. For example, being *open* or *cluttered* are ecological properties of what Gibson calls the "layout" of an environment (an open layout is one which consists of just a ground, horizon and sky; a cluttered layout is one that has objects scattered on the ground). Similarly, containing a hollow or an enclosure is to count as an ecological property of a layout.

This list by no means exhausts the examples that Gibson provides, nor are we to assume that the examples he provides exhaust the category of ecological properties. There is, however, one class of ecological properties which requires special mention: the "affordances." Affordances are certain properties of objects which somehow concern the goals and utilities of an organism. So, being edible is an affordance of certain objects, as is being capable of being used as a weapon or tool, being an obstacle, being a shelter, being dangerous or being a potential mate. Roughly, affordances are *dispositional* properties (because they concern what an organism *could* do with an object); and they are *relational* properties (because different organisms can do different things with objects of a given kind).

According to Gibson then, "the environment of any animal (and of all animals) contains substances, surfaces, and their layouts, enclosures, objects, places, events and other animals. ... The total environment is too vast for description even by the ecologist, and we should select those features of it that are perceptible by animals like ourselves" (p. 36). When, by contrast, Gibson gives examples of properties that are *not* ecological, they tend also to be properties that things *cannot be perceived to have*. "Perceiving" here means something like telling-by-looking. (Perceiving by the use of instruments does not count as a core case for Gibson.) So, properties like being made of atoms, or being a thousand light years away are offered as instances of *non*-ecological properties. This makes it seem as though Gibson has it in mind that "ecological" and "directly perceivable" should be interdefined, as is also suggested by the quotation just cited.

But, of course, that will not work. If the notion of an ecological property is to serve to constrain the notion of direct perception, then it cannot be stipulated to embrace all properties that are "perceptible by animals like ourselves." Consider again the property of being a shoe. This is clearly a property that we can perceive things to have, hence it is a property we can *directly* perceive, assuming that being ecological is a sufficient condition for being perceptible. But this means that introducing the construct "ecological property" has not succeeded in constraining the notion of direct perception in such a way as to rule out vacuous explanations like "the way that you perceive a shoe is by picking up the property it has of *being a shoe*." If all properties that can be perceived are *ipso facto* ecological, then the claim that perception is the pickup of ecological properties is vacuously true. What we need, of course, is some criterion for being ecological *other than perceptibility*. This, however, Gibson fails to provide.

2.2 Second gambit: only the projectible properties of ecological optics are directly perceived

We have just seen that if by "ecological properties" Gibson means *all* perceptible properties, then the notion of an ecological property will not serve to constrain the notion of direct pickup. Perhaps, then, only some independently specifiable subset of the ecological properties should count as directly perceptible. In particular, the directly perceptible properties might be the ones that figure in the laws of the science of "ecological optics."

There are, according to Gibson, *laws* about ecological properties of the environment. The laws that get discussed most in Gibson's text are the ones which connect ecological properties with features of the light that objects in the environment emit or reflect. For example, such laws connect certain sorts of discontinuities in the light array with the spatial overlap of surfaces of environmental objects; and they connect flow patterns in the light array with characteristic alterations of the relative spatial position of the observer and the object being observed. Similarly, Gibson presents the following "tentative hypothesis." "Whenever a perspective transformation of form or texture in the optic array goes to its limit and when a series of forms or textures are progressively foreshortened to this limit, a continuation of the surface of an object is specified as an occluding edge." Presumably, if this hypothesis is true, then the relation between the occlusion and the transformation of the textures is lawful, and the generalization that the hypothesis expresses is a law of ecological optics.

Now, it is generally held that laws of a science are distinguished by, among other things, characteristic features of their vocabulary (see Goodman 1954). Only certain sorts of predicates can appear in a law, those being the ones which pick out natural kinds in the domain that the law subsumes. We need such a notion of "natural kind" in order to explain a striking difference between laws and mere true generalizations: the former hold in counterfactual cases (hence, they apply to unexamined instances) and the latter do not.

Consider, for example, the following two generalizations: *all mammals have hearts* and *all mammals are born before 1982*. The point is that (as of this writing) *both generalizations hold for all the observed cases*. To date, there have been no observations of mammals without hearts, and there have been no observations of mammals born after 1982. The difference between the cases is that, whereas the observation of a large number of mammals with hearts (and none without) is grounds for believing that there *could be* no mammals without hearts, the observation of a large number of mammals born before 1982 (and none born after) provides no reason at all for believing that there could be no mammals born in 1983. The idea, then, is that the property *being born before 1982* fails to subsume a natural kind; it is not the sort of property in virtue of which things enter into lawful relations. Since generalizations about things which happen to have that property are not laws, there is no reason for believing that they will hold in *new* cases. The inductive "confirmation" of such generalizations provides no rational basis for making predictions.

We will borrow a term from the philosophy of science and refer to predicates that appear in laws as "projectible predicates," and we will say that projectible predicates express "projectible properties." To say that a predicate is *not* projectible is thus to say that there are no laws about the property that it expresses. For example, the predicate "is my grandmother's favorite metal" is nonprojectible since, presumably, there are no laws that apply to things in virtue of their being metal of my grandmother's favorite kind. Notice that this is still true even on the assumption that my grandmother's favorite metal is gold and that there *are* laws about gold. This is because *being my grandmother's favorite metal* and *being gold* are different properties, and the laws about gold would continue to hold even if my grandmother's taste in metals were to change. Coextensive properties may differ in projectibility. ...

To return to Gibson: the projectible ecological properties would be the ones which are connected, in a lawful way, with properties of the ambient light. It would thus be in the spirit of much of Gibson's text to suggest that it is the projectible ecological properties, and only those, that are the possible objects of direct visual perception. This would at least rule out the direct perception of such properties as having been painted by Da Vinci since, presumably, there are no laws, ecological or otherwise, which subsume objects in virtue of their possession of that property (whereas, on Gibson's assumptions, there *are* laws which subsume objects in virtue of such of their properties as their surface texture – see above).

As will presently become clear, we think that there is much to be said for explicating the notion of a directly detected property by reference to the notion of projectibility. Nevertheless, this move will not do much for Gibson, for the following reasons:

(a) Not all projectible properties are directly perceived on Gibson's view. For example, the projectible properties of classical optics are not; that is why you need *ecological* optics to construct a theory of visual perception. That classical optics fails to taxonomize properties in the ways that a theory of direct visual perception requires is, in fact, among Gibson's favorite themes. So, then, if the distinction between directly perceptible properties and others is to be explicated by reference to the projectible *ecological* properties, and if the explication is to be noncircular, we need a principled way of distinguishing between ecological laws and laws of other kinds. This, however, Gibson does not provide. Rather, insofar as Gibson is explicit about the matter at all, the notion of an ecological law is introduced by reference to the notion of an ecological property (e.g., ecological laws connect ecological properties to properties of the ambient light). But, as we have seen, the notion of an ecological property appears to be characterizable only by reference to the notion of a property that is directly perceivable (e.g., by "animals like ourselves"). And, of course, it was precisely the notion of direct perception that needed explication in the first place.

(b) Not all of the properties that Gibson wants to be directly perceptible are plausibly considered to be projectible; in particular, affordances usually are not projectible. There are, for example, presumably no laws about the ways that light is structured by the class of things that can be eaten, or by the class of writing implements, though being edible or being a writing implement are just the sorts of properties that Gibson talks of objects as affording. The best one can do in this area is to say that things which share their affordances often (though, surely, not always) have a characteristic shape (color, texture, size, etc.) and that there are laws which connect *the shape* (etc.) with properties of the light that the object reflects. But, of course, this consideration does Gibson no good, since it is supposed to be the affordances of objects, not just their shapes, that are directly perceived. In particular, Gibson is explicit in denying that the perception of the affordances of objects is mediated by inference from prior detection of their shape, color, texture, or other such "qualities."

In short, if we assume (as we should) that being a Da Vinci (or a pencil, or a shoe) is *not* projectible, we are in need of an explanation of how

184 Jerry A. Fodor and Zenon W. Pylyshyn

people perceive that some paintings are Da Vincis (or that some objects are shoes). The natural view would be: the Da Vincihood of an object (or its shoehood) is inferred from those of its (projectible) properties that are directly perceived. But this is the Establishment solution; precisely the one that Gibson is pledged to avoid.

As is customary with dilemmas, Gibson's has two horns. Either you trivialize the notion of a projectible property by stipulating that all perceptible properties are projectible; or you assume that some perceptible properties are not projectible, in which case you need to say how the perception of these nonprojectible properties is possible. The Establishment story is that the detection of nonprojectible properties is inferential, but that is the route that Gibson has eschewed. In either case, projectibility is not doing the job that Gibson needs done: viz. to provide a notion of direct perception that is simultaneously nonvacuous and compatible with the doctrine that perception is immediate.

2.3 Third gambit: only phenomenological properties are directly perceived

Introspection suggests that the world is perceptibly accessible under some descriptions but less so under others. A landscape, for example, is readily seen as containing fields, trees, sky, clouds, houses, shrubs, and stones. But it takes special training to see those properties of a landscape which a convincing *trompe l'oeil* painting would have to duplicate; typically, properties which depend on a fixed locus of observation. It is a matter of considerable significance that properties of the world that seem to be perceptually accessible are generally ones that children learn early to recognize and to name.

Suppose we call these relatively accessible properties of things their *phenomenological* properties. Then much of what Gibson says can be construed as suggesting that it is phenomenological properties, and only those, that are directly perceived. This may be what is at issue in Gibson's injunction that the environment must be described in *meaningful* terms: "the qualities of the world in relation to the needs of the observer are experienced directly", whereas "sensations triggered by light, sound, pressure and chemicals are merely incidental" (p. 246).

Phenomenological properties are accorded a similarly central role in Gibson's discussion of ontogenesis. "... the infant does not begin by first discriminating the qualities of objects and then learning the combinations of qualities that specify them. Phenomenological objects are not built up of qualities; it is the other way around. The affordance of an object is what the infant begins by noticing. The meaning is observed before the sub-stance and the surface, the color and the form, are seen as such" (p. 134).

If we go by introspection alone, the identification of the perceptually accessible properties with those that are directly perceived certainly seems plausible: phenomenological properties are precisely the ones which strike one as "given" rather than inferred. Gibson says such things as that "the perceiving of the world entails the coperceiving of where one is in the world and of being in the world and of being in the world at that place" (p. 200) and "the environment seen-at-this-moment does not constitute the environment that is seen" (p. 195). And these remarks (with which, by the way, Husserl would have been entirely comfortable) seem true enough in light of introspections of perceptual salience. There is a scale of phenomenological accessibility, and locations, objects, and affordances are high on this scale. Contrariwise, the "sensory properties" which function as the bases of perceptual inference in, for example, Helmholtzian versions of the Establishment theory, do seem to be very low in phenomenological accessibility.

There are, however, three objections to the proposal that we take the phenomenological properties to be directly perceived. The first is in-ternal: the proposal fails to include some of Gibson's own favorite examples of ecological invariants. For example, the slant of surfaces, the gradients and flows of textures, the amount of texture occluded by interposing objects, the moving occluding texture edge, etc., are *not* phenomenologically accessible. Witness the fact that it requires delicate experimentation to discover the central role that the detection of such properties plays in perception. Roughly, the present proposal has diffi-culties complementary to those of the suggestion that the object of direct perception is the projectible properties of ecological optics (see above); whereas the projectibility criterion leaves the affordances out, the phe-nomenological criterion lets almost only the affordances in. This is not surprising; you would not really expect the properties in virtue of which objects satisfy laws to be coextensive, in the general case, with those which are phenomenologically accessible. If such a general coextension held, doing science would be a lot easier than it has turned out to be.

Second, it seems at best a dubious strategy to infer direct perception from phenomenological salience: perhaps the latter is *solely* a phenom-enon of conscious access and tells us nothing about the nature of percep-tion *per se*. This is, in any event, a familiar claim of Establishment theories, and it is often rendered persuasive by experimental demonstrations that the perception of phenomenologically salient properties of the stimulus is causally dependent upon the detection of features whose phenomenological accessibility is negligible; properties of the stimulus which may, in fact, entirely escape the conscious notice of the subject. For example, Hess (1975) has shown that a variety of highly accessible perceived properties of faces – including their relative attractiveness – depends on the detection of the relatively *in*accessible property of pupilary diameter. In the light of such findings, Gibson cannot, in any event, establish the identification of directly perceived properties with phenomenologically salient ones by fiat; he cannot simply assume that what is most readily reported is what is noninferentially perceived.

Finally, we are going to need a *mechanism* for the direct perception of phenomenological properties, and it is hard to imagine one that will work in the case of properties like the affordances. It is, for example, not good enough merely to *say* that we directly perceive that a rock can be used as a weapon; we need an account of how the apprehension of such a property *could* be noninferential. We will see, presently, that Establishment theories do propose mechanisms for the direct pickup of certain sorts of stimulus properties; but it is a consequence of the Establishment proposal that affordances (and, indeed, most phenomenologically salient properties) are inferred rather than directly perceived. Gibson sometimes speaks of the perceptual mechanism as "resonating" to the values of ecological parameters that they are "tuned" to. But since a more detailed account does not appear to be forthcoming, the resonance metaphor amounts to little more than whistling in the dark. We shall return to this issue further on.

2.4   Fourth gambit: what is directly perceived is whatever "perceptual systems" respond to

It is a point that we will presently make much of – and that Gibson is reasonably clear about – that *all* theories of perception must acknowledge the direct pickup of *some* properties. In Establishment theories, what is directly picked up is often taken to be the properties to which *transducers* respond. There is a circle of interdefined notions here, a directly detected property being one to which a transducer responds, and a transducer being a mechanism that responds directly to the properties that it detects. One way that Establishment theories have of breaking out of this circle is by specifying – typically by enumeration – which organs are to count as transducers; for example, the retina in the case of vision and the tympanic membrane in the case of audition.

We shall have more to say about how the notion of transduction can be constrained presently, and we will argue that such specification by anatomical enumeration is inadequate. The present point is that Gibson recognizes that to specify what is to count as a perceptual organ is implicitly to constrain what a theory says is directly picked up. For example, if you think that the organ of visual transduction is the retina, and if you can show that the retina responds only to such properties as the wavelength and intensity of light, then you are committed to the view that only those properties are directly detected. Consequently, other properties of the light (and, *a fortiori*, all visual properties of distal objects) are apprehended only *indirectly*, presumably *via* processes that involve inference.

Gibson believes that the perceptual organs have been misidentified by Establishment theorists. Correspondingly, he claims that if one individuates the perceptual organs correctly, one gets a new and better census of the immediately perceived properties. So, "Helmholtz argued that we must deduce the causes of our sensations because we cannot detect them. ...The alternative is to assume that sensations triggered by light, sound pressure, and chemicals are merely incidental, that *information* is available to *perceptual systems*, and that the qualities of the world in relation to the needs of the observer are experienced directly" (p. 246, emphasis added). It is a moral of *The Ecological Approach to Visual Perception*, and it is the main point of *The Senses Considered as Perceptual Systems* (Gibson 1966) that the "perceptual system" for vision is the entire complex consisting of "first, the lens, pupil, chamber and the retina. ...Second, the eye with its muscles in the orbit. ...Third, the two eyes in the head. ...Fourth, the eyes in a mobile head that can turn. ...Fifth, the eyes in a head on a body..." (p. 245). It is the discriminative capacity of this system – *and not the discriminative capacity of the retina* – which determines what vision can, in principle, detect.

We can certainly grant that the class of properties to which this complex system is specifically "tuned" – the class of properties it can "directly respond to" – may not be the class of properties that Establishment theories have usually taken to be visually transduced. (It is far from clear that it will be the class of ecological properties either. But as we remarked above, the criteria we are ascribing to Gibson for selecting candidate objects of direct visual perception are not, in general, coextensive.) So, Gibson is right to claim that reparsing the system of perceptual organs provides for, or at least permits, a new census of directly detected properties. It follows that *if* Gibson had a motivated criterion for deciding what is to count as a perceptual system, he would *ipso facto* have a principled way of constraining the notion of direct pickup.

But Gibson provides *no* criterion for identifying perceptual systems, or even for circumscribing which organs can in general be regarded as parts of the same perceptual system. For example, it is notable that Gibson's enumeration of the parts of the visual system does not include the brain. Inasmuch as Gibson emphasizes that perceptual systems can overlap (different such systems may share anatomically individuated organs) this exclusion seems, to put it mildly, unmotivated. If, however, the brain *is* included as a component of the visual system, then presumably the properties that the visual system can pick up would *ipso facto* be coextensive with the properties that people can visually perceive and we are back where we started. We still want independent characterizations of "perceive" and "pick up directly" if the identification of perception with direct pickup is to amount to an empirical hypothesis.

It is clear from Gibson's discussion of perceptual systems that he intends to individuate them functionally rather than anatomically, a decision which we applaud. The problem is that the proposed criteria of individuation are so flexible that the notion of "perceptual system" actually provides *no* constraint on what might count as a "directly detected" invariant. According to Gibson, there are five overlapping perceptual systems, each of which can "orient, explore, investigate, adjust, optimize, and come to an equilibrium. ..." The functioning of these systems is explicitly *not* limited to the transduction of impinging stimulation. Rather, the responses of perceptual systems are "specific to the qualities of things in the world, especially affordances" (p. 246). Furthermore, the nature of the information which such systems can pick up "becomes more and more subtle, elaborate and precise with practice." Given the unbounded scope of the activities that perceptual systems can perform, there would seem to be nothing in the notion that prevents the detection of shoes, grandmothers, genuine Da Vincis, performances of Beethoven's Kreutzer Sonata, or authentic autographs of George Washington all being possible "achievements of perceptual systems." It looks as though whatever is perceived is *ipso facto* the proper object of a perceptual system, and whatever is the proper object of a perceptual system is *ipso facto* perceived directly; we have, in particular, no independent constraints on the individuation of perceptual systems that will permit us to break into this chain of interdefinitions.

The moral of all this is that to define the directly perceivable in terms of what perceptual systems respond to is merely to shift the locus of trivialization from the former notion to the latter. It puts the same pea under a different shell. We believe that there *are* ways of constraining the notion of a perceptual mechanism – via an independent characterization of transduction – but the price you pay is that many perceptual processes turn out to be *non*transductive, hence presumably inferential. This is Gibson's characteristic dilemma, and we claim that he has no way out of it.

2.5   The problem of misperception

In much of the preceding discussion we have emphasized the undesirable consequences of interdefining "pick up," "invariant," "ecological property," and "directly perceive," but that is not the only difficulty with Gibson's approach. Part of an adequate theory of perception ought to be an account of perceptual *errors*, and it is hard to see how this requirement can be squared with the claim that perception is direct on *any* of the interpretations that Gibson's text suggests.

People who have tried to understand the nature of the mind, at least since Plato, have been particularly worried about the problem of false belief. In the present context, this is the problem of explaining how *misperception* is possible. The standard approach to this problem within Establishment theories is to connect misperception with failed inference. Your perception that something is edible, for example, is said to depend upon inferences from the appearance of the thing (e.g., from its smell, taste, texture, shape, color, and so forth). These inferences depend upon generalizations gleaned from past experience, and the generalizations are themselves nondemonstrative, and hence fallible. So, for these and other reasons, the (perceptual) inference from appearance to edibility sometimes goes wrong, with consequences that are typically painful and occasionally fatal.

Now consider how a noninferential story about misperception might go. Here we get a first glimpse of a dilemma that emerges, in various guises, throughout Gibson's text. If "directly perceive that" is taken to be factive, then by stipulation "x directly perceives that y is edible" will entail that y is edible. It follows that what goes on when one misperceives something as edible cannot be the direct perception of edibility. If, on the other hand, "directly perceive that" is *not* taken to be factive, then it is logically possible to, as it were, directly *misperceive* that something is edible. But Gibson will then need an account of what has gone wrong when misperception is direct. Notice, in particular, that he *cannot* account for such cases by saying that what you pick up when you directly misperceive the edibility of a thing is the property of *apparent* edibility. For, things that are misperceived to be edible *do* have the property of being *apparently* edible, and the problem for a theory of misperception is to explain how things could be taken to have properties that in fact they do *not* have. (A way out would be to say that you pick up the apparent edibility and *infer* the edibility from that; but this just *is* the Establishment way out and, of course, it is closed to Gibson.)

Probably the line that Gibson wants to take is that *if* an affordance is correctly perceived, *then* it is perceived directly; and that is, of course compatible with the factivity of "directly perceive." Notice, however, that such an approach does not help with the problem of misperception, since it does not tell us how we are to describe the cases where the antecedent of the hypothetical is *false.* We will return to this sort of difficulty. Suffice it at present to say that the problem of constraining "directly perceive" so as to provide a nonvacuous construal of the claim that perception is noninferential, and the problem of providing a coherent account of misperception without recourse to the notion of perceptual inference, are two sides of the same coin. No wonder Gibson is so unhappy about the role that appeals to illusions have played in the confirmation of Establishment theories of perception.

If a theory of perception is to be tenable it must not only address the most common (veridical) cases, but also the ones in which perception fails to be veridical and leads to false beliefs. The relative infrequency of the latter sorts of cases does not alter this principle (and, in fact, they are arguably not all that infrequent; only they tend to escape our notice except when the consequences are serious). Gibsonians sometimes urge that we should take very seriously the fact that perception works most of the time (see Reed and Jones 1978), and it is true that this fact is of central importance for epistemology. But the goal of psychological theory construction is not to predict most (or even all) of the variance; it is to explicate the underlying mechanisms upon whose operation the variance depends. It seems quite inconceivable that the psychological mechanisms of perception and the psychological mechanisms of misperception are different *in kind.*

This problem is such a serious one that it sometimes drives Gibsonians to truly desperate recourses. For example, Turvey and Shaw (1979) suggest that we should cope with the issue of perceptual error by "tak[ing] perception out of the propositional domain in which it can be said to be either right or wrong... and relocat[ing] it in a nonpropositional domain in which the question of whether perception is right or wrong would be nonsensical" (p. 182). Apparently, this means either that we should stop thinking of perception as eventuating in beliefs, or that we should stop thinking of beliefs as having truth values. Turvey and Shaw describe this proposal as "radical," but "suicidal" might be the more appropriate term.

Perhaps the most characteristic Gibsonian move in this area is to identify misperception with failure to pick up "all the relevant information" (the bird flies into the window because it failed to pick up the ambient information that specifies *window*). But, of course, pickup of the very light structures which failed to specify *window* for the bird might be adequate to specify *window* for *us*. From a mentalistic point of view, this is not surprising; we know a lot more about windows than birds do. So, the form of the problem for Gibson is to explain how pickup of the very same state of affairs that constitutes an adequate sample of information for one organism could constitute an inadequate sample for another. The Establishment account has an answer: viz. that what you perceive depends not only on the ambient information picked up, but also on the mental processes deployed in processing that information. It is far from clear what alternative the Gibsonian position could propose.

3 The Problem of Direct Detection in Establishment Theories

Our argument thus far has been that unless the notions of pickup and invariant are constrained, it will always be trivially true that there is an invariant property whose pickup is necessary and sufficient for the perception of any object: viz. the property of being that object. We have also argued that some doctrines of Gibson's which can plausibly be construed as attempts to provide the relevant constraints do not succeed in doing so.

Though these considerations raise problems for Gibson's theory, it is important to understand that all other theories, including Establishment theories, have problems of a corresponding sort. This is because even theories that hold that the perception of many properties is inferentially mediated must assume that the detection of *some* properties is direct (in the sense of *not* inferentially mediated). Fundamentally, this is because inferences are processes in which one belief causes another. Unless some beliefs are fixed in some way other than by inference, it is hard to see how the inferential processes could get started. Inferences need premises.[3]

To admit this is not, however, to endorse any "foundationalist" view of epistemology: to say that the pickup of some properties must be non-inferential is not to say that our knowledge of these properties is infallible, or that the justification of perceptual beliefs depends upon assuming that the mechanisms of direct pickup are epistemologically privileged. Many philosophers have held that the deliverances of direct perception must figure centrally in the arguments which justify our perceptually based knowledge claims, but it is quite unnecessary to read this sort of moral from Establishment perceptual psychology.

The psychologist's topic is the causation of perceptual judgments, not the establishment of epistemic warrant in justificatory arguments. One can perfectly well hold – as in fact we are inclined to do – both that matters of epistemic warrant are typically determined by "inference to the best explanation" and that the causation of perceptual judgments typically involves inferences from premises which are not themselves inferred. The causal chain in perception typically flows "inward" from the detection of those properties to which peripheral transducers respond. But the flow of epistemic justification typically goes in every which way since the justification of perceptual knowledge claims is heavily constrained by principles of conservatism, parsimony, and coherence. In what follows, then, the epistemological issues will be put completely to one side: we make no assumptions about the epistemological role of whatever is directly detected;[4] for us, "direct" means only "noninferential."

One can distinguish at least two proposals that Establishment theories have made about how to draw the line between what is directly detected and what is inferentially mediated. On some views, especially the older, epistemologically based theories, the distinction between direct detection and inferential mediation is taken to be coextensive with the distinction between "sensory" properties and the rest. Typically, the sensory properties are characterized by introspective availability, and often enough it is assumed that the deliverances of introspection are infallible; hence the putative connection between perceptual immediacy and epistemic warrant that we noted in the preceding paragraph. Gibson holds, and we think that he is right about this, that the appeal to introspection will not do the job. In fact, as we saw when we discussed the "phenomenological" criterion for direct detection, what is introspectively accessible is typically not the traditional sensory properties (color, two-dimensional form, etc.) but rather "meaningful" properties like the affordances. When Gibson says that "phenomenological objects are not built up of qualities; it is the other way around" (p. 134) he is quite right about the deliverances of introspection. Since, however, traditional theorizing is precisely concerned to treat properties that are on the level of the affordances as *inferred*, it very early abandoned the identification of what is directly detected with what is introspectively available. If, however, the sensory properties are *not* identifiable with the ones that are introspectively available, it does not help much to say that sensory properties are what we detect directly, the former notion being as unclear as the latter.

Recent versions of the Establishment theory have sought to constrain the notion of direct detection by identifying the properties that are available without inferential mediation with those to which transducer mechanisms are sensitive. This transfers the problem of constraining "directly detectible property" to the problem of constraining "mechanism of transduction" and, contrary to assumptions that appear to be widely made, specifying what is allowed to count as a transducer for the purposes of cognitive theory is a nontrivial problem. For example, transducers are technically defined as mechanisms which convert information from one physical form to another. But this definition is entirely compatible with there being transducers for *any* pattern of stimulation to which the organism can respond selectively since *whole organisms* are, in that sense, transducers for any category to which they can reliably assign things; e.g., for sentences, or shoes, or, in Berenson's case, for Da Vincis. This is precisely Gibson's problem as it arises in the context of Establishment theories, and to fail to grasp its seriousness is to fail to understand the challenge that Gibson poses to the Establishment. The theory that perception is typically direct is empty barring an independent construal of pickup; *but so too is the theory that perception is typically inferential.* On the other hand, it should be borne in mind that the Establishment does not accept Gibson's condition on the solution of this problem; viz. that the objects of direct detection (transduction) must be so specified that no perceptual judgments turn out to be inferentially mediated. We think that Gibson's position is hopeless precisely because pickup can be constrained only if that condition is abandoned. ...

4   The First Constraint on Pickup: What is Picked Up in (Visual) Perception is Certain Properties of the Ambient Light

We begin by considering a fundamental construct in Gibson's theory, the notion that states of affairs can *contain information about* one another. The basic idea is that the state of affairs S1 contains information about the state of affairs S2 if and only if S1 and S2 have correlated properties. Suppose that S1 consists of a's having property F and S2 consists of b's having property G. Then if, in general, x's having property F is correlated with y's having property G, then S1 contains information about S2.

As Gibson repeatedly remarks, this is an entirely "objective," nonpsychological notion of information. Information in this sense is something "in the world," just as correlation is. In particular, information-cum-correlation is not something that is encoded, or transmitted, or stored;

though it is, according to Gibson, "picked up" whenever anything is perceived.

But, whereas information is an ontological category, *specification* is an epistemological one. The idea is basically that when two states of affairs are correlated, the organism can use the occurrence of one to find out about the other. Under such circumstances, the first state of affairs is said to *specify* the second (for that organism). Correlation (hence information) is presumably a necessary condition for specification: when S1 specifies S2, S1 and S2 are correlated,[5] and S1 contains information about S2. Gibson's favorite example is the relation of specification that holds between features of the ambient light and features of the distal environmental layout. Features of the light are correlated with features of the layout in virtue of the regularities expressed by laws of ecological optics. The structure of the light therefore contains information about the character of the layout; and, since organisms actually use that information in the perceptual identification of layout features, the structure of the light is said to specify the character of the layout.

Now, the relation of *containing information about* is symmetrical, but, in the general case, the relation of *specifying* is not. Suppose that the state of the layout is correlated in a certain way with the state of the light. While it is then true that the properties of the light contain information about the properties of the layout, it is equally true that the properties of the layout contain information about the properties of the light. However, for no organism that we know of – barring, perhaps, the occasional ecological optician – does the structure of the layout specify the light. Organisms just do not use the properties of the layout to find out how the light is arranged. Notice that that is not because the information is not there. Since the two are correlated you could, in principle, determine the structure of the light given the facts about the layout (and about the correlations) just as you can, in principle, determine the structure of the layout given the facts about the light (and about the correlations). And this raises a problem, though not one that Gibson discusses in these terms: viz. *what determines the direction of specification?*

As soon as the problem is put this way, the principle at issue seems clear enough. What determines the direction of specification is the nature of the detectors (transducers) available to the organism. Light specifies layout and not vice versa precisely because we have transducers for light and no transducers for layout. If we had transducers for layout and no transducers for light, then any specification relation that held between the two would have to go in the opposite direction. The moral is: if we are in a position to say what the direction of specification is for a given organism, then that fact constrains our attribution of transducer mechanisms to the organism. The attribution of transducers must serve (*inter alia*) to explain the facts about the direction of specification for the organism.

So we have a constraint on transduction. But how is this constraint to be applied? In particular, how do you tell which sorts of states of affairs serve as specifiers for a given organism? Given correlated states of affairs, how do you tell which specifies which? The answer is sufficiently obvious. What you do is, you break the correlation experimentally (you set up a case in which the correlation fails) and then you see what happens.[6]

Consider the following simple examples. How do we know that the light specifies the layout and not vice versa? Well, we can create paired situations in one of which we preserve the features of the light without the corresponding layout, and in the other of which we preserve the features of the layout without the corresponding light. The presentation of a hologram would be an example of the first kind; turning out the lights would be an example of the second kind. There is no dispute about what would happen in such experiments. You can vary the layout as much as you like; so long as the properties of the light are unaffected, the perceptual judgments of the organism are unaffected too. On the other hand, leaving the layout intact does you no good if the structure of the light is changed. In the extreme case, take the light away, and the organism cannot see.

In short, the way you determine which of a pair of correlated states of affairs specifies the other is by applying the "method of differences," in which one determines which of two factors is the cause of some effect by setting up a situation in which only one of the factors is operative. . . .

5   The "Information in the Light"

The main point of our discussion was to establish some conditions on the notion *detection* (transduction). We needed to do this because we doubted that the notion *could* be appropriately constrained consonant with the doctrine that perception is, in the general case, not inferentially mediated. We are now in a position to see one of the ways in which the conflict arises; indeed, one of the respects in which the Gibsonian model of visual perception is after all committed to inferential mediation, just as Establishment models are.

The first point to notice is that Gibson actually agrees with much of what we have been saying, although the terminology he employs sometimes obscures the consensus. Gibson makes a distinction (largely implicit, and not invariably honored) between what he describes as "directly perceived" and what he describes as "picked up." The latter locution is usually reserved for features of the light, while the former is usually used for features of the layout. Moreover, Gibson seems to agree that picking up features of the light is causally necessary for "directly perceiving" features of the layout. Notice that, in this respect, Gibson's view is simply indistinguishable from the Establishment theory. Where Gibson speaks of directly perceiving features of the layout in consequence of picking up features of the light, the Establishment theory speaks of perceiving features of the layout in consequence of transducing features of the light. Thus far, the differences are merely terminological. The important fact is the agreement that the subject's epistemic relation to the structure of the light is different from his epistemic relation to the layout of the environment, and that the former relation is causally dependent upon the latter.

There is, however, this difference: the classical theory has a story about *how you get from detected properties of the light to perceived properties of the layout*. The story is that you infer the latter from the former on the basis of (usually implicit) knowledge of the correlations that connect them. Gibson clearly does not like this story, but it is quite unclear how he is going to get along without it. It is all very well to call your epistemic relation to layout features "direct perception," but if it is agreed that that relation is dependent upon an epistemic relation to properties of the light, "direct" certainly cannot be taken to mean "unmediated." The basic problem for Gibson is that picking up the fact that the light is so-and-so is *ipso facto* a *different* state of mind from perceiving that the layout is so-and-so. In the normal case, states of mind like the first are causally necessary to bring about states of mind like the second (and they are normally causally sufficient for organisms which have had appropriate experience of the ways in which light states and layout states are correlated). Some process *must* be postulated to account for the transition from one of these states of mind to the other, and it certainly looks as though the appropriate mechanism is inference. The point is that Gibson has done nothing to avoid the need to postulate such a process; it arises as soon as "direct detection" is appropriately constrained. And he has suggested no alternative to the proposal that the process comes down to one of drawing perceptual inferences from transducer outputs; in the present state of the art that proposal is, literally, the only one in the field. . . .

Notes

1 All references are to Gibson (1979) except as otherwise noted.

2 The problem that we are raising against Gibson is, to all intents and purposes, identical to one that Chomsky (1959) raised against Skinner. Chomsky writes: "A typical example of *stimulus control* for Skinner would be the response...to a painting...*Dutch*. (Such responses are said by Skinner to be) 'under the control of extremely subtle properties of the physical object or event' (p. 108). Suppose instead of saying *Dutch* we said *Clashes with the wallpaper, I thought you liked abstract work, Never saw it before*..., or whatever else might come into our minds when looking at a picture...Skinner could only say that each of these responses is under the control of some other stimulus property of the physical object. If we look at a red chair and say *red*, the response is under the control of the stimulus *redness*; if we say *chair*, it is under the control of (the property) *chairness*, and similarly for any other response. This device is as simple as it is empty...properties are free for the asking..." (p. 52 in Block, 1980; Chomsky's page reference is to Skinner, 1957). If one substitutes "the property picked up in perception" for "the stimulus property controlling behavior," it becomes apparent how similar in strategy are Skinner's antimentalism and Gibson's. There is, however, this difference: Skinner proposes to avoid vacuity by requiring that the "controlling stimulus" be physically specified, at least in principle. Chomsky's critique thus comes down to the (correct) observation that there is no reason to believe that anything physically specifiable *could* play the functional role *vis-à-vis* the causation of behavior that Skinner wants controlling stimuli to play; the point being that behavior is in fact the joint effect of impinging stimuli *together with the organism's mental states and processes*. Gibson has the corresponding problem of avoiding triviality by somehow constraining the objects of direct perception; but, as we shall see, he explicitly rejects the identification of the stimulus properties that get picked up with physical properties.

3 There is, nevertheless, a sense in which all perceptual processes, strictly so called, might be inferential. Perception is usually taken to affect what the organism knows, and it is conceivable that transducer-detected properties are epistemically inaccessible to the organism and subserve no purposes except those of perceptual integration. (Cf. Stich's (1978) discussion of "subdoxastic" states.) In that case, these non-inferential processes are nonperceptual, as it were, by definition. In deference to this consideration, we have generally avoided talking of transduced properties as directly *perceived*, preferring the less tendentious "directly picked up." Of course, this terminological issue does not jeopardize the observation in the text that processes of perceptual inference must begin from premises that are not themselves inferred. The present question is just whether the noninferential processes of

pickup which make such premises available should themselves be referred to as perceptual. ...

4   Some Gibsonians apparently want to read a sort of epistemological Realism as one of the morals of theories of direct perception (see, for example, Turvey 1977), but that would seem quite unjustifiable. On the one hand, *every* theory will have to acknowledge the fact of at least *some* misperception, and if one is going to run skeptical arguments in epistemology, that is the premise one needs to get them started (e.g., "if you admit that perception is sometimes fallible, what reason is there to suppose that it isn't always wrong? ... " etc.). If you find such arguments persuasive, the idea that perception is direct *when it is veridical* will do nothing to soothe the skeptical itch, since that idea is compatible with the possibility that perception is *never* veridical. Correspondingly, an inference based theory of perception is perfectly compatible with a Realistic account of the information that perception delivers. All that is required for a perceptual inference to yield knowledge is that it should be sound. Gibson's views have philosophical implications, but not for epistemology.

5   Strictly, S1 and S2 are tokens of correlated types. We will not be explicit about the type token relation except where the intention is not clear from context.

6   Of course, knowing the physical/physiological structure of the organism can provide some constraints upon the assignment of transducers, since if there is *no* mechanism that is differentially sensitive to a given form of input energy, then that form of input *cannot* be a specifier for that organism. However, as we remarked above, this consideration does less than might be supposed since, in the general case, practically any form of ambient energy is likely to have *some* effect on the organism's neurological condition, and it is functional considerations which must decide which such effects are to count as transductions.

References

Block, N. (ed.) (1980), *Readings in Philosophy of Psychology*, Cambridge, MA: Harvard University Press.

Chomsky, N. (1959), a review of B. F. Skinner's *Verbal Behavior*. Reprinted in N. Block (ed.), *Readings in Philosophy of Psychology*, vol. 1. Cambridge, MA: Harvard University Press.

Gibson, J. (1966), *The Senses Considered as Perceptual Systems*, Boston: Houghton Mifflin.

Gibson, J. (1979), *The Ecological Approach to Visual Perception*, Boston: Houghton Mifflin.

Goodman, N. (1954), *Fact, Fiction and Forecast*, London: Athlone Press.

Hess, E. (1975), The role of pupil size in communication. Reprinted in Atkinson and Atkinson (eds.), *Mind and Behavior: Readings from "Scientific American,"* San Francisco: W. H. Freeman, 1980.

Reed, E. and Jones, R. (1978), Gibson's theory of perception: a case of hasty epistemologizing, *Philosophy of Science* 45: 519–30.

Skinner, B. F. (1957), *Verbal Behavior*, New York: Appleton Century Crofts.

Stich, S. (1978), Beliefs and subdoxastic states, *Philosophy of Science* 45: 499–518.

Turvey, M. (1977), Contrasting orientations to the theory of visual information processing, *Psychological Review* 84: 67–88.

Turvey, M. and Shaw, R. (1979), The primacy of perceiving: an ecological reformulation of perception for understanding memory. In L. G. Nillson (ed.), *Perspectives on Memory Research Essays in Honor of Uppsala University's 500th Anniversary*, New Jersey: Erlbaum.

17

Inference in Perception

Irvin Rock

The thesis of this [chapter] is that perception is intelligent in that it is based on the same kinds of operations that characterize thought. However, the dependence of perception on sensory information makes for certain differences between it and "higher" cognitive functions such as imagination and thinking. Clearly the phenomenal experience of a percept is different from that of thought. Still the processes underlying these different mental end products may be quite similar. Although we know little about the nature of thought, a demonstration that perception results from cognitve operations does constitute an explanation. Others seek to explain perception in very different ways.

To turn the problem around so to speak, it is entirely possible that thinking evolved from perception. Perception might be the evolutionary link between low-level sensory processes that mediated simple detection of environmental changes in phylogenetically primitive organisms and high-level cognitve processes.

To paraphrase what William McDougall said about instinct, perception too seems to be shot through with intelligence. The following example will illustrate this claim. One views either a stereogram such as the one in figure 17.1 or an anaglyph through red and green filters in order to achieve an illusory depth effect. Because the picture is in fact flat, we know we have isolated binocular disparity as the source of depth perception. After looking at the display for a while one experiences a strong, realistic depth. Part of the display, for example the inner rectangle in figure 17.1 should appear to be floating in space well behind the larger one. So much for preconditions.

Irvin Rock, "Inference in Perception," in *Proceedings of the Philosophy of Science Association* 2 (1982), pp. 525–40.

Figure 17.1   To fuse the two half-views of the stereogram one holds a cardboard midway between them at right angles to the page and tries to view the left figure with the left eye and the right one with the right eye by imagining one is looking through them at a more distant object.

What happens when one now moves one's head? As the reader can verify for him- or herself, the object that appears behind, the small rectangle, seems to move in the direction opposite to that in which the head moves. (If the depth should happen to be reversed, with the small rectangle seen in front, then during head movement it will appear to move in the same direction the head moves.) That is the effect. What is the explanation? Although a few authors have referred to this effect from time to time and it is known to most experts in the field, it remains an essentially unexplained phenomenon. Yet it is not so mysterious. If normally a shifting of the retinal images of things (or parallax change) occurs during head motion viewing three dimensional scenes, what should we expect when there is zero parallax change during head motion as is the case here (because there is no real depth)? This anomalous condition must lead to an impression of object motion if the perceptual system is governed in its operations by certain rules. In point of fact, only an object moving at just the right speed could nullify the parallax change that would ordinarily occur with a certain speed of head motion. However, the illusory effect makes very clear that the system is following rules or at least deducing from rules what must be the case under these novel conditions of stimulation. It is worth emphasizing that this effect will undoubtedly occur even though these particular conditions may never have been encountered before.

Yet few students of perception believe that this outcome is actually the result of an intelligent process analogous to reasoning. A phenomenon may appear to be intelligent but the mechanism underlying it may have no common ground with the mechanisms underlying reasoning, logical thought, or problem-solving. Thus, for example, the web of a spider is certainly a remarkable feat of engineering but that hardly means that anything analogous to thought is operating in its construction.

It is fair to say there are good reasons for the majority view. Perception is experienced as instantaneous rather than discursive as is thought. There is no awareness of any thought taking place, i.e., it is unconscious, which many may regard as a contradiction in terms. Perception is usually not affected by what we know on a conceptual level about the prevailing objective state of affairs, e.g., we experience geometrical and other illusions even when we know they are illusions which may lead some to say that perception is inflexible and stupid, not intelligent. There is evidence that the perception of some object or spatial properties is innately determined and not dependent upon past experience although reasoning has been assumed to be closely linked to prior learning and experience. There is good reason for believing that many animal species and young children perceive the world in much the way we do and many would be unwilling to believe that such organisms achieve their perceptions on the basis of a process that parallels those that mediate reasoning in man. These are legitimate objections, but I will have time to address only some of them in this talk.

What distinguishes perception from other modes of cognition (such as imagination or dreaming or thought) is that perception is the mental representation of external objects and events that is based upon or in some way corresponds to the stimuli reaching our sense organs. That being the case, it seems to me that a priori there are only a limited number of theories that can explain perception, in fact three distinct kinds: stimulus theory, spontaneous interaction theory, and cognitive theory.

The basic idea behind the stimulus theory is that for every distinct kind of perceptual property – of color, size, depth, movement, and the like – there is a unique stimulus (or type of stimulus information) reaching the sense organ. Nothing more is considered necessary by way of explanation of perception than to isolate the relevant stimulus (or the neural representation of it in the sense organ or brain). Obviously, by the very definition of perception, there *is* some unique stimulus that enters into the chain of events that leads to any particular percept. Therefore, of course, a particular stimulus is at the very least a necessary determinant of a particular perception. Yet the isolation of the relevant stimulus does not provide a sufficient account of perception.

Logically, a given local stimulus is only an ambiguous indicator of the relevant property of the object producing it. For example, an image of a given size, measured by the visual angle it subtends at the eye, will be produced by a whole family of objects of varying sizes, each at a different distance (see figure 17.2(a)). Thus the perceptual system could never determine from an image's visual angle alone what the size of the object that produced it is. The same is true analogously for image shape with respect to object shape (see figure 17.2(b)) (because the slant of the object can vary), and other aspects of the proximal stimulus with respect to

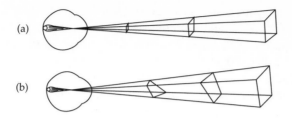

Figure 17.2

other object properties. Nonetheless, such object properties are not ambiguous in perception.

There is another kind of ambiguity of the stimulus that concerns the qualitative character of the percept and here perception *is* ambiguous in that given the same stimulus one may perceive it differently at different times. Moreover the stimulus pattern or sequence is reversible and we speak of reversible figures. Well-known examples of it are Rubin's vase-face figure and reversible perspective patterns such as the Necker cube.

So we see that the same stimulus (at least one defined locally) can give rise to varying percepts. Conversely, differing stimuli (at least if defined in the same way) can give rise to the same percept. Object constancy illustrates this last statement, where for example an object will appear the same in size or shape despite variations in the proximal stimulus it yields.

To get around these central difficulties with a stimulus theory, James Gibson (1950, 1966) and others during the last several decades suggested that we redefine the stimulus. The argument is that perception is based on stimulus relationships, or higher-order features of the stimulus, rather than locally defined absolute features. This step does indeed seem to resolve some of the problems of ambiguity to which I just referred. It builds upon the insights of the Gestalt psychologists who emphasized the importance of stimulus relationships and contextual effects. The trouble with this modified stimulus theory, however, is that the allegedly determining invariant higher-order stimulus information is neither necessary nor sufficient. It is not necessary because one can obtain constancy effects under reduction conditions, e.g., in a dark room where only the single object under study is visible. As long as certain "cues," e.g. cues to distance such as the accommodative state of the lens and the convergence of the eyes, are allowed, the object's properties such as size are perceived more or less veridically. The higher-order stimulus information is not sufficient because, when in a direct test, it is provided (but other kinds of information such as the "cues" just mentioned are eliminated) then object perception is only moderately affected by stimulus relationships.

Moreover there are other serious difficulties with this approach, among which is its failure to deal with the problem of perceptual organization. Such organization is an achievement of the perceptual system, not something that can be said to be given by the stimulus, no matter how the latter is defined.

The final difficulty for a stimulus theory is a fact that can hardly be denied, namely that what we perceive is in certain respects enriched by mental contents *not* given in the present stimulus. For example, by definition, the phenomenal experience of familiarity and meaning derive from past experience. Here, while other perceptual properties remain unchanged, most objects do appear familiar and we do have an immediate sense of what they are or what their function is. The first time we encountered them this was not the case. But other object properties may also be affected by prior experience. It is evident that figures such as the one shown in figure 17.3 look different once they are identified than they do prior to that moment. They take on the perceptual properties of the object they represent – such as three-dimensionality – and they are organized differently. For readers who have not succeeded in recognizing figure 17.3, it may be helpful to identify it: a picture of a child on a tricycle. Clearly there is an enrichment of perception here based on a contribution from memory. The attribute in memory is somehow entering into the overall perceptual experience. Therefore the stimulus alone, no matter how defined, does not do justice to the perception.[1]

One way of resolving these difficulties or some of these difficulties is to maintain that the correlate of a perception is not the stimulus, no matter how defined, but spontaneous interactions between the neural representations of several stimuli. The essence of this kind of theory is that the correlate of a percept is not simply (and perhaps is never) the projected neural representation of the stimulus in question but rather more complex interactive brain events that ensue following stimulation and that can allow for effects such as those already mentioned. But this is *not* a cognitive theory any more than is the stimulus theory since no reference is made or need be made to thoughtlike processes such as description, rule-following, inference, or problem-solving.

Figure 17.3

To give a well-known example, it was suggested by Max Wertheimer (1912) in his research that launched the Gestalt movement, that apparent (or stroboscopic) movement perception results from a flow of electrical energy back and forth from the loci in the brain where the signals from the separately flashing stimuli terminate. While this hypothesis is no longer seriously entertained, it does capture the flavor and intent of this kind of theory better perhaps than any other example. The motion perceived that has no representation in the stimulus is explained by a neural interaction. I will contrast this kind of explanation of apparent movement with a cognitive one shortly.

What I have been trying to do is briefly to give the reader a feeling for the kind of phenomena of perception with which any theory must deal and to give the flavor of the theories that have been advanced to do so. This is not the time for a careful critique of these theories. Suffice to say that while a spontaneous interaction approach also resolves some of the difficulties of a simple stimulus theory, such as that of stimulus ambiguity, perceptual organization, and relational or contextual effects, it has difficulty with the facts about enrichment and about constancy. In general, no more than does Stimulus Theory, it does not directly address the problem raised by phenomena that suggest perceptual intelligence.

In my opinion, the only other way of dealing with the facts is to maintain that the correlate of perception is not the stimulus *per se* nor the interactions to which the stimulus gives rise, but of interpretations or inferences made from it concerning what the object or event is in the world that has produced it.[2] As is true of the Spontaneous Interaction Theory, here too sensory stimulation other than the focal stimulus under consideration can become relevant but, in addition, more central content (memories, schemata, "assumptions," "rules," "hypotheses," "constructions," and the like) enter in as well. When I speak of "interpretations" made from the stimulus as the essence of cognitive theory, I mean nonconscious interpretations that lead to *perceptions*, not merely to conscious judgments. Helmholtz (1867) advocated this kind of theory.

I will now give some examples of perception that seem to me to require or to support a cognitive theory.[3] These examples were deliberately chosen to cover a range of phenomena, namely, form perception, perceptual constancy, and apparent motion, in order to illustrate different kinds of cognitive operations that I suggest are occurring. First on form perception as a process of description: It is a fact that an object will look different depending upon its orientation. Consequently we may fail to recognize something if it is in an abnormal orientation. Quite probably the reader has not recognized the outline drawing in figure 17.4 although it has been

Figure 17.4

visible since turning to this page. It may now be recognized as one searches for its correct orientation. It is in fact an outline drawing of the continent of Africa tilted 90° counterclockwise from its customary position. The difficulty we have recognizing pictures of faces or just identifying the expression when such pictures are inverted is a case in point. A particularly striking fact when one thinks about it is that we cannot read our own writing when it is viewed upside down.

How do students of perception explain this kind of effect? There are good reasons why orientation should *not* affect perceived form. Forms are transposable just as are melodies. Thus changes in size or locus of projection on the retina do not affect phenomenal shape. That seems to imply that what matters for form perception is maintenance of invariant geometrical relationships. Well, if so, why should a figure look so different when the orientation of its retinal image is altered, since the internal geometry is not thereby altered?

However, a very simple experiment demonstrates that the main problem here does not concern the altered orientation of the retinal image. Ernst Mach (1886) had noted the differing appearances of a square and a diamond as shown in figure 17.5. I now invite the reader to be a subject in an experiment. Tilt your head 45° in either direction and hold it there. Does the square look any less like a square or the diamond any more like a square? Not according to the results of a formal experiment I did. Yet the square's image is now the same as that of the diamond as viewed from an upright position and the diamond's image is now the same as that of the square.

So the problem does not lie with a changed visual stimulus of the figure *per se* and it would be a false trail to begin looking for a neuro-

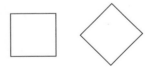

Figure 17.5

physiological explanation along that line (a good example of the prematurity of searching for brain-mechanism explanations when there are still crucial things to be found out on a psychological level of analysis). It would seem that what matters in these cases of orientation affecting form is the orientation as *perceived*. If I perceive the sides of the figure as horizontal and vertical in the world then it looks like a square and if I perceive the corners as at the top and bottom or left and right then it looks like a diamond. Never mind how the retinal image is oriented. If all this is correct (and I have a great deal of data I cannot describe here in support of this conclusion) then we have an example of one perception determining another, namely, perceived orientation affecting perceived shape. See Rock (1973). That kind of causal sequence is not accommodated by stimulus or spontaneous interaction theories.

The question now to be faced is why the perceived orientation of an object should affect its perceived shape. I have not been able to think of any reason other than this: the object would be described differently when it is in different orientations. Consider the example in figure 17.6, the same figure in two different orientations. The figure on the left might be described by observers as an irregular quadrilateral resting on a side. The figure on the right might be described as a symmetrical diamond-like object standing on a point in unstable equilibrium. The symmetry about one axis of this figure is only realized when that axis is vertical and thus this very important figural characteristic is phenomenally absent in one case and present in the other.

I suggest that descriptions of this kind determine phenomenal appearances. The descriptions are based on the internal geometry as well as on how the figure as a whole is seen to be oriented and on other factors that I cannot go into here. Obviously such description must be unconscious and not couched in natural language. It is a hypothetical process more or less propositional in form rather than simply a phenomenal characterization of perception. Where perception by definition is phenomenally concrete and picture-like (Dretske 1981), description is abstract and propositional. In short, I am suggesting, based on the evidence considered plus evidence not discussed, that form perception is governed by a cognitive

Figure 17.6

process and is not explicable simply in terms of the stimulus input (although it is constrained to be faithful to it) or in terms of brain mechanisms that are triggered by stimulus contours or edges in differing orientations.

Note that the kind of cognitive process I am suggesting here, one of unconscious description, is not one of unconscious *inference*. However, in other examples of perception, it *would* seem appropriate to maintain that a process of inference occurs. Helmholtz had suggested this explanation but he seemed to have in mind interpretation of a presently occurring stimulus on the basis of induction from prior experience. What I have in mind is inference that can be formalized according to general predicate logic based on premises entailing relations and, moreover, I don't think we need to assume that the knowledge expressed by the premises is necessarily acquired by past experience.

The example of the false-depth paradox (using an anaglyph or stereo display) is a case in point. The rules of parallax, i.e. angular change of direction occurring during observer movement based on the distance of objects from the observer, are "known" and are employed in the anomalous case where the object that appears farther than the background is in fact not farther. If then the object that appears farther does not shift its location relative to the background as the observer moves (as the parallax rules for stationary objects require) then it can be inferred that that object has changed its location (or moved) during the observer's motion.

Perceptual constancy can be explained in terms of this kind of inference process. Consider the phenomenon of size constancy. If the rule is known that the visual angle subtended by an object is an inverse function of its distance or, what amounts to the same thing, that the size of an object yielding the same visual angle is a direct function of its distance, then size perception can be inferred given the visual angle and the apparent distance of an object. More formally stated: If the visual angle detected is x and the distance perceived is y and if size is a function of visual angle × distance then it follows that size is x times y. Inference and computation become synonymous here.

Of course perception can be no better than the sensory information available, so that if for any reason such information is incorrect, i.e. nonveridical, then the resulting inference-based perception will also be incorrect. In the present example of size perception, where constancy depends upon taking proper account of distance, distant objects often look small, presumably because we do not correctly perceive their true distances.

Still other cases of perception suggest a process of problem-solving, which entails more than just inference. The problem for the perceptual system is to infer what object or event in the world is producing the proximal stimulus. Often several possible hypotheses can account for the stimulus. In my view, unlike the story for thought or imagination or dreaming, for a perception to occur there must be a match or good fit between the hypothesis (or solution) and the stimulus. Not only must the solution account for or conform to the stimulus, but the stimulus must support the solution.

There is space to give only one example. A phenomenon of great interest to students of perception is apparent movement. An object does not have to be in continuous motion to appear to move. It can be presented discontinuously in one position and, a fraction of a second later, in another position and, if the timing and spacing are just right, it will appear to move from one place to the other. As is well known, this effect underlies the perception of moving pictures. Despite a century of research on apparent motion we do not have any explanation of the effect.

I already mentioned Wertheimer's suggestion that apparent motion is based on the flow of electrical energy from the locus of frame 1's projection to the cortex to that of frame 2's projection, a good example of a neural interaction theory. More recent research suggests a sensory explanation, that it is the successive stimulation of different regions of the same receptive field on the retina that yields the effect.

But an alternative approach is an inference theory of apparent movement. On detecting that an object in place 1 has suddenly disappeared and that another object has suddenly appeared in a nearby place 2, the perceptual system infers that one object has moved rapidly from place 1 to place 2. It is interesting to realize that although the motion appears to be continuous over time, only after frame 2 occurs does it make sense for the inference to be drawn that motion had been occurring since the offset of frame 1 so that the phenomenal experience of motion must be retroactively imposed by a process that occurs later.

The motion perceived must do justice to the specific nature of the objects presented in frames 1 and 2. Thus, if 1 is a vertical line and 2 a horizontal one, then not only is motion seen, but it must be a motion that *explains* the differing orientations of the line. Rotary motion fulfills this requirement and that is seen. However, there may be several options as to the kind of motion in space that can "explain" the difference between objects 1 and 2. For example if "1" is ∧ and "2" is ∨ then one can perceive either a figure that bends as it moves, a figure that rotates 180° within the plane as it moves, or a figure that flips over in the third dimension as it moves. The third alternative seems to be preferred. But whatever is seen, it must "explain" the transformation. Why should that be true if perception has nothing to do with thoughtlike, rational processes?

One may say that it is odd to speak of problem-solving under conditions where a psychological outcome seems to be effortless, universal and inexorable. It is true that in most of those perceptual situations where I would invoke the concept of problem-solving, observers always seem to achieve the effect, so there clearly are differences between the process in perception and in thought. However, the outcome is *not* necessarily inexorable.

In the typical experiment on apparent motion, the objects in frames 1 and 2 *inexplicably* disappear and appear. What is meant is that no rationale is provided to the observer of why they appear and disappear such as is the case when things in the environment suddenly move out of the way or in the way. This suggested the following kind of experiment to Arnold Stoper (1964) and later to Eric Sigman and me (Sigman and Rock 1974). Suppose we cause the retina to be stimulated by spots in frame 1 and 2 in just the right places at just the right tempo, etc., but by a method in which we move an opaque object back and forth, alternately covering and uncovering the spots. As far as other theories of apparent movement are concerned there is no obvious reason why these conditions should *not* produce an impression of spots moving and in fact in a control condition where the opaque object is not visible observers do perceive motion. But from the standpoint of problem-solving theory, we have now provided an explanation for the alternate appearance and disappearance of the spots, namely, that they are there all the time but undergoing covering and uncovering. Therefore the perceptual system may prefer this solution or at least we are offering it a viable alternative not usually available. The subjects rarely perceived motion of the spots here.

It should be noted that in these cases where a covering–uncovering effect is perceived there is no reason why movement of the dots could not have been perceived. That is to say, it is possible for the observer to see an opaque rectangle moving back and forth and, *simultaneous with this*, a spot stroboscopically moving in the opposite direction. This solution would also account for the stimulus sequence. Conversely, everything implied by that solution is represented in the stimulus. Therefore the tendency to perceive spots undergoing covering and uncovering rather than spots moving represents a preference for one solution over the other. The preferred solution is obviously related to a very basic characteristic of perception, one might say an axiomatic background characteristic of perception, namely, object permanence, the tendency to assume the continued presence or existence of an object even when it is momentarily not visible for one reason or another. But given the very strong predilection we have to perceive apparent motion even under the most unlikely conditions, it remains a problem as to why it is not perceived in this situation and the object-permanence solution is preferred. A possible answer is that the covering–uncovering solution elegantly accounts for all stimulus change by one "cause": a moving rectangle covering and uncovering spots that are continuously present. The other solution entails two independent events that are coincidentally and unaccountably cor-related: a rectangle moving in one direction and in antiphase to spots moving in the opposite direction. The perceptual system tends to reject coincidental solutions. There is more I could say about this problem-solving approach to the phenomenon of apparent movement, about its strengths and possible weaknesses, but perhaps I have said enough to give the flavor of it.

So much for evidence and illustrations of cognitive factors in percep-tion. If perception *is* the result of intelligent, thoughtlike processing, one may well ask why it is more or less impervious to the influence of knowledge. Perceptual illusions of all kinds, not just the better-known geometrical ones, attest to this fact. The percept is simply not affected at all by what we consciously know to be the fact of the matter. Some may consider this to be a critical paradox for a constructionist theory of perception such as the one I am here advocating.

I believe that the reason for the relative autonomy of perception from conceptually based knowledge is that perception is the joint result of stimulus content and unconscious rules, assumptions, and descriptions, brought to bear on the stimulus. To give an example, a black surface will look light gray or even white if only *it* is illuminated in a dark room. Knowing it is black will not change the outcome in the slightest. On the other hand, placing a white surface next to the black one in the beam of light will result in the black one immediately appearing to be black. There is agreement among the experts that the perception of lightness of color is a function of ratios of light intensities from adjacent regions. Thus to achieve or support the impression of blackness, the stimulus must in-clude at least two regions of very different intensities. The region whose intensity is roughly 1/30 of a neighboring one will look black. Without the second region then, a black surface cannot *look* black although we may know it is black. So this is an example illustrating how perception is grounded in the stimulus.

To give a different example, the moon over the horizon looks much larger than the moon in the elevated sky, a phenomenon that has interested thinkers since Ptolemy. The currently accepted theory of it is that the moon at the horizon appears to be far away, at least as far away as objects on the ground at the horizon whereas the moon in elevation appears to be at some relatively indeterminate but nearer distance. Since size perception is a joint function of visual angle and perceived distance, by the unconscious application of the rule concerning visual angle and distance – which seems to be "known" to the perceptual system – the moon takes on phenomenal size values based on its apparent distance. The observer may consciously know the moon is the same size and distance away in its various elevations but that kind of knowledge has no effect. So, in this example, it is the relevance of the unconsciously based rule and the immediate computation to which it gives rise that is being illustrated.

I hasten to add that the ineffectualness of knowledge about a situation does not imply that past experience cannot affect perception. There is certainly some evidence, albeit not as much as some might think, that such experience can play a role in what we perceive. Obviously, by definition, such experience governs recognition and object identification, but there is reason for believing it affects such perceptual properties as form and depth as well. So the question arises as to how *some* "knowledge" derived from experience can affect perception whereas other kinds of knowledge also derived from experience cannot. One possible answer is that specific visual memories can be tapped by the perceptual process so that a pattern such as the two-dimensional drawing (in figure 17.7) will appear three-dimensional to those with the relevant past experience. This is another example of what I referred to earlier as enrichment. Another answer may be that rules can be acquired on an unconscious level from *prior perceptual encounters* – as in my example of how visual angle varies with distance.

One final thought about the relationship between perception as a process of inference and perception as based on knowledge is this. For some reason the two ideas have become identified with one another historically. It seems to me that inference refers to a certain kind of mental operation and as such is not to be confused with the source of the

Figure 17.7

knowledge that enters into the premises used in such an operation. The Gestaltists were clear on this point when they argued that problem-solving in the domain of thought may or may not make use of past experience but problem-solving is not simply to be defined as the application of past experience to a new situation. I am making the same point about inference in perception.

Various problems with the kind of theory here advocated remain to be sorted out. For example, some argue that if perception is thoughtlike and thus rational we ought not be able to perceive contradictory objects or events. I would agree that the perceptual system does seek to avoid contradiction. For example, take the case of illusory contours shown in figure 17.8. One tends to perceive a triangle with contours that do not exist physically and the triangle is phenomenally whiter than the object-ively equal white background. But now, as Richard Anson and I have demonstrated, if stripes are presented behind this pattern, as shown in figure 17.9, observers do not perceive the illusory triangle (Rock and Anson 1979). It is not simply that the stripes as physical contours interfere with that percept, because if they are placed in front of the pattern, observers do see it. The point is that the white triangle percept is phe-nomenally an opaque thing and thus one cannot simultaneously see white stripes *through* it; thus one avoids perceiving it when stripes are behind it.[4]

What about the following kind of example? If one views a three-dimensional wire figure such as a cube with one eye, one can succeed in reversing it just as one can reverse the apparent depth of a drawing of

Figure 17.8

Figure 17.9

such a cube. This immediately leads to certain size and shape distortions as is to be expected given the automatic application of the incorrect information of the apparent distances of its various parts. But even more dramatic is what happens as the cube now rotates or as one moves around it assuming one can hold on to the reversal during the movement. The object undergoes dynamic transformations and distortions – as is also to be expected from all that is known about perception. But isn't this an example of contradictions or a violation of probabilities? It certainly violates what we know about objects and might be said to violate internalized or intuitive rules we have about physics. Things do not change like this, at least without visible cause or at least not simply because they change their locations.

That the distortions violate what we know is of no account, as I have already pointed out. What about the violation of internalized or intuitive laws of physics? I would argue that perception, at least visual perception, is in no way concerned with laws of physics in contradistinction to the laws of geometrical optics. From this point of view, it is no contradiction that an object appear to enlarge, shrink, or change its shape without apparent cause, or that it appears to rise against the pull of gravity. On the other hand, it is a contradiction if one can simultaneously perceive an opaque surface and an object directly behind it; it is a violation if a surface rotates so as to change its orientation with respect to us without changing its retinally projected shape; and so forth.

In conclusion, perception differs from thought primarily because it is rooted in and constrained by the necessity of accounting for the proximal stimulus. In my opinion dreaming is the cognitive event most similar to perception in that phenomenologically the content of dreams is so much like perception. Things and events are experienced as external in dreams just as in perception but the dream process is unconstrained by the necessity of conforming to or of accounting for a stimulus.

The other major difference between perception and thought is that perception is based on a rather narrow range of internalized knowledge as far as inference and problem-solving is concerned. Perception must rigidly adhere to the appropriate internalized rules so that it often seems unintelligent and inflexible in its imperviousness to other kinds of knowledge. Another difference between the two domains already mentioned is, of course, that the inference or description achieved in the one case has the status of a percept whereas in the other it has the status of a proposition or of an idea.

To come back to the beginning, then, I have tried to show by evidence and argument that perception is thoughtlike and, in that sense, is intelligent. The claim has been that operations that culminate in perceptual experience are of the same kind that characterize thinking. Thought itself is not always as intelligent as it might be (by the criteria of degree of flexibility, valid inferences, creativity, and the like) but when we say of *another* domain that it is governed by operations of the kind that govern thought, then we are attributing intelligence to that domain.

Notes

1   In his commentary on this paper, Stephen Stich, in rejecting the Gibsonian approach, might give the reader the impression that it is not taken seriously by students of perception. That is not at all the case since in fact it has had a major impact on theorizing over the last several decades.

2   For a more complete statement of the kind of theory advocated here, see Rock (1983).

3   In the light of some of the comments of Patricia Churchland on this paper it may be helpful if I clarify two aspects of the position I hold concerning an inference theory. One is that while acknowledging the neural basis of all perception I am suggesting that the brain events underlying perception are much like those underlying thought. One does not deny the intelligence of *thought* by reference to its basis in neuronal activity. The other is that I would agree that processing in perception must begin with low-level operations without benefit of what Churchland calls "descending control" or "high-level hypotheses." In fact there is a very good reason why this must be so, namely, that we access the appropriate memory on the basis of similarity to what is perceived. Thus, for example, recognition normally begins with perception. If, therefore, perception itself manifests descending control it must be because some level of perception is first achieved without it and only then is it modified by memories or internally generated hypotheses. Churchland's distinction between a low-level and a descending-control operation parallels the contemporary distinction in psychology between bottom-up and top-down processing and is quite useful in distinguishing an inference theory from the one she calls computational.

4   The view given here of the illusory contour effect is by no means the dominant one today, since others try to explain it in terms of bottom-up processing, as for example the result of contrast. Churchland points out some but not all of the difficulties for a purely bottom-up approach. In fact, I am not clear at all how Marr would explain it. The effect is not simply one of filling in or interpolation of contours across a gap or the emergence of virtual lines where no abrupt luminance change exists. For example, no such illusory contour occurs for a triangle figure with gaps in it. In the patterns that do produce the effect, what had been ground becomes figure, so that the reversal of organization

must also be explained and an important aspect of the phenomenon is the illusory lightness of the figural region, not just its illusory contour. Moreover, the effect is not automatic, as one might think it should be if it is governed by bottom-up processing. Naive subjects may not achieve it at all, and even those who have experienced the effect may not achieve it in an otherwise "noisy" array. Attention is a factor.

References

Dretske, F. I. (1981), *Knowledge and the Flow of Information*, Cambridge, MA: Bradford Books/MIT Press.

Gibson, J. J. (1950), *The Perception of the Visual World*, Boston, MA: Houghton Mifflin.

——— (1966), *The Senses Considered as Perceptual Systems*, Boston: Houghton Mifflin.

Helmholtz, H. von (1867), *Handbuch der physiologische Optik* (Part III), Leipzig: L. Voss. (As reprinted as *Helmholtz's Treatise on Physiological Optics*, vol. III, tr. J. P. C. Southall, Optical Society of America, 1925.)

Mach, E. (1886), *Beiträge zur Analyse der Empfindungen*, Jena: Gustav Fischer. (As reprinted as *Contributions to the Analysis of Sensations*, tr. C. M. Williams, Chicago: Open Court, 1897.)

Rock, I. (1973), *Orientation and Form*, New York: Academic Press.

——— (1983), *The Logic of Perception*, Boston, MA: Bradford Books/MIT Press.

——— and Anson, R. (1979), Illusory contours as the solution to a problem, *Perception* 8: 665–81.

Sigman, E. and Rock, I. (1974), Stroboscopic movement based on perceptual intelligence, *Perception* 3: 9–28.

Stoper, A. E. (1964), The effect of the structure of the phenomenal field on the occurrence of stroboscopic motion. Paper delivered at *Meeting of the Eastern Psychological Association*.

Wertheimer, M. (1912), Experimentelle Studien über das Sehen von Bewegung, *Zeitschrift für Psychologie* 61: 161–265.

18

Is the Visual System as Smart as It Looks?

Patricia Smith Churchland

1 Introduction

Here is one way to portray the history of research on the visual system. It consists of a rivalry between those who discern the benchmarks of intelligence in visual perception, and those who seek to show how the appearance of intelligence can be stripped away to reveal the reality of essential stupidity. In the main the rivalry has been exciting and productive, as the two egg each other on to ever more extreme exertions; that is, to exhibit demonstrations of ever more cunning ways in which stupid elements can be wired and assembled to yield smart looking results, and by reply, to exhibit demonstrations of ever more subtle and striking performances of the visual system which betoken intelligence and defy reduction by existing reductive hypotheses. The demonstrations of intelligence have typically come from behavioral experiments concerning, for example, illusory contours, and constancy in such things as size perception and orientation perception (see Rock 1975; Rock and Anson 1979; Gregory 1970). The reductive hypotheses have typically come from neurophysiological studies and have been fueled by such discoveries as the centre-surround organization of cells in the visual system, and the possibilities for organizing these cells to produce quite stunning complexity (Ratliff and Hartline 1959).

Both the reductive hypotheses and the behavioral observations are essential to the program aimed at figuring out how the visual system works. What motivates the reductive strategy is the rather obvious point that the visual system is made up of neurons, and neurons are entirely

Patricia Smith Churchland, "Is the Visual System as Smart as It Looks?" in *Proceedings of the Philosophy of Science Association* 2 (1982), pp. 541–52.

stupid, non-intelligent units. Unless one supposes that there is a non-physical intelligence cleverly manipulating the neurons, or that there are special "intelligentrons" whose output is intelligent but whose workings are somehow sheerly intelligent (and not the result of more basic operations), then one must expect that in the last analysis, intelligent behavior is the outcome of suitably orchestrated stupid elements. Just how that story goes, or what is the best reductive strategy to follow, is diabolically difficult to divine. As for the behavioral studies, among other things, they specify the capacities of the visual system which have to be explained, and hence these studies are crucial to finding out *what* the visual system does. Such discoveries sometimes lead quite directly to a neurophysiological hypothesis, as, for example, when Mach's discovery of what are now called "Mach bands" led him to predict a mechanism for contrast enhancement. With the advent of microelectrodes, Ratliff and Hartline eventually went on to discover lateral inhibition in the retina (see also Cornsweet 1970). There is then no in-principle incompatibility between the two research strategies; on the contrary, they are necessary to each other. Lest this all sound a bit too chummy, I should say that the best results will likely come from each approach attempting to outdo, foil, and otherwise amaze the other. The more dedicated the search for complexity in visual performance, the better the characterization of the capacities of the visual system, and hence the better the characterization of the problem which the reductionist must solve.

2   The Computer Vision Strategy

Reductionists regard their failures as predictable if disappointing, for in its early stages, the program's first attempts are bound to be fumbles-in-the-dark. Essentially three things are needed: (1) more psychophysical data, (2) more neurophysiological data, and most particularly (3) new conceptions of what configurations of neurons are doing such that cleverness is got out of stupidity. That is, the desperate need is for new theories of how information is processed in the visual system and about how to characterize what is going on at a level or two above the level of the individual neuron. The need for testable wild ideas and testable inspired guesses is manifest, and theories are needed not only to provide an explanatory toehold, but to motivate the data-gathering. A breakthrough here would be exceedingly important, and I suggest that it is possible that a breakthrough on the theoretical front has recently been made. The main thing I want to do in these comments is to test the idea that the newly emerging reductive models which bill themselves as "computational" or "information processing" models are so powerful and so sophisticated that they appear capable of reducing at least some of the intelligence in perception. The late David Marr from MIT vigorously developed this approach to vision (Marr 1976, 1979, 1982; Marr and Hildreth 1980), and others from his group at MIT have taken up the tools and are plunging ever deeper into the seemingly impenetrable mysteries of visual function. The question I have for Irvin Rock, therefore, is this: Are the Marr models in the right ball park? That is, are they the right sort of model to solve the problem of intelligence in perception? In order to give the question a backdrop, I shall give a summary description of the Marr approach together with some necessary detail.

Marr and Rock agree on a fundamental point: the visual representation of a 3-dimensional objection is radically underdetermined by the intensity distribution on the retina, so that you cannot get from a two-dimensional intensity array on the retina to a visual representation of a three-dimensional object without the injection of extra information. Marr's view is that it makes sense to suppose that the visual system has evolved in such a way that it incorporates certain assumptions about the way the world is. Some of the extra information, therefore, is built in by the artful hand of natural selection. It also makes sense to suppose that the processing of information is handled in stages, and hence that different parts of a task are handled by different components or *modules*. The point is, a large problem can be decomposed into a set of smaller, more manageable subproblems, where the solution to one subproblem becomes the datum on which the next module works. It makes sense to suppose that the evolution of the nervous system proceeded from the periphery inwards, with the innermost layers finding ever more subtle and useful information lying unused in the layer next outwards. Determining the modular profile of the visual system is a fundamental and difficult empirical problem, to be informed by data from wherever you can get it, certainly including data from perceptual psychology, neurophysiology, clinical neurology, ethology, developmental biology, and evolutionary theory.

But having carved up the larger problem into a set of subproblems, the game for the theorist is to figure out what any given module must do in order to accomplish its job. Here the *Marr* approach advises thus:

1 Specify the operations of the modules so that they are computable; that is, modules must execute algorithms, and hence their operations will be programmable on a computer. This is important because a

computable solution is a reductive solution, and because the adequacy of a proposed solution can be tested directly on a computer.

2 Squeeze every ounce of information out of the intensity array before having recourse to intervention by higher centres; e.g., before hypothesizing recognition of an object via descending control. Adding computations to modular operation is cheap, but intervention by higher centres puts the solution out of computational reach.

3 If, in order to keep the module's operation algorithmic, it is necessary to build in assumptions about the world, then do so. The problems here are basically engineering problems – ones which evolution has solved. What we have to do is feel our way to the same solution. Hence building-in is always a better option than descending control.

4 Devise the computation of the module so that it conforms to whatever we know about the underlying physiology, about psychophysics, and about the evolution of the brain.

The result of adopting this advice is a theory of the early stages of visual processing which is reductive in the straightforward sense that it provides a mechanical, algorithmic method for getting inputs from outputs, and where the algorithm's adequacy is testable on a computer and against the neurophysiology. Whilst there is much to reflect on in this approach, for our purposes here the point of emphasis is this: some of the algorithms already conceived and tried are sufficiently fancy that the module spits out answers to very difficult questions, so much so that at arm's length and to the uninitiated, the module looks smart. The effect is that what appears at first to require a bit of reasoning specially tailored to the occasion and supplied from higher centres, turns out to be generable as a stock-in-trade computation performed in the normal course of business by a blind stupid, low-level, blissfully mechanical module. One of the soothing surprises of the computer vision approach is that the complexity in some cases turned out to be far more tractable than might first have been feared.

Before turning to details, several observations are appropriate. First, nobody supposes that by having hewn a solution to the computational problem of how a module *could* accomplish its chores, that we have thereby solved the problem of how the brain *does* accomplish its chores. It is an empirical question whether the brain does it in the same way, and the computational hypothesis can be taken to the wetware for confirmation or disconfirmation. Second, by showing that a particular problem has a computational solution, it is shown that a purely mechanical, fundamentally stupid and local system of operations can produce the smart effect in question. And that is a striking result. *It is therefore a demonstration that perception might well be intelligent without the intelligence deriving from a bit of reasoning on the part of the subject.* Or should one say that it shows that some of the intelligence in perception may not be the genuine article, but a staged cleverness hooked up by evolution and wired into the neurons?

3   Information Processing in the Visual System: A Thumbnail Sketch and Cook's Tour of the Early Stages

The problem for the visual system is to get a representation of an object which specifies its 3-D geometry. In order to get that, we first need a representation of the surface geometry centred on the perceiver; e.g., of where are the boundaries, where are the discontinuities in depth, where are the discontinuities in surface orientation, and so on. Marr calls this more primitive representational description the $2\frac{1}{2}$-D Sketch. Now in order to get *that*, we first need to get an even more basic description of the geometry of the *image*; i.e., of line segments, edges, blobs and end-points, and their positions, orientation, contrast, length, etc. This primitive but rich description he calls the Primal Sketch, and it is constructed from raw intensity data on the image. As well, feeding into the $2\frac{1}{2}$-D component may be information from a stereopsis module which performs computation on binocular disparity and yields a description of depth (Marr and Poggio 1976, 1979). If the object or the perceiver is in motion, there will be output from a module which computes 3-D structure from several distinct sets of Primal Sketches (Ullman 1979).

The first computational problem for the visual system, therefore, is how to get a geometrical description – a Primal Sketch – out of the intensity array on the retina. Briefly, the idea is that the image is convolved with masks of varying sizes and orientations, where the job of a mask is to measure intensity changes across its midline (see figure 18.1). Which mask size is optimal for a situation is determined by a local computation. The primitive sketch is built up by analyzing intensity changes, recording these with tokens which specify position, orientation, contrast, etc., analyzing these tokens further to get a local geometrical organization in terms of lines, blobs, edges, and terminations, then grouping those elements to form larger-scale tokens which may in their turn be analyzed to yield tokens of yet larger scale again (see figure 18.2).

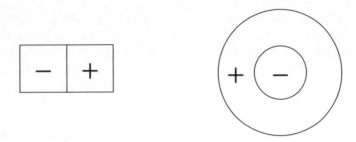

Figure 18.1 Schematic masks (adapted with permission from Marr 1982).

Noise is separated from signal as the analysis proceeds, and some of the blobs and lines from the first go-round will be eliminated. In other cases grouping operations will smooth line segments. One of the functions of the grouping operations is to make explicit information concerning the relative distance between elements on the basis of distance and similarity data. Now the reason I draw attention to this particular grouping operation is that it appears to be the basis for a perceptual phenomenon hitherto reckoned intelligent, namely, subjective or illusory contours (see figure 18.3a). Illusory contours seem to be a shining example of the kind of perceptual effect which should make reductionists tear their hair. The difficulty is that there are no luminance intensity changes in the retinal image which correspond to the contour seen. As Rock (1977: 367) puts it:

> Thus there is no question that the effect is perceptual, yet it would seem to be the end product of an intelligent construction on the part of the perceptual system.

And later in a paper on illusory contours, he and Anson say:

> More specifically, we will argue that the emergence of a percept with illusory contours represents the solution to the problem posed by the stimulus as to what it represents in the world.   (Rock and Anson 1979: 666)

What is particularly fascinating about the grouping operations noted earlier is that they are required to insert lines where there aren't any whenever the algorithm demands it. Specifically, the grouping computations will yield *virtual lines*; i.e., geometrical features not present in the retinal array but constructed in the normal course of primal sketching. Construction of virtual lines is a routine part of low-level processing

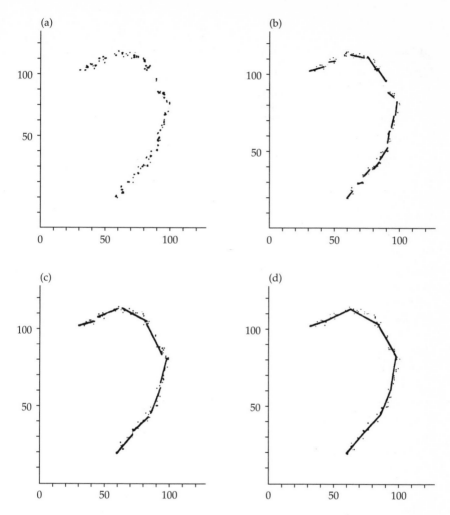

Figure 18.2 Finding a boundary from dot (or place token) density changes. Once a rough assignment of boundary points has been made (a) local line-fitting (b) and grouping (c and d) techniques can recover a rough specification of the boundary quite easily. (Reprinted by permission from Marr 1979, p. 30.)

which yields the basic representation of the geometry of the image, where that representation is to be used in the construction of the $2\frac{1}{2}$-D sketch. The rationale for inserting constructional operations into the computation does not derive from a desire to have a mechanism for giving illusory contours. Rather, those contours appear to be a sometime by-product of normal

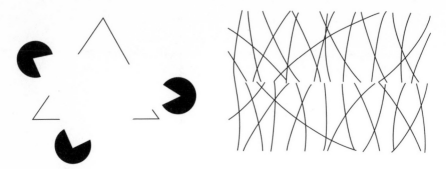

Figure 18.3 Subjective contours. (Reprinted with permission from Marr 1982.)

interpolation; e.g., such mechanisms would account for the perception of a boundary separating the lines in figure 18.3(b). What the rationale for the constructive operations does derive from is the need to figure out what general assumptions about the world the visual system has to make in order that a $2\frac{1}{2}$-D sketch be generable from a Primal Sketch.

Interpolation and filling-in of gaps is also believed to be a standard feature of the computations which construct the $2\frac{1}{2}$-D sketch, and of the construction of depth relations in stereoptic pairs. Evidence for its presence in stereopsis is to be found in the 3–5 percent random dot stereograms (Marr 1982: 121) where only a fraction of a perceived depth boundary will have corresponding retinal intensity changes, yet we perceive an entire smooth length of boundary with uncanny clarity. Pegging a contour as a depth boundary does require adjustments in brightness perception, though what the computation will look like for that has not yet been figured out.

What then are the assumptions about the world which should be built into the algorithm and which result in interpolation in the computation of the $2\frac{1}{2}$-D sketch? Crudely, the assumption goes like this: objects are cohesive and have boundaries. When an object is placed in front of another object, the depth boundary usually progresses smoothly across the image. So discontinuities in depth boundaries should be filled in. In Marr's less crude and more condensed formulation:

> The loci of discontinuities in depth or in surface orientation are smooth almost everywhere. (Marr 1982: 50)

Accordingly, in order to derive surface geometry from raw intensity changes, it will be necessary to construct virtual lines to effect the smoothness required by the physical assumption. Moreover, and this is something of a bombshell, Ullman (1976) has produced an algorithm which fill gaps by means of local (i.e., non-global) computations. This is a computation which proceeds without "knowing" what is in the whole perceptual scene and without knowing what 3-D objects objects are in the scene.

I think there is a difference between Marr and Rock here, and I think the difference is this. On the Marr model, illusory contours are constructed without benefit of high-level hypotheses about what 3-D objects are present; indeed, according to the Marr theory, the construction of a primal sketch and then a $2\frac{1}{2}$-D sketch is necessary for the business of recognizing a specified shape as a pail or a pig or what have you. In contrast to Marr, Rock does seem convinced that the perception of illusory contours involves something analogous to reasoning and framing recognitional hypotheses, and hence involves descending control over low-level computations.

To focus more finely on the contrast, consider Rock and Anson's (1979) account of the perception of illusory contours as mediated by reasoning. I take it that for figures such as that shown in figure 18.3(a), the reasoning-in-perception goes roughly like this:

1   There are three black pies, each with a white wedge.
2   There are three corner contours aligned such that one arm of each corner is cocurvilinear with the arm of the nearest neighbor corner contour.
3   The corner contours could belong either to the pies or to a figure of lighter color lying in front of the pies and occluding parts of them.
4   If a white triangle were positioned in front of a frame triangle and three black pies, that would account for the corner contours and their alignments.
5   My knowledge of the world tells me that well-aligned discontinuities are more likely the result of objects occluding other objects than that objects are discontinuous.
6   Therefore, the best explanation of what I am seeing is three pies and a frame triangle lying behind a white triangle.

This reasoning is an example of inference to the best explanation, and certainly one has occasion to use reasoning in such form quite consciously in puzzling perceptual situations. On the face of it, the contrast between Marr and Rock seems stark: Rock believes the perception of illusory contours involves descending control, and in particular involves recognitional hypotheses about what 3-D objects are in the scene at hand.

Marr does not. He thinks illusory contours are typically, if not always, generable without recognitional hypotheses and without descending control, but generable in the normal course of computational business.

Marr's case, however, is by no means complete. It should be mentioned that while there is an algorithm for generating contours once a decision has been reached that a contour needs generating, the conditions under which gaps are filled and contours generated are not yet fully specified in the Marr models. It seems that a figure/ground specification is first needed in some cases. Nevertheless, even if such specification were required, it may be unproblematically forthcoming from the computations in the 2½-D module and would not require a recognitional hypothesis. Hence it would not require the intervention of descending control.

A number of questions want a voice here, but I shall close by splashing around in some empirical data. *First*: the idea that the early stages of processing advance without recognitional hypotheses does fit with the clinical data on visual agnosia. In these cases, patients with a lesion in the visual association cortex can see but cannot recognize what they are seeing. For example, a patient can faithfully copy a line diagram of a pig or a locomotive, but will be quite unable to say what object they have drawn, though they will try to identify it by suggesting, e.g., that it is something used in the kitchen. Such patients typically can identify the object if allowed to touch, hear, or smell the object (Rubens 1979).

Second: it is striking that we do perceive a depth boundary in a 3–5 percent random dot stereogram, where it appears that there is nothing for a recognitional hypothesis or an inference-to-the-best-explanation to get its hooks into.

Third: To see if the perception of an illusory contour might be altered by a recognitional hypothesis, I doctored the standard Kanizsa figure by putting dots on the pies to make them Pacmen. If the illusory contour essentially involves a recognitional hypothesis, it might be expected to disappear in the Pacman condition (see figure 18.4).

Fourth: I have a question about how well the Primal Sketch to 2½-D to 3-D story works in the case of visual perception of written words. It has been found that fluent readers are better at recognizing whole words than they are at recognizing individual letters when these are flashed for very short durations. For example, a subject may identify the word "dog" when flashed, but fail to identify the single letter "d" flashed for the same duration. This is the so-called word-superiority phenomenon. Possibly related is a rare case of a stroke patient who was able to read whole words, e.g., "cow" but who could not identify single

Figure 18.4 The Pacman condition.

letters. Unfortunately this patient was not thoroughly tested so we do not know whether she could read new words, or what happened when she came across the one-letter word "I."

Fifth: the notion of a module will have to be carefully studied in view of a number of considerations. The distinction between hardware and software does not apply unproblematically to the brain. The brain is plastic, and it learns and grows, where learning and growing bring about physical changes in the brain's wiring. Additionally, it would be a mistake to assume that when brains evolve, a new module is just clapped on to whatever is already there. The changes come as a package: our retina is not just like an alligator retina or a rat retina or even a monkey retina. It may be, in consequence, that when we try to figure out the computation of a single module, we may have to allow for more *inter-modular* communication than hitherto supposed.

Sixth: there is no doubt that previous exposure to illusory contour figures makes it more likely that we shall perceive such contours on other occasions (Rock and Anson 1979), which supports the suggestion that so-called mental set is a factor in the perception of illusory contours. Put another way, it implies that some sort of learning is going on, and hence that there may be more talk between higher centres and low-level modules than Marr's guidelines would permit.

Seventh and finally: we cannot follow Marr's advice on building-in indefinitely, since the plasticity of the brain, and in particular the human brain's ability to learn, suggests we must have real learner computations going on somewhere. Sooner or later, we are going to find "real," "active" intelligence in the visual system. The open question concerns how far down it reaches.

228   *Patricia Smith Churchland*

Acknowledgment

I gratefully acknowledge support for this research by the Social Sciences and Humanities Research Council of Canada, grant no. 410-81-0182.

References

Cornsweet, T. N. (1970), *Visual Perception*, New York: Academic Press.
Gregory, Richard (1970), *The Intelligent Eye*, New York: McGraw Hill.
Marr, David (1976), Early processing of visual information, *Philosophical Transactions of the Royal Society of London* 275: 483–519.
———(1979), Representing and computing visual information. In *Artificial Intelligence: An MIT Perspective*, vol. 1, ed. P. H. Winston and R. H. Brown, Cambridge, MA: MIT Press, pp. 15–80.
———(1982), *Vision*, San Francisco: W. H. Freeman.
———and Poggio, T. (1976), Cooperative computation of stereo disparity, *Science* 194: 283–7.
———and Hildreth, E. (1980), Theory of edge detection, *Proceedings of the Royal Society of London B* 207: 187–217.
———and Poggio, T. (1979), A computational theory of human stereo vision, *Proceedings of the Royal Society of London B* 204: 301–28.
Ratliff, F. and Hartline, H. K. (1959), The response of *Limulus* optic nerve fibres to patterns of illumination on the receptor mosaic, *Journal of General Physiology* 42: 1241–55.
Rock, Irvin (1975), *An Introduction to Perception*, New York: Macmillan.
———(1977), In defense of unconscious inference. In *Stability and Constancy in Visual Perception*, ed. William Epstein, New York: Wiley, pp. 321–73.
———and Anson, Richard (1979), Illusory contours as the solution to a problem, *Perception* 8: 665–81.
Rubens, Alan B. (1979), Agnosia. In *Clinical Neuropsychology*, ed. Kenneth M. Heilmar and Edward Valenstein, New York: Oxford University Press, pp. 233–67.
Ullman, Shimon (1976), Filling-in the gaps: the shape of subjective contours and a model for their generation, *Biological Cybernetics* 25: 1–6.
———(1979), *The Interpretation of Visual Motion*, Cambridge, MA: MIT Press.

19

Tacit Assumptions in the Computational Study of Vision

Simon Ullman

The computational study of vision has two different goals. One is the development of a theoretical foundation and engineering practice for the construction of useful "vision machines." The other is to develop a theory for the processes underlying vision in biological systems and, in particular, human vision.

The belief that computational vision could provide a useful framework for understanding human vision rests on a number of assumptions that are usually taken for granted, without being explicitly stated or called into question. Although these assumptions are shared by researchers in the field, they are not universally accepted, and most of them have been challenged on various grounds. Theses challenges are worth considering, because if some of the main assumptions are in fact invalid, the entire enterprise may turn out to be misguided.

The goal of this paper is to discuss some of the tacit assumptions underlying computational vision, and some of the challenges that have been raised against them.

Assumption I: The Brain is an Information Processing Device

Different artificial devices are constructed for different goals. Some are mechanical devices, constructed, for example, to move things from one place to another. The main function of other devices is to transform energy from one form to another. Yet other devices are constructed to manipulate information. The first assumption means

Simon Ullman, "Tacit Assumptions in the Computational Study of Vision," in A. Gorea (ed.), *Representations of Vision* (Cambridge: Cambridge University Press, 1991), pp. 305–17.

that the brain, although a natural biological system rather than an artificial device, also belongs to the class of information processing devices. The important aspects of the brain are not its mechanical properties (although F. Crick has suggested that tiny muscles in dendritic spines may control synaptic efficacy in the brain), nor properties concerned with energy manipulation (although there are metabolic processes in the brain). The important processes in the brain have to do with the manipulation of signals and information, rather than forces or energy.

According to this view the brain receives sensory signals, these signals get transformed, analyzed, integrated, stored, compared, etc. These processes can then lead, for example, to the generation of patterns of activation of muscles, and thereby to observed behavior. In performing its tasks, the brain may be different from any known artificial information processing device, but it still belongs to the general class of information processing systems. The view of the brain as an information processing device does not mean, of course, that the brain is similar to standard "Von Neuman" digital computers. It may use, for example, distributed representations and massively parallel computation. It is still subject, however, to the same general principles that govern a Turing machine. Its processes can still be studied, at least at a functional level (as opposed to their biological implementation) within the general framework of studying computing devices.

This assumption has important implications to the manner research is conducted in computational vision. First, it justifies the entire enterprise, making it plausible that building artificial vision machines will tell us something relevant about "biological machines." Second, it sets the general framework for computational vision, and determines the kind of questions that should be asked. It suggests the view that vision produces some internal representations, and that other processes manipulate and use these representations. (The representation issue is discussed in more detail below.) It leads to the formulation of certain questions, such as the type of the representations created (e.g., the primal sketch, 2.5-D sketch, etc.), or questions such as "How do different visual modules communicate?" etc.

Challenges to assumption I

A number of objections have been raised against the view of the visual system (and the brain) as an information processing system. Most of these objections contend not only that something in this way of thinking is simplified or incomplete, but that the entire approach is misguided and will lead nowhere.

1 Subjective experience   The basic argument is that when we see, we don't just process information, but we have a conscious experience of what we see. In contrast, machines manipulate signals, but do not have similar experiences.

For a long period this problem has not been a legitimate subject that scientists studying vision and the brain in general were concerned about. As J. Searle (1990) puts it, "since Descartes, we have, for the most part, thought that consciousness was not an appropriate subject for serious science or scientific philosophy of mind." It is interesting to note that more recently it became the subject of much thinking and theorizing within the fields of psychology and biology (e.g. Baars 1988; Crick and Koch 1990; Edelman 1989; Jackendoff 1987; Johnson-Laird 1988; Penrose 1989; Searle 1990).

The subjective experience objection has two versions, a "minimal" and a "maximal" one. The minimal version contends that the theory of vision will be incomplete without explaining subjective phenomena. Some researchers believe that a complete theory will be attainable within the current scientific framework (Crick and Koch 1990; Edelman 1989). Others do not, and believe that the brain is not merely some kind of a biological computer, but also something else. It contains some "extra" mechanisms, above and beyond the ones known today (e.g., according to Penrose's recent theory (Penrose 1989), some quantum effects that make it capable of "surpassing" the limitations of a Turing machine). According to this "minimal" version the computational approach may be incomplete, but it is not fundamentally wrong.

The "maximal" version contends that the fact that the brain somehow "generates" subjective experience and a computer does not, indicates that they are two radically different sorts of entities. It will therefore be entirely misguided to try to explain one in terms of the other.

My own view is close to the "minimal" view. The origin of perceptual experiences lies outside the realm of current theories, and it seems likely to me that radical changes and new insights will be required before such issues will be addressable by scientific theories. At the same time, this problem does not appear to me to undermine the computational approach to vision. The problem is "late" rather than "early" in the sense that one can study much of the brain's structure and function without having to tackle the problem of perceptual experience. At least up to a point, the perceptual systems that have been studied do behave like specialized information processing devices, operating on principles familiar to scientists and engineers. A beautiful example is the owl's sound localization system, which has been studied and analyzed in impressive detail on the levels of both function and mechanism (e.g., Konishi et al. 1985). This is a sophisticated system using components and methods that are entirely expected on the basis of common engineering practices, such as filters, delay lines, coincidence detectors and the like.

2   *The problem of meaning*   This is a philosophical objection that claims, roughly, that "symbol manipulation does not capture meaning." One version of this appears in the form of J. Searle's "Chinese room argument" (Searle 1980). Searle describes a situation where a number of people (or a single person) in a closed room are following the instructions of a "Chinese understanding" program. They receive input symbols, written in Chinese, through an input slot. They then follow a set of instructions, comparing the input string to other symbols stored in various drawers in the room, moving symbols from one place to another, copying some other symbols, etc., and eventually deliver an output string through an output slot. The people in the room can follow this symbol-manipulating procedure and produce a "Chinese understanding" behavior without understanding Chinese at all.

Similarly, the argument goes, when I see something, it has a meaning for me. In contrast, the generation of representations inside a computer does not have any meaning. These representations can only have a meaning for us, for people who can interpret them.

The Oxford philosopher P. Hacker (1990) raises a related argument. In his view:

> a creature that can see . . . can also search for what it wants, look for things it likes, look at objects that interest it . . . flee from those it perceives as threatening and which it fears.

The problem is related to, but not identical with, the problem of perceptual experience. Humans and animals can see, and machines cannot,

> not because they "have minds" . . . nor is it because animals and men are biological structures and industrial robots are not. It is rather because our use of these expressions [e.g. "see"], and so their meaning, are bound up with the highly complex behavioral repertoire of creatures in the rich environment of the world they inhabit, and systematically interwoven with a host of further psychological predicates the application of which is licensed by the same form of behavior.

Seeing thus makes sense only by its relations to other aspects of behavior and "psychological predicates" that give it meaning. For machines, "seeing" does not have such a meaning, therefore they cannot see in the same sense we do.

Personally, I am not convinced that there is a serious problem here that is really distinct from the one concerning perceptual experience. Aspects of this problem are taken up again below, in discussing the problem of internal representations.

3 *Direct perception* The theory of direct perception (e.g. Gibson 1950, 1979) is strongly opposed to any notion of vision as involving computation and information processing. Concepts such as inference, interpretation, or categorization, and processes such as copying, storing, comparing, and matching, have no possible place in the theory of visual perception. The theory similarly rejects notions such as "nervous operations on the signals in the nerves." What is suggested instead is that perception is "the process of direct information pickup."

This position is in strong opposition to any version of a computational approach. It is interesting, therefore, that some researchers in computational vision still regard themselves as Gibsonians, or "neo-Gibsonians." How can computational theories be related to an approach that is entirely opposed to any notion of computation? The answer is that the Gibsonian theory has also emphasized another aspect: the richness of the visual stimulus. The theory stresses the point that the visual stimulus in a natural environment is rich in information (particularly in the form of spatial and temporal texture gradients). This is presented as a contrast to theories that describe the visual stimulus as impoverished, therefore requiring further inference processes.

An example of the theory is its account of binocular stereo vision. The theory begins by describing the source of depth information – the relative position of corresponding points on the two retinae. The next stage, according to the theory, is that this information is directly "picked up." Unlike computational theories of stereo vision, direct perception sees no reason to include in the theory processes that filter the images, extract features, establish correspondence, resolve ambiguities, extract disparity, etc.

This notion of direct perception appears to me to be mistaken and fruitless. Briefly, the main argument is the following (see Ullman 1980). The term "immediate" is relative to a given area of investigation. For example, for the psychologist of vision, it is justifiable to consider the photoreceptors in the eyes as registering "directly" light intensity, or that

Meissner's corpuscle "immediately" registers touch. The response of a retinal rod, for example, to light is in fact a highly complex process, composed of a sequence of many distinct events. A biophysicist will therefore not be satisfied with a description of the rod as registering light "directly." For the psychologist, the details of the biophysical reactions are outside his or her domain of investigation, and it is therefore justified as far as psychology is concerned to view the process of registering light as "direct." In general, then, a process can be called "immediate" in a given domain, if it has no meaningful decomposition into more elementary constituents within the domain of interest. It therefore becomes evident that a satisfactory theory of psychology cannot regard binocular vision, or object recognition, for example, as "direct" information pickup.

Assumption II: Computations Can Be Studied on Their Own

One version of this assumption is Marr's well-known division of the study of vision into three levels – the levels of computation, algorithm, and mechanism. Each of these levels can be studied more or less on its own (although, as emphasized by Marr, they are not entirely independent).

Some form of this assumption is crucial for justifying computational vision as a means for studying aspects of perception. In computational vision one usually proceeds by trying to develop a computational scheme that can solve successfully a given problem, such as recovering binocular disparity, recovering structure from motion, etc. The assumption is that by doing so one studies some general aspects of the problem that will carry over to human vision as well.

The assumption above has two main aspects:

1   Sufficient independence of the mechanism and the computation. If the description of the processes that go on is equivalent to a complete description of the mechanism, then there is little value in studying the "computation" independent of the mechanism.
2   Sufficient constraints on possible solutions. If, for example, there is a large number of very different ways of solving the binocular stereo problem, then the study of possible stereo algorithms on their own is less likely to be of direct relevance to the study of binocular stereo vision performed by the brain. If the set of possible solutions is highly constrained, studying computationally in detail a number of options

is more likely to prove useful to the understanding of how the brain solves the same problem.

Challenges to assumption II

1 Connectionism Some versions of connectionism challenge the distinction between the levels of algorithm and mechanism. The computational properties of the system are "emergent behavior" of the units and their connections, and the studies of function and mechanism cannot be separated. Unlike a standard computer, one cannot distinguish in such a network a program, or an algorithm, using, or "running on", the hardware. The conclusion is that the emphasis should therefore be placed on the study of the unit and network properties. For example, Hopfield (personal communication) has shown that the exact form of the Hebbian learning rule in associative networks can directly influence the overall behavior of the system. In one form of the rule, the system will recall sequences equally well in both forward and backward directions. In a slightly modified form, the forward direction will be highly favored. Other properties, such as the capacity for associative recall, are network properties that arise from the entire pattern of connections in the net.

A real difficulty will indeed arise if it turns out that the simplest description of a network's operation is essentially to describe fully its units and list all their interactions. This is, however, unlikely, for two reasons. First, the distinction between mechanisms and computation is often a conceptual rather than a physical one. For example, one can construct a special purpose piece of hardware for performing edge detection, or FFT, etc. In such a device it is difficult to distinguish an algorithm "running on" the hardware. And yet, one can describe the particular algorithm embodied in the hardware. Similarly, in complex connectionist networks, even when there is no physical distinction between the "hardware" and the computation "using" the hardware, a conceptual description of the computation may very well exist.

The second point is that connectionist networks for difficult tasks, rather than being one large unanalyzable unit, often have structure in terms of sub-components that perform well-specified aspects of the task. For example, the network developed at AT&T's Bell Laboratories for reading handwritten numerals (LeCun et al. 1989) has a number of distinct levels performing different operations involving abstraction and feature detection, etc. In such a structure, although it is still a highly interconnected network of simple units, it becomes easier to give at least a partial description of the network's operation in computational terms.

2   Non-biological solutions   An objection is often raised that computational studies of vision produce "artificial," nonbiological, solutions. The feeling is that the solutions produced by computational vision are sometimes too "logical," "neat" and "symbolic" in nature (Minsky 1990). This objection is related in part to the assumption stated above regarding the constraints on possible solutions. The worry is that the space of possible solutions is in fact large and unconstrained, and the solutions proposed by theoretical studies may bear little relevance to the biological solution. This worry can be addressed at least in part by adopting an appropriate methodology in the field, namely, by taking into consideration constraints imposed by known biological and psychological data. It also appears that in many cases the space of possible solutions is indeed rather restricted. In object recognition, for instance, it is difficult at present to come up with even a single scheme that will be able to perform the task in a reasonable manner. Finally, some aspects of computational vision are sufficiently broad in nature that they are likely to apply to any system, natural or artificial, that performs visual tasks. The main example here is the set of "natural constraints" utilized by the visual system (Marr 1982), such as object continuity in the case of binocular disparity extraction, a rigidity constraint in the case of perceiving structure from motion (Ullman 1979) or the use of smoothness constraint in a number of visual computations (Poggio et al. 1985).

Assumption III: Modularity

The assumption is that the visual system consists of a number of modules that can be studied more or less independently (see also Fodor 1983). Modules that have been studied computationally include edge detection, stereo vision, motion measurement, structure-from-motion, color, texture analysis, shape-from-shading, surface interpolation, segmentation, object recognition, and others. Obviously, there are some inter-relations among them, but the assumption is that to a first approximation they are independent. The integration of modules is assumed to be primarily "late" in nature. That is, it operates primarily on the results obtained by the individual modules. This is the scheme researchers in computational vision follow in practice. Each of the individual modules is usually studied on its own. In addition, some researchers consider separately the problem of their integration, namely, how results of the individual modules are then put together.

Challenges

1   Empirical evidence   The empirical evidence regarding the modularity of visual processes is not entirely clear. Anatomically, there is evidence for multiple parallel pathways, e.g., for motion, binocular vision, and color processing. The processing stream of the color system, for instance, includes the parvo layers of the LGN, the blobs in V1, thin stripes of V2, and area V4 (Livingstone and Hubel 1984). There is also evidence from brain lesions regarding specific deficits of cortical origin in color vision, motion perception, and binocular vision.

In contrast with this evidence for independence, there is also a considerable body of evidence, primarily from psychophysics, for early interactions between modules. For example, Gilchrist (1977) has shown that perceived three-dimensional (3-D) structure can affect perceived lightness. It is known that apparent motion can be established between stereo discontinuities, indicating fairly early interactions between the two modules. There are indications for interactions between motion perception and surface interpolation, and others.

As mentioned above, the empirical data concerning interactions among modules is still fragmentary. It seems to me that the interactions are unlikely to be all of the 'late' type. At the same time, the modularity assumption appears to be sufficiently useful as a starting point. Theoretically, the system could have been one large interconnected entity that resists any attempt to break it down into meaningful modules. This does not appear to be the case, even if interactions among modules do exist at different levels. In future computational studies it would be of interest to explore more fully the nature and usefulness of such interactions. For example, when combining stereo and motion information, there is more room for useful interactions between them than e.g. simply combining the three-dimensional estimates provided by the two modules, with some appropriate weights (such as "60 percent stereo, 40 percent motion"). To mention just a few examples, motion and stereo discontinuities could interact, the two systems could be used to calibrate one another, and motion information, combined with the current depth estimations, could be used to predict an updated depth map (to facilitate the computation of an updated depth map rather than starting it anew).

2   "Society of mind"   This objection is termed after M. Minsky's (1987) description of the mind as a society of a very large number of highly interactive agents. Translated to the domain of vision, this means that the visual process is composed not of a relatively small number of more-or-less independent modules, but of a very large number of highly interdependent processes, with the interactions between them being as complex and as important to the operation of the system as the individual modules themselves. This view is related to Ramachandran's (1985) view of the visual system as a "bag of tricks." The view is again of the visual system as composed of a very large number of highly specialized (and presumably interacting) processes. Ramachandran raises this notion as an alternative to the computational view – the brain does not use computations, it uses "tricks." As far as I can see, this is not really a challenge to the computational view. The "tricks" described by Ramachandran can be equally described as specialized, and often highly complex and sophisticated computations (as in the case of motion capture, that can distinguish, e.g., between the inside and the outside of a closed figure). I think that it is an interesting and a reasonable point of view that the visual system may include considerably more modules than commonly assumed in current computational vision. For example, there may be not one stereo matching computation, but a number of different ones, for different types of inputs, (dense vs. sparse input, with or without clear monocular cues) as well as for different goals (e.g. for manipulation in nearby space, as opposed to distant objects). Such an architecture does not by itself undermine the notion of modularity, but it may change some of the current notions in computational vision.

Assumption IV: Bottom-up Processing

Current computational approaches typically assume a very large and often dominant role to the bottom-up component of the visual process. "Bottom-up" means here an automatic process that is determined by the input, and is not governed by specific goals of the computation, and does not bring to bear specialized knowledge regarding specific objects. In Marr's theory, for example, visual processing proceeds primarily through the bottom-up creation of a sequence of representations, the primal sketch, then the 2.5-D sketch, and finally the 3-D representation. Similarly, in computational theories of most of the visual modules the computations are again primarily bottom-up. For example, in performing stereo matching, current schemes do not "care" what is the purpose of the computation (e.g., manipulation, navigation, or object recognition), or what we know about the specific objects in the scene. This emphasis on bottom-up processing is the dominant approach in current computational vision, but alternative approaches have also been advocated (e.g., Freuder 1974; Tenenbaum and Barrow 1976).

Challenges

1 Empirical evidence There is some psychophysical evidence indicating the effect of high-level knowledge on relatively early visual processing. As mentioned above, Gilchrist (1977) has shown that the interpreted three-dimensional structure of the scene can have effects on the perceived lightness of surfaces. When we see hollow shaded masks of faces, the visual system "resists" seeing them as concave, it seems that our knowledge about faces tends to enforce a convex interpretation (Gregory 1970). The recognition of objects in some cases, e.g., the well-known image of a Dalmatian dog by R. C. James (Gregory 1970; Marr 1982) does not appear amenable to bottom-up processing. From an anatomical standpoint, interactions going "back down" can certainly be supported by the extensive back projections between visual areas.

It should be noted, however, that the empirical evidence is not entirely unequivocal. There are also a large number of cases where early processes appear "impenetrable" to higher influence. An interesting and perhaps somewhat unexpected example is certain segmentation processes (described e.g. by Nakayama et al. 1989). It appears that in many cases the visual system "decides" for us what goes with what in the scene, i.e., which regions belong together as a part of a single object and which are separate, and that high-level influence on these decisions is severely limited. Physiologically, it has been shown (Livingstone and Hubel 1981) that, at least in V1, responses in natural sleep, barbiturate anesthesia, and different levels of arousal, are quite similar, suggesting that the processing up to that level is not highly dependent (although may still be modulated to some degree) by higher-level activity.

It seems to me that in most of the earlier processes, such as edge detection, stereo, motion processing, or shading analysis, there may be some higher-level effects, but they are not of major influence. Even segmentation processes appear to have a very significant bottom-up component. Object recognition may, however, be quite different. I find the bottom-up creation of 3-D models and matching to memory (as in Marr's scheme) unlikely. A scheme in which stored knowledge about objects' shapes and information from the image can interact in both directions appears more likely for the purpose of visual object recognition.

Assumption V: Explicit Representations

The "final" goal of the visual process, according to this assumption, is to produce a set of representations that are useful to the observer, and are not cluttered by irrelevant information (such as Marr's sequence of representations mentioned above). In the words of J. Frisby (1980):

> it is an inescapable conclusion that there must be a symbolic description in the brain of the outside world.

The main question in computational vision can therefore be formulated as follows:

> When we see, what are the symbols inside our head that stand for things in the outside world.

For example, the goal of the binocular stereo process is to produce a three-dimensional representation, perhaps in the form of a depth map. Other processes that extract 3-D information, such as structure-from-motion and shading analysis, may then add depth information to the same representation.

This view is in the spirit of cognitive science in general. On this view cognition is described in terms of processes operating over internal representations. The picture is that the visual system delivers representations of depth, shape, motion, color, etc., and later processes then manipulate and use these representations for tasks such as recognizing objects, planning and controlling movements in the environment, and navigation.

Having a common representation of this type, e.g., for depth information, has some advantages from a computational standpoint. A common representation can integrate contributions from various sources, and then different modules could all use the same representations, rather than having to create unnecessary duplications of the same information.

This general picture guides much of the thinking about visual processes. For example, work on binocular depth is usually not concerned directly with controlling an arm, or avoiding obstacles, etc., but with the creation of a depth representation, with the assumption that subsequent processes will somehow use this representation to plan and guide behavior.

Challenges

1 Multiple direct pathways Although arguments could be raised in favor of using some common explicit representations, alternative schemes are also possible. It may be that there are no common representations but many separate ones, and that quantities such as depth, surface orientation, direction of motion, etc., are not represented explicitly anywhere in the system. For example, it may be that information derived from the motion perception system is used to create patterns of activity that will guide the hand to catch a moving object without an explicit representation of direction or speed. Furthermore, there may be multiple pathways of this type for performing different tasks. The control of eye movements, for example, may not share a common representation with the hand control pathway. In such a structure there may not be an identifiable common and explicit representation of properties such as depth and velocity.

The work of R. Brooks on the so-called subsumption architecture for motor control (Brooks 1986) is close to this alternative view. Some of the objections raised by the philosopher H. Dreyfus against artificial intelligence are also related to this view. He points in his argument to the distinction between "knowing that" and "knowing how." "Knowing that" relates to facts that we store and explicit rules for actions we follow. "Knowing how" on the other hand is akin to the skill of riding a bicycle. This knowledge is not stored in the form of a list of facts and rules to follow, but is somehow incorporated into the behavior of the system. Similarly, it may be that in a variety of perceptual skills and visually guided behavior we "know how" to perform different tasks without having an explicit representation of the state of the world and rules for manipulating these representations.

2 Empirical evidence The empirical evidence regarding common and explicit vs. distributed and implicit representations is not yet clear. Physiologically, something like an internal "depth map" has not been found, but this may simply reflect our very partial knowledge of the visual system. Some evidence appears to be in broad agreement with the general notion of common, explicit, representations. For example, the primary visual area V1 appears to make explicit properties such as orientation and direction of motion, and this representation subserves different areas involved in different tasks. Area MT may be a common "motion representation" that is used for different tasks requiring motion information.

Other physiological evidence agrees more with the picture of a more direct pathway with an implicit form of encoding. In area 7a of the posterior parietal lobe cells appear to be involved in the transformation from retinal to head-based coordinates (see Zipser and Andersen 1988 for a description and a model of this transformation.) Many of the cells in this area are affected by both the retinal location of the stimulus and eye position. From this combined response it is possible to deduce the spatial coordinates relative to the head coordinated system. No cells were found, however, that encode explicitly the spatial position of the stimulus with respect to the head.

3   *Philosophical objections*   Objections have been raised on philosophical grounds against the use of terms such as "representations" and "internal descriptions". It has been argued that it is a categorical mistake to say that events in the brain can represent or describe something. "Representation" is the use of symbols of a formal system by a cognizant agent who can interpret them. In the case of the brain, there is no cognizant agent outside the brain that will interpret brain representations. This type of argument is expressed, e.g., by P. Hacker (1990):

> neural firings are not symbols, do not have definitions of rules of syntax, are not employed by symbol-using creatures, cannot be used correctly or incorrectly, cannot be grammatical or ungrammatical, and are not part of a language.

This and related arguments are considered to be sufficiently devastating to the computational approach to conclude that (ibid.).

> [Computational vision] as an explanatory theory of vision is a non-starter since such a theory is not conceptually coherent.

In contrast with this view, it seems to me that there is a reasonable notion of "representation" that can be meaningful in describing patterns of activity in the brain. When we say that a certain device can be viewed as a symbolic system we imply that some (but not all) of the events within the system can be consistently interpreted as having a meaning in a certain domain. For example, some of the events within an electronic calculator have a consistent interpretation in terms of entities in arithmetic. Other events inside the calculator, for example, in the power supply, do not have such an interpretation. Similarly for the brain: according to the representational view some of the events inside the brain may have a consistent interpretation in terms of depth, surface orientation, reflectance, and the like. This is apparently not what Hacker and others would like the term "representation" to stand for, and it may be given a different name, say, representation*. The claim that certain brain patterns can be viewed as representations* is a statement that is testable, at least in part, by empirical means. In this sense we can ask whether or not we find in the brain a common explicit representation* of depth, for instance, used for a number of different tasks.

It is probably true that the notion of representation and perhaps the entire computational approach do not provide an explanation to epistemological questions related to knowledge, meaning, or awareness. In my view, this is also not the goal of current computational vision. As far as the notion of representation is concerned, it seems to me that in the manner it is used in computational vision it has a reasonable and potentially useful meaning. At the same time, the use of common, explicit, representations by (or in) the visual system is still an unsettled issue.

Assumption VI: Links to the Brain

This assumption has to do with the link between computational theories and their interpretation in terms of physiological events. In making this connection it is usually assumed that the firing rates of individual units represent the meaningful physiological variables. When we look for, say, depth representation in the brain, we will try to discover single units whose firing rates correlate with perceived depth.

This assumption is more technical in nature then the previous ones. It is an important assumption for making the link between theoretical models and empirical studies of the brain. This assumption does not mean, however, that a single unit by itself codes the meaningful variable. The brain could use a population encoding, e.g., for orientation, in which a single unit codes for a possible range of orientations. In this case the firing rate of a single unit is ambiguous and does not code a unique orientation value. The value is determined instead by a distributed activity across a population.

There is a body of physiological evidence that supports this general notion. Starting from low-level features, units in V1 seem to signal (either individually or within a population encoding) the presence of oriented features, their orientation, contrast, direction of motion, etc. More surprisingly, single units in an area of the STS of the macaque monkey seem to function as some sorts of "face analyzers". Their individual firing rates have clear correlations with the presence of, e.g., specific faces, observed from a restricted set of viewing directions. In a recent study by W. Newsome and his collaborators (Salzman et al. 1990) microstimulation of single units in area MT of the monkey were sufficient to bias the animal's judgments towards the direction of motion encoded by the stimulated neurons.

The reason for bringing up this assumption is that there have been recently some challenges that, if verified, may change this picture, and may have important implications to the "physiological link" assumption.

Challenges

Oscillations and temporal coding   There have been a number of challenges and alternatives to the notion of the firing rate of a fixed set of neurons as the main variable encoded by neurons. One example is the temporal coding notion of B. Richmond and his co-workers (Richmond et al. 1987). They have shown some evidence that the temporal firing pattern of neurons may carry important information, e.g., about the shape of the stimulus. According to this evidence, a neuron may respond to two different stimuli with the same mean firing rate, but signal two different events by the shape of the temporal firing pattern. In such a case it is not meaningful to ask merely how strongly a given unit responds to a given stimulus; the more relevant variable is the temporal pattern of the response.

Another possibility that has attracted considerable attention recently is based on the findings of correlated oscillations in the cortex. Gray, Singer, and others (e.g., Gray et al. 1989) have shown correlated oscillations of about 40–60 Hz in the cat's visual cortex in response to moving stimuli. For example, they have stimulated two cortical sites separated by 7 mm in the cortex, that had non-overlapping receptive fields, arranged colinearly, and with similar orientation preference. When the separate receptive fields were stimulated by a single long bar, the responses at the two sites were oscillatory at about 50 Hz and phase locked. When the single line was replaced by two shorter lines moving together the phase locking was reduced, and when the shorter lines moved independently the correlation disappeared completely. This and related experiments raise the possibility of the use by the cortex of temporary ensembles that oscillate coherently together. On this view the firing rate of an individual unit has little meaning, if its firing is not a part of an oscillating ensemble.

A number of experiments have suggested this mode of activity, but their interpretation is still not entirely clear and unequivocal. If this notion of oscillating ensembles turns out to be a fundamental cortical mechanism, it will not change the computational theories on their own, but it will change significantly the relations between theory and modeling. It will change the way physiological data are interpreted for the purpose of modeling, the form of the predictions, and the forms of the models themselves.

Acknowledgment

This work was partially supported by NSF grant 8900267.

References

Baars, B. J. (1988), *A Cognitive Theory of Consciousness*, Cambridge: Cambridge University Press.

Brooks, R. A. (1986), A robust layered control system for a mobile robot, *International J. of Robotics Research*, 2: 14–23.

Crick, F. H. C. and Koch, C. (1990), Toward a neurobiological theory of consciousness, *Seminars in Neuroscience*, 2: 263–75.

Edelman, G. R. (1989), *The Remembered Past*, New York: Basic Books.

Fodor, J. A. (1983), *The Modularity of Mind*, Cambridge, MA: MIT Press.

Freuder, E. C. (1974), A computer vision system for visual recognition using active knowledge, *MIT AI Lab. Tech. Report* 345.

Frisby, J. P. (1980), *Seeing: Illusion, Brain and Mind*, Oxford: Oxford University Press.

Gibson, J. J. (1950), *The Perception of the Visual World* Boston, MA: Houghton Mifflin.

Gibson, J. J. (1979), *The Ecological Approach to Visual Perception*, Boston, MA: Houghton Mifflin.

Gilchrist, A. (1977), Perceived lightness depends on perceived spatial arrangement, *Science*, 195: 185–7.

Gray, C. M., Konig, P., Engel, K. and Singer, W. (1989), Oscillatory responses in cat visual cortex exhibit inter-columnar synchronization which reflects global stimulus properties, *Nature* 338: 334–7.

Gregory, R. L. (1970), *The Intelligent Eye*, London: Weidenfeld and Nicolson.

Hacker, P. M. S. (1991), Seeing, representing, and describing: an examination of David Marr's computational theory of vision. In *Investigating Psychology: Sciences of the Mind after Wittgenstein*, ed. John Hyman, London: Routledge, pp. 119–54.

Jackendoff, R. (1987), *Consciousness and the Computational Mind*, Cambridge, MA: MIT Press.

Johnson-Laird, P. N. (1988), *The Computer and the Mind*, Cambridge, MA: Harvard University Press.

Konishi, M., Sullivan, W. E. and Takahashi, T. (1985), The owl's cochlear nuclei process different sound localization cues, *J. Acoust. Soc. Am.* 78: 360–4.

LeCun, Y., Boser, B., Denker, J. S., Henderson, D., Howard, R. E., Hubbard, W. and Jackel, L. D. (1989), Backpropagation applied to handwritten zip code recognition, *Neural Computation* 1(4): 541–51.

Livingstone, M. L. and Hubel, D. H. (1981), Effects of sleep and arousal on the processing of visual information in the cat, *Nature* 291: 554–61.

Livingstone, M. L. and Hubel, D. H. (1984), Anatomy and physiology of a color system in the primate visual cortex, *J. of Neuroscience* 4(1): 309–56.

Marr, D. (1982), *Vision*, San Francisco: W. H. Freeman.

Minsky, M. (1987), *Society of Mind*, New York: Simon and Schuster.

Minsky, M. (1990), Logical vs. analogical, symbolic vs. connectionist, neat vs. scruffy. The 1990 Japan Prize Lecture. Circulated manuscript.

Nakayama, K., Shimojo, S. and Silverman, G. H. (1989), Stereoscopic depth: its relation to image segmentation, grouping, and the recognition of occluded objects, *Perception*, 18: 55–68.

Penrose, R. (1989), *The Emperor's New Mind*, New York: Oxford University Press.

Poggio, T., Torre, V. and Koch, C. (1985), Computational vision and regularization theory, *Nature*, 6035: 314–19.

Ramachandran, V. S. (1985), The neurobiology of perception. Guest editorial, *Perception*, 14: 97–103.

Richmond, B. J., Optican, L. M. and Gawne, T. J. (1987), Evidence of an intrinsic temporal code for pictures in striate cortex neurons, *Abstracts Soc. Neuros., 17 Ann. Meeting, New Orleans, LA, Nov. 16–21* 178.11: 631.

Salzman, C. D., Britten, K. H. and Newsome, W. T. (1990), Cortical microstimulation influences perceptual judgements of motion direction, *Nature* 346: 174–7.

Searle, J. R. (1980), Minds, brains, and programs, *Behavioral and Brain Sciences* 3: 417–57.

Searle, J. R. (1990), Consciousness, explanatory inversion and cognitive science. *Behavioral and Brain Sciences* 13: 585–642.

Tenenbaum, J. M. and Barrow, H. G. (1976), Experiments in interpretation-guided segmentation, *Stanford Research Institute Tech. Note* 123.

Ullman, S. (1979), *The Interpretation of Visual Motion*, Cambridge, MA: MIT Press.

Ullman, S. (1980), Against direct perception, *Behavioral and Brain Sciences* 3: 373–415.

Zipser, D. and Andersen, R. A. (1988), A back-propagation programmed network that simulates response properties of a subset of posterior parietal neurons, *Nature* 331: 679–84.

20

"Why Do Things Look as They Do?" What Koffka Might Have Said to Gibson, Marr and Rock

William Epstein

I begin with an autobiographical note. My generation of graduate students in the late 1950s were, on the whole, hearsay-knowers of Gestalt psychology. What they knew they learned from secondary sources whose sources were themselves often secondary sources. This is often the way of prejudice that passes as knowledge.

My personal circumstances at the time were decidedly different. With Solomon Asch, Mary Henle and Hans Wallach among my teachers I was no stranger to Gestalt psychology. Despite the efforts of these remarkable teachers, my first encounters with Gestalt theory left me cold. Köhler's *Gestalt Psychology* seemed to me out of touch with the urgent controversies, since forgotten, that filled the pages of North American journals and his *Dynamics in Psychology* baffled me.[1]

My state of mind was promptly altered when Hans Wallach directed me to the segment in Koffka's *Principles*, titled *Why Do Things Look as They Do?*[2] Merely to recognize the question was exciting and Koffka's style of argumentation was compelling.

Koffka wrote in 1935. Since that time much has happened in the analysis of perception. Particularly noteworthy has been the development in the 1970s and 1980s of two new and apparently antithetical theoretical approaches. One, introduced and promoted by J. J. Gibson, is called the theory of direct perception or the ecological approach to perception; the other, popularized by David Marr, is offered under the

William Epstein, " 'Why do things look as they do?' What Koffka might have said to Gibson, Marr and Rock," in S. Pogg (ed.), *Gestalt Psychology: Its Origins, Foundations and Influence* (Florence: Leo S. Olschki, 1989), pp. 175–89.

generic label of computational theory. In addition to these new approaches, the work of Irvin Rock over the last two decades represents a serious effort toward a working out of classical Helmholtzian inferential theory. How does Koffka's analysis of the problem of perception seem in the light of these contemporary developments? That is the question I will address today.

Gibson's Theory of Direct Perception

In his progress toward the "true answer,"[3] Koffka considers and dismisses three false answers. The second of these answers is "that things look as they do because the proximal stimuli are what they are."[4] Despite Koffka's reasoned rejection, this answer, in revised form, is the centerpiece of J. J. Gibson's theory of direct perception.[5] Here is a capsule rendering of Gibson's theoretical approach: (*a*) Proximal stimulation at the level of spatiotemporal optical structures carries information about the world; information in optical structures specifies environmental properties and events. (*b*) Owing to the fact that the visual system has evolved in this optical environment the hardware of the system has been engineered to ensure sensitivity to the informative optical structures. (*c*) The principal function of the perceptual system is not the generation of representations of the world for contemplation by the mind. The principal function of the perceptual system is to support action. Successful action depends on contact with the environment. For this reason the perceptual system is driven to detect the optical structures that can insure contact with the environment. In summary, Gibson's answer to Koffka's question is that things look as they do because the information in proximal stimulation is what it is.

What might Koffka have said to Gibson? I believe that Koffka would have found much that he liked in Gibson's approach but in the end one sticking point would have kept Koffka from embracing Gibson's position. Koffka would certainly have applauded Gibson's emphasis on higher-order variables of stimulation. Any move away from an explanation that takes as its premise a link between perception and punctiform aggregates of receptor inputs would appeal to Koffka.

Moreover, Koffka would have appreciated that in important respects Gibson's theory does not share the vulnerabilities of the older proximal hypothesis. For Koffka, the facts of perceptual constancy counted as a telling rebuttal of the older account. Koffka argued that contrary to the proximal account, the constancies, e.g. perceived size remains unchanged over variations in viewing distance, are evidence that perception is independent of local variations in the correlated proximal variable, e.g. projective size. Moreover, two objects that have identical local proximal correlates, e.g. A at distance D and 2A at distance 2D, are distinguished readily under natural viewing conditions. As in the preceding case, Koffka argued, perception exhibits an independence from local proximal states that does not conform to the proximal account.

Gibson's answer is not vulnerable to this line of argumentation. Gibson proposes that perception is the detection of information and he explicitly denies that information is carried by static local proximal states. Information is a property of spatiotemporal optical structures and these higher-order dynamic structures are not subject to the vagaries that are characteristic of the local static proximal correlate. The constancies are the rule because the optical structures that specify properties and events are as a rule invariant over the variables that generate changes in the local proximal correlate.

These aspects of Gibson's theory and more would have exercised a strong pull on Koffka. But in the end, as I have suggested, Koffka would have been put off by Gibson. And paradoxically, Koffka's dissatisfaction would have arisen with respect to that very aspect of Gibson's theory that initially elicited approval. At the core of Gibson's theory is the proposition that stimulation is structured, that is, that structure is there in the optic array. In a sense, for Gibson optical input is organized; it is an organization that is contingent on the structure of the physical environment and the laws governing ambient light. In sharp contrast, Koffka repeatedly insists that optical input is not structured. The perceptual world is organized and by hypothesis the underlying brain process is structured, but proximal stimulation is not structured. To refer to optical structures, as Gibson does, is to commit a variant of the "stimulus error." Gibson, Koffka might have said, has mistaken the facts known to the ecological psychologist, that is, that ambient light may be construed as optical structure, as facts for the perceptual system.

Koffka's insistence that optical input is in principle unstructured warrants scrutiny. The claim rests on an assumption that Koffka took over from the orthodox position which he so urgently wished to undermine. The orthodox view took the retina as the frame of reference for assessing the nature of optical input. Adopting this anatomical frame of reference, the orthodox view concluded that optical input is a mosaic of independent receptor activations. And this was also the frame of reference adopted by Koffka. This is nowhere more evident than in the physical metaphor Koffka deployed in developing his thesis that stimulation does not exhibit the properties of structure. Optical input is described by analogy with light delivered to a photographic plate:

> if you have taken a regular picture, what is on your developed plate? A picture? Yes and no; yes, when you include the person who looks at the plate in the situation, but *no*, if you consider the plate by itself. On this plate you have a great number of particles which, before the plate was developed and fixed, were sensitive of the light which struck them... the developed plate can be adequately described if you divide it up into small areas and measure the thickness of the layer in each of these areas. A complete table of these thicknesses would be a complete description of the developed plate. There is *no* picture on it, if we mean by picture more than this complete table. Break off a corner of your plate, rub off a part of the photographic layer, the rest will remain as it was before, each point having its characteristics independently of all the others.
>
> ...And now let us go back to our eyes. When they have focused on an object... what is on the retinae? Pictures of these objects? Yes, only when we mean by a picture just such a table as we have described in the case of the photographic plate; only instead of the individual particles we have to list the sensitive elements of the retinae, the cones and rods, and instead of the thickness of the layer the *kind* and amount of stimulation which each of these elementary receptors receives. But apart from this difference the immediate cause of our vision of any object is just such a mosaic of stimulation as that of the photographic plate.[6]

The photographic plate and the independent granular photochemical changes are offered by Koffka as counterparts of the retina and the biochemical changes in the receptors. If this anatomical frame of reference is accepted, Koffka's rejection of the possibility of structure in optical input is persuasive.

However, the anatomical frame of reference is not the only one available. In fact, Gibson has adopted a different frame of reference, one that is centered in the ambient light itself. It is the ambient light converging on a point of observation that is structured by the environment. This structuring does not depend on the arrangement of receptors. The coordinates of Gibson's frame of reference are in the ambient light, not in the retina.

The great difference between Gestalt theory and Gibson's theory turns on this point. Koffka, seeing no possibility of imputing structure to stimulation, looked to processes in the brain to impart organization. Gibson, judging that stimulation is structured, saw no requirement to look elsewhere for organizing processes.

We need to be clear that Gibson's theory of direct perception does not object to talk about brain processes although there is little such talk in the canonical works of the theory. The stance that I attribute to Gibson is that theorizing about brain processes will inevitably be shaped by the function that is assigned to the putative brain process in the perceptual system. If the function is supposed to be to impose organization, then one is encouraged to formulate a conception of brain process that can satisfy this need. On the other hand, if the function is to detect optical structures, that is, to pick up information, then speculation about underlying brain processes will assume a different form, e.g. resonance.

One final comment on Koffka and Gibson before I turn to consideration of Rock's position. We know that Koffka objected strongly to the thesis that things look as they do because past experience is what it is. But we also know, contrary to popular reports, that the Gestalt theorists did not rule out effects of past experience; they only wished to keep the effects of past experience in proper perspective. For example, while denying that past experience can be the basic organizing principle of form perception, Wertheimer, Köhler, and Koffka always accepted that when an organization has been achieved in the past on the basis of the primary principles of grouping, this previously achieved organization can influence current perceptual organization.[7]

The admission by Gestalt theory of a role for past experience or learning in perception is a necessary concession to the facts of the matter. Nevertheless, it seems to me a troublesome admission inasmuch as the admission is not accompanied by a special formulation of the learning process that would reconcile perceptual learning with the general Gestalt theory of perception. The orthodox associationist conceptions favored by Koffka's contemporaries would certainly be unnatural grafts on to the main body of Gestalt theory.

Gibson also confronted the problem of learning in his theory. His solution was to offer a special conception of learning in perception that does not threaten the integrity of his theory. I think Koffka would have appreciated Gibson's intent to render to learning its due without granting it unlimited license. Gibson's conception is that learning in perception is a process of tuning the perceptual system to higher levels of sensitivity to information in stimulation. What is learned is to pick up informational structures previously neglected. In this way, learning is kept entirely within the bounds of Gibson's claim that things look as they do because the information in proximal stimulation is what it is.

Rock's Neo-Helmholtzian Constructivism

Helmholtz is alive and well and living in the pages of the contemporary journals. The *Physiological Optics* remains among the most widely cited works. The standing of the *Physiological Optics* owes much to its masterly organization of the fundamental facts of perception. But to a degree that is remarkable, Helmholtz's currency is due to his theoretical analysis of the perceptual process which he set out in the opening chapter of volume 3 of the *Physiological Optics*. Helmholtz advanced the following perceptual heuristic: "such objects are always imagined as being present in the field of vision as would have to be there in order to produce the same impression on the nervous mechanism, the eyes being used under ordinary normal condition."[8]

Underlying this heuristic, according to Helmholtz, is a ratiomorphic, inference-like process which takes the optical input and stored representations of the circumstances under which the optical input has typically been encountered and from these premises draws a conclusion about the occurrent state of affairs. The logical structure is akin to inductively strong inference in that if the premises are true then the conclusion is highly likely, but not certain. Notice that Helmholtz has posited an interactive model of the perceptual process, one in which bottom-up and top-down constraints interact to pick out the best-fitting conclusion.

Irvin Rock's theoretical analysis, set out in *The Logic of Perception*, is a variant of Helmholtz's thesis.[9] How would Rock reply to Koffka's question? Let Rock speak for himself: "My answer to Koffka's query – Why do things look as they do? – would be: because of the cognitive operations performed on the information contained within the stimulus."[10] In common with other variants of constructivism, Rock assumes that the process of perception is a hierarchically ordered multistage process. The output of the first stage is a description of the proximal input. This proximally correlated representation is itself a cognitive construction owing its organization to the interpretive activities of a central executive. Rock considers the Gestalt principles of grouping not as descriptions of the properties of a self-organizing process but as descriptions of the rules followed by the central executive in generating a description of the optical input.

The first stage is necessary but the output of the first stage is not sufficient to support adaptive behavior. The proximally correlated description is necessary as a source of constraints on the later interpretation generated by the central executive. The later interpretation must accommodate the facts that are made explicit in the proximally correlated description. At the same time, the early output is not sufficient. For one, it is viewer-centered, not environment-centered; in addition, the proximally correlated description will, as a rule, be equivocal with respect to candidate distal attributions.

For this reason, Rock postulates a higher level of processing which operates on the output of the first stage. The higher level of processing picks out one description of the distal state of affairs from the candidate descriptions. The process by which the lower-level representation is superseded is characterized by Rock as a cognitive process. The executive of the perceptual system deploys a repertoire of perceptual heuristics to arrive at a solution to the problem posed by the occurrent first-level representation.

The following example selected from Rock's program of experimentation will help to clarify his approach.[11] The subject views a single luminous line which oscillates in the frontal parallel plane behind an invisible rectangular viewing aperture. The dimensions of the aperture and the length of the line are such that the ends of the line never come into view. The first perceptual description of the display is true to the proximal state of affairs: a single line undergoing concurrent changes in retinal orientation and length. Notice that this description may be assigned two distal interpretations, one that recapitulates the actual state of affairs and another quite different, a line of constant length oscillating *in depth*. Which distal interpretation will be favored? The decision is determined by the *nonaccidentalness rule*. Systematic concurrent changes in optical input, e.g. changes of orientation and length, do not occur by chance. The association is due to a common cause that effects both changes. In this case a distal event that could cause concurrent changes in orientation and length is oscillation of the line in depth. In fact, this is the interpretation favored by subjects. However, if the rectangular viewing aperture is made visible the favored interpretation shifts owing to the activation of rules concerning occlusion and disocclusion.

We can be certain that Koffka would not find much to like in Rock's theory. Rock's approach would put Koffka in mind of the "interpretation" theory which he and Köhler criticized so roundly. Like Rock's theory, the interpretation theory postulated two levels of representation, one proximally determined, the other determined by interpretation of the former based on experience. In rebutting the interpretation theory, Koffka set out four arguments: (1) If the perceptual world is the product of interpretation of sensation then it ought to be possible to observe sensation but in fact the presumed sensations are as a rule not noticed.

(2) If perceiving the world depends on cognitive operations then one would expect that the perceptual world of the infant should be severely impoverished but in fact in many respects, e.g. the perceptual constancies, the perceptual world of the infant resembles the adult perceptual world. (3) If perception depends on knowledge and knowledge depends on perception how does perception get off the ground? (4) Finally, if interpretation is based on knowledge then why is it the case that so often knowledge fails to affect perception, e.g. illusions do not yield to knowledge?

Rock is quite sensitive to these lines of attack and he has tried to fortify his position against these arguments. First, in Rock's view the output of the first stage is in fact accessible: While it is superseded by the later representation it is not overwritten in the operations that compute the environment-centered representation. Moreover, the proximally related representation is available for report under appropriate conditions. The description of the proximal state is an explicit premise not an unnoticed sensation. The paradox, interpreting a sign which itself is unregistered, does not trouble Rock.

What of Koffka's other questions? Rock proposes to fend off the second and third thrusts by distinguishing between cognitive theory and empiricist theory. Koffka's criticisms are telling objections to classical empiricist theory but Rock insists that a cognitive theory need not be an empiricist theory. It is not necessary to suppose that the rules, assumptions and logical structures that govern perception are learned. This form of knowledge is in the nature of the deep structure of the language of perception and may well be part of the inherited competence of the organism. Rock wants to distinguish between claims concerning the origins of the syntax of the language of perception (empiricist theory) and claims that the syntax of the language shapes the interpretation of optical input (cognitive theory).

From this stance the fact that the perceptual world of the infant does not differ greatly from the adult world does not pose a problem. For example, it is likely, given the results of recent studies of the perception of structure from motion by very young infants, that if infants were used as subjects in Rock's experiment the infants would respond the same way as adults. The nonaccidentalness rule is a basic rule of the syntax of perception [that will be conformed to] from the outset.

Koffka's objection from the invulnerability of perception to the introduction of knowledge also loses force if one distinguishes between the syntax and semantics of the language of perception. In Rock's view it is syntax that matters not semantics or specific contents. It is the rule that relates visual angle, registered distance and perceived size will not modify differences of perceived size when the differences are dictated by the rule that links visual angle, perceived distance and perceived size.

Would Koffka's unhappiness with Rock be allayed by these counterarguments? I am certain that Koffka's dissatisfaction would remain. Rock's insistence that percipients can have access to the proximally correlated description is based on certain experimental results but even if these results have been correctly interpreted they do not establish that these proximally correlated representations function in the perceptual process in the way Rock proposes. As for the other counterarguments they seem to be a form of special pleading; that is, the claims do not emerge from facts but seem to have been designed specifically to accommodate troublesome facts.

There is another, yet more fundamental concern that Koffka would have with Rock's approach. The approach stressing inference, problem-solving and choosing among alternatives seems to require a reasoner, problem-solver or decision-maker. Indeed Rock does not shrink from this necessity. He explicitly posits a homuncular executive agent. This postulation runs counter to the physicalist orientation of Gestalt theory. Postulation of a homunculus borders on vitalism, that is, attributing to the biological organism some special property not captured by the laws of physics. In summarizing his reasons for rejecting vitalism, Koffka noted that "the vitalistic solution is no solution, but a mere renaming of the problem." It is hard to escape the feeling that Rock's executive agent is a fair target for the same criticism.

Marr's Computational Theory

The latest fashion in styles of perceptual theory is known as computational theory. David Marr's *Vision* published in 1982 was the first integrated statement of the computational approach.[12] In common with other successful fashions, the computational approach owes its favorable reception both to its novelty and to its continuity with established tradition.

The traditional aspect of Marr's approach is recognized readily. Marr himself aptly characterized his approach as a modern extension of the representational theory of mind. The aim of the perceptual system is to deliver useful representations of the world and the process that sustains this achievement is a process of representational transformation.

What distinguishes Marr from his predecessors is the exacting standards of explicitness that he has adopted in realizing his instantiation of the representational theory. For each of the three major levels of representation, the primal sketch (imagine descriptions), the 2.5D sketch (scene surfaces) and the 3D model, Marr begins by formulating a "computational theory" – an account of the nature of the task confronting the visual system and a description of the input and the output. The description of the nature of the task must be complete and explicit. The success of the next phase in development of the theory depends on it. In this phase Marr sets out to write algorithms that can operate on the input to generate the prescribed output. The test of a computational algorithm is in the running. An algorithm that generates a unique representation of the form that can serve as useful input to the next stage of processing passes the test of efficacy. In deciding among candidate algorithms for the human visual system Marr looks for direction to psychophysical data and to a lesser degree to current conceptions of the hardware of the visual system. It is Marr's aim to proceed as far as possible without recourse to knowledge. Marr is determined to develop a data-driven process theory. It is only as a last recourse that Marr admits top-down processes.

Gibson and Rock are complete competitors. It is hard to suppose that they could co-exist. How does Marr stand in relation to Gibson and Rock? Obviously Gibson would have found Marr's constructivist/representational metatheory decidedly uncongenial while Rock would find little to quarrel about with Marr on the level of metatheory. Nevertheless, I think there is better prospect of a reconciliation of Gibson and Marr than of Rock and Marr.

This assertion rests on my reading of the Marr program. I take it that unlike Rock but like Gibson, Marr holds that there is information in stimulation; that when the environment satisfies certain constraints, variables of optical stimulation are related to the environment in an unequivocal manner. But, according to Marr, the information is implicit; needed are computational algorithms that will make the information explicit. These computational algorithms play the role in Marr's theory that the unelaborated construct "pickup" plays in Gibson's theory. Gibson talks about the detection or pickup of optical structures; Marr faces the demands of such claims squarely and proposes algorithms that do the computational work that makes the information in optical structure explicit.

How would Koffka have reacted to Marr? I think that the first impulse of a perfect promoter of Gestalt theory would be to reject Marr in entirety on the grounds that the computational theory is nothing but the old-style constructivist theory in new dress. But on reflection a more balanced assessment would replace outright rejection.

To begin with, not since Wertheimer and Köhler has anyone written so perceptively about the problems of sensory organization. Like the Gestalt theorists Marr recognized that retinal stimulation does not present itself as organized structures. The organization of retinal input is the product of processes that exploit environmental regularities to generate a representation, the primal sketch, that will be the basis for construction of distally correlated representations. In fact, the regularities or constraints that Marr deploys can be aligned closely with the Gestalt principles of grouping. The grouping principles in Marr's treatment have a different warrant than the principles have in Gestalt theory. In Marr's theory they are rules that reflect regularities in the environment and that owe their status to the evolution of the processes of early vision in response to the environment. For Koffka the principles of grouping are descriptions of the rules of perceptual organization that owe their status to the self-organizing properties of brain fields. Despite this difference Koffka would have appreciated Marr's recognition of the problems of organization. Marr cannot be charged with the "stimulus error."

Next, consider the constructivist cast of Marr's theory. It cannot be constructivism as such to which Koffka would have objected. After all in a nontrivial sense Gestalt theory is a constructivist theory – the perceptual world is a construction of dynamic global brain processes; perception is not a direct response to stimulation. So it must be Marr's particular brand of constructivism that requires assessment. One feature that is decidedly unacceptable is Marr's insistence that the constructive process is a sequential generation of representations. Koffka might grant that postulation of these representational stages does useful work in support of the development of successful computational algorithms. But Koffka would caution Marr not to confuse the possible with the actual. Nowhere in Marr's monograph is there evidence in the form of phenomenological reports or experimental data that implicates these stages in the human perceptual system. Marr, the scientist, may need the "primal sketch" but there is no evidence that Marr, the percipient, instantiates the primal sketch in his perceptual system. I don't believe that there can be a reconciliation on this matter. My judgment is that the burden of proof falls squarely on Marr's shoulders.

A second feature of generic constructivism that is obvious in the writings of Rock, Gregory, and Hochberg is the cognitive coloration in which they paint the operations that construct the perceptual world. As I noted in discussing Koffka's reaction to Rock, Koffka finds the attribution of cognitivie operations unacceptable. If the algorithms that Marr proposed are inherently cognitive then Marr must also be found unacceptable. But are Marr's computational algorithms cognitive?

This question must be considered twice, once for the algorithms of early vision, the algorithms that compute the primal sketch and the 2.5D sketch and once for the algorithms that compute the final object-centered representation, the 3D model.

There can be little doubt about these latter algorithms. These definitely have a cognitive cast: they make use of a collection of stored mental models and these models serve as the interpretative context for transforming the viewer-centered representation into an object-centered representation. It has never been clear to me why Marr felt compelled to make this move to conceptually-driven processing. But this move places these algorithms out of bounds as far as Koffka is concerned.

Turning next to the algorithms of early vision the matter is not so straightforward. Nevertheless, one compatible interpretation of the processes of early vision is that they are noncognitive computational algorithms. While the representations they generate are intelligent solutions, the process is not of the sort that is intelligibly characterized as intelligent. It is not a process guided by an intelligence, nor is it a process resembling logical thinking, deductive or inductive. The algorithms are executed by special computational modules that have evolved for specific problems and that incorporate relevant constraints. For example, the correspondence problem in stereoscopic vision is solved by a highly interactive, massively parallel algorithm that incorporates the constraints of uniqueness and uniformity. The process is not one of deciding among candidate solutions or inferring the correct solution. Instead it is a process of settling into a solution under the prevailing constraints.

At issue here is not whether the particular algorithms developed by Marr are in fact up to the tasks of a biological vision system but whether when characterized in this way Marr's algorithms might be more congenial to Koffka. I would be greatly relieved were Koffka to appear to speak for himself. It seems to me that the cooperative algorithms of Marr and the general class of algorithms that may be characterized as highly interactive massively parallel and which are gaining widespread currency among contemporary computational approaches offer a prospect that Koffka never considered. The prospect is of a process that is noncognitive and nonteleological that settles into a solution as a consequence of dynamic interaction among networks of individual processing units. This conception does not ignore the activity of elementary processing units. Nevertheless, the process is not elementaristic. Nor does the conception deny that the solution reflects more than the and-summative aggregation of the outputs of the individual unit. Nevertheless, the process is not wholistic. In their polemical drive against the atomistic apporoach and their fervor for a dynamic field approach the Gestalt theorists were persuaded that these two conceptions exhausted the set of viable options. But the newer conceptions cannot be assigned to either category. They would have presented a challenge and an opportunity for Koffka.

Concluding Comment

Shortly before his death, Gibson delivered an unpublished lecture to a conference on Processes of Perceptual Organization and Representation that was held in Abano.[13] Gibson called his talk "The Ecological Approach to Perception: An Extension of Certain Features of Gestalt Psychology." In this way, at the end of his life, Gibson recognized a debt which had its origins over 40 years earlier during Gibson's tenure as Koffka's colleague at Smith College. Given the profound differences between Gibson and Koffka it may seem odd that Gibson should have construed his theoretical work as an extension of aspects of Gestalt theory. The resolution of this seeming anomaly is suggested in an earlier talk that Gibson presented in 1969 (publ. 1971) to commemorate Koffka's *Principles* 35 years after its publication.[14] In commenting on the relationship of his ideas to the ideas of Koffka, Gibson observed: *"my ideas about visual perception depend on his ideas, if not by agreement then by contrast....* His book, more than any other book of its time, set the psychology of perception on the course it is now following."[15] I think that although to a lesser degree than was true in 1969 the questions raised by Koffka continue to shape the general agenda of contemporary work on the problems of perception.

Notes

1 W. Koehler, *Gestalt Psychology*, New York, Liveright, 1929, 2nd edn 1947; idem., *Dynamics in Psychology*, New York, Liveright, 1940.
2 K. Koffka, *Principles of Gestalt Psychology*, New York, Harcourt Brace, 1935.
3 Cf. ibid., p. 98.
4 See ibid., p. 80.
5 Cf. J. J. Gibson, *The Ecological Approach to Visual Perception*, Boston, Houghton Mifflin, 1979.

6   Koffka, op. cit., pp. 74–5.
7   Cf. e.g. Koehler, *Gestalt Psychology*, op. cit., pp. 192–3.
8   H. von Helmholtz (orig. edn. 1866), Eng. tr. *Treatise on Physiological Optics* (J. P. C. Southall, trs.), New York, Optical Society of America, 1924–5, vol. III, p. 2.
9   See I. Rock, *The Logic of Perception*, Cambridge, MA, MIT Press, 1983.
10   I. Rock, *Perception*, New York, Scientific American Books, 1984, p. 231.
11   See I. Rock and D. Smith, Alternative Solutions to Kinetic Stimulus Transformations, *Journal of Experimental Psychology: Human Performance and Perception* 7, 1981: 19–29.
12   D. Marr, *Vision: A Computational Investigation into the Human Representation and Processing of Visual Information*, New York, W. H. Freeman, 1982.
13   Cf. J. J. Gibson, *The Ecological Approach to Perception: An Extension of Certain Features of Gestalt Psychology*. Paper presented at conference on Processes of Perceptual Organization and Representation, Abano (Italy), June 1979.
14   J. J. Gibson, The Legacies of Koffka's Principle, *Journal of the History of the Behavioral Sciences*, 7, 1971: 3–9.
15   Ibid., p. 16.

Part IV

Perception and Conception

Introduction to Part IV

Almost everyone agrees that there is a significant line to be drawn between perception and cognition. The acutest eye needs to have language or other conceptual apparatus available in order to determine *that* the person is the son of Diares or *that* the painting is a Da Vinci. Yet, where and how are we to draw this boundary between perceptual and conceptual knowledge and awareness? Or might this supposed difference, itself, depend on intuitions that are no longer sustainable? At this point, perennial epistemological issues and concerns would seem to establish close contact with ongoing vision theory (Crane 1992).

Dretske argues that it is important for both visual science and philosophy to distinguish cases of "seeing objects" from cases of "seeing that." For example, someone may see a cat, without seeing *that* it is a cat. The person may not have a concept of "cat" available to categorize the object and so cannot perceive that the object is in fact a cat. This minimal type of seeing Dretske labels "sensory seeing" or "sensory perception." The more conceptually dependent type he calls "cognitive seeing" or "cognitive perception". Dretske's appeal to sensory seeing is not meant to revive older notions of visual sensations as two-dimensional displays of color experience. At the same time, it is meant to capture what Dretske thinks can often be visually alike between a person who only sees a cat and a person who in addition sees that it is a cat. Dretske is aware of the many obstacles to be faced in formulating a satisfactory distinction between sensory and cognitive perception. One difficulty, that he mentions toward the end of his paper, is the need to square his account with the facts of perceptual learning. Dretske deals with this and related problems more fully and with ingenuity in other writings (Dretske 1981, 1995).

Dretske also discusses the relationship between his sensory perception/ cognitive perception distinction and the direct/indirect dichotomy considered in Part III of this volume. He argues that the latter controversy in visual science is to be distinguished from philosophical worries over the non-immediacy of perception and ensuing metaphysical debates over Realism (Gibson 1967). If Dretske is correct, it then becomes an interesting question to what extent this disconnection both diminishes the significance of the problem for vision theory and deprives the philosophical controversies of their empirical content (Schwartz 1994).

The Fogelin piece is an excerpt from his book on Wittgenstein, and some prior familiarity with Wittgensteinian ideas is helpful to appreciate Fogelin's commentary. In this selection, Fogelin attempts to make sense of Wittgenstein's thoughts on several puzzling perceptual phenomena. These cases are usually referred to as "seeing as" or "aspect seeing" (Budd 1989). In particular, Wittgenstein asks how best to characterize the following: (i) the changes that take place when we come to see a hitherto unnoticed likeness between two people or things, and (ii) the changes that take place when a picture undergoes figure/ground reversal or when it perceptually switches its apparent shape (as with the much cited duck-rabbit drawing). Everyone seems to agree that in these cases something remains constant and something alters. But what is it that remains the same and what accounts for the changes noticed in (i) and (ii)? Is it necessary to bring in some notion of a constant sensation or sensory core to capture the phenomena? Are the experienced shifts to be accounted for in terms of the application of different concepts?

According to Fogelin, Wittgenstein thinks that neither of these options is quite right. Fogelin believes that in the end Wittgenstein's position is that perceptual phenomena do not fit into a few clearly delineated categories. There is a range of significant differences among the cases. For example, not only do the phenomena in (i) and (ii) differ, but the duck/rabbit perceptions may depend on a type of conceptualization not required to experience figure/ground reversals. Wittgenstein thinks that the best, and perhaps only, thing to do is to point out the relevant likenesses and dis-likenesses among the cases. We should not insist on forcing them all into a few familiar and convenient categories. If perceptual phenomena, though, do constitute such a motley collection, then there may be no sharp perception/conception dichotomy on which to hang philosophical theses and psychological theories.

As Dretske reminds us, the assumption that people with normal functioning vision can see the same things, despite their conceptual differences, has a powerful grip. Of course, it may be necessary to make allowances for perceptual learning. With practice and training, powers of detection and discrimination can be considerably altered. Colors, sounds, and tastes that formerly could not be distinguished may come to be experienced as qualitatively quite distinct. Hanson builds on this and related aspects of perceptual development. He goes on to argue that *conceptual* skill and knowledge can itself alter the very content of what we see. People with different backgrounds and understandings of the world do not see the same things. For Hanson all perception is *theory-laden*.

If earlier philosophers thought that we "really" (directly, immediately) see very little, only sensations or sense data, Hanson goes to the other extreme. Appropriately informed observers can "really" see everything from atomic particles to complex human interactions. But then how is a theory of vision to cope with or explain the domain of seeing thus expanded? And what if there is no empirically sound way to separate those aspects of perception that are due to purely *visual* factors from those that accompany the acquisition of new concepts or beliefs?

Hanson's ideas continue to play a prominent role in debates over observation and scientific objectivity. After all, observation is supposed to supply the ground, the "neutral" evidence for the evaluation of theories. So if, as Hanson maintains, all seeing is theory-laden and different theorists actually see different worlds, there might be no non-relative way to adjudicate among competing theories (Fodor 1984, 1988; Churchland 1988).

Peacocke has long been concerned with characterizing the nature and content of visual experience (Peacocke 1983). Moreover, he believes that any adequate theory of perception must confront the following problem. On the one hand, perceptions serve to inform us about the state of things in the environment. On the other hand, the information so provided is often not readily captured in words or concepts that can be articulated. For example, we may be able to see the distance from here to there or between the couch and the table without being able to assign any specific numerical length measures to the spaces so perceived. But if such perceptions are not conceptually cloaked, in what manner do they have "representative" content?

Peacocke's answer to this question requires him to provide both a basis for individuating experiential states and a scheme for assigning them content. Peacocke sketches a solution to the first problem in terms of matching profiles, a method of qualia individuation related to that which Goodman (1951) developed in *The Structure of Appearance*. Peacocke then goes on to suggest that the type of representation employed in these non-conceptual cases is analogue in form. They differ in this way from the digital type of schemes associated with linguistic symbols. Peacocke's solution, therefore, depends critically on the details of his account of matching profiles and on his analysis of the analogue/digital distinction. Peacocke is also aware that much of his project hinges on a proper treatment of the content of demonstrative thought (Peacocke 1989).

Spelke asks how we come to experience the world as consisting of enduring physical bodies. She rejects the answers she finds not only in the Berkeley/Helmholtz tradition but in work done along Gestalt, Gibsonian and Marr-inspired lines. Spelke's main complaint is that all of these approaches assume that objects are *perceived*. In contrast, she maintains that they are conceived. This does not mean, though, that the apprehension of objects appears late in human development. Spelke and her colleagues have produced a body of experimental evidence they believe shows that infants are innately endowed with a basic object concept. In this abridgment of the paper, Spelke's detailed examination of alternative accounts of the development of the object concept is not included.

Of course, all this requires being clear about (i) what it means to experience the world as a layout of objects (Kellman and Arterberry 1998; Schwartz 2001), and (ii) where perception ends and conception begins. Spelke argues that the dividing line between perception and thought cannot be determined by introspection. Nor can it be drawn in terms of impenetrability, learning, passivity, directness, or simplicity. Her claim is that the end product of pure perception is a simple specification of the layout that assigns no distinct spatial or temporal object boundaries.

As discussed above, the manner and degree to which perceptions are experientially embodied and conceptually rich remains a controversial topic. Less controversial is the idea that the visual system does generate an end product, percepts or perceptions. These perceptions, in turn, are "passed along" to cognition, where they serve to inform thought and instigate action. Dennett's radical move is to challenge the idea of there being any final or finished perceptual state that plays this sort of role.

According to Dennett, there is no point or time in processing at which a complete percept emerges. Instead, the nervous system encodes the stimulus for a variety of properties, both over time and in accord with task demands. Seeing is believing, for Dennett, in that there are no independent experiential states with qualities distinct from these encodings. For example, cases of phenomenal filling-in are to be understood as the system enriching its report of the stimulus rather than its actually generating a detailed or more complete image. Dennett does puzzle over the form these encoded representations might take, and how differences in representational format might or might not affect perceptual experience. Dennett's paper is best read against a background of his theory of consciousness and other of his writings on qualia (Dennett 1988, 1991). But the paper also raises a host of independent issues about how best to understand Koffka's question and what might count as an appropriate answer to it.

References

Budd, M. (1989), *Wittgenstein's Philosophy of Psychology*, London: Routledge.
Churchland, P. (1988), Perceptual plasticity and theoretical neutrality, *Philosophy of Science*, 55: 167–87.
Crane, T. (ed.) (1992), *The Contents of Experience: Essays on Perception*, Cambridge: Cambridge University Press.
Dennett, D. (1988), Quining qualia. In *Consciousness in Contemporary Science*, ed. A. Marcel and E. Bisiach, New York: Oxford University Press.
Dennett, D. (1991), *Consciousness Explained*, Boston: Little, Brown.
Dretske, F. (1981), *Knowledge and the Flow of Information*, Cambridge, MA: MIT Press.
Dretske, F. (1995), *Naturalizing the Mind*, Cambridge, MA: MIT Press.
Fodor, J. (1984), Observation reconsidered, *Philosophy of Science*, 51: 23–43.
Fodor, J. (1988), A reply to Churchland's "Plasticity and theoretical neutrality," *Philosophy of Science*, 55: 188–98.
Gibson, J. J. (1967), New reasons for realism, *Synthese* 17: 162–72.
Goodman, N. (1951), *The Structure of Appearance*, Cambridge, MA: Harvard University Press.
Kellman, P. and Arterberry, M. (1998), *The Cradle of Knowledge*, Cambridge, MA: MIT Press.
Peacocke, C. (1983), *Sense and Content*, Oxford: Clarendon Press.
Peacocke, C. (1989), Perceptual content. In *Themes from Kaplan*, ed. J. Almog, J. Perry, and H. Wettstein, Oxford: Oxford University Press.
Schwartz, R. (1994), *Vision: Variations on Some Berkeleian Themes*, Oxford: Blackwell.
Schwartz, R. (2001), The concept of an object in perception and cognition. In *From Fragments to Objects: Segmentation and Grouping in Vision*, ed. T. Shipley and P. Kellman, Amsterdam: Elsevier, pp. 3–17.

21

Seeing, Believing, and Knowing

Fred Dretske

Epistemology is a branch of philosophy devoted to the study of knowledge and topics – such as truth, memory, perception – relating to knowledge. Epistemology is a philosopher's version of cognitive studies.

Truth is an important part of this study because a central conception of knowledge is knowledge *of the truth*. Though you can know that something isn't so – that, say, the cat *isn't* under the sofa – you can't know something – that the cat *is* under the sofa – that isn't so. To know the whereabouts of the cat requires one to be in possession of the truth about the cat's location. This being so, the idea of truth, as a necessary condition for knowledge, has figured prominently in philosophical discussions of cognition.

Memory and perception also occupy a prominent place in epistemology. Much of our knowledge (some would say *all* of our knowledge) is acquired by perceptual means: we come to know where the cat is by seeing it on the sofa. We might also hear, smell, and feel the cat. These are some of the ways we have of finding out, ways of coming to know, the content and character of our world. The general term for such ways of finding out, ways of coming to know, is *perception. Memory* is the name we give to the ways we have for retaining (through time) the acquired knowledge. Powerful mechanisms for acquiring knowledge (keen eyesight, for example) are of little value to animals that cannot remember, if even for a few seconds, anything they learn. A large storage capacity, on the other hand, is wasted on systems with no way of getting information to be stored.

Fred Dretske, "Seeing, believing, and knowing," in D. Osherson, S. Kosslyn, and J. Hollerbach (eds.), *Visual Cognition and Action*, vol. II (Cambridge, MA: MIT Press, 1990), pp. 129–48.

...There has been a dramatic increase in our scientific understanding of *how* we know some of the things we know. Nevertheless, despite this progress, certain classical philosophical problems, problems concerning the nature, scope, and limits of visual cognition, remain unanswered – or, better, remain without answers that command widespread assent. As we learn more about the way things actually work, these problems tend to be expressed in somewhat different ways. In the past forty years, for instance, computer terminology, a terminology that is embodied in information-processing models of perception and cognition, has become popular. Nomenclature aside, though, the problems are still the old problems, the ones philosophers have pondered and debated for centuries. John Locke, the famous seventeenth-century philosopher, would have little trouble understanding the issues discussed here. Indeed, he had well-developed views on most of these topics.

Although some find it frustrating, this continuing lack of agreement about the right answers to certain puzzling questions – the so-called philosophical questions – is not unexpected. Problems tend to be classified *as* philosophical when they elude established methods, including scientific methods, of solution. But this is no reason to belittle the problems or to despair of their eventual solution. Solutions may lie in finding better methods. This chapter is an attempt to survey some of the more intractable of these problems, to indicate options for dealing with them, and to introduce, when it seems useful, appropriate distinctions and clarifications.

1   Seeing Objects and Seeing Facts

When cognitive scientists speak of visual perception, it seems reasonable to suppose that they are referring to something that we normally describe using the verb *to see*. Seeing the cat on the sofa is to visually perceive the cat on the sofa.

To avoid misunderstanding, though, one should ask, at the very beginning, whether visual perception (or seeing) is to be reserved for objects facts, or something else. After all, we normally speak of seeing objects (like cats and sofas), the properties of objects (the color of a cat, the size of the sofa), events (the cat's jumping on to the sofa), states of affairs (the cat's being on the sofa), and facts (*that* the cat is on the sofa). If these are all to be counted as instances of visual perception, as they appear to be in ordinary language, then care must be taken in a scientific study of visual perception to specify *what* is being perceived: an object, a property, an event, a state of affairs, or a fact. For it is not at all clear that the *same* processes and mechanisms are, or need be, involved in the perception of these different things. Quite the contrary.

Consider, for example, a small child glancing at the sofa and mistaking a sleeping cat for an old sweater. Does the child see an object? Yes, of course. Besides the sofa there is an object, the black cat on the sofa, that the child mistakenly believes to be a black sweater. Though the child does not recognize the cat (*as* a cat), she must, in some sense, see the cat in order to mistake it for a sweater. Nevertheless, though the child sees a black cat on the sofa, sees an object fitting this description, she does not realize that this is a correct description of what she sees. She thereby fails to see the corresponding fact: *that* there is a black cat on the sofa. She sees an object (the black cat on the sofa) but not the fact (that there is a black cat on the sofa) corresponding to it. Shall we say, then, that the child *perceives* the black cat on the sofa? The answer to this question will obviously depend on whether one is thinking of objects (black cats) or facts (that they are black cats).

We can, of course, merely stipulate that visual perception is a way of seeing objects that involves, in some essential way, a knowledge of the object. So when a child – or, indeed, any other kind of animal (an unsuspecting mouse, for instance) – sees a cat on the sofa without realizing what it is, without learning or coming to know that it is a cat, then this way of seeing the cat will not count as *perceiving* the cat. To perceive a cat is, according to this way of using words, to come to know, by visual means, by the use of one's eyes, that it is a cat. Perception is restricted to seeing facts – to seeing that a cat is a cat.

We are free to use words as we please. There is nothing to prevent our restricting visual perception to visual cognition, to a coming-to-know-by-visual-means. It would seem that this particular restriction is, in fact, rather widespread in cognitive psychology. Interested, as they are, in what subjects learn in their perceptual encounters with objects, cognitive psychologists tend to focus on a subject's recognition or identification of objects, ways of seeing (hearing, smelling) things that require some knowledge of what is seen (heard, smelled). So, for instance, recognizing a geometric figure *as* a triangle requires the subject to realize, to come to know, upon seeing it, that it *is* a triangle. If he, upon seeing it, doesn't know what kind of figure it is, doesn't at least distinguish it from other sorts of figures, then he doesn't *recognize* it – not, at least, *as* a triangle. Recognizing triangles is a way of seeing a fact – the fact, namely, that they are triangles.

We are indeed free to use words as we please. But this proposed restriction of visual perception to the perception of facts, to recognition, to a way of seeing things that requires a knowledge of the thing seen, has unfortunate consequences. For we now have no natural way of describing the child who mistakes the cat for a sweater. Since the child does not know it is a cat, she does not, on this way of using words, *perceive* the cat. What, then, is the relation that exists between the child and the cat? The child is not blind. Light rays, reflected from the cat, are entering the child's eyes and, in some perfectly normal way, causing within her a visual experience that would be quite different if the cat were not there. This being so, it seems most natural to say, from a commonsense standpoint, that the child sees the cat but does not realize that this is what she sees. If, because of the way we have decided to use the word *perception*, this does not count as perceiving the cat, it must surely count as *seeing* the cat. Using the word *perception* in this restricted way, then, would not let us count, as visual perception, a person's seeing a cat in perfectly normal circumstances.

It seems preferable, therefore, to distinguish between seeing objects and seeing facts, not (as above) by artificially reserving the word *perception* for one way of seeing, the way of seeing that requires knowledge of the thing seen (that is, seeing facts), but rather by distinguishing two forms of perception, two ways of seeing. We are then free to speak of seeing a black cat without necessarily realizing (knowing or believing) that it is a black cat (or, indeed, an animal at all) as, say, *sense perception* (of a black cat), and another, recognitional, way of seeing the cat as, say, *cognitive perception* (that it is a black cat). This brings our use of the term *visual perception* (including as it now does both cognitive and sense perception) into closer harmony with the ordinary verb *to see* and at the same time allows us to preserve the important distinction between seeing a cat on the sofa and seeing what it is that is on the sofa.

Given this way of using words, we are then free to describe the efforts of cognitive scientists as investigating the processes underlying these forms of perception, examining their differences and commonalities. Perhaps it will turn out, for instance, that processes described as early vision are merely the processes involved in sense perception, the seeing of objects, and later vision comprises whatever additional conceptual or cognitive processes are essential to the perception of facts (cognitive perception) relating to these objects. Perhaps, also, debates about whether perceptual processes are top-down or bottom-up, about the inferential or constructive character of perceptual processes, about whether these processes are massively parallel or sequential, and about their modularity are all debates that can be given sharper focus by distinguishing between the *kind* of perception the debate is a debate about. Discussions or perceptual learning and development will also benefit by a close observance of the difference between cognitive and sensory forms of perception.

For these reasons we will adopt in this chapter the device of speaking of sensory and cognitive perception. The first is a way of seeing (or perceiving) cats (or triangles) that does not require (though it may in fact be accompanied by) knowledge that it is a cat (or a triangle) that is seen. This is what we have been calling *object perception. Cognitive perception* of a cat (or triangle) will be reserved for that way of seeing the cat (triangle) that necessarily involves a coming to know, a cognition (in fact, a recognition), that it is a cat (a triangle). If one, as we ordinarily describe things, sees a cat (a triangle) and recognizes it only as an animal (a figure) of some sort, fails (for whatever reason) to know or realize that it is a cat (a triangle), then one has sensory, but not cognitive, perception of a cat (triangle). Cognitively one perceives only an animal (figure) of some (unspecified) sort. I leave open the question . . . of whether it is possible to have sensory perception of an object without *any* cognitive perception of it – whether, for instance, one might see a cat without recognizing it as anything whatsoever (not even as an animal of some sort).[1]

2   Perceptual Objects

Many, perhaps most, of our cognitive perceptions, the facts we come to know by visual means, are mediated in some way. Our visual knowledge of A depends on, and derives from, our visual knowledge of B. We see that we need gas (come to know, by visual means, that we need gas) by seeing that our fuel gauge registers "empty." We see one fact (that our gas tank is nearly empty) by seeing another fact (that our gauge registers "empty"). We see *by the newspapers* that there has been a tragic plane crash, *by the tracks* that the animal went this way, *by her frown* that she is displeased, and *by the thermometer* that the patient has a fever.

Given this dependence of some visually known facts on other visually known facts, the question naturally arises whether some facts are basic in the sense of being known directly and without this kind of dependence on other visually known facts. If my knowledge of the plane crash derives, or is somehow inferred, from my knowledge of what is printed in the newspapers, if my knowledge of what other people are thinking and feeling is somehow inferred from what I can see of their observable behavior and expression, are the latter pieces of knowledge themselves derived from some more fundamental, even more basic, kind of knowledge – possibly a knowledge of how the light (reflected from a newspaper page or a person's face) is structured, how this light is affecting my eyes, or how my brain is reacting to all these external events? Might it turn out, as some philosophers have argued, that all our knowledge of external, objective, facts – that there was a plane crash, that the newspaper reports a plane crash, that Susan is displeased, that she is frowning – derive, ultimately, from our knowledge of subjective facts, facts about the current state of our own mind (how things look)?

This is a question about cognitive perception, about the structure of our knowledge. Are there some facts we know that are fundamental – *foundational*, as philosophers like to put it – in the sense that all other things we know are derived from them? Is our knowledge of the way the world *is* derived from, and ultimately dependent upon, our knowledge of the way the world *appears*?

The answer to this question depends on the answer to a somewhat different question, a question about sense perception. What objects do we see? Do we see cats, sofas, newspapers, and people? If not, then it would seem that our knowledge of these things (the fact, for instance, that the newspapers say there was a plane crash and the fact that Susan is frowning) must derive from our factual knowledge about other things (whatever objects we do see). My knowledge of the plane crash derives from my knowledge of the newspapers because I did not *see* the plane crash. I see only the newspaper. Hence, whatever facts I learn about the plane crash, including the fact that there was a plane crash, must derive from facts I learn about the newspaper.

What facts we see, and which of these facts are fundamental, therefore depends on what objects we see. If you don't see the gas tank, then your visual knowledge of the gas tank, that it still contains gas, must derive from your visual knowledge about whatever objects you do see – in this case, typically, facts about your fuel gauge. You see that you have some gas left *by* seeing what your gauge registers, and this dependence among cognitive perceptions (your knowledge of the gauge being primary) derives from a fact about sensory perception, from the fact, namely, that you see the gauge but not the tank.

Even when we speak of perceiving one object *by, through,* or *in* perceiving another – in the way we speak, for instance, of seeing the game *on* TV or seeing someone *in* a movie (or photograph) – our knowledge of the game or person will be secondary relative to our knowledge of the electronic or photographic image. Insofar as we regard the image appearing on our television or movie screen as the primary, or real, *object* of perception, we regard facts about these images as cognitively primary. Facts about the people and events being represented are secondary. For instance, we learn (see) that a player kicked a field goal by observing the behavior of the electronically produced images of the player, the ball, and the goalposts appearing on our television screen.

Hence, a question about the structure of cognitive perception – whether in fact there is a fundamental level of visual knowledge, and if so, whether this is knowledge of objective or subjective facts – awaits the answer to a prior question: What is the structure of sense perception? What objects do we see? The answer to this question will constrain, if not determine, the answer to the questions about cognitive perception. If we do not see physical objects, if we are (in sense perception) always aware of mental images (representations) of external objects (as some philosophers and psychologists seem to believe), then our knowledge of objective reality (if, indeed, we have such knowledge) will necessarily be derivative from and secondary to our knowledge of our own mental states.

Discussions of these issues are often clouded by failure to appreciate the difference between cognitive perception and sense perception. It is sometimes argued, for instance, that we do not perceive ordinary physical objects because, for whatever reason (the reason is usually skeptical in character), we do not know, or cannot be absolutely certain, that there *are* physical objects. For all we know, all experience, even the experience we take to be *of* a real external world, may be illusory. It could all be a dream. This argument, though it has a distinguished history, is a fairly obvious conflation of cognitive perception and sense perception. One does not have to know, let alone know for certain (whatever that might mean), that there are physical objects in order to see (sense perception) physical objects. Such knowledge is only required for cognitive perception. Just as the child described above saw a cat on the sofa without knowing what it was, it may turn out that we see ordinary physical objects (including cats and sofas) every moment of our waking life without ever being able to know (if the philosophical skeptic is right) that this is what we are seeing. Questions about what objects we see are quite different from questions about what facts we know.

Failure to keep the distinction between sense and cognitive perception clearly in mind also tempts students into mistakenly supposing that if our knowledge of physical objects is somehow derivative from the way they *appear* to us, from the way they *look*, then what we really perceive when (as we ordinarily say) we see a cat is an internal mental image of the cat. We see (as it were) the *look* or *appearance* of the cat. Such an inference would be fallacious because even if our cognitive perceptions rest on subjective foundations (on the way things look to us), our sense perceptions need not rest on similar foundations. We may know that there are physical objects by the way they appear to us (so that cognitive perception has, in this sense, a subjective basis), but our sense perception of objects is itself direct and unmediated. In other words, we may come to know (see) it is a cat (a fact) by the way it appears, but what we see (the object) is the cat itself, not its appearance.

Aside from these possible confusions, though, there are a variety of positions that have been, and continue to be, taken on the nature of both cognitive and sense perception – on what facts and objects are most immediately and directly seen. Though these theories, in both their classical and their modern form, are often hard to classify because of their failure to be clear about whether it is cognitive perception or sense perception they are talking about, they can be roughly characterized as follows.

Direct (Naive) Realism (sometimes said to be the view of the person-on-the-street) holds (1) that there is a real physical world, objects and facts whose existence is independent of our perception of them (this makes the view a form of physical *realism*) and (2) that under normal conditions we are, in a direct and unmediated way, perceptually aware of these objects and facts (hence, *direct* and therefore, according to its detractors, *naive* realism). In other words, what we are directly aware of in sense perception is, unlike a headache or an afterimage, something physical that continues to exist when we are no longer aware of it.

Representative Realism (also called the *Causal Theory of Perception*) shares with Direct Realism (and common sense) the first of these two doctrines. It disagrees, though, about the second. According to Representative Realism, our perception of physical objects is indirect, mediated by a more direct apprehension of something mental, some internal representation (hence the name *representative* realism) of external physical reality. These mental representations have been given various names: sensátions, ideas, impressions, percepts, sense-data, experiences, and so on. But the idea is almost always the same. Just as we see what is happening on the playing field *by* seeing what is happening on our television screen (so that our knowledge of the game, when viewed on television, is indirect), so knowledge of even the most obvious physical fact – the fact, say, that there is a table (or, indeed, a television set) in front of us – is itself indirect. We see that there is a table in front of us *by* seeing, or somehow being aware of, its internal, mental representation. When we are watching a game on television, then, our knowledge of the actual game is *doubly* indirect: we know about a game occurring 1,000 miles away by knowing what is happening on a television screen a few feet away, and we come to know what is happening a few feet away by becoming aware of what is happening (presumably *no* distance away) in our own minds. In the last analysis, then, all our knowledge of object-ive (physical) fact rests on a knowledge of subjective (mental) fact be-cause the only objects perceived (directly) are mental objects – the way things appear.

Going beyond these forms of realism are various forms of *idealism* (sometimes called *phenomenalism*), theories that deny an objective phys-ical reality altogether. Everything that exists depends for its existence (like a headache or an afterimage) on someone's awareness of it; hence, everything is in the nature of a mental entity like an idea (hence, *ideal-ism*). Since these extreme views have few, if any, serious advocates within the philosophical (not to mention cognitive science) community today, we will leave them without further comment.

As indicated earlier, one might be a Direct Realist on sense perception but an Indirect Realist on cognitive perception. The objects we see are physical objects, but we know about them via their effect on us (the way they appear to us) in sense perception. The problem with this mixed position is the problem of saying just how one might come to know how objects look – which, according to some theorists, is a knowledge of how, in sense perception, we internally represent them – without thereby becoming aware of, and hence perceiving, the internal represen-tations themselves (thereby becoming an Indirect Realist on sense per-ception also). To put it crudely, how can one *know* how things look without perceiving, or somehow being aware of their look?

The debate between Direct and Indirect Realists becomes very tech-nical at this point. Indirect Realists maintain that we are directly aware of mental objects – images – in hallucinations and dreams. Aside from the *cause* of the experience, though, there is no reason to distinguish between these illusory experiences and our ordinary veridical perception of (phys-ical) objects. In both cases we are directly aware of the internal mental representation. When we speak, as we commonly do, of seeing an ordin-ary object (like a cat), we are, if we speak truly, being caused to experi-ence some catlike image by a real cat (a real cat that we do not directly perceive). When we hallucinate or dream of a cat, there is no such external cause – hence, we speak of these experiences as illusory. In all cases, though, it is the image that we directly experience. Only the cause of the experience is different. Direct Realists try to counter this, and related, arguments by insisting that although sensory perception of real objects requires the having (and thereby the existence) of internal representations, and though such representations in fact determine the way these objects look or appear to us, there is no reason to suppose we perceive these representations themselves. We perceive a cat by (internally) representing a cat, not by perceiving an internal representation of a cat.

3   Perceptual Processes

The debate about the objects of perception is related to a debate (not always clearly distinguished from it) about the kind of processes underlying perception. Do perceptual processes, those culminating in our seeing something, exhibit the qualities of reason and intelligence? Do they, despite being unconscious, have an inferential or computational character, moving from premise to conclusion (deductive reasoning), or from data to explanatory hypothesis (inductive reasoning), in something like the way human agents consciously solve problems? When I see a cat on the sofa, or that there is a cat on the sofa, does my visual system do something similar to what clever detectives do when they infer, on the basis of certain clues and signs, that a certain state of affairs not directly apprehended *must be* the case?

We can, of course, metaphorically describe the operations of anything, even the simplest machine, in thoughtlike, semicognitive terms. We are especially fond of doing this with computers. We say they know, that they remember, recognize, infer, and conclude. If one counts arithmetical operations as forms of computation, even dime store calculators perform (or are *described* as performing) impressive feats of reasoning – multiplying, taking square roots, and calculating percentages in fractions of a second. We even speak of such comparatively humble devices as thermostats and electric eyes in quasi-perceptual terms – as, for example, "sensing" a drop in room temperature or the approach of a person and responding by turning the furnace on or opening a door. The question, then, is not whether we *can* speak this way, not even whether it is sometimes useful to talk this way (to adopt what Dennett (1987) calls the *intentional stance*), but whether this is anything more than a metaphorical crutch – a figure of speech that conceals or masks our ignorance about underlying causal processes and mechanisms. Do visual systems ever literally solve problems, infer that something is so, formulate (on the basis of sensory input) hypotheses about the distant source of stimulation in the way that rational agents do this at the conscious level?

Hermann von Helmholtz, the great nineteenth-century physiologist, thought so, and many investigators today (see, for example, Gregory 1974a, 1978; Rock 1977, 1983; Ullman 1980) are inclined to agree. At least they view the processing of visual information as a form of problem solving and hence as a form of reasoning that, though unconscious, exhibits enough of the essential properties of fully rational thought and judgment to make it, in a fairly literal sense, an instance of problem solving itself. The light reaching the receptors (sometimes called the *proximal stimulus*) carries information – fragmentary and impoverished (and thereby ambiguous) information to be sure, but information nonetheless – about distant situations (the *distal stimuli*). The visual system's function is to take these data and to construct, as best it can, a reasonable conjecture (hypothesis, judgment) about the distal source of this stimulation. It begins with premises describing receptor activity, data concerning the distribution and intensity of energy reaching the receptor surface, and is charged with the task of arriving at useful conclusions about the distal source of this stimulation. The conclusion it reaches (for instance, it must be a cat out there causing this pattern of retinal activity) constitutes the subject's perception of a cat. If the visual system reaches a different conclusion – that, for instance, it is probably an old black sweater – the subject sees an old black sweater instead of a fluffy black cat. If the perceptual system can't make up its mind, or keeps changing its mind (it's a cat; no, on second thought, it's probably a sweater; no, that can't be right, it's probably a cat), the subject sees first a cat, then a sweater, then a cat again. Though such flip-flopping seldom occurs when we are looking at real cats (because, in normal circumstances, light from real cats is generally richer in information – hence, less ambiguous – about the kind of object that has structured the light), it sometimes happens with specially constructed figures viewed under restricted (say, monocular) conditions – Necker cubes, for instance. Since so much emphasis is placed on the visual system's efforts at constructing a reasonable interpretation or hypothesis (about the distal stimulus) from information reaching the receptor surfaces, this approach to perceptual processing is often described as a *Constructivist* or *Computational* approach to visual perception.

Since Constructivists regard sensory stimulation, even in the best of viewing conditions, as inherently ambiguous (there are always a variety of distal arrangements that could have produced that pattern of proximal stimulation), they view perceptual processing as primarily a matter of *adding* information to the stimulus (or *supplementing* the information available in the stimulus) to reach a perceptual outcome: seeing a cat. Since the proximal stimulation does not unequivocally specify the distant object as a cat, and since we nonetheless (under optimal viewing conditions) see a cat (the visual system reaches this conclusion), the perceptual system must exploit some other source of information to reach this judgment – adding or supplementing (via some inductive inference) the information contained in the stimulus.

There has been a vigorous challenge to this (more or less) orthodox position in the last forty years. Gibson, in a series of influential books (1950, 1966, 1979) and articles (1960, 1972) has argued that the stimulus, *properly understood*, contains all the information needed to specify the distal state of affairs. If the proximal stimulus is understood, not as a static distribution of energy occurring on the receptor surfaces *at a time*, but as the total dynamic pattern of stimulation reaching a mobile observer *over time*, there is no need for inference, reasoning, and problem solving. There is sufficient information in the stimulus (thus broadly conceived) to specify (unambiguously determine) the character of the distal object. Why reason about what is out there when the stimulus tells you what is out there? Why suppose, as Constructivists do, that perceptual systems are smart detectives when all they really have to be (given reliable informants – that is, information-rich stimuli) is good listeners, good extractors of the information in the signals reaching the receptors? Since this approach tends to eliminate all intervening cognitive (indeed, all intervening psychological) mechanisms from the processes resulting in our perception of objects, it is often referred to as a *Direct Theory* of perceptual processing.

Relevant to the question of whether perceptual systems are more like good detectives doing their best with ambiguous data (Constructivism) or more like good listeners faithfully registering stimulus information (Direct Theory) is what Fodor (1983) describes as the *modularity* of information-processing systems. A system is (comparatively) modular when it is (comparatively) insulated from information available to other parts of the total system. If I am told (and thereby know) that it is a cat on the sofa, for instance, does this, *can* this, affect my visual perception of the cat? If not, my visual system exhibits modularity with respect to this kind of information (information available to the central processor from auditory sources). If this collateral information is capable of affecting what I see, then the visual system (understood as that subsystem responsible for my seeing what I see) is not modular in relation to this kind of information.

If the visual system is modular, its operation (and therefore presumably what the subject perceives) is unaffected by what other information may be available to other parts of the system (or what the subject may know as a result of information received from these other parts). Modular systems are therefore described as *stimulus-driven* (the processing is bottom-up rather than top-down): it is the stimulus itself (information at the bottom, as it were), not the system's (possibly variable) hypotheses about that stimulus (information available at the top) that guides the processing of incoming signals and thereby determines what the subject perceives. Modular systems are therefore most naturally thought of in the second of the two ways described above – as good extractors of pre-existent information, information that is already in the stimuli, not as good detectives or problem solvers about the best interpretation of informationally ambiguous stimuli. There is no point in supposing that a process of reasoning is occurring in modular systems when the process, being modular, is not allowed to use information (other than what is in the stimulus itself) to generate perceptual conclusions. Modular systems are not intelligent. They don't have to be. They have no problems to solve. They just do what the stimulus tells them to do.

It is by no means obvious that these two approaches to the analysis of perceptual processes are incompatible. It may turn out, for example, that although the stimulus, properly understood, *is* rich in information about distal objects, rich enough (let us suppose) to unambiguously determine what distal objects produced it, it nonetheless requires inferential (reason-like) processes to decode the signal, to extract this information from the stimulus. Fingerprint's, being unique to their bearers, may unambiguously determine or specify (in an information-theoretic sense) who held the gun. It nevertheless takes a good deal of problem solving, after one has discovered the incriminating prints, to figure out who held the gun. One has to know which people go with which prints, and this may take memory, inference, and prior learning (the sort of cognitive work that organizations like the FBI invest into the creation of a fingerprint file). As Ullman (1980: 380–1) puts it, the role of processing may not be to create information, but to extract it, integrate it, make it explicit and usable.

There are, then, a variety of ways of expressing questions about the nature of those processes underlying our perception of the world. But these questions should not be confused, as they often are, with questions about the objects of perception, the questions discussed in section 2. Gibson's views have been described (by both Gibson and others) as a theory of *direct* perception. This can be misleading. It certainly is confusing. The sense (if any) in which this theory is direct is much different from the sense in which Direct Realism is direct. Direct Realism is a theory about the *objects* of perception, about *what* we see. The kind of direct realism we are now talking about, the kind associated with Gibson's work, is a theory about the processes underlying perception, about *how* we see what we see. One can be a Direct Realist about the objects of perception, holding that we directly apprehend physical objects (not sensations or mental intermediaries), and be a Constructivist about the processes underlying our (direct) perception of these objects. One can suppose that intelligence, some kind of thought-like process, is involved in the construction of internal representations without supposing that one thereby sees (or in any way perceives) the representations so constructed. One can, in other words, be a Direct Realist about the objects of perception and an Indirect Realist, a Constructivist, about the processes underlying this direct relationship.

Once again, though, controversy about the intelligence, or lack of it, of perceptual processes is often muddled by failure to be clear about exactly which processes are in question. It should be obvious that cognitive perception – our perception of facts, our seeing *that* (and hence coming to know that) there is a cat on the sofa – is the result of a process that is strongly influenced by higher-level cognitive factors. Cognitive perception is clearly not modular. A subject who does not already know what a cat is, or does not already know what they look like – a small child or an inexperienced animal, say – will be unable to *see* (recognize) *what* is on the sofa, unable to *see that* there is a cat there (to be carefully distinguished from an ability to see the cat there). For cognitive perception of the cat on the sofa, in contrast to sense perception of the cat, requires not only the appropriate concepts (for *cat* and *sofa*) but some intelligence in the application of these concepts to the objects being perceived (the cat and the sofa). The upshot of cognitive perception is some *known fact* (say, that there is a cat on the sofa) and such facts are not learned without the cooperation of the entire cognitive system. By changing a subject's cognitive set – changing what the subject knows or believes about the way things look, for instance – one easily changes what the subject learns, comes to know, hence perceives in a cognitive way, about the objects it sees (in a sensory way). Some form of Constructivism or Computationalism is therefore inevitable for seeing *facts*.

The real question is, or should be, whether that part of the visual system given over to *sense perception*, to seeing objects (like cats and sofas), is also intelligent. Does *it* exhibit some (any? all?) of the marks of reasoned judgment? Is *it* modular?

The answer to this question will depend on just what one takes to be involved in the perception of objects, in seeing, say, a cat on the sofa or a person in the room. If the upshot or outcome of cognitive perception is some known fact – that there is a cat on the sofa or a person in the room – what is the upshot or culmination of sense perception? When, at exactly what stage in the processing of incoming information, do we see the cat on the sofa and the person in the room? If recognizing the object *as* a cat or *as* a person is not necessary to the sensory perception of these objects (as it is to their cognitive perception), what is necessary? Since we can see a cat at a distance, in bad lighting, or in unusual conditions (circumstances in which it does not even look like a cat), we cannot suppose, following Gibson, that to see a cat is to have information in the stimulus that specifies the cat *as* a cat. For in such cases there may be no information in the stimulus about what it is we see. That does not prevent our seeing it.

It is true, but unilluminating, to be told that the sensory perception of an object occurs when the visual system constructs a sensory representation of the object. What we want to know is what kind of representation a sensory representation is. If cognitive perception of a cat occurs when the system constructs a cognitive representation of the cat, an internal judgment or belief that it is a cat (some kind of internal description of the cat *as a cat*), what is a sensory representation of the cat, the kind of internal representation whose occurrence constitutes a sensory perception of the cat? Is it something like what philosophers and psychologists used to call a *sensation*? Or is it more like what they (or some of them) now call a *percept*? Or, to use even more fashionable jargon, is it more like what Marr (1982) and his associates call a $2\frac{1}{2}$-*D* sketch?

Until these questions are answered, we can expect little progress on questions about the nature of perception itself. How can we tell whether sensory perception is best thought of in terms of a clever detective or a good listener if we cannot say, in any clear way, what final product, what kind of internal representation, this kind of perception is supposed to produce?

4   Perceptual Change

Do we learn to see things? Does prolonged experience of the world change what we perceive or the way we perceive it? Do people with radically different languages, radically different ways of describing their surroundings, see their surroundings differently? Do completely different world views – what Kuhn (1962), for instance, calls *incommensurable scientific theories* – generate differences in what people can observe and, hence, in the data on which their theoretical differences rest?

Such questions have fascinated philosophers and psychologists, linguists and anthropologists, for centuries. The answers to these questions are not easy. Nevertheless, some things seem reasonably clear – if not the final answers themselves, then at least the sorts of considerations that must inform the search for final answers.

The first point, a point that has been made repeatedly in this chapter, is that before rushing in with answers to any of these questions, one should first be very clear about the question. What kind of perception is the question a question about?

As a case in point, the question about whether we learn to see things has a reasonably straightforward answer if it is a question about cognitive perception, about the facts we come to know by visual means. The first time (as a very small child presumably) I saw a maple tree I probably didn't know what kind of tree it was. Having no experience or knowledge of maple trees, being ignorant of what maple trees looked like (or, indeed, of what maple trees were), I didn't recognize what I saw *as* a maple tree. I didn't see what kind of tree it was. Now, however, I am quite expert in this kind of identification. I can look at maples, at least the more common varieties, and quickly recognize them as maples. I can see, by their general shape, their bark and leaf structure, *what kind of tree* they are, that they are maple trees. There has been a change, therefore, in my ability to cognitively perceive objects around me, a change that came about by experience, learning, and (in this case) diligent study and practice. Learning of this kind is a pervasive and familiar phenomenon.

But if the question about perceptual learning is a question about sensory perception, about the objects we see, about whether we learn to see maple trees themselves (and not just the fact that they are maple trees), the answer appears to be quite different. I did not learn to see maple trees. I could do that when I was a very young child – before I learned to recognize them. What I learned is how to identify the things I saw, things I therefore saw before I learned to identify them. Sensory perception of objects normally comes before the cognitive perception of these same objects. If it did not, there would be no way to learn what objects look like. How can you learn what objects look like if you cannot see them? Humans do not see things at the moment of birth, of course. Certain physiological changes must first occur before we can, for instance, focus on objects and coherently process information contained in light. But these maturational processes are not to be classified as *learning* in any ordinary sense. We no more learn to see solid objects than we learn to digest solid food.

This is not to say that some changes in our perception, our sensory perception, of objects may not occur after prolonged experience. Perhaps objects start looking different after they become familiar or after we know certain things about them. Does a familiar face – the face of a loved one, say – look different after it has become familiar from the way it looked the first time you saw it? Do coins look larger to poor children than they do to rich children? Do lines in an optical illusion that look to be of different lengths start looking the same after you learn (by measuring them) that they are the same length? These questions are questions about the way things look, about the character of our visual experience, about something we earlier dubbed (without really knowing or explaining what it was) the *sensory representation* of objects. They are not questions about the way we cognitively represent objects, about our perceptual beliefs or judgments. Changes and differences in cognitive representations are an obvious and familiar fact of life. That such changes exist is not worth arguing about (though the changes themselves are certainly worth studying). Changes, if any, in our sensory representations are not so obvious. Quite the contrary. To document such changes one has to be very clear about what sensory representations are and what constitutes a change in them. To answer questions about whether we learn to see in this sense, then, requires a clear, at least a much better, understanding of the nature of sensory representation, of what kind of internal response to an external object constitutes our seeing the object.

Similar remarks can be made about various forms of perceptual *relativity*. Is perception relative? Well, cognitive perception is certainly relative to many things – everything, in fact, capable of influencing what one comes to believe. If not having a word for X or a theory about X means I cannot come to have certain beliefs about X, then not having a word (or a theory) for X will prevent me from cognitively perceiving X. Without an appropriate language for talking about oxygen, without some knowledge (however crude) of chemical theory, I can hardly be expected to see *when* oxidation is occurring (see *that* it is occurring) even when it happens under my nose. I just will not recognize it – certainly not *as* oxidation. So the cognitive perception of oxidation is relative to those factors – factors like possession of the right concepts and knowledge of the appropriate scientific theories – that are essential to a knowledge that oxidation is occurring. For the same reason, people who have badly mistaken astronomical views will not be able to see what others see when a lunar eclipse occurs – that the moon is moving into the earth's shadow. They will not see that a lunar eclipse is occurring because, with mistaken views about what is happening (they think the gods are showing displeasure by extinguishing the moon), they will not learn what everyone else learns when they see the same thing: that the earth is casting a shadow on the moon.

But though cognitive perception is obviously relative in this way, there is no reason to think – in fact, there is a lot of reason *not* to think – that sensory perception is similarly relative. Though the astronomically ignorant may not see that an eclipse is occurring, they certainly see *the eclipse* (= the earth's shadow moving across the face of the moon). That, in fact, is what frightens them. And though the chemically ignorant can hardly be expected to see that oxidation is occurring, they can, given normal eyesight, witness the oxidation, the blazing fire, as well as everyone else.

To say that perception is relative to a certain factor is to say that our perception of things depends on that factor. Change that factor (enough) and we change what is perceived or, possibly, whether anything at all is perceived. To suggest, then, that sense perception is *not* relative to a variety of factors affecting our perception of facts is a way of suggesting that sense perception is comparatively modular. It is *not* sensitive to the cognitive influences (a subject's language, conceptual scheme, or scientific world view) that determine one's perception of facts. The issue of perceptual relativity, and more generally of perceptual change and learning, then, is merely another way of approaching questions raised in earlier sections of this chapter about perceptual processes in general. It seems, therefore, that the answers to a variety of questions, both philosophical (raised in this chapter) and scientific (addressed in earlier chapters), depends on a deeper understanding of perceptual processes and the different outcomes, sensory versus cognitive, that they support. Achieving deeper understanding of this sort will require the combined efforts of investigators from many fields.

Note

1   The topic of *seeing as* – at one time a fashionable topic in the philosophy of perception – is a hybrid form of perception, a way of seeing that goes beyond sensory perception (requiring a fairly specific cognitive or judgmental attitude or tendency on the part of the perceiver) but falling short of full cognitive perception (knowledge not being required). One sees a stick as a snake. The stick obviously does not have to *be* a snake for one to see it as a snake. Hence, this cannot be cognitive perception, at least not cognitive

perception of a snake (for this would require one to recognize it as a snake, something one cannot do of something, like a stick, that is not a snake). Nonetheless, one sees (sensory perception) the stick and takes or judges it to be a snake. The knowledge required of cognitive perception (knowing that the X is an X) is replaced by some variant of belief: one believes, or is inclined to believe, or would believe if one did not know better, of the object (it may or may not be an X) that it is an X.

References

Dennett, D. (1987), *The Intentional Stance*, Cambridge, MA: MIT Press.

Fodor, J. (1983), *The Modularity of Mind*, Cambridge, MA: MIT Press.

Gibson, J. J. (1950), *The Perception of the Visual World*, Boston: Houghton Mifflin.

Gibson, J. J. (1960), The concept of the stimulus in psychology, *American Psychologist* 15: 694–703.

Gibson, J. J. (1966), *The Senses Considered as Perceptual Systems*, Boston: Houghton Mifflin.

Gibson, J. J. (1972), A theory of direct visual perception. In J. R. Royce and W. W. Rozeboom (eds), *The Psychology of Knowing*, New York: Gordon and Breach.

Gibson, J. J. (1979), *The Ecological Approach to Visual Perception*, Boston: Houghton Mifflin.

Gregory, R. (1974a), Choosing a paradigm, for perception: In E. C. Carterette and M. P. Friedman (eds), *Handbook of Perception*, vol. 1: *Historical and Philosophical Roots of Perception*, New York: Academic Press.

Gregory, R. (1978), *Eye and Brain: The Psychology of Seeing*, 3rd edn. New York: McGraw-Hill.

Kuhn, T. S. (1962), *The Structure of Scientific Revolutions*, Chicago: University of Chicago Press.

Marr, D. (1982), *Vision: A Computational Investigation into the Human Representation and Processing of Visual Information*, San Francisco: W. H. Freeman.

Rock, I. (1977), In defense of unconscious inference. In W. Epstein (ed.), *Stability and Constancy in Visual Perception*, New York: Wiley.

Rock, I. (1983), *The Logic of Perception*, Cambridge, MA: MIT Press.

Ullman, S. (1980), Against direct perception, *Behavioral and Brain Sciences* 3: 373–415.

22

From *Wittgenstein*

Robert Fogelin

Seeing As

Part II of the *Investigations* contains a famous (and perplexing) discussion of the phenomenon of changing aspects. We look at a drawing of a double cross and first see it as a black figure on a white ground, then as a white figure on a black ground. More famously, we look at a drawing of a duck and then, to our surprise, it strikes us as a drawing of a rabbit. Wittgenstein begins his discussion of these cases by distinguishing two uses of the word "see":

> The one: "What do you see there?" – "I see *this*" (and then a description, a drawing, a copy). The other: "I see a likeness between these two faces" – let the man I tell this to be seeing the faces as clearly as I do myself. ([Wittgenstein, *Philosophical Investigations*, Basil Blackwell, 1953; hereafter] PI, p. 193)

Thus if A and B are asked to sketch the faces they have seen, it could come out that they have seen the same thing through the striking similarities in the drawings they produce. Yet A may notice a likeness between the faces that B fails to recognize. This shows, according to Wittgenstein, a categorical difference ([ein] *kategorische Unterschied*) between these two "objects" of sight (PI, p. 195). Wittgenstein calls this later sort of seeing "noticing an aspect" (PI, p. 193). Noticing an aspect is a common phenomenon, but it appears in its most arresting form in the so-called ambiguous figures of the kind mentioned at the beginning of this section. Here we see something first under one aspect, then under

Robert Fogelin, *Wittgenstein*, 2nd edn. (London: Routledge, 1987), pp. 201–5.

another. For example, we first see the drawing as a flight of stairs falling away from us, then we see it as coming toward us, as if from underneath. In a case like this, we are inclined to say that we really *see* the drawing one way and then *see* it the other. This is not something we make up; it is, we might say, a part of our visual experience.

In an enigmatic passage, Wittgenstein makes the following remark about visual experience:

> What is the criterion of the visual experience? – The criterion?
>   What do you suppose?
>   The representation of "what is seen".   (PI, p. 198)

I'm not entirely sure what Wittgenstein means by this passage, but one plausible reading squares with the general development of his argument. Suppose that two people, A and B, are looking at a duck-rabbit drawing. A sees it as a duck drawing; B sees it as a rabbit drawing. There is a sense in which they are seeing the same thing and another sense in which they are not. This difference could be brought out by asking each to produce a set of drawings corresponding to what he sees. We might first ask each to produce an accurate *copy* of what he has seen, and then a series of drawings of other things that have the same look. Though too pat to occur in real life, we can imagine the result. The similarities between the attempted copies would reveal the sense in which they have seen the same thing. The sharp difference between the remaining drawings would reveal the sense in which they have seen something different (see PI, p. 197).

Wittgenstein's basic point is that we fall into confusion when we merge these categorially different uses of the word "see". An attempted assimilation can go in either direction: (i) all cases of seeing can be treated as cases of seeing-as, or (ii) seeing-as can be viewed as just another kind of seeing.

(i)   The idea that seeing is always a matter of seeing-as has the ring of a profound discovery. Indeed, many people suppose that psychological investigation has put this contention beyond dispute. Wittgenstein treats it as a conceptual confusion:

> One doesn't "take" what one knows as the cutlery at a meal *for* cutlery; any more than one ordinarily tries to move one's mouth as one eats, or aims at moving it.   (PI, p. 195)

For example, if I say "Now I am seeing this as a knife," I will not be understood, unless, that is, the knife appears in a strange context where it is not easily recognized. Against this, someone might argue that when I recognize a knife I am recognizing a similarity between this item and other items that are called knives. So every act of seeing involves noticing an aspect; cases only differ in their novelty or vividness. Wittgenstein would probably reply that this cannot be the fundamental account of perceptual recognition, for, in order for there to be perceptual recognition at all, there must be a form of recognition that is *not a matter of interpretation*. None of this commits Wittgenstein to naive realism in the theory of perception. He can easily acknowledge that perception is mediated by *causal* factors, that is, causal factors enter into what we can see and how we see it. But we do not get an account of these causal factors by the conceptual trick of reducing all cases of seeing to cases of seeing-as. Indeed, nothing is accomplished by this move since the notion of seeing-as presupposes the notion of seeing and gains its significance from the contrast it enjoys with it.

(ii)   A different kind of confusion can arise if we treat seeing-as as just another sort of seeing. Here Wittgenstein maintains that it is a mistake to put the organization of the visual impression on the same level with colors and shapes (PI, p. 196). He associates this with the "idea that the visual impression is an inner object" which makes it, he suggests, "into a chimera; a queerly shifting construction" (PI, p. 196). One reason that we might invoke such an inner object is to explain where the change of organization takes place. Since the figure visibly does not alter, something *else* must alter. An inner image has often commended itself at this point. But how will an inner image help? Is it an image of the ambiguous duck-rabbit drawing? This will not do, for now we are confronted with an inner object that undergoes aspect-change and, although the seat of the mystery has been shifted, the mystery itself has not been solved. Then are the inner pictures a series of unambiguous duck-image followed by an unambiguous rabbit-image, etc.? We find nothing in experience corresponding to this, for part of our experience is that the thing we see, in an important sense, does not change. Our difficulty is that we want the inner picture to play *both* roles: we want it to be an exact copy since, in noticing an aspect-change, we notice, in some strong sense, that nothing changes at all. We also want the inner picture to be like those other pictures of ducks and rabbits that we invoke to explain what does seem to change. But now we are making incompatible demands upon the picture. This incompatibility is not relieved by making the picture an inner picture.

Wittgenstein's own remarks about aspect-change are broad and programmatic. He suggests that "the flashing of an aspect on us seems half visual experience, half thought" (PI, p. 197). It seems both "seeing and thinking" or even an "amalgam of the two" (PI, p. 197). How then are we to characterize this phenomenon? One thing we might do is simply describe how this phenomenon is related to others – both in relevant similarities and differences. We could simply stop with this description. This, I think, is Wittgenstein's suggestion, although he recognizes that the task of the description may be highly complicated:

> Is being struck looking plus thinking? No. Many of our concepts cross here.   (PI, p. 211)

Wittgenstein also ties the phenomenon of seeing-as to his central idea of mastering a technique:

> "Now he is seeing it like *this*", "now like *that*" would only be said of someone *capable* of making certain applications of the figure quite freely.
>   The substratum of this experience is the mastery of a technique.
> (PI, p. 208)

This suggests that an aspect-change seems natural to us because we are able to apply the figure freely (or as a matter of course) to represent a duck or to represent a rabbit. Our experience of the diagram is a reflection of our ability to employ the diagram smoothly in a given way. This, I think, provides the background for understanding the following startling remark:

> [W]hat I perceive in the dawning of an aspect is not a property of the object, but an internal relation between it and other objects.   (PI, p. 212)

This is the only mention of *internal relations* in the *Investigations*, and it needs some explaining. I think that Wittgenstein's explanation of internal relations would follow his treatment of necessity. When things appear as if they *have to be* connected in a certain way, this shows that we are bringing them under a rule that we have mastered and apply routinely (blindly). Although Wittgenstein does not use the phrase in that context, this is how he explains the internal relations in the numerical sequence 2, 4, 6, 8. . . .

But isn't it really peculiar that an ability to apply a figure in a given way should be a *logical* condition for a certain kind of experience? We have, of course, seen a position somewhat similar to this with respect to the emotions. Since hoping is a manifestation of a complicated form of life involving complex propositional attitudes toward the future, it seems that only a creature who has mastered the use of language can hope (PI, p. 174). Yet the situation with respect to the duck-rabbit figure seems somehow different. Couldn't a child, perhaps, notice that the diagram undergoes a strange alteration without having a command of either the concept duck or the concept rabbit? Wittgenstein, in fact, acknowledges that this might happen with a simpler diagram – the double cross where figure and ground seem to alternate:

> Those two aspects of the double cross (I shall call them the aspects A) might be reported simply by pointing to an isolated black cross.
> One could quite well imagine this as a primitive reaction in a child even before it could talk. (PI, p. 207)

In speaking of a *primitive* reaction, Wittgenstein surely means a reaction that antedates a particular training or the particular mastering of a technique. So, at least in some cases, Wittgenstein freely acknowledges that the phenomenon of aspect-change cannot be explained by a previous mastery of concepts. Now for most philosophers an admission of this kind would seem completely fatal to the view being presented. Wittgenstein seems wholly undisturbed. That we cannot extend the application of aspect-change from one case to another merely shows, according to him, that they are less similar than we originally supposed:

> You only "see the duck and rabbit aspects" if you are already conversant with the shapes of those two animals. There is no analogous condition for seeing the aspect A. (PI, p. 207)

There is something deeply unsatisfying about a move of this kind, but, of course, we have met it before. It seems that those things which we will call aspect-changes form only a family, where certain features that are logically crucial in some cases simply drop out in others. We have no right to insist that there must be a single theory of aspect-change that covers both the duck-rabbit and the double cross. We can explain what we can explain, but very quickly Wittgenstein leaves explaining alone and falls back upon describing similarities and differences in various cases.[1]

Note

1 The *Brown Book* exemplifies this approach better than any of his other writings.

23

From *Patterns of Discovery*

Norwood Russell Hanson

Observation

Were the eye not attuned to the Sun,
The Sun could never be seen by it.
(Goethe[1])

A

Consider two microbiologists. They look at a prepared slide; when asked what they see, they may give different answers. One sees in the cell before him a cluster of foreign matter: it is an artefact, a coagulum resulting from inadequate staining techniques. This clot has no more to do with the cell, *in vivo*, than the scars left on it by the archaeologist's spade have to do with the original shape of some Grecian urn. The other biologist identifies the clot as a cell organ, a 'Golgi body'. As for techniques, he argues: 'The standard way of detecting a cell organ is by fixing and staining. Why single out this one technique as producing artefacts, while others disclose genuine organs?'

The controversy continues.[2] It involves the whole theory of microscopical technique; nor is it an obviously experimental issue. Yet it affects what scientists say they see. Perhaps there is a sense in which two such observers do not see the same thing, do not begin from the same data, though their eyesight is normal and they are visually aware of the same object.

Norwood Russell Hanson, *Patterns of Discovery* (Cambridge: Cambridge University Press, 1965), pp. 4–13, 15–18.

Imagine these two observing a Protozoon – *Amoeba*. One sees a one-celled animal, the other a non-celled animal. The first sees *Amoeba* in all its analogies with different types of single cells: liver cells, nerve cells, epithelium cells. These have a wall, nucleus, cytoplasm, etc. Within this class *Amoeba* is distinguished only by its independence. The other, however, sees *Amoeba's* homology not with single cells, but with whole animals. Like all animals *Amoeba* ingests its food, digests and assimilates it. It excretes, reproduces and is mobile – more like a complete animal than an individual tissue cell.

This is not an experimental issue, yet it can affect experiment. What either man regards as significant questions or relevant data can be determined by whether he stresses the first or the last term in 'unicellular animal'.[3]

Some philosophers have a formula ready for such situations: 'Of course they see the same thing. They make the same observation since they begin from the same visual data. But they interpret what they see differently. They construe the evidence in different ways.'[4] The task is then to show how these data are moulded by different theories or interpretations or intellectual constructions.

Considerable philosophers have wrestled with this task. But in fact the formula they start from is too simple to allow a grasp of the nature of observation within physics. Perhaps the scientists cited above do not begin their inquiries from the same data, do not make the same observations, do not even see the same thing? Here many concepts run together. We must proceed carefully, for wherever it makes sense to say that two scientists looking at x do not see the same thing, there must always be a prior sense in which they do see the same thing. The issue is, then, 'Which of these senses is most illuminating for the understanding of observational physics?'

These biological examples are too complex. Let us consider Johannes Kepler: imagine him on a hill watching the dawn. With him is Tycho Brahe. Kepler regarded the sun as fixed: it was the earth that moved. But Tycho followed Ptolemy and Aristotle in this much at least: the earth was fixed and all other celestial bodies moved around it. *Do Kepler and Tycho see the same thing in the east at dawn?*

We might think this an experimental or observational question, unlike the questions 'Are there Golgi bodies?' and 'Are Protozoa one-celled or non-celled?' Not so in the sixteenth and seventeenth centuries. Thus Galileo said to the Ptolemaist '... neither Aristotle nor you can prove that the earth is *de facto* the centre of the universe...'.[5] 'Do Kepler and Tycho see the same thing in the east at dawn?' is perhaps not a *de facto* question either, but rather the beginning of an examination of the concepts of seeing and observation.

The resultant discussion might run:

'Yes, they do.'

'No, they don't.'

'Yes, they do!'

'No, they don't!'...

That this is possible suggests that there may be reasons for both contentions.[6] Let us consider some points in support of the affirmative answer.

The physical processes involved when Kepler and Tycho watch the dawn are worth noting. Identical photons are emitted from the sun; these traverse solar space, and our atmosphere. The two astronomers have normal vision; hence these photons pass through the cornea, aqueous humour, iris, lens and vitreous body of their eyes in the same way. Finally their retinas are affected. Similar electro-chemical changes occur in their selenium cells. The same configuration is etched on Kepler's retina as on Tycho's. So they see the same thing. ...

... [But] seeing the sun is not seeing retinal pictures of the sun. The retinal images which Kepler and Tycho have are four in number, inverted and quite tiny.[7] Astronomers cannot be referring to these when they say they see the sun. If they are hypnotized, drugged, drunk or distracted they may not see the sun, even though their retinas register its image in exactly the same way as usual.

Seeing is an experience. A retinal reaction is only a physical state – a photochemical excitation. Physiologists have not always appreciated the differences between experiences and physical states.[8] People, not their eyes, see. Cameras, and eye-balls, are blind. Attempts to locate within the organs of sight (or within the neurological reticulum behind the eyes) some nameable called 'seeing' may be dismissed. That Kepler and Tycho do, or do not, see the same thing cannot be supported by reference to the physical states of their retinas, optic nerves or visual cortices: there is more to seeing than meets the eyeball.

Naturally, Tycho and Kepler see the same physical object. They are both visually aware of the sun. If they are put into a dark room and asked to report when they see something – anything at all – they may both report the same object at the same time. Suppose that the only object to be seen is a certain lead cylinder. Both men see the same thing: namely this object – whatever it is. It is just here, however, that the difficulty arises, for while Tycho sees a mere pipe, Kepler will see a telescope, the instrument about which Galileo has written to him.

Unless both are visually aware of the same object there can be nothing of philosophical interest in the question whether or not they see the same thing. Unless they both see the sun in this prior sense our question cannot even strike a spark.

Nonetheless, both Tycho and Kepler have a common visual experience of some sort. This experience perhaps constitutes their seeing the same thing. Indeed, this may be a seeing logically more basic than anything expressed in the pronouncement 'I see the sun' (where each means something different by 'sun'). If what they meant by the word 'sun' were the only clue, then Tycho and Kepler could not be seeing the same thing, even though they were gazing at the same object.

If, however, we ask, not 'Do they see the same thing?' but rather 'What is it that they both see?', an unambiguous answer may be forthcoming. Tycho and Kepler are both aware of a brilliant yellow-white disc in a blue expanse over a green one. Such a 'sense-datum' picture is single and uninverted. To be unaware of it is not to have it. Either it dominates one's visual attention completely or it does not exist.

If Tycho and Kepler are aware of anything visual, it must be of some pattern of colours. What else could it be? We do not touch or hear with our eyes, we only take in light.[9] This private pattern is the same for both observers. Surely if asked to sketch the contents of their visual fields they would both draw a kind of semicircle on a horizon-line.[10] They say they see the sun. But they do not see every side of the sun at once; so what they really see is discoid to begin with. It is but a visual aspect of the sun. In any single observation the sun is a brilliantly luminescent disc, a penny painted with radium.

So something about their visual experiences at dawn is the same for both: a brilliant yellow-white disc centred between green and blue colour patches. Sketches of what they both see could be identical – congruent. In this sense Tycho and Kepler see the same thing at dawn. The sun appears to them in the same way. The same view, or scene, is presented to them both.

In fact, we often speak in this way. Thus the account of a recent solar eclipse:[11] 'Only a thin crescent remains; white light is now completely obscured; the sky appears a deep blue, almost purple, and the landscape is a monochromatic green... there are the flashes of light on the disc's circumference and now the brilliant crescent to the left. ...' Newton writes in a similar way in the *Opticks*: 'These Arcs at their first appearance were of a violet and blue Colour, and between them were white Arcs of Circles, which...became a little tinged in their inward Limbs with red and yellow. ...'[12] Every physicist employs the language of lines, colour patches, appearances, shadows. In so far as two normal observers use this language of the same event, they begin from the same data: they are making the same observation. Differences between them must arise in the interpretations they put on these data.

Thus, to summarize, saying that Kepler and Tycho see the same thing at dawn just because their eyes are similarly affected is an elementary mistake. There is a difference between a physical state and a visual experience. Suppose, however, that it is argued as above – that they see the same thing because they have the same sense-datum experience. Disparities in their accounts arise in *expost facto* interpretations of what is seen, not in the fundamental visual data. If this is argued, further difficulties soon obtrude.

B

Normal retinas and cameras are impressed similarly by figure 23.1.[13] Our visual sense-data will be the same too. If asked to draw what we see, most of us will set out a configuration like figure 23.1.

Do we all see the same thing?[14] Some will see a perspex cube viewed from below. Others will see it from above. Still others will see it as a kind of polygonally-cut gem. Some people see only criss-crossed lines in a plane. It may be seen as a block of ice, an aquarium, a wire frame for a kite – or any of a number of other things.

Do we, then, all see the same thing? If we do, how can these differences be accounted for?

Here the 'formula' re-enters: 'These are different *interpretations* of what all observers see in common. Retinal reactions to figure 23.1 are virtually identical; so too are our visual sense-data, since our drawings of what we see will have the same content. There is no place in the seeing for these differences, so they must lie in the interpretations put on what we see.'

This sounds as if I do two things, not one, when I see boxes and bicycles. Do I put different interpretations on figure 23.1 when I see it now as a box from below, and now as a cube from above? I am aware of

Figure 23.1

no such thing. I mean no such thing when I report that the box's perspective has snapped back into the page.[15] If I do not mean this, then the concept of seeing which is natural in this connexion does not designate two diaphanous components, one optical, the other interpretative. Figure 23.1 is simply seen now as a box from below, now as a cube from above; one does not first soak up an optical pattern and then clamp an interpretation on it. Kepler and Tycho just see the sun. That is all. That is the way the concept of seeing works in this connexion.

'But', you say, 'seeing figure 23.1 first as a box from below, then as a cube from above, involves interpreting the lines differently in each case.' Then for you and me to have a different interpretation of figure 23.1 just *is* for us to see something different. This does not mean we see the same thing and then interpret it differently. When I suddenly exclaim 'Eureka – a box from above,' I do not refer simply to a different interpretation. (Again, there is a logically prior sense in which seeing figure 23.1 as from above and then as from below is seeing the same thing differently, i.e. being aware of the same diagram in different ways. We can refer just to this, but we need not. In this case we do not.)

Besides, the word 'interpretation' is occasionally useful. We know where it applies and where it does not. Thucydides presented the facts objectively; Herodotus put an interpretation on them. The word does not apply to everything – it has a meaning. Can interpreting always be going on when we see? Sometimes, perhaps, as when the hazy outline of an agricultural machine looms up on a foggy morning and, with effort, we finally identify it. Is this the 'interpretation' which is active when bicycles and boxes are clearly seen? Is it active when the perspective of figure 23.1 snaps into reverse? There was a time when Herodotus was half-through with his interpretation of the Graeco-Persian wars. Could there be a time when one is half-through interpreting figure 23.1 as a box from above, or as anything else?

'But the interpretation takes very little time – it is instantaneous.' Instantaneous interpretation hails from the Limbo that produced unsensed sensibilia, unconscious inference, incorrigible statements, negative facts and *Objektive*. These are ideas which philosophers force on the world to preserve some pet epistemological or metaphysical theory.

Only in contrast to 'Eureka' situations (like perspective reversals, where one cannot interpret the data) is it clear what is meant by saying that though Thucydides could have put an interpretation on history, he did not. Moreover, whether or not an historian is advancing an interpretation is an empirical question: we know what would count as evidence one way or the other. But whether we are employing an interpretation when we see figure 23.1 in a certain way is not empirical. What could count as evidence? In no ordinary sense of 'interpret' do I interpret figure 23.1 differently when its perspective reverses for me. If there is some extraordinary sense of the word it is not clear, either in ordinary language, or in extraordinary (philosophical) language. To insist that different reactions to figure 23.1 *must* lie in the interpretations put on a common visual experience is just to reiterate (without reasons) that the seeing of *x must* be the same for all observers looking at *x* . . .

The sun, however, is not an entity with such variable perspective. What has all this to do with suggesting that Tycho and Kepler may see different things in the east at dawn? Certainly the cases are different. But these reversible perspective figures are examples of different things being seen in the same configuration, where this difference is due neither to differing visual pictures, nor to any 'interpretation' superimposed on the sensation.

Some will see in figure 23.2 an old Parisienne, others a young woman (à la Toulouse-Lautrec).[16] All normal retinas 'take' the same picture; and our sense-datum pictures must be the same, for even if you see an old lady and I a young lady, the pictures we draw of what we see may turn out to be geometrically indistinguishable. (Some can see this *only* in one way, not both. This is like the difficulty we have after finding a face in a tree-puzzle; we cannot thereafter see the tree without the face.)

When what is observed is characterized so differently as 'young woman' or 'old woman', is it not natural to say that the observers see different things? Or must 'see different things' mean only 'see different objects'? This is a primary sense of the expression, to be sure. But is there not also a sense in which one who cannot see the young lady in figure 23.2 sees something different from me, who sees the young lady? Of course there is . . . .

Figure 23.2

How does one describe the difference between the *jeune fille* and the *vieille femme* in figure 23.2? Perhaps the difference is not describable: it may just show itself.[17] That two observers have not seen the same things in figure 23.2 could show itself in their behaviour. What is the difference between us when you see the zebra as black with white stripes and I see it as white with black stripes? Nothing optical. Yet there might be a context (for instance, in the genetics of animal pigmentation), where such a difference could be important.

A third group of figures will stress further this organizational element of seeing and observing. They will hint at how much more is involved when Tycho and Kepler witness the dawn than 'the formula' suggests.

What is portrayed in figure 23.3? Your retinas and visual cortices are affected much as mine are; our sense-datum pictures would not differ. Surely we could all produce an accurate sketch of figure 23.3. Do we see the same thing?

I see a bear climbing up the other side of a tree. Did the elements 'pull together'/cohere/organize, when you learned this?[18] You might even say with Wittgenstein 'it has not changed, and yet I see it differently...'.[19] Now, does it not have '...a quite particular "organization"'?

Organization is not itself seen as are the lines and colours of a drawing. It is not itself a line, shape, or a colour. It is not an element in the visual field, but rather the way in which elements are appreciated. Again, the plot is not another detail in the story. Nor is the tune just one more note. Yet without plots and tunes details and notes would not hang together.

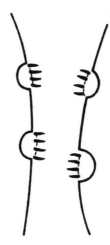

Figure 23.3

Similarly the organization of figure 23.3 is nothing that registers on the retina along with other details. Yet it gives the lines and shapes a pattern. Were this lacking we would be left with nothing but an unintelligible configuration of lines. . . .

A trained physicist could see one thing in figure 23.4: an X-ray tube viewed from the cathode. Would Sir Lawrence Bragg and an Eskimo baby see the same thing when looking at an X-ray tube? Yes, and no. Yes – they are visually aware of the same object. No – the *ways* in which they are visually aware are profoundly different. Seeing is not only the having of a visual experience; it is also the way in which the visual experience is had.

At school the physicist had gazed at this glass-and-metal instrument. Returning now, after years in University and research, his eye lights upon the same object once again. Does he see the same thing now as he did then? Now he sees the instrument in terms of electrical circuit theory, thermodynamic theory, the theories of metal and glass structure, thermionic emission, optical transmission, refraction, diffraction, atomic theory, quantum theory and special relativity.

Contrast the freshman's view of college with that of his ancient tutor. Compare a man's first glance at the motor of his car with a similar glance ten exasperating years later.

'Granted, one learns all these things', it may be countered, 'but it all figures in the interpretation the physicist puts on what he sees. Though the layman sees exactly what the physicist sees, he cannot interpret it in the same way because he has not learned so much.'

Figure 23.4

Is the physicist doing more than just seeing? No; he does nothing over and above what the layman does when he sees an X-ray tube. What are you doing over and above reading these words? Are you interpreting marks on a page? When would this ever be a natural way of speaking? Would an infant see what you see here, when you see words and sentences and he sees but marks and lines? One does nothing beyond looking and seeing when one dodges bicycles, glances at a friend, or notices a cat in the garden.

'The physicist and the layman see the same thing', it is objected, 'but they do not make the same thing of it.' The layman can make nothing of it. Nor is that just a figure of speech. I can make nothing of the Arab word for *cat*, though my purely visual impressions may be indistinguishable from those of the Arab who can. I must learn Arabic before I can see what he sees. The layman must learn physics before he can see what the physicist sees. ...

The infant and the layman can see: they are not blind. But they cannot see what the physicist sees; they are blind to what he sees.[20] We may not hear that the oboe is out of tune, though this will be painfully obvious to the trained musician. (Who, incidentally, will not hear the tones and *interpret* them as being out of tune, but will simply hear the oboe to be out of tune.[21] We simply see what time it is; the surgeon simply sees a wound to be septic; the physicist sees the X-ray tube's anode overheating.) The elements of the visitor's visual field, though identical with those of the physicist, are not organized for him as for the physicist; the same lines, colours, shapes are apprehended by both, but not in the same way. There are indefinitely many ways in which a constellation of lines, shapes, patches, may be seen. *Why* a visual pattern is seen differently is a question for psychology, but *that* it may be seen differently is important in any examination of the concepts of seeing and observation. Here, as Wittgenstein might have said, the psychological is a symbol of the logical.

You see a bird, I see an antelope; the physicist sees an X-ray tube, the child a complicated lamp bulb; the microscopist sees coelenterate mesoglea, his new student sees only a gooey, formless stuff. Tycho and Simplicius see a mobile sun, Kepler and Galileo see a static sun.[22]

It may be objected, 'Everyone, whatever his state of knowledge, will see figure 23.1 as a box or cube, viewed as from above or as from below.' True; almost everyone, child, layman, physicist, will see the figure as box-like one way or another. But could such observations be made by people ignorant of the construction of box-like objects? No. This objection only shows that most of us – the blind, babies, and dimwits excluded – have learned enough to be able to see this figure as a three-dimensional box.

This reveals something about the sense in which Simplicius and Galileo do see the same thing (which I have never denied): they both see a brilliant heavenly body. The schoolboy and the physicist both see that the X-ray tube will smash if dropped. Examining how observers see different things in x marks something important about their seeing the same thing when looking at x. If seeing different things involves having different knowledge and theories about x, then perhaps the sense in which they see the same thing involves their sharing knowledge and theories about x. Bragg and the baby share no knowledge of X-ray tubes. They see the same thing only in that if they are looking at x they are both having some visual experience of it. Kepler and Tycho agree on more: they see the same thing in a stronger sense. Their visual fields are organized in much the same way. Neither sees the sun about to break out in a grin, or about to crack into ice cubes. (The baby is not 'set' even against these eventualities.) Most people today see the same thing at dawn in an even stronger sense: we share much knowledge of the sun. Hence Tycho and Kepler see different things, and yet they see the same thing. That these things can be said depends on their knowledge, experience, and theories. . . .

Notes

1   Wär' nicht das Auge sonnenhaft,
     Die Sonne könnt' es nie erblicken;

> Goethe, *Zahme Xenien* (*Werke*, Weimar, 1887–1918), bk. 3, 1805.

2   Cf. the papers by Baker and Gatonby in *Nature*, 1949–1965.
3   This is not a *merely* conceptual matter, of course. Cf. Wittgenstein, *Philosophical Investigations* (Blackwell, Oxford, 1953), p. 196.
4   (1) G. Berkeley, *Essay Towards a New Theory of Vision* (in *Works*, vol. 1, London, T. Nelson, 1948–56), pp. 51 ff.
    (2) James Mill, *Analysis of the Phenomena of the Human Mind* (Longmans, London, 1869), vol. 1, p. 97.
    (3) J. Sully, *Outlines of Psychology* (Appleton, New York, 1885).
    (4) William James, *The Principles of Psychology* (Holt, New York, 1890–1905), vol. 2, pp. 4, 78, 80 and 81; vol. 1, p. 221.
    (5) A. Schopenhauer, *Satz vom Grunde* (in *Sämmtliche Werke*, Leipzig, 1888), ch. 4.
    (6) H. Spencer, *The Principles of Psychology* (Appleton, New York, 1897), vol. 4, chs. 9, 10.

(7) E. von Hartmann, *Philosophy of the Unconscious* (K. Paul, London, 1931), B, chs. 7, 8.

(8) W. M. Wundt, *Vorlesungen über die Menschen und Thierseele* (Voss, Hamburg, 1892), 4, 13.

(9) H. L. F. von Helmholtz, *Handbuch der Physiologischen Optik* (Leipzig, 1867), pp. 430, 447.

(10) A. Binet, *La psychologie du raisonnement, recherches expérimentales par l'hypnotisme* (Alcan, Paris, 1886), chs. 3, 5.

(11) J. Grote, *Exploratio Philosophica* (Cambridge, 1900), vol. 2, pp. 201 ff.

(12) B. Russell, in *Mind* (1913), p. 76. *Mysticism and Logic* (Longmans, New York, 1918), p. 209. *The Problems of Philosophy* (Holt, New York, 1912), pp. 73, 92, 179, 203.

(13) Dawes Hicks, *Arist. Soc. Sup.* vol. 2 (1919), pp. 176–8.

(14) G. F. Stout, *A Manual of Psychology* (Clive, London, 1907, 2nd edn), vol. 2, 1 and 2, pp. 324, 561–4.

(15) A. C. Ewing, *Fundamental Questions of Philosophy* (New York, 1951), pp. 45 ff.

(16) G. W. Cunningham, *Problems of Philosophy* (Holt, New York, 1924), pp. 96–7.

5 Galileo, *Dialogue Concerning the Two Chief World Systems* (California, 1953), 'The First Day', p. 33.

6 '"Das ist doch kein Sehen!" – "Das ist doch ein Sehen!" Beide müssen sich begrifflich rechtfertigen lassen' (Wittgenstein, *Phil. Inv.* p. 203).

7 Cf. Whewell, *Philosophy of Discovery* (London, 1860), 'The Paradoxes of Vision'.

8 Cf. e.g. J. Z. Young, *Doubt and Certainty in Science* (Oxford, 1951, The Reith Lectures), and Gray Walter's article in *Aspects of Form*, ed. by L. L. Whyte (London, 1953). Compare Newton: 'Do not the Rays of Light in falling upon the bottom of the Eye excite Vibrations in the Tunica Retina? Which Vibrations, being propagated along the solid Fibres of the Nerves into the Brain, cause the Sense of seeing' (*Opticks* (London, 1769), Bk. III, part I).

9 'Rot und grün kann ich nur sehen, aber nicht hören' (Wittgenstein, *Phil. Inv.* p. 209).

10 Cf. 'An appearance is the same whenever the same eye is affected in the same way' (Lambert, *Photometria* (Berlin, 1760)); 'We are justified, when different perceptions offer themselves to us, to infer that the underlying real conditions are different' (Helmholtz, *Wissenschaftliche Abhandlungen* (Leipzig, 1882), vol. II, p. 656), and Hertz: 'We form for ourselves images or symbols of the external objects; the manner in which we form them is such that the logically necessary (*denknotwendigen*) consequences of the images in thought are invariably the images of materially necessary (*naturnotwendigen*) consequences of the corresponding objects' (*Principles of Mechanics* (London, 1889), p. I).

Broad and Price make depth a feature of the private visual pattern. However, Weyl (*Philosophy of Mathematics and Natural Science* (Princeton, 1949), p. 125) notes that a single eye perceives qualities spread out in a two-dimensional field, since the latter is dissected by any one-dimensional line running through it. But our conceptual difficulties remain even when Kepler and Tycho keep one eye closed.

Whether or not two observers are having the same visual sense-data reduces directly to the question of whether accurate pictures of the contents of their visual fields are identical, or differ in some detail. We can then discuss the publicly observable pictures which Tycho and Kepler draw of what they see, instead of those private, mysterious entities locked in their visual consciousness. The accurate picture and the sense-datum must be identical; how could they differ?

11   From the BBC report, 30 June 1954.

12   Newton, *Opticks*, bk. II, part I. The writings of Claudius Ptolemy sometimes read like a phenomenalist's textbook. Cf. e.g. *The Almagest* (Venice, 1515), VI, section II, 'On the Directions in the Eclipses', 'When it touches the shadow's circle from within', 'When the circles touch each other from without'. Cf. also VII and VIII, IX (section 4). Ptolemy continually seeks to chart and predict 'the appearances' – the points of light on the celestial globe. *The Almagest* abandons any attempt to explain the machinery behind these appearances.

Cf. Pappus: 'The (circle) dividing the milk-white portion which owes its colour to the sun, and the portion which has the ashen colour natural to the moon itself is indistinguishable from a great circle' (*Mathematical Collection* (Hultsch, Berlin and Leipzig, 1864), pp. 554–60).

13   This famous illusion dates from 1832, when L. A. Necker, the Swiss naturalist, wrote a letter to Sir David Brewster describing how when certain rhomboidal crystals were viewed on end the perspective could shift in the way now familiar to us. Cf. *Phil. Mag.* III, no. I (1832), 329–37, especially p. 336. It is important to the present argument to note that this observational phenomenon began life not as a psychologist's trick, but at the very frontiers of observational science.

14   Wittgenstein answers: 'Denn wir sehen eben wirklich zwei verschiedene Tatsachen' (*Tractatus*, 5. 5423).

15   'Auf welche Vorgänge spiele ich an?' (Wittgenstein, *Phil. Inv.*, p. 214).

16   From Boring, *Amer. J. Psychol.* XLII (1930), 444 and cf. Allport, *Brit. J. Psychol.* XXI (1930), 133; Leeper, *J. Genet. Psychol.* XLVI (1935), 41; Street, *Gestalt Completion Test* (Columbia Univ., 1931); Dees and Grindley, *Brit. J. Psychol.* (1947).

17   'Was gezeight werden kann, kann nicht gesagt werden' (Wittgenstein, *Tractatus*, 4. 1212).

18   This case is different from figure 23.1. Now I can help a 'slow' percipient by tracing in the outline of the bear. In figure 23.1 a percipient either gets the perspectival arrangement, or he does not, though even here Wittgenstein

makes some suggestions as to how one might help; cf. *Tractatus*, 5. 5423, last line.

19 Wittgenstein, *Phil. Inv.* p. 193. Helmholtz speaks of the 'integrating' function which converts the figure into the appearance of an object hit by a visual ray (*Phys. Optik*, vol. III, p. 239). This is reminiscent of Aristotle, for whom seeing consisted in emanations from our eyes. They reach out, tentacle-fashion, and touch objects whose shapes are 'felt' in the eye. (Cf. *De Caelo* (Oxford, 1928), 290a, 18; and *Meteorologica* (Oxford, 1928), III, iv, 373 b, 2. (Also Plato, *Meno*, London, 1869), 76c–D.) But he controverts this in *Topica* (Oxford, 1928), 105b, 6.) Theophrastus argues that 'Vision is due to the gleaming... which [in the eye] reflects to the object' (*On the Senses*, 26, tr. G. M. Stratton). Hero writes: 'Rays proceeding from our eyes are reflected by mirrors... that our sight is directed in straight lines proceeding from the organ of vision may be substantiated as follows' (*Catoptrics*, 1–5, tr. Schmidt in *Heronis Alexandrini Opera* (Leipzig, 1899–1919)). Galen is of the same opinion. So too is Leonardo: 'The eye sends its image to the object... the power of vision extends by means of the visual rays...' (*Notebooks*, C.A. 135 v.b. and 270 v.c.). Similarly Donne in *The Ecstasy* writes: 'Our eyebeams twisted and... pictures in our eyes to get was all *our* propagation.'

This is the view that all perception is really a species of touching, e.g. Descartes' *impressions*, and the analogy of the wax. Compare: '[Democritus] explains [vision] by the air between the eye and the object [being] compressed... [it] thus becomes imprinted... "as if one were to take a mould in wax"...' (Theophrastus, *op. cit.*, 50–3). Though it lacks physical and physiological support, the view is attractive in cases where lines seem suddenly to be forced into an intelligible pattern – by us.

20 Cf. 'He was blind to the *expression* of a face. Would his eyesight on that account be defective?' (Wittgenstein, *Phil. Inv.* p. 210) and 'Because they seeing see not; and hearing they hear not, neither do they understand' (Matt. xiii. 10–13).

21 'Es hört doch jeder nur, was er versteht' (Goethe, *Maxims*, in *Werke*, Weimar, 1887–1918).

22 Against this Professor H. H. Price has argued: 'Surely it appears to both of them to be rising, to be moving upwards, across the horizon... they both see a moving sun: they both see a round bright body which appears to be rising.' Philip Frank retorts: 'Our sense observation shows only that in the morning the distance between horizon and sun is increasing, but it does not tell us whether the sun is ascending or the horizon is descending...' (*Modern Science and its Philosophy* (Harvard, 1949), p. 231). Precisely. For Galileo and Kepler the horizon drops; for Simplicius and Tycho the sun rises. This is the difference Price misses, and which is central to this essay.

24

Analogue Content

Christopher Peacocke

Consider someone who has to furnish a room. He may see how far the door is from the bookshelf; and he may raise the question of whether he can fit a piano between them. His question will not necessarily be answered by a catalogue of pianos, however large, which gives the lengths of pianos in feet and inches. For when he sees the distance from the door to the shelf, he does not see it as having a certain length in feet and inches; and he does not necessarily learn its length in feet and inches. Conversely, we can consider a salesman who is presented with a plan of a room he has not seen, a plan which states in feet and inches the distance from door to shelf. Faced with a showroom full of pianos, the salesman need not be in a position to answer the question of which if any of the pianos he perceives will fit. It seems that there is a way of perceiving distance, and a way of thinking of distances based on perceptions of them, neither of which are captured by specifications of distance in feet and inches. What are these ways, what is distinctive of them, and what is their significance?

The phenomenon seems to be present for virtually all perceptible magnitudes. A tourist may be standing looking at a baroque facade, and see a particular carving to be in a particular direction. This is not to see it as 37 degrees left of straight ahead and as at 64 degrees of elevation, even if the carving is in that direction and the tourist is perceiving accurately. It is informative that a particular perceived direction is 37 degrees left and 64 degrees up. A tourist who learns from a guidebook the carving's direction in degrees need not be in a position to know which

Christopher Peacocke, "Analogue Content," in *The Aristotelian Society*, supplementary vol. 60 (1986), pp. 1–17.

one it is out of the many carvings he sees. Similarly to look out of the window and see how fast the train is moving is not to be in a position to know its speed in miles per hour; to know which particular note above middle C is sounded goes beyond what can be learned from simply hearing that note sounded; and so forth.

We can make two major divisions within the class of philosophical questions raised by these distinctive ways of perceiving and ways of thinking of magnitudes. We can distinguish on the one hand questions about the correct formulation of these ways, their individuation, their internal relations to one another, and what distinguishes them as a class; on the other hand there are questions about what abilities a subject must have if he is to be capable of enjoying mental states which have such contents. Questions of the sort in the second class are now often described as 'substantive', though of course questions in the first class are genuine and need investigation. Answers to questions in each class constrain the acceptability of answers to questions in the other. In this [chapter] my concern will be with questions of the first sort, and I will only brush the second. The other major division we can make is between questions about the content of experiences of perceptible magnitudes and questions about the content of judgements constitutively linked to such experiences. We should not assume in advance that the relevant components of the content of the experience and of the contents of the judgement are identical; in fact I will argue that they are not. But let us return to considering what the content of these experiences is.

The difficulty we had with expressing the content of the room furnisher's experience of the distance from the door to the shelf in terms of feet is nothing to do with scope. It is not as though it would be correct to say 'The furnisher does not see the distance as 7.22 feet, but *of* the number 7.22, he does see the distance as being that number of feet'. That would not be correct: the notion of distance in *feet* ought not to enter a specification of the content of his experience at all.

Nor is the problem resolved merely by introducing what we may call a *unit-free* conception of distance. There is such a conception, and there may be good reasons for saying that what we perceive are distances given in unit-free terms. This would be a conception on which we can say that there is something, D, which is the distance between two points; numerical measures can then be applied to this distance D itself, using any units one may choose. No one who accepts the standard practice of treating distance as a relation between two points and a number ought to reject such unit-free distances: for the unit-free distance between a and b is identical with the unit-free distance between c and d if and only if the distance in feet between *a* and *b* is the same as the distance in feet between *c* and *d*. But for all their intelligibility, unit-free distances (and their ilk for the other magnitudes) help us only with the question of *what* is perceived, and not with the question of the *way* in which it is perceived. Of course someone may maintain that there is no such distinction to be drawn here; but that would be a highly substantial thesis needing a defence which draws upon some account of the ways in which these magnitudes are perceived. It cannot be a triviality written into the identification of ways in which magnitudes are perceived.

There is one last preliminary before we turn to a positive account. It is always tempting in this area to use, for instance, the idea of the precise direction or distance experienced. Since humans do not have arbitrary powerful senses, we know that 'the precise direction experienced' cannot be exactly the direction from the subject as origin to some three-dimensional coordinate given by real numbers. In fact the idea of the precise direction experienced is incoherent in a familiar way if it is supposed to conform to the following principle: that experiences of discriminably different directions are ones in which different directions are experienced, and experiences of non-discriminably different directions are experiences in which the same direction is experienced. This is just the parallel notion for direction of an incoherent notion of shade in the case of colour.[1] For any dimension along which matching (non-discriminable difference) is non-transitive, contradiction results if we suppose there are what correspond to shades or to precise directions experienced. If *a* matches *b*, *b* matches *c* but *a* does not match *c*, there is no precise direction experienced which is coherently assignable to *a* – since it must both be the same as that of *c* (by virtue of being the same as that of *b*, which both *a* and *c* match), and different from it (by virtue of *a*'s not matching *c*). But though we know there is no such coherent notion of precise direction experienced, it seems clear from our three examples that we had nevertheless better make some sense of perceiving something to be in a particular direction, and of perceiving something to be a particular length. It may be that we cannot vindicate all our pretheoretical intuitions if they implicitly use the notion of precise direction experienced: as in many projects which respond to a derivation of a contradiction, there will be elements which reconstruct some but not all of our intuitions, and there may not be a uniquely correct way of building such a reconstruction. Still, we cannot simply dismiss our initial examples. The experiential phenomena and the judgements based on them seem real enough: and I will argue below that they play an essential part in the psychological explanation of spatial actions. I would also hold that they have a crucial role in the individuation of many concepts. So we cannot just abandon the project of giving a positive account of them.

Suppose you perceive the end of one arm of a television aerial to be in a particular direction from you. We can use the notion of the *matching profile* of your experience in respect of the perceived direction of the end of the presented arm. This matching profile is a set of directions: a given direction is in the set if and only if it is not discriminably outside the apparent direction of the end of the perceived arm. For the purposes of this definition, the directions in the set may be arbitrarily finely individuated. In the case of directions, a matching profile could naturally be taken as a particular solid angle, centred on the subject's location at the time of the experience. In the case of perceived distance, the matching profile would be a set of distances. Many refinements could be made to the definition of the matching profile, but the details would not affect the essential uses to which it will be put here. The matching profile of an experience is sensitive to the subject's perceptual acuity in a way Goodman's *qualia* are not.[2] If two experiences have the same matching profile in respect of perceived direction of an object presented in a given way, it follows that they have the same 'direction quale' as determined by Goodman's identity conditions. But the converse condition is not true, as in effect some of Dummett's remarks on Goodman brought out:[3] the size of the matching profile will depend on visual acuity. The matching profile of an experience is not meant to function as the precise perceived direction: we already know that nothing can have such a function. But matching profiles can serve several purposes, the primary one of which is in stating what is required for an experience to be veridical in a given respect. For a perceived object really to be where it seems to be the object itself must be located relative to the subject in roughly the directions contained in the matching profile. On the definition given, these may not be the real directions of the object perceived: the light may be bending, there may be mirrors, or some patch of the subject's retina may have slipped.

Whenever someone perceives something – an object, a property, a magnitude – he perceives it in a particular way, or, as I shall say, in a particular *manner*. These manners comprise part of the content of perceptual experience, and it is of them that we have to give some account in saying what that content is. To say that these things are perceived in a particular manner is not at all to imply that these things are not themselves perceived. On the contrary: the notion has been introduced here in the context of the phrase 'thing perceived in a particular manner'.

What properties must these manners have? Suppose we are concerned with the manners in which things of a given kind may be perceived, say distances. Then, first, we should require that if μ is the manner in which one distance is perceived and μ' is the manner in which a second distance is perceived by the same subject at the same time, and $\mu = \mu'$, then the distances are experienced as the same by that subject (they match in Goodman's sense). Anything failing this principle would be too crude to capture the manner of perception of things of the kind in question. We know from the nontransitivity of matching that this necessary condition of identity of manner cannot also be sufficient. For the time being, let us follow Goodman and take matching by exactly the same things as sufficient for identity of manner. As we saw, we could instead take something more sensitive to perceptual acuity: but let us keep things simple for the present.

Dummett (op. cit.) would point out that, on classical assumptions about space, this will commit us to distinguishing continuum many $(2\aleph0)$ manners of perception of distance. Is it just absurd to suppose that we need to use such manners in the description of the mental states of finite beings? I offer two related defences. First, the use of such manners does not float free of real psychological facts about humans because their individuation supervenes on facts about the matching relations sustained by a subject's mental states. Second, it is indeed plausible that humans can be in only finitely many significantly different brain states (central states). But if a subject's *environment* is infinitely divisible or variegated, the finitude of the possible central states is consistent with the subject having the capacity for being in any one of infinitely many different relational states; and a substantive theory of what is involved in perceiving something in a particular manner will have to advert to his environmental relations. These defences are related because if they are both correct, it follows that facts about matching do not supervene solely on the subject's central states.

In the case of the particular contents in our examples, those concerning distance and direction, there is a second requirement on the manners. This is the requirement that they be *amodal*, in the sense that the same manner can enter the content of experiences in different sense modalities. You may hear a birdsong as coming from the same direction as that in which you see the top of a tree: we would omit part of how the experience represents the world as being were we to fail to mention this apparent identity. It also makes sense to say that something feels roughly the same size as it looks. This is not necessarily to say that all manners of perception of spatial magnitudes are amodal: only that some are.

The title of this paper derives from the fact there is a sense in which manners of perception conforming to these principles and which featured in our initial examples can be described as *analogue*. As a first approximation, a type of manner is analogue provided that there is some dimension of variation such that for any pair of distinct points d, d' on that dimension, there are two manners of the given type one of which is a manner of perception of something which is or includes d but not d', and the other of which is a manner of perception of something which is or includes d' but not d.[4] The dimension may be direction or size, but it is neither confined to these, nor to spatial characteristics. One type of nonspatial content falling under this definition is the type of manner in which a note, when played on a violin, is perceived: here the relevant dimension will be a range of pitches. This first approximation, which certainly covers the examples we gave, is slightly too stringent: for it excludes some conceivable cases of 'digitized' vision. We can conceive of our visual experience being digitized in points of light arranged in a 1000×1000 square matrix. A visually perceived straight line could then be perceived in a distinctive manner that ought, intuitively, to be of analogue type: but it would not be so counted under the first approximation, with its requirement about every pair of points on the relevant dimension. This case would be covered by modifying the criterion to require just that there is some way of segmenting the dimension in question such that for points d and d' *not in the same segment*, there are manners. . . . & c.

In the recent psychological and philosophical literature the idea of something's being analogue has featured prominently. The notion has been applied both to mental representations and to processors on representations.[5] It has been closely linked with Shepard's famous idea of a second-order isomorphism. Shepard wrote:

> isomorphism should be sought – not in the first-order relation between (*a*) an individual object, and (*b*) its internal representation – but in the second-order relation between (*a*) the relations between alternative external objects, and (*b*) the relations among their corresponding internal representations. Thus, although the internal representation for a square need not itself be square, it should (whatever it is) at least have a closer functional relation to the internal representation for a rectangle than to that, say, for a green flash or the taste of persimmon.[6]

The present [chapter] is not about internal representations, claims about which need experimental investigation, constrained as they should be by their ability to explain empirical psychological phenomena. The present paper is concerned rather with the correct description of some of the more familiar phenomena themselves. But there is a corresponding notion of second-order isomorphism applicable in connection with analogue contents. Consider manners of perception of directions. If one such manner is of a direction d and another is of a direction d', and d is sufficiently above d', then the perceiver will have the impression that the first direction is above the second direction. In the case of directions, this will hold for a range of spatial relations, not just that of being above; for other things presented by analogue contents, there will be a comparable range of relations. Here we have an isomorphism between some of the relations really holding between what the contents are *of* and the relations of which the subject has the impression that they hold between the perceived objects; in fact formulated that way, in successful perception, it is not just an isomorphism, it is an identity.[7]

How does the present sense of 'analogue' relate to others' uses of the term? It is hard not to agree with the suspicion voiced by Haugeland that these uses constitute a motley rather than a unified single kind (op. cit.). Nevertheless there are links between analogue content and, for instance, Haugeland's own definition of an analogue device. Haugeland concentrates on the character of the device's write-read cycle. For him, the procedures used in that cycle for an analogue device have this property: there is a notion of margin of error such that the narrower it is, the harder it is to stay within it; the actual procedures stay within a relatively small margin; better procedures are always possible, but not procedures guaranteed to be perfect.[8] Perhaps memory may be regarded as 'reading' states with analogue content. But even then there is no *cycle*: these memories are not distinctively involved in the production of other states with analogue content. Nevertheless, there is still a connection with Haugeland's excellent definition. If the manners of perception of spatial magnitudes which give the content of our own experience are as finely individuated as we have sliced them, there is certainly no operation of memory guaranteed to produce an image with precisely the same analogue content.[9] The very idea of memory or any other faculty yielding a state with a content which only *approximates* some other content implicitly relies on notions in our characterization of analogue content: approximation makes sense only where there is a dimension of variation which is covered by the kind of content in question.

Manners of perception constitute a genuine level of content in their own right, intermediate between two more familiar levels. On one side, manners are distinct from the things of which they are manners of perception; on the other, they are distinct from perceptual-demonstrative thought constituents (Fregean modes of presentation) of the form 'that distance', 'that direction', and so on. That is, they are also distinct from the components which enter the content of judgements based on perceptual experience. Both these claims of distinctness need argument. As a preliminary, I should mention that in what follows I use the phrase 'mode of presentation' only for Fregean thought-constituents and never for manners of perception. If only we could ignore history, 'mode of presentation' would be an excellent term for what I have been calling manners of perception: but the fact is that the use of 'mode of presentation' as an English rendering of Frege's notion is now part of ingrained philosophical practice, and I will not try to change it.

Suppose you see two straight lines at oblique angles, one to your right and one to your left. In some such cases, you neither see one line as longer than the other, and nor do you see the lines as of the same length, as matching in length. It follows that the distance between the ends of the one line and the distance between the ends of the other are not presented in the same manner: this follows from our condition on manners that things presented by the same manner must be experienced as matching in the relevant respect. Since the lines may in fact be of the same length, manners of perception of distance are in a many–one relation to the distances perceived. By a similar argument, manners of perception of distance are also in a many–one relation to the matching profiles of the two lengths. Similar points could be developed for the perception of direction, at least when it is radial rather than spherical direction which is in question. Suppose you are standing on the observation floor at the top of a skyscraper in Manhattan. In the dense patchwork of buildings stretching away from you on the ground, you may see two buildings, one much closer to you than the other. These buildings may not appear to you to be in exactly the same direction, nor does it look as if they are in different directions. Again, the manners in which the directions of the two buildings are perceived cannot be identified with the directions themselves; for the directions may well be identical, while the manners are not. These points are of course not a proof that there is no way of identifying manners of perception with something on the level of things perceived: but I do conjecture that the same form of consideration just given against particular identifications could be applied against other candidates.

It is much less obvious that manners of perception are not modes of presentation. But it is so, for the supposition that manners are so much as in one–one correlation with modes of presentation leads to a contradiction. Here is the argument for the case of length. Let us return to the tourist looking at the baroque facade, and let us suppose that he notices a column and a window parallel to it which match in respect of apparent length. Now suppose that in fact not merely do they match in this way, but that they are in fact exactly the same length, and that they are perceived in exactly the same manner. We will also assume for *reductio* that once the subject's context is fixed, there is for each length *presented in a given manner* a unique demonstrative mode of presentation of it of the form 'that length'. We can call this 'the uniqueness assumption'. Since we have assumed that the lengths are perceived in exactly the same manner, the uniqueness assumption implies that the modes of presentation ('m.p.'s') 'that length' used in connection with the column and the window are identical. Nevertheless, it is consistent with everything in this example so far that the tourist suspect that the column and the window are not precisely the same length (and not because his perceptual systems are malfunctioning): he suspects that there could, as things actually are, be objects matching the column in length which do not match the window. For all he knows, a few moments later he may actually notice something on the facade which matches one but not the other. So our tourist is certainly not willing to judge, concerning the length of the column and the window, that the former is identical with the latter. For our tourist, the thought 'that length [used in connection with the window] is that length [used in connection with the column]' is informative. But this is incompatible with the identity of the demonstrative modes of presentation of the length, in the presence only of Frege's Principle – the Principle that if m.p.'s m and m' are identical, the thought that the thing presented by m is identical with the thing presented by m' is uninformative. So we have a contradiction.

It seems to me that the only plausible way out of this contradiction is to reject the uniqueness assumption. We can hardly say that the contradiction establishes that it is incoherent to suppose that there are perceptually based thought constituents of the form 'that distance', 'that direction' and the rest: they are ubiquitous in our everyday thought. There is no real possibility of rejecting Frege's Principle, which is constitutive of modes of presentation: anything not conforming to that Principle will be inadequate for capturing the phenomenon of distinctive contributions to cognitive significance, a phenomenon we surely must capture. Nor does the derivation of the contradiction depend upon taking the referents of the perceptual-demonstratives as finely sliced magnitudes. We can reproduce the argument if the referents are wider bands: we can do so as long as there are distinct bands which match, which there must be if our perceptual powers are finite.

If the uniqueness assumption is false, then *a fortiori* manners of perception cannot be identified with modes of presentation. This conclusion ought not to be surprising to us. The distinctness of the constituents of the contents of perception from constituents of the contents of judgement flows ultimately from the difference between the considerations which respectively individuate the two types of content. Individuation of the content of perception is answerable to considerations of phenomenology in the first instance, while the content of attitudes is answerable to considerations of epistemic possibility: there is no reason these different notions must coincide, and the contradiction shows that in fact they do not.

This leaves outstanding the question of what relation *does* hold between manners of perception and modes of presentation of such forms as 'that length', 'that direction' and the rest. The contradiction may show that the modes are distinct from the manners, but there is a sense in which it does not show why they are. We will have an independent motivation for our particular way out of the contradiction if we can give a substantial theory of what individuates such modes of presentation as those of the form 'that length', a theory from which it follows that 'that length' thought in connection with the column and 'that length' thought in connection with the window are distinct.

Consider a partially parallel example concerned with perceptual modes of presentation of shades of colours. Suppose two surfaces which a subject sees match in colour, and are in fact of the same Goodmanian shade. The subject may entertain the hypothesis that in fact there is something which would match the one and not the other; and so the m.p.'s of the shade used in the content of the hypothesis are distinct. This case seems unproblematic, because the surfaces are perceived as distinct: they apparently occupy different regions of the space around the perceiver. Here it seems right to say that there are two m.p.'s in thought of the one shade in part because there are two modes of presentation of the form 'that surface'. The surfaces may really be the same – a single surface may have a reflection in an unnoticed mirror – but as long as they are apparently in different regions of space, egocentrically identified, then the subject's hypothesis is epistemically possible.

This simple case has three features which will be shared by the cases in which we are interested. First, it suggests that to individuate a perceptual m.p. of the shade we need to mention three things: the manner of its perception, the mode of presentation of the surface perceived to have it, and (arguably) the concept *shade*. Second, the conditions leading to contradiction are not fulfilled with such individuation: the modes of presentation of the shade are manifestly distinct, given the distinct modes of presentation of the surface(s) perceived to have the shade. Third, a m.p. of this type is not to be identified with one of the form 'the shade of that surface', that is, with one which applies a descriptive functor to a perceptual m.p. of a surface. The former m.p. can only be used by a subject who can see (or takes himself to be able to see) the shade in question: whereas the mixed descriptive-demonstrative can be used by someone who, in near darkness, can see the surfaces but cannot see their colours.

Now consider demonstrative m.p.'s of lengths. I suggest that the m.p. 'that length' used in connection with the column is individuated by three things: the manner in which that length is perceived, the perceptual mode of presentation of the column, and the concept 'length'. It is then distinct from the m.p. 'that length' used in connection with the window, since the two differ in respect of the second component of the triple of factors by which they are individuated: the perceptual mode of presentation of the column is distinct from the perceptual mode of presentation of the window. Contradiction is avoided because the antecedent of Frege's Principle is not fulfilled. Similarly, these m.p.'s are to be distinguished from the mixed descriptive-demonstrative m.p.'s which apply a descriptive functor to a demonstrative m.p. of an object. Perhaps this is clearest in the case of directions. The m.p. 'that direction' used in connection with a perceived tree is distinct from the m.p. 'the direction of that tree', where 'that tree' expresses a demonstrative m.p. of the tree in question: for a person may reasonably think that a tree on the horizon is not in the direction it seems to be. The thought '*That* direction [used in connection with the perceived tree] is not in fact the direction of that tree' is then epistemically possible: indeed, it could be true. Can we at least identify the m.p. 'that direction [used in connection with the perceived tree]' with the m.p. 'the *apparent* direction of the tree'? This is indeed immune to the objections just brought against an identification with 'the direction of that tree'. But it is one thing for an object to appear to be in a certain direction from a subject, and another for that subject to have the *concept* of apparent direction. A subject who does have that concept may indeed reflect and realize that 'that direction is the apparent direction of that tree' is true. But the former demonstrative mode of presentation could be employed without the subject having the conceptual apparatus for so reflecting. The same points may be made *pari passu* for demonstrative contents concerning the other magnitudes we considered.

If these claims about individuation are true, then the analogue perceptual contents, the manners, have a dual role in contributing to the individuation of the corresponding modes of presentation of the form 'that direction', 'that distance' and the rest. They contribute not only in the most obvious way, in the first component of the individuating triple. They also contribute at a prior stage to the individuation of the perceptual mode of presentation which constitutes the second component: for they will have to be used in specifying the way in which the presented object is perceived.

The above discussion strongly supports one feature of Evans' position in *The Varieties of Reference*. He insisted on a sharp distinction between what he called the 'nonconceptual' content of experience and the conceptual content of judgement and other propositional attitudes.[10] The contradiction which we noted would result from an identification of manners with modes provides an additional argument for the need to distinguish the two levels: though the argument I have been giving for distinguishing them has remained neutral on the issue of whether the content of experience is wholly nonconceptual. One might, naively, have thought that at least in the case of perceptual demonstratives of the form 'that direction', it ought to be permissible to identify a thought component with a component of perceptual content: if what I have been saying is right, it is not possible even in this case.

Another consequence of this discussion can be introduced by considering some further analogue spatial contents of perception. These are by no means exhausted by manners of perception of direction and distance. Visual perception and some other modalities have analogue contents concerning the two- and three-dimensional shape of surfaces and objects in the environment. When we enter a room, even a room full of abstract sculptures, we perceive things in it as having particular shapes: and there is no question of this requiring that we had in advance *concepts* of these particular shapes.

When we say that an object looks octagonal to a perceiving subject, we are saying something which covers each of two rather different sorts of case. One is that in which the perceiver has the concept 'octagonal', necessarily exercisable whether or not something is presented as octagonal to him, and has a perceptual experience as of something falling under that concept. That experience also has, of course, a more fine-grained analogue content given by the particular manners in which the shapes in his environment are perceived. The other type of case is that in which the subject does not himself have the concept 'octagonal' in his repertoire, but in which in a clear sense, he still sees the object as having the same shape as does our first perceiver. Our second perceiver sees the object as having the shape, perceived in a manner given by an analogue shape content, which octagonal things present when placed in a certain relation to him. It would be a mistake, not clearly avoided by the author of *Sense and Content*, to assimilate the second case to the first.[11] In particular in chapter 1 of that work, I said that a perceiver must have the concepts used in specifying the representational content of his experiences. That would be true if the 'concepts' are explicitly analogue contents: but I gave no examples of these, and used only specifications like 'looks spherical'. A perceiver can have an experience whose representational content has as a component an analogue shape content in fact applicable to spheres without having the concept 'sphere' in his conceptual repertoire. Perhaps he must be able to introduce it, but that can hardly be the same as already having it. I was probably tempted into trampling on this distinction as a result of failure to appreciate that demonstrative thought-contents like 'that shape' cannot also be manners of perception of shapes. Once this is granted, it is clear that one cannot hope to maintain that such a demonstrative can specify the fine-grained content of an experience as opposed to that of a judgement.[12]

A third observation is that the demonstratives of the form 'that direction', 'this length' and so forth display the features characteristic of other demonstrative thought constituents. In earlier work I formulated what I called the Indispensability Thesis: this Thesis states that no set of attitudes gives a satisfactory propositional attitude explanation of a subject's acting on a particular object unless the content of those attitudes includes a demonstrative mode of presentation of that object. (This was a generalization inspired by ideas of Perry.[13]) Demonstratives of the form 'that direction', 'this length' and others based on the analogue content of a perceptual experience can be the crucial components of content which make for rationally intelligible action upon an object or magnitude. There is no rational propositional attitude explanation for our tourist near the beginning of this paper pointing in the direction of the carving he wishes to see, even if by chance he succeeds in doing so: this is because he lacks any belief of the form '*that* direction is 37 degrees left and 64 degrees up'. We can also note that in examples in which the subject does have the appropriate demonstrative attitudes for action relating him to a particular property or magnitude, the actions are made intelligible under descriptions which relate (for instance) to the spatial directions themselves, and not to directions as identified with reference to some particular coordinate and metric system. This dovetails with the acknowledged unit-free character of the magnitudes picked out by the manners and modes.

The topics of this paper have some intrinsic interest; but in the offing are at least two deeper and more general questions. One is the nature of the constitutive relations of concept mastery to states with analogue and analogue-based contents; the other is the substantive issue of what it is to be in particular kinds of states with given analogue contents. I take the main point of considering the topics of this paper to be the need to provide the project of answering those deeper questions with clear and correct goals.

Notes

1   See, for instance, my 'Are vague predicates incoherent?', *Synthese* 46 (1981) 121–41, esp. p. 131. The point that such a notion is incoherent is implicit in Dummett's writings.
2   Qualia of a given kind are distinct if and only if there is something which matches one and not the other (in the respect of the given kind): *The Structure of Appearance* (Indianapolis: 2nd edn, Bobbs-Merrill, 1966), pp. 272 ff.
3   'Wang's paradox', reprinted in *Truth and Other Enigmas* (London: Duckworth, 1978), esp. p. 267.
4   This 'is or includes' formulation is to leave room for the possibility that manners are manners of perception of something with boundaries sufficiently broad that they are in one–one correlation with the matching profiles mentioned earlier.
5   See, amongst much else, R. Shepard's review of Neisser's *Cognitive Psychology* in *The American Journal of Psychology* 81 (1968), 258–89; R. Shepard and S. Chipman, Second-order isomorphism of internal representations: shapes of states, *Cognitive Psychology* 1 (1970) 1–17; N. Goodman, *Languages of Art* (Indianapolis: Bobbs-Merrill, 1968), pp. 159–64; D. Lewis, Analog and digital, *Nous* 5 (1971), 321–7; J. Haugeland, Analog and Analog, *Mind, Brain and Function* ed. J. Biro and R. Shahan (Norman, OK: University of Oklahoma Press, 1981); R. Shepard and L. Cooper, *Mental Images and Their Transformations* (Cambridge, MA: MIT Press, 1982); N. Block, Mental pictures and cognitive science, *Philosophical Review* XCII, no. 4 (1983), 499–541.
6   Shepard and Chipman, op. cit., p. 2.
7   I have not said, and it would not be true to say, that whenever analogue contents are in question, analogue processes operate upon them. Since their content derives from the content of experiences, both imaginings and memory images have analogue content. But I do not know of any evidence that analogue processes in Shepard's sense (see Shepard and Cooper, op. cit.) are operative when a subject moves from one imagined musical tone to another.
8   Op. cit., p. 221.

9　There are some ways of fleshing out a possible case in which a subject uses the digitized point matrix contents for which this claim would not be true. A more circumspect statement of the connection with Haugeland's notion would, in outline, be this. Let us say that a type of content is *merely approximately readable by x* if, using its current procedures, there is a margin of error in its reading of states with contents of that type on which *x* cannot improve. Then the claim would be that our analogue contents are each of a type such that it is possible that there is a mind by which it is merely approximately readable.

10　Oxford: OUP, 1982, at p. 227. This may be an appropriate point to record that I withdraw footnote 6, p. 17 of my *Thoughts: An Essay on Content* (Oxford: Blackwell, 1986): it is not, on my present views, an analogue content itself which enters the content of judgement, but rather something individuated by means of analogue content. This would be entirely consonant with the position of *The Varieties of Reference*. Of course others have also insisted on senses in which experience has a nonconceptual character: see, for instance, T. Burge, Belief *De Re, Journal of Philosophy* LXXIV (1977), 338–62; and F. Dretske, *Knowledge and the Flow of Information* (Cambridge, MA: MIT Press, 1981). This is not to say they have offered the kind of account of nonconceptual content I have been beginning to outline here. I discuss Dretske's views in slightly more detail in 'Perceptual content', op. cit.

11　Oxford: Clarendon Press, 1983.

12　The distinction between the two cases covered by 'looks octagonal' also shows that a certain style of consideration is not sufficient to establish that (say) visual experience has a conceptual content of a given type. This is the consideration that by virtue of his having such experiences, it is correct to say that something looks so-and-so to the subject, where so-and-so is of the type in question. This is not enough to establish the point, because the case may be of the second, and not the first, of our two sorts.

13　The problem of the essential indexical, *Nous* 13 (1979), 3–21.

25

Where Perceiving Ends and Thinking Begins: The Apprehension of Objects in Infancy

Elizabeth S. Spelke

Introduction

Human adults experience the world as a layout of physical bodies that endure through time. Our ability to do this is both mysterious and fascinating, because the information we receive about physical objects is potentially so misleading. Consider the case of vision. Objects are bounded, but the visual scenes in which they appear are continuous arrays of surfaces. Somehow, we must determine which of the many surfaces that touch or overlap in a visual array are connected to one another. Objects are also integral units, but they are only partly visible at any given time and their visible surfaces are often separated from one another by nearer occluding objects. Somehow, we must recover the integrity of each object from this mosaic of visible fragments. Finally, objects exist and move continuously through space and time, but they are frequently occluded and disoccluded by movements of surfaces or of the observer. Somehow, we must apprehend the continuous existence of an object from our sporadic encounters with it. Vision, moreover, appears to provide the richest information for objects. The problems of apprehending objects only seem to increase when humans explore by listening or touching.

Elizabeth S. Spelke, "Where Perceiving Ends and Thinking Begins: The Apprehension of Objects in Infancy," in A. Yonas (ed.), *Perceptual Development in Infancy* (Hillsdale, NJ: Lawrence Erlbaum Associates, 1988), pp. 196–9, 220–30.

For centuries, philosophers and psychologists have attempted to understand how humans organize the world into objects by focusing on the origins of that ability. The most influential proposal has come from the empiricists. Perception, on this collection of views, begins with capacities to detect just the sensible properties of a scene, such as the surface fragments that reflect light to the eyes or resist the fingers' touch. Children construct a world of objects from this sensory tableau by learning about the consequences of their actions (e.g., Helmholtz 1924; see also Piaget 1954), and/or by learning how to use words to refer to parts of the world (e.g., Berkeley 1910; Quine 1960). One influential alternative to this view has come from the gestalt psychologists, who proposed that perceivers have an unlearned disposition to organize experience into maximally simple and regular units (Koffka 1935; Kohler 1929; Wertheimer 1958). Even infants will perceive the unity, boundaries, and persistence of most objects, because objects tend to be relatively homogeneous in substance and regular in shape. Learning influences object perception, on the gestalt view, by modulating this organizing tendency.

These theories have been joined in recent years by several further approaches to perception. One is the ecological approach of James and Eleanor Gibson, which posits that perceivers apprehend properties of the world that are relevant to action by detecting invariant relationships in arrays of stimulation (E. J. Gibson 1969, 1984; J. J. Gibson 1966, 1979). Since the unity and boundaries of objects are highly relevant to early-developing human actions such as prehension and manipulation, mechanisms for detecting invariants that specify objects should become functional for humans at an early age. A different approach posits that perception depends on a hierarchy of computations performed by modality-specific and largely autonomous mechanisms. For example, a set of visual "modules" transforms the optic array into a succession of representations, each capturing deeper properties of the world (e.g., Marr 1982). Although aspects of this view are akin to that of Helmholtz (1924), the empiricist background of Helmholtz's theory has been abandoned. Some or all of the mechanisms performing visual computations may be innate, on this view, and subsequent changes in their operation may depend primarily on maturation.

We have conducted research that suggests that all these approaches to object perception are wrong. In our studies of human infants, the organization of the perceptual world does not appear to mirror the sensory properties of scenes, it does not appear to follow from gestalt principles of organization, and it does not appear to depend either on invariant-detectors or modality-specific modules. Our research suggests that these views are wrong for a common reason. All assume that objects are *perceived*: that humans come to know about an object's unity, boundaries, and persistence in ways like those by which we come to know about its brightness, color, or distance. I suggest, in contrast, that objects are *conceived*: Humans come to know about an object's unity, boundaries, and persistence in ways like those by which we come to know about its material composition or its market value. That is, the ability to apprehend physical objects appears to be inextricably tied to the ability to reason about the world. Infants appear to understand physical events in terms of a set of principles that guide, as well, the organization of the perceived world into units.

The search for the mechanisms of object perception serves to organize the present chapter. In the first section, I consider whether objects are constructed from a sensory tableau, by asking if infants who cannot yet reach for objects or talk about them nevertheless organize the visual world into unitary bodies. A review of research with partly occluded objects suggests that they do, contrary to the empiricist thesis. Next, I consider whether object perception could arise from gestalt forces, by asking if infants group surfaces into objects in accord with gestalt principles of organization. Further research with partly hidden objects and with adjacent objects provides evidence against this thesis. In the third section, I consider whether objects are perceived through the detection of invariants in stimulation, by asking if infants perceive objects through a direct analysis of properties of the optic array. Studies of the interaction of different sources of information for object boundaries, as well as studies of the role of motion in specifying object unity, provide evidence that infants apprehend objects by analyzing properties of the perceived surface layout, not simply by detecting optical invariants. In the fourth section, I consider whether object perception depends on a modular visual process, by asking if separate mechanisms underlie infants' apprehension of objects in the visual and haptic modes. Research on haptic perception of objects provides preliminary evidence that a common, more central mechanism serves to organize the surface layout.

That last suggestion leads to a positive proposal: The apprehension of objects is a cognitive act, brought about by a mechanism that begins to operate at the point where perception ends. This mechanism begins not with the optic array but with the perceived surface layout, and it carves that layout into entities whose central properties are abstract. At a functional level, this mechanism can be considered a conception of the physical world. A review of research on infants' understanding of events involving fully hidden objects is presented as evidence for this proposal.

That review also illustrates the fourfold conception of the physical world with which, I believe, infants are endowed: the initial object concept. In the final section, I attempt to sketch a general distinction between perception and thought, suggested by the foregoing analysis. ....[1]

Objects as Products of Thought

Central mechanisms for understanding the world do more than give sense and order to perceived events: They carry perceivers beyond their immediate surroundings and allow them to apprehend properties of the world that cannot be sensed. Thus, as Piaget (1954) and others have proposed, a true object concept enables one to keep track of the existence, the behavior, and the location of objects that are fully hidden and to predict, to some degree, the future course of events involving those objects. The next experiments investigated whether infants have such abilities.

When an object moves fully out of view for more than several seconds, most adults would no longer say that it is "perceived": Awareness of objects does not long keep the character of an immediate experience (Michotte et al. 1964). Under many conditions, nevertheless, a witness to an object's disappearance knows if the object still exists, where it is, and what it is doing. Notions of various kinds contribute to her understanding of events in which objects move from view. Consider, for example, the case of a pencil that is dropped behind a screen that stands on a table. An adult who observed this event would predict that the pencil will come to rest upon the table, and not above or below it, in accord with the notion that *objects are subject to gravity* and cannot stand unsupported in midair, and the notion that *objects are substantial* and cannot pass freely through other objects. She would also predict that the pencil will reach its resting place on the table by following a connected path. This prediction follows from the notion that *objects are spatiotemporally continuous*: They cannot pass from one place to another without moving on a continuous path between them. Further predictions might concern the pencil's direction and speed of motion, in accord with notions concerning physical forces (some of which are erroneous: e.g., Clement 1982; McCloskey et al. 1980). Finally, an adult would predict that the hidden pencil will remain a yellow, elongated object that affords writing; this prediction follows from notions concerning the constancy of object substances, forms, and functions over free movements through the layout.

What are the origins of capacities to make sense of events involving hidden objects? An enormous collection of studies has addressed this question using search tasks developed by Piaget (1954). These studies reveal that the ability to search for and recover occluded objects develops over the first 18 months in a regular sequence of stages. A predictable developmental sequence can be discerned not only when infants search manually but also when they search visually, although the development of visual search is more rapid (Harris 1983). Studies of object-directed search do not reveal, however, whether these developments stem from changes in infants' conceptions of hidden objects or changes in infants' capacities to act. Curiously, research by Piaget (1952) provides strong presumptive support for the latter possibility. For example, Piaget found that young infants cannot coordinate separate acts into means–ends relationships, as systematic search requires. The inability to coordinate means with ends would limit young infants' search for hidden objects, even if the infants conceived of such objects as existing continuously. It appears necessary, therefore, to investigate infants' knowledge of the continued existence of occluded objects by means of methods requiring no coordinated search. Our research, and a growing body of research by Renée Baillargéon, have begun this task.

One series of experiments, conducted with Roberta Kestenbaum and Debra Wein, used a habituation method to investigate whether infants apprehend the locations and movements of hidden objects in accord with the principle that objects move on spatiotemporally continuous paths (Spelke and Kestenbaum 1986; Spelke et al. in preparation). Four-month-old infants were presented with events involving objects that moved successively behind two spatially separated screens. The events were borrowed from Moore, Borton, and Darby (1978), whose ingenious studies of visual tracking revealed dramatic developmental changes, over the second half of the first year, in infants' patterns of looking at objects that move behind occluders. In the "continuous event," a narrow object moved in and out of view behind the separated screens; in the "discontinuous event," one object moved behind the first screen and after a pause, a second object emerged from behind the second screen (figure 25.1). These events are superficially similar; only the presence or absence of a visibly moving object between the two screens distinguishes them. Adults understand the events differently, however, reporting that one object participates in the continuous event and that two objects participate in the discontinuous event (Spelke et al., in preparation). This inference follows from the principle that objects move on continuous paths.

326   *Elizabeth S. Spelke*

Continuous event   Discontinous event

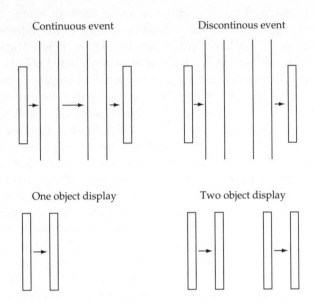

One object display   Two object display

Figure 25.1   Habituation displays (top) for three experiments on infants' understanding of continuous and discontinuous occlusion events. Test displays (bottom) presented one or two objects undergoing different motions in different experiments; the motion patterns for one of the experiments is indicated. (From Spelke & Kestenbaum 1986.)

Three habituation experiments investigated how infants apprehend these events. In each experiment, one group of infants was habituated to the continuous event and one group of infants was habituated to the discontinuous event, and then all the infants were presented with events involving one or two objects with no occluders. The positions and movements of the test objects were varied in different experiments so that only the number of objects served as a consistent basis for generalizing habituation (see Spelke and Kestenbaum 1986). The results of the studies were the same: Infants who were habituated to the continuous event generalized habituation to the one-object test display and looked longer at the two-object test display, whereas infants who were habituated to the discontinuous event did the reverse. These looking patterns provide evidence that infants, like adults, understand the continuous event as involving one object and the discontinuous event as involving two objects. Infants apprehend these events in accord with the principle that objects move on spatiotemporally continuous paths.

Our next experiments focused on events in which objects disappeared behind one wide screen. In these events, one object moved toward the screen at a constant speed and disappeared behind it, and then a second visually indistinguishable object appeared at the opposite side of the screen, moving at the same speed. All that varied in these events was the occlusion time. In the constant speed event, the occlusion time corresponded to the time it would have taken one object moving at a constant velocity to traverse the region behind the occluder; in the too-fast reappearance event, the occlusion time was one third as long; in the immediate reappearance event, the second object began to emerge from behind the screen as soon as the first object was fully hidden. Adult subjects reported that a single object participated in the constant speed and the too-fast events. They reported that two objects participated in the immediate reappearance event. Adults were less confident about all these judgments than they were when judging the continuous and discontinuous events from the first experiments (Spelke et al., in preparation).

To investigate how infants apprehend these events, separate groups of subjects were habituated to each of the three events and then all the infants were tested with events involving one versus two objects, without occluders. The visible velocities of the objects and the occlusion times were varied in two separate experiments so that only the number of objects provided a consistent basis for responding to the test events. Patterns of dishabituation did not differ across the three experimental conditions. Unlike adults, infants do not appear to apprehend occlusion events in accord with the notion that objects move at constant (or gradually changing) speeds.

The conclusions we draw from these experiments are exactly opposite to those drawn by Moore et al. (1978) and Bower (Bower et al. 1971; Bower and Paterson 1973). In their studies, young infants interrupted their visual tracking of objects if the objects appeared to move at changing speeds, but not if the objects appeared to move discontinuously. In view of our findings, however, it seems likely that these tracking patterns stem from properties of the eye-head movement system and do not reflect infants' apprehension of the numerical identity or distinctness of objects. If the head and eyes tend to move on relatively smooth trajectories, infants will have difficulty following an object if it suddenly changes speed. Such a deficiency does not indicate that infants conceive of objects as entities that can only move at constant speeds, as Bower (1982; Bower et al. 1971; Bower and Paterson 1973) suggested. Moreover, infants will track smoothly any movement at a uniform speed, whether or not that movement traces a connected path. This does not imply that infants understand both continuous and discontinuous movements as involving a single object.

In brief, young infants appear to apprehend events involving objects that move out of view in accord with the principle that objects are spatiotemporally continuous. This principle allows infants to trace the paths of objects through time and to infer how objects behave when they are fully occluded. Stronger evidence for the same ability comes from experiments by Baillargéon investigating whether infants understand occlusion events in accord with the principle that objects are substantial.

Baillargéon's first study focused on two events involving a stationary block and a rotating screen (Baillargéon et al. 1985). At the start of each event, the screen lay flat on the table and the block could be seen behind it. Then the screen began to rotate upward toward the block, fully occluding it. In one event, the screen continued rotating until it reached the place where the occluded block stood; in the other event, the screen continued rotating through the place that the block had occupied until it lay flat on the table. Once the screen came to a halt in each event, it reversed its direction of rotation and returned to its initial position, revealing the object (see figure 25.2). Adults judge that the first of these events is expected and the second is impossible. These judgments follow from the principle that objects exist continuously in space and time (thus, the occluded block continues to exist behind its occluder) and the principle that objects are substantial (thus, the screen cannot pass through the place that the block occupies).

To investigate how infants apprehend these events, 5-month-old infants were first habituated to the screen with no object present, moving as it would later move in the impossible event. After habituation, the block was introduced and the two events were presented. Infants looked markedly longer at the impossible event, even though it presented a

Possible event

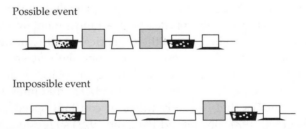

Impossible event

Figure 25.2   Test displays for an experiment on knowledge of object persistence and substance. (From Baillargéon et al., 1985.)

familiar motion. The experiment provided evidence that infants understand occlusion events in accord with notions that objects are spatiotemporally continuous and substantial.

Further research by Baillargéon provides evidence that even 3- and 4-month-old infants understand the rotating-screen events as adults do (Baillargéon 1987). Six- to 8-month-old infants respond appropriately to even more complex events involving an occluder, a moving object, and an occluded barrier in the path of the hidden object's motion (Baillargéon 1986). In understanding such events, infants take account of the location, the orientation, and the size of both the hidden obstacle and the hidden or visible object that moves toward that obstacle (Baillargéon, in press). For example, 7-month-old infants respond to a large rotation of a screen as impossible if a tall thin object stands behind the screen in a vertical orientation; if the same object is oriented horizontally, the infants appropriately treat the same rotation as a possible event.

In summary, these experiments provide evidence that infants are able to make sense of their successive encounters with objects, keeping track of the existence and the movements of objects that are hidden. Like adults, infants appear to understand physical events as involving substantial entities that exist continuously. Infants would seem to appreciate two fundamental object properties, substance and spatiotemporal continuity, before they can search for objects that are hidden and even before they can reach for objects that are visible. Prior to the development of most object-directed actions, infants are endowed with mechanisms that carry them beyond the immediately perceivable world.

The Object Concept

The findings of all the experiments described in this chapter can be explained by proposing that young infants have a fourfold conception of the physical world. Infants appear to endow the world with entities that are *cohesive, bounded, substantial*, and *spatiotemporally continuous*. Each of these properties is abstract: It cannot be seen or smelled or touched. These properties can be known, however, because each constrains how objects can be arranged and how they can move. Cohesion limits an object's movements to those that preserve its integrity: When objects move freely, they move as wholes. Boundedness limits an object's movements to those that preserve its distinctness: Unlike water or mercury, objects do not blend into other objects when they are freely displaced. Substance restricts an object to movements through unoccupied places:

When objects move freely, they do not pass through one another. Spatio-temporal continuity restricts an object to movements along connected paths: An object does not move from one place to another without tracing a continuous path between them.

Because these properties constrain the behavior of objects in space and time, infants can find objects by analyzing the perceived arrangements and motions of surfaces. That is why, I suggest, the infants in our experiments used the common and independent motions of surfaces to discover the unity and boundaries of objects in space, and also why they used the continuous and discontinuous motions of surfaces to discover the identity and distinctness of objects through time. Because an object's properties determine its behavior, infants can also predict the future state of an object under certain conditions. Thus infants predict that an object will stop moving when it arrives at a place occupied by a second object.

The properties of unity, boundedness, substance, and spatiotemporal continuity appear jointly to constitute an initial *object concept*. Although this concept is less rich than our conceptions of objects as adults, it may constitute the core of those conceptions. Adults come to believe many things about the behavior of objects, some of them idiosyncratic and incorrect (e.g., Gentner and Stevens 1983), but everyone seems to believe intuitively that objects move as cohesive and bounded bodies on continuous paths through unoccupied space. We believe these things so strongly that we hesitate to consider something a physical object if its parts are scattered around a room, if it appears in different places without ever moving between them, or if other solid bodies can pass through it. Learning may enrich human conceptions of objects, but learning does not appear to overturn the conceptions humans hold as infants.

Perception and Thought

The proposal that infants apprehend objects by virtue of an object concept raises old and difficult questions about the distinction between perception and thought. Intuitively, these activities seem to differ greatly: *Perceiving* that a tree is green is different from *thinking* that it is in the state of New York; *perceiving* that the shape of some cookies is round is different from *thinking* that their number is prime. But how do these activities differ, and where is the boundary between them? Intuition does not provide ready answers to these questions.

One traditional attempt to distinguish perception from thought relies on introspection. Both structuralist and gestalt psychologists suggested that perceptual processes are opaque to consciousness and give rise to immediate and vivid impressions of the surrounding world. In contrast, processes of thought were said to be relatively slow, deliberate and transparent, yielding fainter impressions that bear the traces of the reasoning behind them. Insofar as introspection is a guide, however, the identification of thought with deliberateness and transparency to consciousness appears to be wrong. Numerous experiments suggest that central cognitive systems can be as opaque as perceptual systems and can give rise to experiences that are as immediate and unanalyzable (Humphrey, 1951, discusses some examples). It is not surprising, therefore, that introspective methods have failed clearly to distinguish perception from thought.

A second, related proposal is that mechanisms of perception are distinguished from mechanisms of thought by their degree of autonomy: Whereas central cognitive systems are open to the influence of what we believe, perceptual systems are "impenetrable" by explicit knowledge and thought (Fodor 1983; Pylyshyn 1980; see also J. J. Gibson 1966, 1979; Helmholtz 1924; Michotte 1963). Distinguishing perception from thought on this basis raises the considerable practical difficulty of determining whether a given system has been penetrated, in its operation, by belief (see Fodor 1983). Insofar as the penetrability of a system can be determined, however, mechanisms of thought appear to be as impenetrable as mechanisms of perception. Studies of intuitive reasoning about geometry and physics provide examples. One may learn in school that space is non-Euclidean and is furnished with particles that move discontinuously. Despite this learning, humans appear to continue to experience a Euclidean world of spatiotemporally continuous matter and objects (see Gentner and Stevens, 1983, for other examples of students' resistance to certain scientific theories; see Cheng, 1986, and Cheng and Gallistel, 1984, for an extended demonstration of the modularity of spatial knowledge in the rat). The current attempt to distinguish perceiving from thinking on grounds of cognitive penetrability will fail, I believe, as did its predecessor.

At least four other distinctions between perception (or more narrowly, "sensation") and thought (or "judgment") have been suggested: (a) perception is partly innate whereas thought depends wholly on learning (e.g, Helmholtz 1924); (b) perception is "passive" whereas thought is "active" (e.g., Piaget 1969); (c) perception is "direct," involving no intermediate representations, whereas thought depends on representations and rule-governed inferences (e.g., J. J. Gibson 1966, 1979); and (d) perception is relatively simple whereas thought is complex: It requires more of the brain, it is beyond the capacities of lower animals, and so forth (see Fodor 1983). Although these suggestions cannot be evaluated adequately, all of them appear to be wrong. Thought, like perception, appears to be innately based (e.g., Antell and Keating 1983). Perception, like thought, appears sometimes to be active (e.g., E. J. Gibson 1970), representational (e.g., Marr 1982), and dependent on mechanisms of considerable complexity (e.g., Rock 1984). Perceptual and cognitive mechanisms both give sense to the world, and they appear to grow and to operate in similar ways.

If perception can be distinguished from thought, I suggest it is because human perceptual and cognitive systems take different kinds of input and bring different kinds of sense and order to experience. Human perceptual systems appear to analyze arrays of physical energy so as to bring knowledge of a continuous layout of surfaces in a state of continuous change. We perceive the layout and its motions, deformations, and ruptures. This continuous layout contains no spatially bounded "things" and no temporally bounded "events": Perceptual systems do not package the world into units. The organization of the perceived world into units may be a central task of human systems of thought. Different systems of thought seem to specialize in units of different kinds: They cut up the world in different ways for different purposes. All cognitive systems seem to function, however, to divide the continuous perceived world into things.

My research has concerned one kind of entity that a central cognitive system appears to find in the world: physical bodies. Other cognitive systems may find entities of other kinds. For example, *events* may be known by virtue of systems of thought. Our conceptions of the world may lead us to break the constantly changing layout into units such as a greeting (defined in part by the actor's intentions), or a battle (defined in part by geographical and political arrangements). As further examples, students of physics or biology develop theories that carve the world into such entities as particles and cells (see Jacob 1973; Kuhn 1962), and children and adults develop systems of mathematical thought that find in the world such entities as classes (with numerical properties) and paths (with geometric properties). Paths form part of the layout that children perceive; even infants can see the ground that extends in front of them, and this perception can guide behaviors such as locomotion (E. J. Gibson and Walk 1960). Perception of the layout, however, does not bring knowledge of paths as geometric objects whose properties allow one to determine which of several routes to a goal is the shortest and how the layout is arranged beyond one's view. The parsing of the world into things may point to the essence of thought and to its essential distinction from perception. Perceptual systems bring knowledge of an unbroken surface layout in an unbroken process of change. Conceptual systems organize that layout into things whose properties and relations specify where each begins and ends, both within and beyond the immediately perceivable world, and how different things are related to one another.

The notion that perception brings knowledge of a continuous and continuously changing layout seems to me implicit in the work of J. J. Gibson (1950, 1966, 1979), whose attempts to develop a theory of perception as unmediated by thought focused on perception of the layout and of the continual, unbounded happenings within it. This same notion is raised explictly by Marr (1982), who suggested that the representation of the surface layout (his "2½-D sketch") "marks the end, perhaps, of pure perception" (p. 268). The notion that thought begins with a continuous universe and carves it into things seems to lie behind certain analyses of scientific thought, in which theories are said to divide the world into objects (e.g., Jacob 1973; Kuhn 1962; Quine 1960) and some analyses of commonsense thinking as well, in which notions about certain kinds of objects are said to provide the conditions for singling out those objects (e.g., Wiggins 1980). With this distinction between perception and thought, it may be possible to hold simultaneously to two theses that seemed incompatible: the thesis that observing the world is different from theorizing about it, and the thesis that theories about the world determine the objects that are "observed" to inhabit it. By granting, further, that both perception and thought are innately based, it may become possible to envisage how different people could come to develop similar theories; indeed, how any person could develop any theory at all.

What then are concepts? I suggest that concepts are best understood in terms of the work of organizing the perceived world into units: They correspond to those entities into which systems of thought divide the world. To have a concept "object," "oxygen," "three," or "triangle" is just to have a central mechanism that carves the perceived world into physical bodies, molecules, sets, or geometric forms. Although this notion leads in a circle, it may give some sense to the claim that concepts are the inhabitants of theories (e.g., Carey 1985; Keil 1989; Kuhn 1962) while leaving open certain issues about the nature of concepts that are best not prejudged, such as whether concepts can be innate, or not expressible through language, or unconscious, or found in lower animals. The object concept, on this view, arises from an intuitive theory of the physical world and its behavior. It is present, albeit in impoverished form; near the beginning of life. Its emergence does not depend on language, on sensorimotor activity, or on associative learning. It reveals itself through the ways infants organize and make sense of the world they perceive.

Note

1   [The two previous paragraphs provide a summary of the points made in more detail by Spelke but not included in the reprint. RS.]

References

Antell, S. E. and Keating, D. P. (1983), Perception of numerical invariance in neonates, *Child Development* 54: 695–701.

Baillargéon, R. (1986), Representing the existence and the location of hidden objects: object permanence in 6- and 8-month-old infants, *Cognition*, 23: 21–42.

Baillargéon, R. (1987), Object permanence in 3½- and 4½-month-old infants, *Developmental Psychology*, 23, 5: 655–64.

Baillargéon, R. (in press), Young infants' reasoning about the physical and spatial properties of a hidden object, *Cognitive Development*.

Baillargéon, R., Spelke, E. S. and Wasserman, S. (1985), Object permanence in five-month-old infants, *Cognition*, 20: 191–208.

Berkeley, G. (1910), *Essay toward a New Theory of Vision*, London: Dutton.

Bower, T. G. R. (1982), *Development in Infancy* (2nd edn), San Francisco: W. H. Freeman.

Bower, T. G. R., Dunkeld, J. and Wishart, J. G. (1979), Infant perception of visually presented objects (technical comment), *Science* 203: 1137–8.

Bower, T. G. R., Broughton, J. M. and Moore, M. K. (1971), Development of the object concept as manifested in tracking behavior of infants between 7 and 20 weeks of age, *Journal of Experimental Child Psychology*, 11: 182–93.

Bower, T. G. R. and Paterson, J. G. (1973), The separation of place, movement, and object in the world of the infant, *Journal of Experimental Child Psychology*, 15: 161–8.

Carey, S. (1985), *Conceptual Change in Childhood*, Cambridge, MA: Bradford/MIT Press.

Cheng, K. (1986), A purely geometric module in the rat's spatial representation, *Cognition*, 23: 149–78.

Cheng, K. and Gallistel, C. R. (1984), Testing the geometric power of an animal's spatial representation. In H. L. Roitblat, T. G. Bever and H. S. Terrace (eds), *Animal Cognition* (pp. 409–23), Hillsdale, NJ: Lawrence Erlbaum Associates.

Clement, J. (1982), Students' preconceptions in introductory mechanics, *American Journal of Physics*, 30 (1): 66–71.

Fodor, J. (1983), *The Modularity of Mind*, Cambridge, MA: Bradford/MIT Press.

Gentner, D. and Stevens, A. L. (1983), *Mental Models*, Hillsdale, NJ: Lawrence Erlbaum Associates.

Gibson, E. J. (1969), *Principles of Perceptual Learning and Development*, New York: Appleton-Century-Crofts.

Gibson, E. J. (1970), The development of perception as an active process, *American Scientist*, 58: 98–107.

Gibson, E. J. (1984), Perceptual development from the ecological approach. In M. E. Lamb, A. L. Brown, and B. Rogoff (eds), *Advances in Developmental Psychology*, Hillsdale, NJ: Lawrence Erlbaum Associates.

Gibson, E. J. and Walk, R. D. (1960), The "visual cliff," *Scientific American*, 202: 64–71.

Gibson, J. J. (1950), *The Perception of the Visual World*, Boston: Houghton-Mifflin.

Gibson, J. J. (1966), *The Senses Considered as Perceptual Systems*, Boston: Houghton-Mifflin.

Gibson, J. J. (1979), *The Ecological Approach to Visual Perception*, Boston: Houghton-Mifflin.

Harris, P. (1983), Cognition in infancy. In M. M. Haith and J. Campos (eds), *Infancy and Biological Development* (vol. 2, pp. 689–782), New York: Wiley.

Helmholtz, H. von (1924), *Treatise on Physiological Optics* (vol. 3) (J. P. C. Southall, tr.), New York: Dover.

Humphrey, G. (1951), *Thinking*, New York: Wiley.

Jacob, F. (1973), *The Logic of Life*, New York: Pantheon.

Keil, F. (1989), *Concepts, Word meaning and Cognitive Development*, Cambridge, MA: MIT Press.

Koffka, K. (1935), *Principles of Gestalt Psychology*, New York: Harcourt, Brace and World.

Kohler, W. (1929), *Gestalt Psychology*, London: Liveright.

Kuhn, T. (1962), *The Structure of Scientific Revolutions*, Chicago: University of Chicago Press.

Marr, D. (1982), *Vision*, San Francisco: Freeman.

McCloskey, M. Caramazza, A. and Green, B. (1980), Curvilinear motion in the absence of external forces: naive beliefs about the motion of objects, *Science*, 210: 1139–41.

Michotte, A. (1963), *The Perception of Causality* (T. R. Miles and E. Miles, tr.), London: Methuen.

Michotte, A., Thinès, G. and Crabbé, G. (1964), *Les compléments amodaux des structures perceptives*, Louvain, Belgium: Publications Universitaires de Louvain.

Moore, M. K., Borton, R. and Darby, B. L. (1978), Visual tracking in young infants: evidence for object identity or object permanence? *Journal of Experimental Child Psychology*, 25: 183–98.

Piaget, J. (1952), *The Origins of Intelligence in Children*, New York: International Universities Press.

Piaget, J. (1954), *The Construction of Reality in the Child*, New York: Basic Books.

Piaget, J. (1969), *The Mechanisms of Perception*, London: Routledge.

Pylyshyn, Z. (1980), Computation and cognition: issues in the foundation of cognitive science, *Behavioral and Brain Sciences*, 3: 111–69.

Quine, W. V. (1960), *World and Object*, Cambridge, MA: MIT Press.

Rock, I. (1984), *The Logic of Perception*, Cambridge, MA: Bradford/MIT Press.

Spelke, E. S. and Kestenbaum, R. (1986), Les origines du concept d'objet, *Psychologie Française*, 31: 67–72.

Spelke, E. S., Kestenbaum, R. and Wein, D. (in preparation), *Spatiotemporal Continuity and the Object Concept in Infancy*.

Wertheimer, M. (1958), Principles of perceptual organization (M. Wertheimer, tr.). In D. C. Beardslee and M. Wertheimer (eds), *Readings in Perception*, Princeton, NJ: Van Nostrand.

Wiggins, D. (1980), *Sameness and Substance*, Cambridge, MA: Harvard University Press.

26

Seeing Is Believing – or Is It?

Daniel C. Dennett

We would all like to have a good theory of perception. Such a theory would account for all the known phenomena and predict novel phenomena, explaining everything in terms of processes occurring in nervous systems in accordance with the principles and laws already established by science: the principles of optics, physics, biochemistry and the like. Such a theory might come to exist without our ever having to answer the awkward "philosophical" question that arises:

What exactly is *the product* of a perceptual process?

There seems to be an innocuous – indeed trivial – answer:

The product of a perceptual process is *a perception*!

What could be more obvious? Some processes have products, and the products of perceptual processes are perceptions. But on reflection, is it so obvious? Do we have any idea what we might mean by this? What are perceptions? What manner of thing – state, event, entity, process – is a perception? It is merely a state of the brain, we may say (hastening to keep dualism at bay), but what could make a state of the brain a *perceptual* state as opposed to, say, merely a metabolic state, or – more to the point – a *pre*-perceptual state, or a *post*-perceptual state? For instance, the state of one's retinas at any moment is surely a state of the nervous system, but intuitively *it* is not a perception. It is something more like the raw

Daniel C. Dennett, "Seeing Is Believing – or Is It?" in K. Akins (ed.), *Perception* (Oxford: Oxford University Press, 1996), pp. 158–72.

material from which subsequent processes will eventually fashion a perception. And the state of one's motor cortex, as it triggers or controls the pressing of the YES button during a perceptual experiment is intuitively on the *other* side of the mysterious region, an effect of a perception, not a perception itself. Even the most doctrinaire behaviourist would be reluctant to identify the button-pressing behaviour of your finger as itself the perception; it is a *response* to . . . what? To a stimulus occurring on the retina, says the behaviourist. But now that behaviourism is history we are prepared to insist that this peripheral response is mediated by another, internal response: a perception is a response to a stimulus, and a behavioural reaction such as a button-press is a response to a perception. Or so it is natural to think.

Natural or not, such ways of thinking lead to riddles. For instance, in a so-called computer vision system does any internal state count as a perception? If so, what about a simpler device? Is a Geiger counter a perceiver – *any* sort of perceiver? Or, closer to home, is thermoregulation or electrolyte balance in our bodies accomplished by a *perceptual* process, or does such manifestly unconscious monitoring not count? If not, why not? What about "recognition" by the immune system? Should we reserve the term "perception" for processes with *conscious* products (whatever they might be), or is it a better idea to countenance not only unconscious perceptual processes but also processes with unconscious *perceptions* as their products?

I said at the outset that a good theory of perception *might* come into existence without our ever having to get clear about these awkward questions. We *might* achieve a theory of perception that answered all our detailed questions without ever tackling the big one: what is a perception? Such a state of affairs might confound the bystanders – or amuse or outrage them, but so what? Most biologists can get on with their work without getting absolutely straight about what life is, most physicists comfortably excuse themselves from the ticklish task of saying exactly what matter is. Why should perception theorists be embarrassed not to have achieved consensus on just what perception is?

"Who cares?" some may say. "Let the philosophers haggle over these stumpers, while we scientists get on with actually developing and testing theories of perception." I usually have some sympathy for this dismissive attitude, but I think that in this instance, it is a mistake. It leads to distortion and misperception of the very theories under development. A florid case of what I have in mind was recently given expression by Jerry Fodor (in a talk at MIT, November 19, 1991): "Cognitive Science is the art of pushing the soul into a smaller and smaller part of the playing field." If this is how you think – even if this is only how you think *in the back of your mind* – you are bound to keep forcing all the phenomena you study into the two varieties: pre-perceptual and post-perceptual, forever postponing a direct confrontation with the product at the presumed watershed, the perception or perceptual state itself. Whatever occupies this mysterious middle realm then becomes more and more unfathomable. Fodor, on the same occasion, went on to say in fact that there were two main mysteries in cognitive science: consciousness and the frame problem – and neither was soluble in his opinion. No wonder he thinks this, considering his vision of how Cognitive Science should proceed. This sort of reasoning leads to viewing the curving chain of causation that leads from pre-perceptual causes to post-perceptual effects as having not only a maximum but a pointed summit – with a sharp discontinuity just where the corner is turned. (As Marcel Kinsbourne has put it, people tend to imagine there is a gothic arch hidden in the mist; see figure 26.1.)

There is no question that the corner must be turned somehow. That's what perception is: responding to something "given" by *taking* it – by responding to it in one interpretive manner or another. On the traditional view, all the taking is *deferred* until the raw given, the raw materials of stimulation, have been processed in various ways. Once each bit is "finished" it can enter consciousness and be *appreciated* for the first time. As C. S. Sherrington put it: "The mental action lies buried in the brain, and in that part most deeply recessed from outside world that is furthest from input and output" (1934: 23).

I call the mythical place somewhere in the centre of the brain "where it all comes together" for consciousness the Cartesian Theater (Dennett 1991;

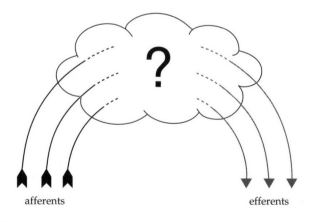

afferents   efferents

Figure 26.1

Dennett and Kinsbourne 1992). All the work that has been dimly imagined to be done in the Cartesian Theater has to be done somewhere, and no doubt all the corner-turning happens in the brain. In the model that Kinsbourne and I recommend, the Multiple Drafts Model, this single, unified taking is broken up in cerebral space and real time. We suggest that the judgmental tasks are fragmented into many distributed moments of micro-taking (Kinsbourne 1988). There is actually very little controversy about the claim that there is no place in the brain where it all comes together. What people have a hard time recognizing – and we have a hard time describing – are the implications of this for other aspects of the traditional way of thinking.

I want to concentrate here on just one aspect: the nature of "takings." An accompanying theme of Cartesian materialism, what with its sharp discontinuity at the summit, is the almost irresistible tendency to see a sharp distinction between, on the one hand, the items that presumably reside at the top, and, on the other hand, the various items that are their causes and effects. The basic idea is that until some content swims all the way up from the ears and retinas into this Theater, it is still just pre-conscious, pre-experienced. It has no moxie; it lacks the *je ne sais quoi* of conscious experience. And then, as the content completes its centripetal journey, it abruptly changes status, bursting into consciousness. Thereafter, the effects that flow, directly or indirectly, from the Audience Appreciation that mythically occurs in the Cartesian Theater count as post-conscious, and these effects, too, lack some special something.

Let's consider a garden variety case of this theme in slow motion, working backwards from peripheral behaviour to conscious perception. Suppose you tell me you believe in flying saucers. Let us further suppose that that behaviour – the telling – is an indirect effect of your once having been shown a highly detailed and realistic photograph of what purported to be a flying saucer. The behaviour of telling is itself an indirect effect of your belief that there are flying saucers – you are telling me what you actually believe. And that belief in turn is an effect of yet another prior belief: your belief that you were shown the photograph. And this belief that you were shown the photograph was originally supported by yet prior beliefs of yours about all the details in the photograph you were shown. Those beliefs about the particular details of the photograph and the immediate perceptual environment of your looking at it were themselves short-lived *effects* – effects of having seen the photograph. They may all have faded away into oblivion, but these *beliefs* had their onset in your memory at the very moment – or very shortly thereafter – that you had the conscious visual perception of the photograph. You believe you saw the photograph because you did see the photograph; it didn't just irradiate your retinas; you saw it, consciously, in a conscious experience.

It looks as if these perceptual beliefs are the most immediate effect of the perceptual state itself.[1] But they are *not* (it seems) the perception itself, because they are (it seems) *propositional*, not... um, *perceptual*. That at least is a common understanding of these terms. Propositional, or conceptual, representations are more abstract (in some hard-to-define way), and less, well, vivid and colourful. For instance, V. S. Ramachandran draws our attention to the way the brain seems to "fill in" the region of our blind spots in each eye, and contrasts our sense of what is in our blind spot with our sense of what objects are behind our heads: "For such objects, the brain creates what might be loosely called a logical inference. The distinction is not just semantic. Perceptual and conceptual representations are probably generated in separate regions of the brain and may be processed in very different ways" (Ramachandran 1992: 87). Just what contrast is there between perceptual and conceptual? Is it a difference in degree or kind, and is there a sharp discontinuity in the normal progression of perceptual processes? If there is, then one – and only one – of the following is the right thing to say. Which is it to be?

1 *Seeing is believing.* My belief that I see such-and-such details in the photograph in my hand is a perceptual state, not an inferential state. I do, after all, *see* those details to be there. A visually induced belief to the effect that all those details are there just *is* the perception!

2 *Seeing causes (or grounds) believing.* My belief that I see such-and-such details in the photograph in my hand is an inferential, non-perceptual state. It is, after all, *merely* a belief – a state that must be inferred from a perceptual state of actually seeing those details.

Neither, I will argue, is the right thing to say. To see why, we should consider a slightly different question, which Ramachandran goes on to ask: "How rich is the perceptual representation corresponding to the blind spot?" Answers to that eminently investigatable question are simply neutral with regard to the presumed controversy between (1) and (2). One of the reasons people tend to see a contrast between (1) and (2) is that they tend to think of perceptual states as somehow much richer in content than mere belief states. (After all, perceptions are like pictures, beliefs are like sentences, and a picture's worth a thousand words.) But these are spurious connotations. *There is no upper bound on the richness of content of a proposition.* So it would be a confusion – a simple but ubiquitous confusion – to suppose that since a perceptual state has such-and-such richness, it cannot be a propositional state, but must be a perceptual state (whatever that might be) *instead*.

No sane participant in the debates would claim that the product of perception was either literally a picture in the head or literally a sentence in the head. Both ways of talking are reckoned as metaphors, with strengths and shortcomings. Speaking, as Kinsbourne and I have done, of the Multiple *Drafts* Model of consciousness leans in the direction of the sentence metaphor, in the direction of a language of thought. (After all, those drafts must all be *written*, mustn't they?) But our model could just as readily be cast in picture talk. In Hollywood, directors, producers and stars fight fiercely over who has "final cut" – over who gets to authorize the canonical version of the film that will eventually be released to the public. According to the Multiple Cuts Model, then, nobody at Psycho-mount Studios has final cut; films are made, cut, edited, recut, re-edited, released, shelved indefinitely, destroyed, spliced together, run back-wards and forwards – and no privileged subset of these processes counts as the Official Private Screening, relative to which any *subsequent* revisions count as unauthorized adulterations. Different versions exist within the corridors and cutting rooms of Psychomount Studios at different times and places, and no one of them counts as the definitive work.

In some regards the Multiple Cuts version is a more telling metaphor – especially as an antidote to the Cartesian Theater. There are even some useful elaborations. Imagine cutting a film into its individual frames, and then jumbling them all up – losing track of the "correct" order of the frames. Now consider the task of "putting them back in order." Numbering the frames in sequence would accomplish this, provided that any process that needs access to sequencing information can then extract that information by comparing frame numbers. There is no logical necessity actually to splice the frames in order, or line them up in spatial order on the film library shelf. And there is certainly no need to "run" them through some projector in the chosen temporal order. The chosen order can be unequivocally secured by the numbering all by itself. The counterpart in our model of consciousness is that it *does not follow* from the fact that we are equipped to make sequence judgments about events in our experience that there is *any* occurrence in real time of a sequence of neural representations of the events in the order judged. Sometimes there *may* be such a sequence occurring in the brain, but this cannot be determined simply by an analysis of the subjective content of experience; it is neither a necessary nor sufficient condition for a like-ordered subjective sequence.

In other regards, however, the Multiple Cuts version of our model is altogether too vivid, what with its suggestions of elaborate *pictorial* renderings. We should be leery of metaphor, but is there any alternative at this point? Are there any non-metaphorical ways of talking that capture the points that need making? How about the terms being popularized by the connectionists: "vector coding and vector completion"? This new way of talking about content in cognitive science is appealing partly because whatever it is, vector coding is obviously neither pictures nor words, and partly, I suspect, because none of the uninitiated dare to ask just what it means!

Let me tell you what it means, so far as I can tell. Think of an enormous multi-dimensional hyperspace of possible contents – all the possible contents a particular organism can discriminate. A vector, if I may indulge yet again in metaphor, can be considered a path leading into a particular quadrant or subspace in this hyperspace. Vector completion is just the process of pursuing a trajectory to an ultimate destination in that hyperspace. Most of the hyperspace is empty, unoccupied. When something (some *sort* of thing) has been encountered by an organism, it renders the relevant portion of the organism's hyperspace *occupied*; recognizing it again (or being reminded of it by another, similar one) is getting back to the same place, the same coordinates, by the same or a similar path. Vector completion creates a path to a location in content-hyperspace.

"Vector completion" talk is just as metaphorical as "language of thought" talk or "pictures in the head" talk; it is simply a *more abstract* metaphorical way of talking about content, a metaphor which neatly evades the talk of pictures versus sentences, while securing the essential informational point: to "discriminate" or "recognize" or "judge" or "turn the corner" is simply to determine some determinable aspect of content within a space of possibilities.

Vector-completion talk is thus like *possible-world semantics*; it is propositional without being sentential (see, e.g., Stalnaker 1984). It provides a way of asserting that a particular "world" or "set of worlds" has been singled out from all the possible worlds the organism might single out for one purpose or another. Acknowledging that perception or discrimination is a matter of vector completion is thus acknowledging something so uncontroversial as to be almost tautological. Vector completion is a cognitive process in the same way growing old is a biological process; short of dying, whatever you do counts.

Almost tautological, but not quite. What the connectionists argue is that as long as you have machinery that can traverse this huge state-space efficiently and appropriately (completing the vectors it *ought* to complete most of the time), you don't have to burden the system with extra machinery – scene-painting machinery *or* script-writing machinery. A highly particular content can be embodied in the state of a nervous system without having any such further properties – just so long as the right sort of transitions are supported by the machinery. Given the neutrality of vector-coding talk, there is no particular reason for the machinery described to be connectionist machinery. You could describe the most sentential and logistic of representation-systems in vector-coding terms if you wished. What you would lose would be the details of symbol-manipulation, lemma-proving, rule-consulting that carried the system down the path to completion – but if those features were deemed beneath the level of the intended model, so much the better. But – and here is the meat, at last – connectionist systems are particularly well-suited to a vector-coding description because of the way they actually accomplish state transitions. The connectionist systems created to date exhibit *fragments* of the appropriate transitional behaviour, and that's a promising sign. We just don't know, yet, whether whole cognitive systems, exhibiting all the sorts of state transitions exhibited by cognizing agents, can be stitched together from such fabrics.

One of the virtues of vector-coding talk, then, is its neutrality; it avoids the spurious connotations of pictures or sentences. But that very neutrality might actually prevent one from thinking vividly enough to dream up good experiments that reveal something about the actual machinery determining the contents. Ramachandran has conducted a series of ingenious experiments designed to shed light on the question of how rich perceptual representations are, and the metaphor of pictorial filling-in has apparently played a large role in guiding his imaginative transition from experiment to experiment (Ramachandran and Gregory 1991; Ramachandran forthcoming). I have been sharply critical of reliance on this "filling-in" metaphor (Dennett 1991, 1992), but I must grant that any perspective on the issue that encourages dreaming these experiments up is valuable for just that reason, and should not be dismissed out of hand, even if in the end we have to fall back on some more neutral description of the phenomena.

One of the most dramatic of these experiments is Ramachandran and Gregory's "artificial scotoma" which the brain "fills in" with "twinkle." According to Ramachandran (1992), it can be reproduced at home, using an ordinary television set. (I must confess that my own efforts to achieve the effect at home have not been successful, but I do not doubt that it can be achieved under the right conditions.)

Choose an open channel so that the television produces "snow," a twink-ling pattern of dots. Then stick a very tiny circular label in the middle of the screen. About eight centimeters from the label, tape on a square piece of gray paper whose sides are one centimeter and whose luminance roughly matches the gray in the snow ... If you gaze at the label very steadily for about 10 seconds, you will find that the square vanishes completely and gets "replaced" by the twinkling dots. . . . Recently we came up with an interesting variation of the original "twinkle" experiment. When a volun-teer indicated that the square had been filled in with twinkling dots, we instructed the computer to make the screen uniformly gray. To our sur-prise, the volunteers reported that they saw a square patch of twinkling dots in the region where the original gray square had been filled in. They saw the patch for as long as 10 seconds.   (Ramachandran 1992: 90)

In this new perceptual illusion, the illusory *content* is *that there is twinkling in the square*. But, one is tempted to ask, how is this content *rendered*? Is it a matter of the representation being composed of hundreds or thousands of individual illusory twinkles or is it a matter of there being, in effect, a label that just says "twinkling" attached to the representation of the square?

Can the brain represent twinkling, perceptually, without representing individual twinkles?

This is a good mind-opening question, I think. That is, if you ask yourself this question, you are apt to discover something about how you have been tacitly understanding the issues – and the terms – all along. Real twinkling – twinkling in the world – is composed of lots of individual twinkles, of course, happening at particular times and places. That's what twinkling is. But not all representations of twinkling are composed of lots of representations of individual twinkles, happening at particular times and places. For instance, this essay frequently represents twinkling, but never by representing individual twinkles. We know that during the induction phase of this experiment, over a large portion of your retina, there are individual twinkles doing their individual work of getting the twinkle-representation machinery going, by stimulating particular groups of cells at particular times and places. What we don't yet know is whether, when neurally represented twinkling "fills in" the neurally represented square area – an area whose counterpart on the retina has no individual twinkles, of course – this represented twinkling consists of individual representations of twinkles. This is part of what one might want to know, when the question one asks is: *how rich* is the neural representation? It is an empirical question, and not at all an obvious one. It does not follow from the fact that *we see the twinkling* that the individual twinkles are represented. They may be, but this has yet to be determined. The fact that the twinkling is remarkably vivid, subjectively, also settles nothing. There are equally stunning illusory effects that are *surely* not rendered in individual details.

When I first saw Bellotto's landscape painting of Dresden at the North Carolina Museum of Art in Raleigh, I marvelled at the gorgeously rendered details of all the various people walking in bright sunlight across the distant bridge, in their various costumes, with their differences in attitude and activity (see figure 26.2)

I remember having had a sense that the artist must have executed these delicate miniature figures with the aid of a magnifying glass. When I leaned close to the painting to examine the brushwork, I was astonished to find that all the little people were merely artfully positioned single blobs and daubs of paint – not a hand or foot or head or hat or shoulder to be discerned (see figure 26.3)

Nothing shaped remotely like a tiny person appears on the canvas, but there is no question that my brain represented those blobs *as* persons. Bellotto's deft brushwork "suggests" people crossing the bridge, and my brain certainly took the "suggestion" to heart. But what did its *taking* the suggestion amount to? We may want to say, metaphorically, that my brain "filled in" all the details, or we may want to say – more abstractly, but still metaphorically – that my brain completed the vector: *a variety of different people in various costumes and attitudes*. What I doubt very much, however, is that any particular neural representations of hands or feet or hats or shoulders were created by my brain. (This, too, is an empirical question, of course, but I'll eat my hat if I'm wrong about this one!)

How can we tell, then, how rich the content of the neural representation actually is? As Ramachandran says, by doing more experiments. Consider for instance another of his embellishments on the artifical scotoma theme, in which the twinkling background is coloured pink, and there is a "conveyor belt" of spots coherently moving from left to right within the gray square region (Ramachandran forthcoming). As before, the square fades, replaced by pink, but the conveyor belt continues for a while, before its coherent motion is replaced by the random jiggling of the rest of the background. Ramachandran concludes, correctly, that there must be two separate "fill in" events occurring in the brain; one for the background colour, one for the motion. But he goes on to draw a second conclusion that does not follow:

Figure 26.2 Bernardo Bellotto, *View of Dresden with the Frauenkirche at left*, 1747. Reproduced courtesy of North Carolina Museum of Art, purchased with funds from the State of North Carolina.

Figure 26.3 Detail from figure 26.2

The visual system must be actually seeing pink – i.e., creating a visual representation of pink in the region of the scotoma, for if that were not true why would they actually see the spots moving against a pink background? If no actual filling in were taking place they would simply have been unable to report what was immediately around the moving spots. (Ramachandran forthcoming, ms. 14)

Of course in some sense "the visual system must be actually seeing pink" – that is, the subject is actually seeing pink that isn't there. No doubt about it! But this does not mean the pink is represented by actually filling in between the moving spots on the conveyor belt – and Ramachandran has yet another experiment that shows this: when a "thin black ring" was suddenly introduced in the centre of the square, the background colour, yellow, "filled the interior of the ring as well; its spread was not 'blocked' by the ring." As he says,

This observation is especially interesting since it implies that the phrase "filling in" is merely a metaphor. If there had been an actual neural process that even remotely resembled "filling in" then one would have expected its progress to be blocked by the black ring but no such effect occurred. Therefore we would be better off saying that the visual system "assigns" the same color as the surround to the faded region. (Ramachandran forthcoming, ms. 16)

In yet another experiment, Ramachandran had subjects look at a fixation point on a page of text which had a blank area off to the side. Subjects duly "filled in" the gap with text. But of course the words were not readable, the letters were not identifiable. As Ramachandran says: "It was as though what was filled in was the 'texture' of the letters rather than the letters themselves" (forthcoming, ms. 15). No rendering of individual letters, in other words, but rather a representation *to the effect that* there was no gap in the text, but just more of the same – more 12-point Times Roman, or whatever. The effect is, of course, perceptual, but that does not mean it is not conceptual, not propositional. The content is actually *less rich* than it would have to be, if the gap were filled with particular letters spelling out particular words (or non-words).

Let's now return to the opening question: what is *the product* of perception? This question may have seemed at first like a good question to ask, but it gets one off on the wrong foot because it presupposes that perceptual processes have a single kind of product. To presuppose this, however, is already to commit oneself to the Cartesian Theater. There are in fact many different ways of turning the corner, or responding to the given, and only a few of them are "pictorial" (or for that matter "sentential") in any sense at all. For instance, when something looms swiftly in the visual field, one tends to duck. Ducking is one sort of taking. It itself is not remotely pictorial or propositional; the behaviour is not a speech act; it does not express a proposition. And there is no reason on earth to posit an intermediary state that "represents" in some "code" or "system of representation."

Suppose a picture of a cow is very briefly flashed in your visual field, and then masked. You might not be able to report it or draw it, but it might have the effect of making you more likely to say the word "milk" if asked to name a beverage. This is another sort of corner-turning; it is presumably accomplished by activating or sensitizing a particular semantic domain centered around cows, so your visual system must have done its interpretive work – must have completed the *cow* vector – but its only "product" on this occasion may be just to turn on the cow-neighbouring portion of your semantic network.

The magician moves his hand just so, misdirecting you. We know he succeeded, because you exhibit astonishment when he turns over the cup and the ball has vanished. What product did he produce by this manipulation of your visual system? Astonishment now, but that, like ducking, is not a speech act. The astonishment is caused by failed expectation; you had *expected* the ball to be under the cup. Now what sort of a "product" is this unarticulated expectation? Is it a sentence of mentalese, "The ball is under the cup" swiftly written in your belief-box, or is it a pictorial representation of the ball under the cup? It's something else, propositional only in the bland sense that it is content-specific; it is *about the ball being under the cup*, which is not the same thing as being *about the cup being on the table* or being *about the magician having moved his hands away from the cup*. Those are *different* products of visual perception, vectors into different regions of your content hyperspace.

This state that you have been put into not only grounds your astonishment if the magician now turns over the cup, but also influences how you will perceive the next move the magician makes if he doesn't turn over the cup. That is, this "product" of perception can immediately go on to influence the processes producing the *next* products of perception, and on and on. Ramachandran illustrates this point with an experiment in which a field of yellow rings is shown to subjects in such a way that one of the rings has its inner boundary obscured by the blind spot (see figure 26.4).

What will their brains do? "Fill in" with yet another ring, just like all the other rings, or "fill in" the center of the obscured ring with yellow,

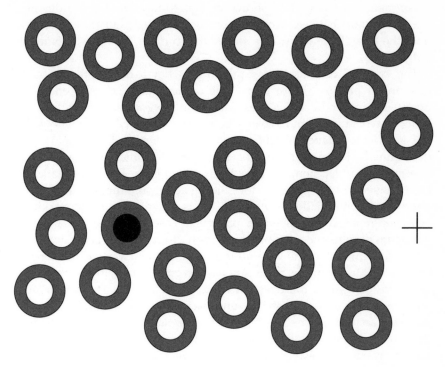

Figure 26.4

turning it into a yellow disk? The latter, it turns out; the solid yellow disk "pops out" as the exception in the field of yellow rings. But even this is not a demonstration of *actual* filling in; in this case, the brain has evidence that there is a yellow region with a circular perimeter, and it has no *local* evidence about whether or not the whole region is yellow. Not having any contrary evidence, it draws the inference that it must be "more of the same" – *more yellow*. This is a fine example of a micro-taking, for this *"conclusion"* amounts to the creation of the content *yellow disk*, which in turn becomes a *premise* of sorts: the odd-one-out in a field represented as consisting of yellow rings, which then triggers "pop out." It might have turned out otherwise; the micro-taking process first invoked for the blind-spot region might have had access to the global information about the multitude of rings, and treated this global content as evidence for a different inference: considered globally, "more of the same" is *more rings*. In that case there would have been no pop-out, and the field would have been seen, veridically, in fact, as a uniform field of rings. So the experiment very definitely shows us something about the order and access relations between a variety of micro-takings, but in neither case does the brain have to provide something in order to arrive at its initial judgment.

The creation of conscious experience is not a batch process but a continuous process. There is not one corner that is turned, once, but many. The order in which these determinations occur determines the order in which they can have effects (no backwards causation allowed!), but is strictly independent of the *order represented* in the contents thus determined. The micro-takings have to interact. A micro-taking, as a sort of judgment or decision, can't just be inscribed in the brain in isolation; it has to have its consequences – for guiding action and modulating further micro-judgments made "in its light." This interaction of micro-takings, however it is accomplished in particular cases, has the effect that a modicum of coherence is maintained, with discrepant elements dropping out of contention, and all without the assistance of a Master Judge. Since there is no Master Judge, there is no *further* process of being-appreciated-in-consciousness, so the question of *exactly* when a particular element was *consciously* (as opposed to unconsciously) taken admits no non-arbitrary answer. And since there is no privileged moment at which to measure richness of content, and since the richness of content of micro-takings waxes and wanes, the idea that we can identify *perceptual* – as opposed to conceptual – states by an evaluation of their contents turns out to be an illusion.

Note

1   This is what I called the β-manifold in "Two Approaches to Mental Images," in Dennett (1978).

References

Dennett, D. C. (1978), *Brainstorms*, Cambridge, MA: MIT Press.
——— (1991), *Consciousness Explained*, Boston, MA: Little, Brown.
——— (1992), Filling in versus finding out: a ubiquitous confusion in cognitive science. In P. van den Broek, Herbert L. Pick, Jr., and D. Knill (eds.), *Cognition: Conceptual and Methodological Issues*, Washington, DC: American Psychological Association.

Dennett, D. C., and M. Kinsbourne (1992), Time and the observer: the where and when of consciousness in the brain, *Behavioral and Brain Sciences*, 15, 2 (June): 183–201.

Kinsbourne, M. (1988), Integrated field theory of consciousness. In A. J. Marcel and E. Bisiach (eds.), *Consciousness in Contemporary Science*, Oxford: Oxford University Press.

Ramachandran, V. S. (1992), Blind spots, *Scientific American*, 266 (May): 86–91.

——(forthcoming), "Filling in gaps in perception," in *Current Directions in Psychological Science*.

Ramachandran, V. S., and Gregory, R. L. (1991), Perceptual filling in of artificially induced scotomas in human vision, *Nature* 350, 6320: 699–702.

Sherrington, C. S. (1934), *The Brain and Its Mechanism*, Cambridge: Cambridge University Press.

Stalnaker, R. (1984), *Inquiry*, Cambridge, MA: MIT Press.

Index